THE CALVO CLAUSE

The Calvo Clause

A PROBLEM OF INTER-AMERICAN AND INTERNATIONAL LAW AND DIPLOMACY

by Donald R. Shea

UNIVERSITY OF MINNESOTA PRESS

Minneapolis

PRINTED AT THE LUND PRESS, INC., MINNEAPOLIS

Library of Congress Catalog Card Number: 55-9371

PUBLISHED IN GREAT BRITAIN, INDIA, AND PAKISTAN BY
GEOFFREY CUMBERLEGE: OXFORD UNIVERSITY PRESS, LONDON, BOMBAY, AND KARACHI

To

CHARLES H. McLAUGHLIN

Preface

PERHAPS the greatest asset of the United States in the present condition of tension in international relations is its strong national economy. It is this economic strength which, in large measure, is responsible for the rise of this nation to a position of tremendous power and influence, and for the development of an unrivaled standard of living for its citizenry. Economically powerful though the United States may be, however, it is not self-sufficient. The world is, in fact, economically interdependent. The continued economic prosperity of America depends on that of the entire world, and, reciprocally, the economic prosperity of the world depends to a considerable extent on that of the United States.

Of tremendous importance to this economic strength are America's commercial and investment relations with the rest of the world. The United States has now become the dominant commercial and investor power. Direct private investment in foreign countries has risen from $3 billion in 1914 to $8 billion in 1943 to well over $16 billion at the end of 1953. Along with this investment expansion, the number of Americans living abroad has risen from 13,239 in 1939 to an estimated more than 500,000 in 1952.

A substantial portion of these commercial and investment relations are with our neighbors to the south, the Latin American republics. The importance of this region to American foreign investment is shown by the fact that 40 per cent of the total direct private investment abroad is in Latin America. This investment in Latin America has been increasing since World War II at the rate of approximately $440 million per year, and there is every indication that this increase will continue. Latin America is a region of great economic potential, and the rate of its industrial progress in the postwar period has been little short of phenomenal. As this development continues, so also will the importance of this region increase in the international economy.

Although the economic relations between the Latin American republics and the United States have been mutually advantageous and, on the whole, quite harmonious, they have also produced a number of vexatious problems. Some of the most controversial of these are involved in the relations between the Latin American governments and the increasingly large number of aliens, many of them United States citizens, who reside in their territory in order to pursue business interests and aid in the development of natural resources. The presence of a number of foreign citizens, who possess the necessary capital and know-how, is essential for the advancement of the underdeveloped region, but it also has not infrequently resulted in serious conflicts of interest between the Latin American states and the investor powers over the treatment that is accorded to resident aliens. Because of this tension and conflict of interests, international law, the body of principles that govern relations on the international level, has evolved certain rules concerning the status, rights, and duties of resident aliens.

One of the most contentious issues in this area of international law is the validity and effectiveness of the Calvo Clause. This concept has produced sharp and seemingly irreconcilable differences of opinion in inter-American and international diplomacy and jurisprudence. Operating on the belief that the utility and effectiveness of the principles of international law are closely related to the preciseness of their definition, I shall attempt in this study to determine as precisely as possible the rule of law on the Calvo Clause in contemporary international law.

I wish to express to Professor Charles H. McLaughlin of the University of Minnesota, to whom this book is dedicated, my

Preface

profound gratitude for his many valuable suggestions and his penetrating criticism. Professor McLaughlin, who by his scholarly and stimulating teaching first enkindled my interest in the field of international law, read the entire manuscript, and whatever merit this book may have is due in large measure to his wise and incisive counsel, which was always available and very frequently used. I also wish to thank Professor Asher N. Christensen of the University of Minnesota, who originally suggested the desirability of further inquiry into the question of the validity of the Calvo Clause, and my colleague Professor Charles D. Goff of the University of Wisconsin (Milwaukee Extension) for his enthusiastic encouragement and readily available advice. I am also indebted to Dr. E. Taylor Parks and Stanley D. Metzger of the Department of State who furnished me with much invaluable information, to the United States ambassadors and their staffs in the various Latin American republics who expended considerable time and effort in assisting me in the determination of the current utilization of the Calvo Clause, and to the various foreign offices which supplied me with current definitions of position on the Calvo Clause.

I am happy to acknowledge a very special debt of gratitude to Elsa Jaeck, librarian at the University of Wisconsin (Milwaukee Extension), who so very graciously and competently assisted me in the tedious task of locating and securing innumerable diplomatic and legal documents. I also received very courteous service from the staff of the Reference and Documents Division of the Milwaukee Public Library and the interlibrary loan divisions of the major American libraries, especially those of the Library of Congress, the Department of State, and the Columbus Memorial Library.

I wish to thank Doris and Henry Cyrak for proofreading the entire manuscript and offering valuable stylistic suggestions, and Mary Jo Schoofs for very efficient stenographic service. I am indebted to the staff members of the University of Minnesota Press for their skillful assistance. Last, but most certainly not least, I wish to record my profound appreciation to my wife,

Patricia, who laboriously and competently typed the entire manuscript, offered many valuable suggestions, and was the source of continual encouragement and inspiration.

Although this book would not have been possible if it were not for the assistance of those mentioned above and the many more who, of necessity, must remain unnamed, I alone, of course, am responsible for any errors of omission or commission.

D. R. S.

Milwaukee, Wisconsin
June 1, 1955

List of Abbreviations

AJIL: American Journal of International Law

APSR: American Political Science Review

BYIL: British Yearbook of International Law

Decisions and Opinions of the Commissioners: Decisions and Opinions of the Commissioners in Accordance with the Convention of November 19, 1926, between Great Britain and the United Mexican States

Further Decisions and Opinions of the Commissioners: Further Decisions and Opinions of the Commissioners in Accordance with the Conventions of November 19, 1926, and December 5, 1930, between Great Britain and the United Mexican States. Subsequent to February 15, 1930

Opinions of Commissioners, I: Opinions of Commissioners under the Convention Concluded September 8, 1923, between the United States and Mexico. February 4, 1926 to July 23, 1927

Opinions of Commissioners, II: Opinions of Commissioners under the Convention Concluded September 8, 1923, as extended by the Convention Signed August 16, 1927, between the United States and Mexico. September 26, 1928 to May 17, 1929

Opinions of Commissioners, III: Opinions of Commissioners under the Convention Concluded September 8, 1923, as Extended by Subsequent Conventions, between the United States and Mexico. October, 1930 to July, 1931

Recueil des Cours: Recueil des Cours de l'Académie de droit international de la Haye

RDDI: Revista de derecho internacional (Havana)

RDI: Revue de droit international (A. de Lapradelle)

RDILC: Revue de droit international et de législation comparée

RGDIP: Revue générale de droit international public

RPDDI: Revista Peruana de derecho internacional

U.S. For. Rel.: Papers Relating to the Foreign Relations of the United States

U.S. Stat. L.: United States Statutes-at-Large series

U.S. Treaties: United States Treaties and Other International Agreements series

Table of Cases

Table of Contents

THE CALVO CLAUSE

Introduction

INTERNATIONAL law, like all systems of law, evolves to meet conflicts of interest. In few areas of relations on the international level is there a more real clash of interests than in the relations between the state and citizens of foreign states. Although the international law governing the settlement of conflicts of interest in this area is one of the most highly developed branches of that law, it is, paradoxically, also one of the most highly controversial.

When a citizen of a state resides and does business in a foreign country, he becomes subject to a conflict of jurisdictions. Under the rules of international law, he is considered to be subject to the territorial jurisdiction of the state in which he resides. This means that the alien owes a temporary obedience to the state of residence. He is therefore governed by the local civil, criminal, and commercial codes, and must normally turn to the local judicial processes to seek redress for any injury to his person or property. Furthermore, a state is held to have even wider power over an alien who more or less permanently makes his residence within its territory, to the extent that the state can, for example, make the alien pay taxes, and in case of need can even compel him, under the same conditions as citizens, to serve in the local police and the local fire brigade for the purposes of maintaining public safety. In turn the alien is considered, under the rules of international law, to be possessed of the procedural and substantive rights of citizens, with the exception of certain special civil and political rights and privileges that may be reserved to the local citizenry. That is, the law of nations would compel every state to grant to aliens at least equality before the law with its own citizens as far as safety of person and property is concerned, but would not compel a state to grant the alien equality in voting and in holding public office, or in the practice of the professions.

If this were the complete situation in regard to a citizen of one state residing in the territory of another, then the position of the alien would not be particularly complicated or controversial, for his rights and obligations would be determined solely in accordance with the laws of the state of residence. However, international law also holds that, while the alien is subject to the territorial jurisdiction of the foreign state, he is also subject to the personal jurisdiction of the state of origin. This means, for example, that the alien is still subject to the taxation and treason laws of his home state. It also means that the alien remains under the protection of his home state. By a customary rule of international law, every state has the right to protect its citizen wherever he may be if the treatment accorded him does not measure up to what are considered to be internationally recognized standards.[1]

It is thus apparent that the presence of the alien can be the cause of a great deal of conflict and controversy between the state of origin and the state of residence. This has been particularly true in situations involving the underdeveloped regions of the world where the legal systems and remedial processes were not considered to measure up to "civilized" standards. In response to pressures brought to bear by the resident aliens and their associated business interests, the major investor powers sought to institutionalize procedures whereby their citizens would not suffer by being subjected to inferior standards of law and justice.

In some of the underdeveloped areas of the world, such as

---

[1] For a brief analysis of the rights and duties of aliens, with references and documentation, see L. Oppenheim, *International Law*, I (7th ed. by H. Lauterpacht, London, 1948), pp. 619–630. These general introductory comments on the principles of international law that govern the status of aliens will be examined in more detail in the course of this analysis.

Introduction

Asia, the Middle East, and parts of Africa, the pressures thus created led to the institution of the system of extraterritorial jurisdiction, whereby the alien, upon entering a country in which the legal institutions and laws were considered to be inferior to or radically different from those that existed in the Occidental states, would, by treaty stipulation, be removed from the territorial jurisdiction of the state of residence and would remain under the jurisdiction of the home state, whose consuls would exercise this jurisdiction, try civil and criminal cases, and determine rights in accordance with their own municipal law.[2] In the Western Hemisphere, however, partly because of the sensitiveness of Latin American states to the prerogatives of sovereignty, partly because Latin American legal and political systems were of European origin, and partly because of the better bargaining position of the states due to the adherence of the United States to the Monroe Doctrine, the principle of extraterritoriality was never established. In this underdeveloped region, protection of the rights and interests of aliens was sought through the utilization of procedures that came to be known as the institution of diplomatic protection. This provided that citizens abroad could appeal to their own governments for protection if, after an injury had been committed to their persons or property, satisfaction was not obtained through the remedial processes available in the foreign state.

The Latin American republics, fearful that this institution of diplomatic protection might be employed as a tool of economic or political imperialism, have employed many ingenious legal devices designed to prevent the alien from appealing to his government for diplomatic protection. The most successful and the most widely used technique has been to require the alien to agree, as part of any contract concluded with a Latin American government, to the so-called Calvo Clause by which the alien

[2] With the political advancement of these underdeveloped countries in Asia, the Middle East, and Africa, extraterritorial privileges have now been abandoned. For an excellent analysis on the subject of extraterritoriality, and an extensive bibliography, see C. C. Hyde, *International Law Chiefly as Interpreted and Applied by the United States* (3 vols., Boston, 1947), II, pp. 849–871.

agrees to waive the right of diplomatic protection and to resort for redress of any grievances exclusively to the local judicial remedies. The validity of the Calvo Clause has become one of the most controversial questions of contemporary international diplomacy and jurisprudence. Perhaps no other problem in international law has been so indecisively arbitrated before international tribunals or as vehemently disputed among nations. This appears even more remarkable in view of the nearly unanimous concurrence of the leading publicists of the United States and Europe regarding this problem. Certainly any subject so theoretically positive, and yet so practically indecisive provides a fertile field for investigation and research. Moreover, when investigation of the decisional law appears to confirm conclusions that differ from the opinions of the majority of publicists, the subject becomes of even greater importance. The present volume is the result of such an investigation.

It is true that the Calvo Clause controversy by itself is but a minute phase of the interrelations of states; however, the Calvo Clause dispute is closely linked with the general problems involved in the diplomatic protection of citizens abroad and with the gradual evolution of international law toward recognizing the rights and duties of the individual as well as of the state. Since international law is not static, but evolves with the changing environmental conditions of the world community, care will be taken here to analyze the development of the Calvo Clause against this changing background. Conclusions regarding the validity of the Clause that might have been acceptable several decades ago will have to be carefully re-examined in order to determine whether they are accurately reflective of present-day circumstances.

The disagreement over the validity of the Calvo Clause is not a result of lack of careful consideration. It has been the subject of a great deal of diplomatic correspondence as well as an issue in more than thirty cases before international arbitral tribunals. Nearly all the general treatises on international law, as well as all the standard treatises on the international responsibility of states for injuries to aliens, deal in part with this concept. Numerous articles in leading legal periodicals have discussed its various aspects, although specialized studies of this problem have appeared only in Latin America.

The Calvo Clause controversy is not solely one of law, however, but also one of politics. It has played an important role in the political relations of the Americas. While the approach here will be primarily legal, a complete understanding of the problem necessitates an examination of the political considerations involved. Political conditions have had an important bearing on the inception and development of this concept.

In the present approach, emphasis will be placed on the problem as it has developed in the Americas, for the Calvo Clause controversy has been almost unique to this hemisphere, with the United States the chief protagonist of the opposition and the Latin American countries the chief defenders of the concept. I believe that the Latin American position has never been adequately presented in English and therefore will attempt to do so here. Necessarily I shall rely primarily on Latin American publications.

The primary purpose of this analysis, however, will be to determine what the precise rule of law is on the Calvo Clause. A survey of the writings of the leading publicists would indicate that such an inquiry is unnecessary, for there is general agreement on the invalidity of the Calvo Clause as a bar to diplomatic interposition. But relying solely on the writings of the publicists is apt to be misleading. The attitudes of the states and the decisions of the international tribunals must be considered carefully, for the opinions of writers, no matter how authoritative, may not correspond with the practice of states or the rulings of the courts. It is my contention that the actual rule of law on the Calvo Clause as determined primarily by state practice and court rulings does not, in fact, correspond with the views expressed by the majority of publicists.

In order to determine this rule of law, therefore, attention will be devoted to all three chief law-determining agencies—governments, courts, and publicists.[3] Chapters III and IV will deal with the official position of the leading nations of the world, paying particular attention to the attitude of the American states which have been obliged to deal with this problem the most. Chapters VI, VII, and VIII will consider the decisions of international tribunals that have involved the Calvo Clause. Chapter V will deal with the opinions of the leading publicists, although, of necessity, their opinions will also be interspersed throughout the analysis. This particular approach, it seems to me, holds the greatest promise for penetrating the confusion, contradiction, and disagreement that have characterized so many treatments of this subject.

[3] Georg Schwarzenberger, *International Law as Applied by International Courts and Tribunals* (London, 1945), pp. xlvii, 8ff.

II

The Origins of the Calvo Clause

Originating Conditions

AN UNDERSTANDING of the Calvo Clause controversy in its contemporary manifestations is dependent upon a knowledge of the historical conditions surrounding its inception and evolution.

The Calvo Clause has existed as a legal and diplomatic problem for about eighty years. It is closely related to, and a result of, the development and exploitation of the natural resources in the underdeveloped regions of the world that occurred in the latter part of the nineteenth century and the early part of the twentieth. In some areas of the world this exploitation took the form of outright colonization in various forms and degrees. However, where independent governments existed in the underdeveloped regions, the exploitation generally came in the form of large foreign investments and a consequent migration of foreigners to these countries to supervise and direct the development of their natural resources.

This investment and migration were both necessary and mutually profitable. However, they inevitably carried with them a certain amount of tension and conflict between the resident aliens and the native governments. The tension and conflict were greatly enhanced by the chronic social, economic, and political instability that characterized many of these underdeveloped regions.

This was particularly true of the Latin American republics in their formative years. These newly organized governments, although sovereign in name, were not yet solidly established in their communities. Superficially, at least, the Latin American republics were patterned after the liberal-democratic ideal, and they vociferously embraced the Western concepts of democracy and justice. But basic experience with the democratic process was lacking, and in many ways the democratic form of government proved ill-adapted to the requirements of these new countries.[1]

The instability and disorder bred by these conditions led inevitably to a certain number of injuries to the persons and property of the resident aliens. Although the Latin American republics provided judicial machinery for the redress of such wrongs, the natural inclination of the resident aliens to question the merit of the foreign justice, reinforced by many examples of maladministration of this justice, led to strong demands for international protection of their persons and property and for redress of wrongs through intervention by their home governments. The pressures thus created led to the institution of procedures by which citizens abroad could appeal to their governments for protection of their persons, property, and rights.

Originally, the interposition of governments on behalf of their citizens abroad was based upon the principle of comity.[2] However, as a body of precedent grew up, these interventions were more often exerted as a matter of legal right. It is from these beginnings that the institution of the diplomatic protection of citizens abroad originated.[3]

---

[1] Frederick S. Dunn, *The Protection of Nationals* (Baltimore, 1932), p. 54 (hereinafter referred to as Dunn, *Prot. of Nat.*).

[2] *Ibid.*, p. 55. Diplomatic interposition in the technical sense consists in "the pressure of a claim by official representations, under the authority and in the name of the government." See Edwin M. Borchard, *The Diplomatic Protection of Citizens Abroad* (New York, 1915), p. 441 (hereinafter referred to as Borchard, *Dip. Prot.*). Borchard asserts (*ibid.*, pp. 441–442) that the term "interposition" is considered preferable to "intervention" in this expression, inasmuch "as the latter term has a long-established meaning of armed interference in the internal affairs of another state." However, as will become apparent *infra*, "intervention" when qualified by the adjective "diplomatic" is quite commonly used as equivalent to "diplomatic interposition," and may be so considered for the purposes of this study.

[3] The best treatment of the historical evolution of the institution of diplomatic protection is found in Dunn, *Prot. of Nat.*, especially pp. 53–66. See also Borchard, *Dip. Prot.*, pp. 836–838.

The principal authorities have concluded that the institutionalization of the adjustment of disputes of this character is of relatively recent origin, actually dating back only to the last half of the nineteenth century.[4] The interposition to assure citizens justice in foreign lands was defended on various grounds. The great powers argued that it was their duty to extend the protection of international law to citizens wherever they might be. Such protection was believed necessary to facilitate the continued growth of international trade and intercourse. Without this protection, the risks involved in foreign investment and exploitation would serve to discourage mutually profitable relationships. This doctrine found its legal sanction in the writings of Emmeric de Vattel, who formulated the principle that an injury to an alien was actually an injury to the state of that alien, and thereby justified measures by the state to seek redress and compensation for the injury.[5] It became the practice for states to intervene on behalf of their citizens and present international claims for the alleged injuries. Although these claims were based on injuries to individuals, the theory held that it was the state itself that was the injured claimant, and hence the state was entitled to compensation under international law. These claims would be honored through diplomatic negotiation, international arbitration, economic or political pressure, or sometimes through the use of armed force.

Defects and Abuses of the Institution of Diplomatic Protection

Although the institution of diplomatic protection arose to meet a legitimate need, and had for its objective the laudable purpose of obtaining justice for citizens when such was not obtainable from local judicial remedies, certain inherent imperfections soon arose in its operation. Redress for injuries was dependent more on political than on legal considerations. The strength

[4] Luis A. Podestá Costa, *Manual de derecho internacional público* (2nd ed., Buenos Aires, 1947), p. 199.

[5] Emmeric de Vattel, *The Law of Nations*, Book II, Chapter vi, text of 1758, "Classics of International Law" ed., III, p. 136. See Dunn, *Prot. of Nat.*, p. 48.

The Calvo Clause

of an alien's state quite often determined his rights of recovery. Most authorities who have given special study to this problem are agreed on its inherent imperfections, which tend to defeat its purpose. The late Edwin M. Borchard, probably the outstanding American authority on this area of international law, asserted that the defects of this system of protection produced a situation in which "all three parties to the issue, the individual, the defendant nation, and the claimant nation, are in a precarious and unhappy condition." [6] Latin American scholars have vigorously endorsed and elaborated these criticisms.[7]

Coupled with these intrinsic defects were certain abuses of the right of protection. Nationals often felt entitled to complete security of their persons and property, and appealed to their governments on rather flimsy evidence and without any real effort to obtain local redress. The petitioned government, acting on limited, one-sided evidence, and often under domestic political pressure, sponsored claims that frequently were not based upon strict justice.[8] Utilization of armed force to compel the weaker nations to honor these dubious claims was not infrequent, and it sometimes happened that the severity of the measures adopted in seeking compensation for the alleged injuries was far out of proportion to the extent of the initial damages suffered.

Then, too, the weaker nations often saw international claims used as the immediate justification for armed intervention and

[6] Borchard, "Limitations on Coercive Protection," *AJIL*, XXI (April 1927), p. 303. See, by the same author, "How Far Must We Protect Our Citizens Abroad?" *New Republic*, L (April 13, 1927), pp. 214–215. Also, Eugene Staley, "Une critique de la protection diplomatique des placements à l'étranger," *RGDIP*, XLII (1935), pp. 557–558; Alwyn V. Freeman, "Recent Aspects of the Calvo Doctrine and the Challenge to International Law," *AJIL*, XL (January 1946), p. 144.

[7] E.g., T. Esquível Obregón, "Protección diplomática de los ciudadanos en el extranjero," *Memoria de la Tercera Conferencia de la Federación Interamericana de Abogados* (Mexico, 1944), III, pp. 218–236; Alfonso García Robles, "La protección diplomática, la Cláusula Calvo y la salvaguardia de los derechos internacionales del hombre," *Memoria de la Tercera Conferencia*, Apéndice, pp. 5–25; Ramón Beteta and Ernesto Henríquez, "La protección diplomática de los intereses pecuniarios extranjeros en los estados de América," *Proceedings of the Eighth American Scientific Congress* (Washington, D.C., 1940), X, pp. 27–35.

[8] For a list of some of these ill-founded claims, see A. Alvarez, *Le droit international américain* (Paris, 1910), pp. 118–119. See also Podestá Costa, "La responsabilidad internacional del estado," *Cursos Monográficos*, II (1952), pp. 171–193.

12

occupation. The French interventions in Mexico in 1838 and 1861, the American interventions in Santo Domingo (1904) and Haiti (1915), and the German, British, and Italian intervention in Venezuela (1902–1903) seemed to justify the fears of weak nations that international reclamations would serve as the basis for foreign domination and control.[9] The late nineteenth and early twentieth centuries saw a rebirth of mercantilism in the form of imperialistic competition for colonies. The areas susceptible to colonization, however, were soon occupied, and the large nations had to turn elsewhere for markets for their goods, sources of raw materials, and defensive outposts. With this atmosphere of world politics, it is not surprising that the weaker nations of the world, especially in Latin America, interpreted the frequent presentation of international claims, and the occasional armed interventions, as the first overture of outright occupation and colonization.

The unhappy experience of the Latin American republics with loans and bond issues negotiated with nationals of the powerful investor states also greatly reinforced their fears of what they considered to be flagrant economic imperialism. The history of Mexico, in particular, reveals a number of instances in which an underdeveloped region was victimized by foreign creditors. The first foreign loan to be negotiated by Mexico after the establishment of her independence was the Goldschmidt loan. This loan, contracted with British creditors, involved the issuance of 5 per cent bonds with a face value of 16,000,000 pesos, of which 8,000,-000 pesos was placed at the disposal of the Mexican government, subject, however, to the prior deduction of 2,000,000 pesos for interest, sinking fund, and commissions, thereby leaving Mexico with a net of only 6,000,000 pesos. Goldschmidt sold the government bonds at 58 per cent of their face value and grossed a profit of a quarter of a million pounds plus subsequent commissions.[10]

[9] Dunn, *Prot. of Nat.*, p. 57.

[10] See Edgar Turlington, *Mexico and Her Foreign Creditors* (New York, 1930), pp. 35–37. The investors extracted these huge interest, discount, and commission payments on the basis of the great risk of default involved. They then pressed their governments to intervene to force full payment and thus remove the risk.

The notorious Jecker claim further intensified Latin American suspicion and fear of foreign creditors. In this case, the Swiss-French banking firm of J. B. Jecker and Company lent a nominal 75,000,000 francs to the Mexican government, of which Mexico received only 3,750,000 francs. Nonpayment of 100 per cent of this loan, which Mexico had borrowed at a cost of about 90 per cent per annum, was one of the justifications used by the French government under Napoleon III for the armed intervention in Mexico in 1861–1862, which led to the imposition of the Maximilian regime.[11]

Not surprisingly, the Latin American republics saw in these "imperialistic encroachments" an enemy to be greatly feared. The Latin Americans needed foreign capital and supervision to develop their natural wealth, but did not wish to pay the price of being subjected to the real or imagined abuses of either diplomatic protection of aliens living within their territory or armed intervention in behalf of foreign creditors. Unable to resist these abuses by force, they attempted to build up strong logical, moral, and legal defenses. Much of the literature of diplomacy and jurisprudence of Latin America in the last half of the nineteenth and the first half of the twentieth centuries has been devoted to this objective.

Since the great powers insisted that their actions were based on international law, it was on this front that the major attack was made. Many different Latin American legal theories and principles designed to substantiate the justice and legality of their resistance to the institution of diplomatic protection and armed intervention have been set forth. One of the most famous of these was the so-called Drago Doctrine.

First advanced by the Argentinian foreign minister, Dr. Luis Drago, in a note to the United States on December 29, 1902, and intended to be a corollary to the Monroe Doctrine, the Drago Doctrine held that "the public debt of an American State can not

---

[11] *Ibid.*, pp. 116–117, 141. When Jecker failed in 1860, the Duc de Morny, half brother of Napoleon, entered into an arrangement by which he was to receive 30 per cent of the profits from the collection of the loan. See Dexter Perkins, *The Monroe Doctrine, 1826–1867* (Baltimore, 1933), p. 383, n. 48.

occasion armed intervention, nor even the actual occupation of the territory of American nations by a European power." [12] Under the leadership of the United States, the Hague Peace Conference of 1907 adopted the Porter Convention, which prohibited the use of force for the collection of any contract debts, but, as Philip Jessup has aptly stated,[13] the convention left a loophole through which a fleet of warships could sail in providing that the renunciation of the use of force was not applicable "when the debtor state refuses or neglects to reply to an offer of arbitration, or, after accepting the offer, prevents any *compromis* from being agreed on, or, after the arbitration, fails to submit to the award." [14] Because this convention quite obviously still leaves the question of armed intervention up to the investor powers, and because not all states have subscribed to it, this "acceptance" of the Drago Doctrine did not allay the fears and suspicions of the Latin American republics.[15]

Furthermore, the Drago Doctrine, even if fully accepted, would never really meet the needs of the Latin Americans, for its area of applicability was too limited. It dealt only with the question of intervention by force for the collection of public debts, and

[12] The text of the Drago note will be found in *U.S. For. Rel.* (1903), pp. 1–5. Drago's note was immediately motivated by the joint intervention of Great Britain, Italy, and Germany against Venezuela in 1902. For a more detailed exposition of this doctrine, see Drago, "State Loans in Their Relation to International Policy," *AJIL*, I (July 1907), pp. 692–726.

[13] *A Modern Law of Nations* (New York, 1948), p. 113.

[14] The complete text of the convention and the many reservations attached will be found in *Hague Conventions and Declarations of 1899 and 1907* (ed. by James Brown Scott, New York, 1915), pp. 242ff.

[15] The general dissatisfaction of the Latin American republics with this convention is indicated by the fact that only Guatemala, Nicaragua, Haiti, El Salvador, Panama, and Mexico ratified it. Of these, only Mexico and Panama ratified without reservation. Mexico, in 1931, denounced the convention according to Article 6 which allows withdrawal after one year's notice. At the Eighth International Conference of American States (Lima, 1938), the Mexican delegation urged the denunciation of the Porter Convention by the few American states that had ratified it or adhered to it. See Samuel Flagg Bemis, *The Latin American Policy of the United States* (New York, 1943), p. 229. Jessup, *op. cit.*, p. 172, asserts that in view of the provisions of the United Nations Charter restricting the use of force, and since according to Article 103, the Charter prevails over any conflicting agreement, "the loophole in the Porter Convention could now be considered to be filled."

did not consider the all-important broader and more continuing problem of the diplomatic protection of resident aliens.[16]

A number of other Latin Americans have set forth theories and doctrines designed to limit or eliminate the right of diplomatic protection,[17] but the legal theory that most adequately met their needs, and the one upon which their strongest attack on diplomatic protection has been based, is that known as the Calvo Doctrine.

The Calvo Doctrine

The patron saint of the Latin American efforts to restrict diplomatic intervention, the man who more than any other symbolized the hopes and aspirations of our southern neighbors, was an Argentinian publicist, Carlos Calvo.

Calvo was born at Buenos Aires in 1824.[18] In 1852 he began his diplomatic career when he was made vice-consul at Montevideo, and he served there as consul-general and diplomatic representative of Buenos Aires from 1853 to 1858. From 1860 to 1864 he represented Paraguay as *chargé d'affaires* at Paris, and also was accredited to Great Britain. At later periods in his career he served as envoy extraordinary to Berlin, Russia, Austria, the Holy See, and Paris.

Although Calvo was by profession a diplomat, it is as a writer in international law that he is best remembered. Calvo was a man of whom it can rightly be said that he was "learned in the law."[19] His gift was mainly that of compiler and organizer, and he is not considered to have been a great thinker or innovator.[20] His works exhibit a practical historical positivism rather than analytical strength, but he "greatly influenced the development

[16] Podestá Costa, "La responsabilidad internacional del estado," *Cursos Monográficos*, II (1952), pp. 199–202.

[17] R. F. Seijas, *El derecho internacional Hispano-Americano* (Caracas, 1884), I, pp. 77, 518; Salvador Mendoza, *La doctrina Cárdenas; texto, antecedents, comentarios* (Mexico, 1939), pp. 29–31, 47; Podestá Costa, *Manual de derecho internacional público*, pp. 211–223.

[18] For a brief sketch of Calvo's life, see Percy Bordwell, "Calvo and the Calvo Doctrine," *Green Bag*, XVIII (July 1906), p. 381.

[19] *Ibid.*, p. 383.

[20] Ed. comment, *AJIL*, I (January 1907), p. 138.

of international law and widened its orbit immensely."[21] The work upon which his fame chiefly rests is his massive, six-volume treatise, *Le droit international théorique et pratique*. First published in Spanish in 1868, it went through five editions, appearing in its final and complete form in Paris in 1896. A virtual storehouse of information, it is considered to be the theoretical source of the Calvo Doctrine.

Calvo's lack of a keen analytical mind, and his inclination to give both sides of a particular question without recognizing the conflict between them, make it extremely difficult to determine his position on disputed points of law. Even when he is advocating the principles of the famous doctrine that bears his name, he falls into inconsistencies and qualifications that tend somewhat to undermine the current interpretation and application of his views.[22] This has led some to assert that it is not his famous treatise but his private correspondence with the leading publicists of Europe over the Drago Doctrine that is really the source of his doctrine.[23] However, most authorities agree that in spite of the vagueness and inconsistency with which he sets forth his views it is really his treatise that is the source or at least the formalization of the Latin American Calvo Doctrine.[24]

In view of the foregoing considerations, it is difficult to cite any one passage of Calvo's treatise as the source of the Calvo Doctrine. The doctrine stems from a series of assertions that must be considered together to understand his advocacy of the principles underlying the Latin American attempt to restrict or eliminate diplomatic protection.

The most representative passages of Calvo are the following:

America as well as Europe is inhabited today by free and in-

[21] A. S. de Bustamante, "Carlos Calvo," *Encyclopaedia of the Social Sciences*, III (1930), p. 153.

[22] Freeman, "Recent Aspects of the Calvo Doctrine and the Challenge to International Law," *AJIL*, XL (January 1946), pp. 132–133.

[23] Mendoza, *op. cit.*, p. 24.

[24] Daniel Antokoletz, *Tratado de derecho internacional público en tiempo de paz* (2nd ed., Buenos Aires, 1928), I, p. 420; Borchard, *Dip. Prot.*, pp. 791–793; Francisco Lopez Gonzalez, *México y la Cláusula Calvo* (Mexico, 1936), pp. 12–13.

dependent nations, whose sovereign existence has the right to the same respect, and whose internal public law does not admit of intervention of any sort on the part of foreign peoples, whoever they may be.[25]

Aside from political motives these interventions have nearly always had as apparent pretexts, injuries to private interests, claims and demands for pecuniary indemnities in behalf of subjects. . . . According to strict international law, the recovery of debts and the pursuit of private claims does not justify *de plano* the armed intervention of governments, and, since European states invariably follow this rule in their reciprocal relations, there is no reason why they should not also impose it upon themselves in their relations with nations of the new world.[26]

It is certain that aliens who establish themselves in a country have the same right to protection as nationals, but they ought not to lay claim to a protection more extended. If they suffer any wrong, they ought to count on the government of the country prosecuting the delinquents, and not claim from the state to which the authors of the violence belong any pecuniary indemnity.[27]

The rule that in more than one case it has been attempted to impose on American states is that foreigners merit more regard and privileges more marked and extended than those accorded even to the nationals of the country where they reside.

This principle is intrinsically contrary to the law of equality of nations . . .[28]

To admit in the present case governmental responsibility, that is the principle of an indemnity, is to create an exorbitant and fatal privilege, essentially favorable to the powerful states and injurious to the weaker nations, establishing an unjustifiable inequality between nationals and foreigners. From another stand-

[25] *Le droit international théorique et pratique* (5th ed., Paris, 1896), I, p. 350. My translation.
[26] *Ibid.*, pp. 350–351. My translation. It should be pointed out that although Calvo refers to armed intervention in this passage, he condemned with equal vigor diplomatic intervention: "La forme sous laquelle a lieu l'intervention n'en altère pas le caractère. L'intervention se produisant par l'emploi des procédés diplomatiques, n'en est pas moins une intervention; c'est une ingérence plus ou moins directe, plus ou moins dissimulée, qui très souvent n'est que le prélude de l'intervention armée." *Ibid.*, p. 267.
[27] *Ibid.*, VI, p. 231. My translation.
[28] *Ibid.*, III, p. 140. My translation.

point, in sanctioning the doctrine that we are combating, one would deal, although indirectly, a strong blow to one of the constituent elements of the independence of nations, that of territorial jurisdiction; here is, in effect, the real extent, the true significance of such frequent recourse to diplomatic channels to resolve the questions which from their nature and the circumstances in the middle of which they arise come under the exclusive domain of the ordinary tribunals.[29]

The responsibility of governments toward foreigners cannot be greater than that which these governments have toward their own citizens.[30]

Although it should be noted that several of these passages were written with specific reference to injuries arising from civil war rather than those arising out of contracts,[31] nevertheless it seems clear, as Borchard states, that

. . . the inference drawn from the whole text, read together with the general principle that foreigners are subject to the local law and must submit their disputes to local courts, has given the Spanish-American countries a basis to assert the doctrine that in his private litigation the alien must exhaust his local remedies before invoking diplomatic interposition and that in his claims against the state he must make the local courts his final forum.[32]

Calvo, basing his theories on the generally accepted rules of national sovereignty, equality of states, and territorial jurisdiction, set forth two cardinal principles which constitute the core ideas of his doctrine: First, that sovereign states, being free and independent, enjoy the right, on the basis of equality, to freedom from "interference of any sort" ("ingérence d'aucune sorte") by other states, whether it be by force or diplomacy, and second, that aliens are not entitled to rights and privileges not accorded to nationals, and that therefore they may seek redress for grievances only before the local authorities. These two concepts of nonintervention and absolute equality of foreigners with nation-

[29] *Ibid.*, p. 142. My translation.
[30] *Ibid.*, p. 138. My translation.
[31] Freeman, "Recent Aspects of the Calvo Doctrine and the Challenge to International Law," *AJIL*, XL (January 1946), pp. 132–133.
[32] Borchard, *Dip. Prot.*, p. 793.

als are the essence of the Calvo Doctrine.[33] It is apparent that the acceptance of these two concepts would result in the elimination of the "enemy" of diplomatic protection.

The sweeping statements set forth by Carlos Calvo failed both in Europe and in the United States to obtain the approval of international lawyers.[34] Arbitration as an alternative to intervention was attracting increasing attention, and the proposal to treat claims of a proprietary nature brought by aliens as claims within municipal law, subject to the exclusive jurisdiction of the courts of the defendant state, had little to commend itself. Although the acceptance of the Calvo Doctrine would eliminate the abuses of diplomatic protection, it would also eliminate the institution itself, without substituting an acceptable alternative. Abolishing diplomatic intervention to cure its abuses would leave the citizen abroad totally at the mercy of native justice, and the possible abuses inherent in such a situation would be considerably greater than those that exist now. This would work to the disadvantage of not only the citizens of the investor nations but also the citizens of the underdeveloped countries, for such a situation well might end or greatly retard mutually profitable investment and development relationships.[35] The practice of states and the decisions of the arbitral commissions have been equally emphatic in their rejection of the ideas of Calvo. As regards winning acceptance on its intrinsic merit, it can be asserted that the Calvo Doctrine has failed to receive recognition as a principle of international law,[36] and as such is now dead.[37]

---

[33] César Sepúlveda Gutiérrez, *La responsabilidad internacional del estado y la validez de la Cláusula Calvo* (Mexico, 1944), pp. 41–45; Green H. Hackworth, *Digest of International Law* (Washington, D.C., 1940–1944), V, p. 635 (hereinafter referred to as Hackworth, *Digest*); Herbert W. Bowen, "The Monroe, Calvo and Drago Doctrines," *Independent*, LXII (April 18, 1907), p. 903.

[34] K. Lipstein, "The Place of the Calvo Clause in International Law," *BYIL*, XXII (1945), p. 130.

[35] Borchard, "Remarks by Professor Edwin Borchard on Papers of Dr. Beteta and Dr. Cruchaga Ossa," *Proceedings of the Eighth American Scientific Congress*, X, p. 74.

[36] Abraham H. Feller, *The Mexican Claims Commissions, 1923–1934* (New York, 1935), p. 185 (hereinafter referred to as Feller, *Mex. Claims Com.*).

[37] Lionel M. Summers, "The Calvo Clause," *Virginia Law Review*, XIX (March 1933), p. 464.

The theories of Calvo were, however, enthusiastically received in Latin America, as would be expected. Their failure to win acceptance on their own merits has compelled the Latin Americans to resort to various devices and techniques to implement the Calvo Doctrine. They have attempted to accomplish this by treaty, by constitutional provision, by municipal law, and by contractual stipulation. Each of these efforts will be examined and evaluated separately.

Attempts to Implement the Calvo Doctrine by Treaty

The Latin American states have shown considerable ingenuity in devising schemes to avoid liability for injuries to aliens. One method they have employed in their attempts to implement the Calvo Doctrine is to incorporate the principle of limited or no responsibility in treaties concluded with other states.

An early effort in this direction was initiated by Venezuela in 1852. In an attempt to avoid frequent diplomatic interventions Venezuela endeavored to obtain an agreement among the Latin American states not to recognize any of the claims presented by foreign governments in the matter of private interests. Although this particular attempt failed, it was indicative of a strong desire by the Latin American republics to use treaties and conventions as a means to restrict or eliminate diplomatic protection.[38] And quite a few of these restrictive treaties have since been concluded among the Latin republics. These generally have provided that aliens are limited to local remedies. An example of this type of treaty would be the General Treaty of Peace and Amity, Arbitration, and Commerce, concluded on September 25, 1906, among the republics of Costa Rica, Salvador, Guatemala, and Honduras. Article 6 of this treaty stated:

The diplomatic agents of each of the high contracting parties shall exercise their good offices in order that due justice shall be administered their fellow citizens. It is well understood, however, that in the defense and protection of their rights and interests,

[38] Borchard, *Dip. Prot.*, p. 794, n. 2.

and in their claims and complaints against the nation or private individuals, no other proceedings shall be resorted to than those which the laws of each signatory Republic may provide for their respective citizens, and they must conform to the final decision of the courts of justice.[39]

European states and the United States have for the most part been unwilling to conclude treaties providing for the complete surrender of the private claims of their citizens to the local courts.[40] Treaties that were accepted generally made a specific exemption for cases of denial of justice. Typical would be the treaty of December 5, 1882, between Mexico and Germany. Article 18, paragraph 2, of this treaty provided:

[The two Contracting Parties,] animated by the desire to avoid disputes which might disturb their friendly relations, agree . . . that with respect to the claims or complaints of individuals in matters of a civil, criminal or administrative character, their diplomatic agents shall not intervene except in case of a denial of justice, illegal or extraordinary delays, failure to execute a definitive judgment; or, after all the legal remedies have been exhausted, for express violation of treaties existing between the Contracting Parties, or of the rules of public and private international law generally recognized by civilized nations.[41]

While such treaties would have the advantage of curbing certain abuses of diplomatic interposition, they are, as Freeman points out, "little more than declaratory of existing international law governing the right of diplomatic protection." [42] Latin American nations, have, however, on some occasions, managed to include a very restricted definition of denial of justice in such treaties, and thereby come closer to their objective of limiting or eliminating diplomatic interposition. An example of this more restrictive type of treaty would be that concluded between Spain and Peru on June 18, 1898. Article 6 asserted: "Spaniards in Peru, and Peruvians in Spain, shall have no right to diplomatic

---

[39] *U.S. For. Rel.* (1906), I, p. 858.

[40] Borchard, *Dip. Prot.*, p. 794; Alwyn V. Freeman, *The International Responsibility of States for Denial of Justice* (London, 1938), p. 493 (hereinafter referred to as Freeman, *Denial of Justice*).

[41] Quoted in Freeman, *Denial of Justice*, pp. 491–492.

[42] *Ibid.*, p. 492.

intervention except in the event of manifest denial of justice, that is, refusal to administer it or negligence in its administration." [43]

Treaties such as these, designed to restrict interposition, were quite common during the closing years of the nineteenth century.[44] Latin American states, in urging the inclusion in treaties of provisions against interposition, argued that the provisions would do nothing more than place foreigners on an equal footing with nationals, thus eliminating the unfair practice of allowing the alien element in the community greater benefits than nationals on account of the undue diplomatic pressure that may be brought to bear on the weaker states.[45] While such treaties are, of course, binding on the contracting parties, most publicists have considered them unwise.[46] The Institute of International Law, at its session in 1910, unanimously adopted the following resolution:

The Institute of International Law recommends that states should refrain from inserting in treaties clauses of reciprocal irresponsibility. It thinks that such clauses are wrong in excusing states from the performance of their duty to protect their nationals abroad and their duty to protect foreigners within their own territory. It thinks that states which, by reason of extraordinary circumstances, do not feel able to assure in a manner sufficiently efficacious the protection of foreigners in their territory, can escape the consequences of such a state of things only by temporarily denying to foreigners access to their territory.[47]

In view of the fact that the United States and European states have in recent years refused to conclude these treaties, their

[43] Quoted in *ibid.*, p. 491.

[44] Harmodio Arias, "The Non-Liability of States for Damages Suffered by Foreigners in the Course of a Riot, Insurrection, or a Civil War," *AJIL*, VII (October 1913), pp. 759–760, n. 58, lists 25 treaties that have restricted aliens to local redress except in case of denial of justice. See also Julius Goebel, "The International Responsibility of States for Injuries Sustained by Aliens on Account of Mob Violence, Insurrections and Civil Wars," *AJIL*, VIII (October 1914), pp. 838–841.

[45] Arias, *op. cit.*, p. 760.

[46] Clyde Eagleton, *The Responsibility of States in International Law* (New York, 1928), p. 105 (hereinafter referred to as Eagleton, *Resp. of States*); Freeman, *Denial of Justice*, p. 495.

[47] *Annuaire de l'Institut de Droit International*, XVIII, p. 253. Translation

23

effectiveness as an attempt to restrict or eliminate interposition has been greatly limited. Treaties formerly concluded are no longer in force, and therefore, outside of Latin America itself, treaty stipulations of irresponsibility for injuries to aliens no longer operate.[48] Thus the attempt to implement the Calvo Doctrine by treaty has largely failed.[49]

Attempts to Implement the Calvo Doctrine by Constitutional Provisions

The importance of the Calvo Doctrine to the Latin American nations is indicated by the widespread inclusion in their constitutions of the principle of limitation of state responsibility for injuries to aliens. By this method they have attempted to restrict the alien to local redress and forbid diplomatic interposition. A typical example of this technique is found in the constitution of Peru:

Article 31. Property, whoever may be the owner, is governed exclusively by the laws of the Republic and is subject to the taxes, charges, and limitations established in the laws themselves.

The same provision regarding property applies to aliens as well as Peruvians, except that in no case may said aliens make use of their exceptional position or resort to diplomatic appeals.[50]

Several countries exempt from the general prohibition of diplomatic interposition the case of denial of justice. The constitution of Bolivia, in Article 18, asserts:

Foreign subjects and enterprises are, in respect to property, in the same position as Bolivians, and can in no case plead an exceptional situation or appeal through diplomatic channels unless in case of denial of justice.[51]

from John Bassett Moore, *A Digest of International Law* (Washington, D.C., 1906), VI, pp. 323–324 (hereinafter referred to as Moore, *Digest*).

[48] Podestá Costa, *Manual de derecho internacional público*, p. 203.

[49] Attempts to implement the Calvo Doctrine by resolutions and conventions of the International Conferences of American States will be considered *infra*, Chapter IV.

[50] Constitution of April 9, 1933, in Russell H. Fitzgibbon, *Constitutions of the Americas* (Chicago, 1948), pp. 670–671.

[51] Constitution of November 23, 1945, *ibid.*, p. 35.

The constitution of Honduras has a similar provision:

Article 19. Aliens may not have recourse to diplomatic channels except in cases of a denial of justice. For this purpose, denial of justice is not understood to mean an executed verdict that is unfavorable to the claimant.

Should this provision be contravened, and claims are not terminated amicably, resulting in loss to the country, the claimant shall forfeit his right to live in the country.[52]

Latin Americans have argued that the widespread inclusion of such constitutional provisions restricting diplomatic protection has created an American "common law" principle which validates the Calvo Doctrine. It would appear, however, that where such constitutional provisions exempt cases of denial of justice in the true sense of that term,[53] they would be only confirmatory of general international practice and not truly expressive of the Calvo Doctrine. Where the constitutional provisions attempt to go farther and purport to bar completely diplomatic interposition that would otherwise be justifiable under the generally recognized principles of international law, state practice, arbitral decisions, and the opinions of the publicists clearly demonstrate their invalidity on the grounds that the limits of diplomatic protection and the responsibility of states for injuries to aliens are determined by international law, and not by domestic constitutions.[54] Prominent Latin American publicists agree with this viewpoint.[55]

It can therefore be concluded that attempts to implement the Calvo Doctrine by constitutional provision have not been successful.

[52] Constitution of March 28, 1936, *ibid.*, pp. 470–471. The constitution of Nicaragua (March 22, 1939) has a nearly identical provision in Article 25 (*ibid.*, p. 558). For additional Latin American constitutional provisions that attempt to limit or eliminate the institution of diplomatic protection, see Gonzalez, *op. cit.*, pp. 15–17, and Carlos Sanchez i Sanchez, *Curso de derecho internacional público americano* (Ciudad Trujillo, 1943), pp. 634–635.

[53] See *infra*, pp. 114–116.

[54] Eagleton, *Resp. of States*, pp. 105–106; Borchard, *Dip. Prot.*, p. 845.

[55] Arias, *op. cit.*, p. 762, asserts that such constitutional provisions are unwise and juridically wrong, for they "involve the mistaken and baseless assumption that the alien's right to demand the protection of his government depends on local law and not upon that of his own country."

Attempts to Implement the Calvo Doctrine by Municipal Legislation

The Latin American countries have also attempted to give validity to the Calvo Doctrine by incorporating its principles in their municipal legislation, with results no more satisfactory than those of constitutional stipulations. The law of Ecuador, passed on February 16, 1938, is typical of such legislation. It provides:

Article 26. Foreigners, by the act of coming to the country, subject themselves to the Ecuadorean laws without any exception. They are consequently subject to the Constitution, laws, jurisdiction, and the police of the Republic, and may in no case, nor for any reason, avail themselves of their status as foreigners against the said conditions, laws, jurisdiction, and police.

. . . .

Article 30. Contracts concluded between the Ecuadorean Government and foreign persons, either individuals or firms of any kind, are subject to the laws of Ecuador, and the rights and obligations deriving from said contracts will be subject to the exclusive jurisdiction of the national judges and courts.

Article 31. The renunciation of diplomatic claims will be an implicit and essential condition of all contracts concluded by foreigners with the state, or of all contracts obligating the state or individuals to foreigners, or of all contracts whose effects should be felt in Ecuador.

Foreigners who have been employed or carried out a commission subjecting them to the Ecuadorean laws and authorities may not claim indemnification through diplomatic channels.[56]

The effectiveness of these attempts to limit diplomatic interposition by municipal legislation falls before the same principle that invalidated constitutional provisions, i.e., that the international responsibility of states is determined by international law, not municipal enactment. The attitude of the United States and European countries, the decisions of international tribunals, and the opinions of the leading publicists all confirm this position.[57]

[56] Printed in *AJIL*, XXXII, Suppl. (1938), p. 168. For additional examples of this type of legislation, see Freeman, *Denial of Justice*, pp. 456–463; Goebels, *op. cit.*, pp. 834–838; Moore, *Digest*, VI, pp. 309–323.

[57] Eagleton, *Resp. of States*, pp. 106–107; Borchard, *Dip. Prot.*, p. 845; Free-

This view was ably expressed by Secretary of State Frelinghuysen, in a memorandum to Señor Soteldo, the Venezuelan minister, on April 4, 1884:

A foreigner's right to ask and receive the protection of his government does not depend upon the local law, but upon the law of his own country. . . . Such a [local] law cannot control the action or duty of his government, for governments are bound among themselves only by treaties or by the recognized law of nations and there is nothing in the existing treaties between the two countries or in the law of nations which recognizes as pertaining to Venezuela the right by the enactment of a municipal law to say how, or where, or under what circumstances the government of the United States may or may not ask justice in behalf of one of its own citizens.[58]

It may be concluded that Latin American attempts to implement the Calvo Doctrine by municipal legislation have not proved successful.

Attempts to Implement the Calvo Doctrine by Contractual Stipulation: The Calvo Clause

We have seen that the Latin Americans have failed to establish the Calvo Doctrine as a theory of international law, and their attempts to win support for this theory by its incorporation into treaties, constitutions, and municipal legislation have been largely unsuccessful. The doctrine has been repudiated by publicists, by governments, and by international courts, and one can say that the Calvo Doctrine has lost whatever efficacy it may have had.[59]

However, although the Calvo Doctrine has failed to receive recognition as a principle of international law, it has "fathered the ubiquitous and difficult problem of the Calvo Clause."[60] This

man, *Denial of Justice*, p. 461; Arias, *op. cit.*, p. 762. Podestá Costa, "La responsabilidad internacional del estado," *Cursos Monográficos*, II (1952), p. 193, observes that "experience shows that these provisions of internal law are frequently ineffective." My translation.

[58] *U.S. For. Rel.* (1884), p. 599. For additional examples of the United States' attitude, see Moore, *Digest*, VI, pp. 309–324.

[59] Summers, *op cit.*, p. 464.

[60] Feller, *Mex. Claims Com.*, p. 185. It is to be noted that the basic Calvo

heir of the defunct doctrine is very much alive, and its validity, as indicated earlier, is a highly controversial issue of contemporary international law and diplomacy.

The Calvo Clause is an attempt to implement the Calvo Doctrine by including in contracts concluded with aliens a provision which binds the alien to local redress and obligates him to forgo his right of appeal for diplomatic protection in case of any dispute or controversy which might arise from the contractual relationships. Its purpose is the same as the other attempts to implement the Calvo Doctrine — to limit strictly or eliminate the abuses of diplomatic protection.[61] It is but a specific application of the Calvo principle that aliens must be satisfied with treatment equal to that received by nationals.[62] However, it differs from the Calvo Doctrine and the previously considered attempts to implement it in one very important respect. The enforcement of the Calvo Doctrine was a *unilateral* act whereas in the case of the Clause the *individual has consented* of his own free will to the surrender of the right of recourse to his government in case of *contractual* controversies or disputes.[63] We have seen previously that constitutional or statutory provisions cannot

Clause principle of restricting the alien to local redress had been inserted in concession contracts before the publication of the first edition of Calvo's treatise in 1868. See, for example, the contract provisions in the *Milligan* case (*infra*, p. 126) and the *Tehuantepec* case (*infra*, pp. 130–131). However, the contractual provision, even though somewhat antecedent to Calvo's treatise, has always been defended and justified on the basis of the theories formalized in his doctrine, and hence properly has borne the title "Calvo Clause."

[61] Beteta and Henríquez, *op. cit.*, p. 44; Lucio M. Moreno Quintana and Carlos M. Bollini Shaw, *Derecho internacional público* (Buenos Aires, 1950), pp. 155–156.

[62] *Ibid.*; Freeman, *Denial of Justice*, p. 469, n. 1; T. Esquível Obregón, *México y los Estados Unidos ante el derecho internacional* (Mexico, 1926), pp. 165–166.

[63] The importance of this distinction was emphasized by the commission in the *North American Dredging Company of Texas* case (*infra*, Chapter VII), *Opinions of Commissioners*, I, p. 21 at 31, where it asserted that it would not honor "any [renunciatory] provision in any constitution, statute, law, or decree, whatever its form, to which the claimant has not in some form expressly subscribed in writing . . ." Some publicists apply the term "Calvo Clause" to statutory and constitutional provisions, as well as to contractual stipulations (e.g., Feller, *Mex. Claims Com.*, p. 185). However, it is properly applied only to cases of voluntary renunciation of diplomatic protection by contract. See Sepúlveda Gutiérrez, *op. cit.*, pp. 57, 60.

modify the right of a state to intervene diplomatically on behalf of one of its citizens. Does the fact that the interested citizen voluntarily surrendered this right of protection modify or affect the right of diplomatic interposition? This question has been the subject of a great deal of controversy and confusion, and it is the purpose here to suggest an answer, based on state practice, arbitral rulings, and the principles of contemporary international law.

The Calvo Clause has appeared in various forms.[64] Typical, however, would be the Clause inserted in the contract between Mexico and the North American Dredging Company of Texas, which provided:

Article 18. The contractor and all persons, who as employees or in any other capacity may be engaged in the execution of the work under this contract either directly or indirectly, shall be considered as Mexicans in all matters, within the Republic of Mexico, concerning the execution of such work and the fulfillment of this contract. They shall not claim, nor shall they have, with regard to the interests and the business connected with this contract, any other rights or means to enforce the same than those granted by the laws of the Republic to Mexicans, nor shall they enjoy any other rights than those established in favor of Mexicans. They are consequently deprived of any rights as aliens, and under no conditions shall the intervention of foreign diplomatic agents be permitted, in any matter related to this contract.[65]

The usual Calvo Clause involves a commitment to submit disputes to the jurisdiction of local courts,[66] where they will be resolved in accordance with the laws of the country in which the contract is made.[67] Some provision is usually included which

---

[64] See Schwarzenberger, *op. cit.*, p. 64; Gonzalez, *op. cit.*, p. 15; Lipstein, *op. cit.*, pp. 131–134. Examples of the Calvo Clause as it has figured in international arbitral jurisprudence will be found in Chapters VI, VII, and VIII, *infra*.

[65] *United States (North American Dredging Co.) v. United Mexican States, Opinions of Commissioners*, I, p. 21 at 22.

[66] For example, in the *United States (Turnbull) v. Venezuela*, *infra*, pp. 179–182, the parties agreed that disputes shall be decided "by the competent tribunals of the respondent Government," and in the *United States (International Fisheries Co.) v. Mexico*, *infra*, pp. 231–240, it was agreed that the parties are subject "to the jurisdiction of the Courts of the Republic."

[67] For example, in the *Great Britain (Nitrate Railroad Ltd.) v. Chile, infra,*

defines the scope of coverage of the contractual stipulation. This coverage is generally confined to the terms of the contract, or disputes or controversies arising out of the contract.[68] However, the tendency in recent years has been to expand the coverage of the contractual renunciation to all matters related to the execution of the contract, and this had been interpreted as including even revolutionary damages suffered by the company or its personnel.[69] The Clause also generally contains a waiver of the protection of the home state,[70] and, to a growing extent, a surrender, in substance, of all future claims based on rights under international law.[71] The tendency in recent years has been to couch the Clause in broader language, and to make the renunciation of diplomatic protection more emphatic and inclusive.[72]

The purpose of the Calvo Clause, as has been pointed out, is to accomplish what the Latin American republics have failed to accomplish by other techniques: to limit, or if possible eliminate, diplomatic interposition. The ultimate objective of this voluntary renunciation is to prohibit completely diplomatic recourse and restrict the alien entirely to local redress for claims of a proprietary nature.[73] However, in order to make the Clause more

pp. 148–152, the Clause provided that the contract is "subject to the laws of the Republic."

[68] E.g., *United States (North and South American Construction Co.) v. Chile, infra,* pp. 141–145.

[69] See the *Great Britain (Mexican Union Railway Co.) v. United Mexican States* case, *infra,* pp. 240–247.

[70] For example, the Clause in the *United States (North American Dredging Co. of Texas) v. United Mexican States, infra,* Chapter VII, provided that "under no conditions shall the intervention of foreign diplomatic agents be permitted in any matter related to the contract."

[71] For example, *ibid.,* the Clause provided that "the contractor . . . shall be considered as Mexican . . . he shall never claim . . . any right as an alien under any form whatsoever."

[72] Borchard, *Dip. Prot.,* p. 800, asserts that the variations in the language of the Clause do not modify the basic principles involved. In recent years, however, international tribunals have closely examined the specific language of the Clause involved. See *infra,* Chapters VII and VIII. For an excellent discussion of the various elements of the Calvo Clause, with examples and analysis, see Lipstein, *op. cit.,* pp. 131–134.

[73] Antonio Gómez Robledo, *The Bucareli Agreements and International Law* (Mexico, 1940), pp. 175–176; Gonzalez, *op. cit.,* p. 15; J. G. De Beus, *The Jurisprudence of the General Claims Commission United States and Mexico, under*

compatible with the generally recognized principles of international law, it has sometimes been interpreted more narrowly as forbidding diplomatic interposition until all local remedies have been exhausted and a denial of justice has been suffered.[74] This more limited interpretation of the Calvo Clause, permitting interposition in case of a denial of justice, would tend to reconcile it with the general principles of international law, but since it would appear to be only confirmatory of the general rule of exhaustion of local remedies, some publicists have concluded that the Clause, in its restricted form, is superfluous.[75] Much of the confusion and contradiction in the diplomacy and jurisprudence involving this problem is due to the failure to distinguish between these two different interpretations of the Calvo Clause.

The Calvo Clause, as a technique to implement the Calvo principles, has proved to be the most successful method of limiting the exercise of diplomatic protection. It is, perhaps, the only such means available now to the Latin American states.[76] Although its validity is a highly controversial matter, nevertheless it has actually served to bar a number of international claims before arbitral tribunals that would have otherwise been admissible under international law.[77] The Latin American states, encouraged by this success, have incorporated provisions into their constitutions and laws requiring the insertion of such clauses in all contracts concluded with aliens. The previously cited law of Ecuador (February 16, 1938) is typical of the enactments, providing:

the *Convention of September 8, 1923* (The Hague, 1938), pp. 68–70; Freeman, *Denial of Justice*, p. 470. It should be noted that the Clause is intended to prohibit submission of claims to international claims tribunals as well as to bar diplomatic intervention as such. For example, the Clause in the *United States (Coro and La Vela Railroad and Improvement Co.) v. Venezuela, infra,* pp. 165–166, provided that "in no case . . . will any international claims be admitted on account of this concession."

[74] For a distinction between these two interpretations of the Calvo Clause, and the implications of such a distinction, see Sepúlveda Gutiérrez, *op. cit.*, pp. 59–60, and Borchard, "The Calvo and Drago Doctrines," *Encyclopaedia of the Social Sciences*, III (1930), pp. 154–155.

[75] E.g., Eagleton, *Resp. of States*, p. 168.

[76] Feller, *Mex. Claims Com.*, p. 198.

[77] See *infra*, Chapters VII and VIII.

The Calvo Clause

Article 31. The renunciation of diplomatic claims will be an implicit and essential condition of all contracts concluded by foreigners with the state, or of all contracts obligating the state or individuals to foreigners, or of all contracts whose effects should be felt in Ecuador.[78]

It has been shown that the Calvo Clause arose out of the same historical conditions as did its parent concept, the Calvo Doctrine. However, while the doctrine as a principle of law has been pretty generally discredited, the Calvo Clause lives on. Based as it is on the voluntary renunciation of the interested individual, the question of its validity opens up entirely new problems. Although most United States and European publicists usually consider it invalid, it has fared considerably better at the hands of governments and tribunals.

[78] Quoted in *AJIL*, XXXII, Suppl. (1938), p. 168. The constitution of Mexico (February 5, 1917) has a similar provision in Article 27. See Fitzgibbons, *op. cit.*, p. 507. For further examples of constitutional and legislative provisions requiring such contractual stipulations, see Borchard, *Dip. Prot.*, pp. 795–796; Freeman, *Denial of Justice*, p. 470.

III

Governmental Attitudes toward the Calvo Clause Controversy

In the investigation of an international law problem, it is imperative to give ample attention to the official attitudes of the governments of the world. Since there is no international legislature to formulate the basic rules governing relations in the world community, these rules are determined, in the first instance, by the positions taken by the various foreign offices.

As indicated earlier, the Calvo Clause controversy has figured in a relatively large amount of diplomatic correspondence and international negotiations. Including the Latin American republics and the United States, some forty-one governments have had occasion in the past few decades to state more or less officially their positions on this controversy. The attitude of the United States, on the one hand, and of the Latin American republics on the other, will be discussed in some detail, since they have been the principal participants in the dispute over the validity of the Calvo Clause. The positions of the other nations in the world will be more briefly summarized, since their positions roughly coincide with that of either the United States or Latin America, depending, to a large extent, on their size and stage of economic development. The larger and more economically advanced nations have generally supported the position of the United States in denying the validity of the Calvo Clause as a bar to diplomatic interposition on behalf of their citizens abroad, while the smaller nations, and those which have been victims of economic exploitation, have generally supported the position of Latin America in condemning the abuses inherent in the institution of diplomatic protection and upholding the voluntary contractual renunciation of protection by the alien as valid and binding.

The Attitude of the Latin American States

The attitude of the Latin American republics toward the Calvo Clause is determined by their attitude toward the institution of diplomatic protection itself. They eagerly embrace any legal principle that holds promise of restricting or eliminating this dread "enemy." As was indicated previously,[1] the Calvo Clause is perhaps the only legal concept that has furnished some meaningful degree of protection against the real and imagined abuses of diplomatic interposition. Certainly, it has proved to be the only means of implementing the Calvo Doctrine that has won a limited recognition in contemporary international jurisprudence.[2] At the same time, it perhaps holds the greatest promise of some day achieving full recognition and thereby greatly curtailing the practice of securing redress for injuries to aliens by the unilateral interposition of the state of the injured alien.[3] It should not be overlooked that the latter is the ultimate objective of the Calvo Clause.

The Latin Americans can construct a strong and logical argument in defense of the Calvo Clause.[4] They generally preface such a defense with a bitter criticism of diplomatic intervention, both as it has operated in the past and as it might serve as a tool of imperialism and exploitation in the future.[5] They argue that the Calvo Clause seeks to serve a legitimate function by attempting to curb the many flagrant abuses inherent in this process of diplomatic intervention, and hence is morally sound.

[1] *Supra*, p. 31.

[2] *Infra*, Chapters VII and VIII.

[3] *Infra*, Chapter IX.

[4] Borchard, "Remarks by Professor Edwin Borchard on Papers of Dr. Beteta and Dr. Cruchaga Ossa," *Proceedings of the Eighth American Scientific Congress*, X, p. 74; Dunn, *Prot. of Nat.*, p. 169; Feller, *Mex. Claims Com.*, p. 198.

[5] An excellent presentation of the Latin American view can be found in Beteta and Henríquez, *op. cit.*, pp. 27–48.

Governmental Attitudes

According to Latin Americans, the individual under the Calvo Clause, in order to share in the riches and natural resources of the underdeveloped region, agrees to be governed exclusively by the laws of the country in which the contract is made insofar as any dispute or determination of rights arising out of the contract is concerned. He thereby waives his right to diplomatic interposition, being content to receive treatment equal to that received by the nationals of the region. The alien makes such an agreement as part of the contract, and in expectation that, for such a concession, he will be amply compensated by the anticipated profits. Is it not equitable and just to hold the individual to such a waiver, voluntarily given, as part of the *quid pro quo* of contract negotiation? The national has signed away his right; therefore he has none. Since no force or compulsion was employed to compromise the voluntary nature of the act, it should be binding and valid.

If the individual, having thus voluntarily waived his right to diplomatic protection, has no right, then neither does his nation. Contrary to the legal subterfuge of the Vattelian fiction, an injury to an alien is not normally an injury to the state of that alien, and to argue the contrary is to allow a historical anachronism to pervert the true interests of justice.[6]

The Calvo Clause commitment merely places the alien in a position of equality with the nationals.[7] Such equality is all that aliens can justly demand. If they wish to share in the wealth of a region, they should be willing to accept the judicial standards of that community. The alien would not be denied justice, for he would have full and free access to the local tribunals. This is all that he has a right to expect. To hold otherwise would place the alien in a favored position. This would be not only inequitable, but an affront to the Latin American people and the quality of their republican institutions.[8]

---

[6] Esquível Obregón, "Protección diplomática de los ciudadanos en el extranjero," *Memoria* (3rd Inter-American Bar Association Conference, Mexico, 1944), pp. 233–234.

[7] García Robles, *op. cit.*, p. 25.

[8] *Ibid.*, pp. 24–25; Beteta and Henríquez, *op. cit.*, p. 34.

This, in essence, is the attitude of Latin Americans.[9] They feel that the Calvo Clause is both morally and juridically sound. The large majority of the Latin American states not only defend the legality of this principle, but vigorously adhere to the use of the Calvo Clause to the extent that many require, in their constitutions and laws, the insertion of such clauses in all contracts concluded with aliens.[10] They have also energetically attempted to win acceptance of the validity of the Clause in inter-American conferences,[11] and in the writings of their leading publicists.[12]

It is important to point out, however, that Latin America, in the face of strong opposition to the complete validity of the Calvo Clause as a bar to interposition, has admitted, in recent years, two major qualifications to this concept. Most Latin American states would now exempt a real denial of justice from the contractual ban on intervention, and Mexico, the leader of the Latin American republics in this controversy, has admitted that the Clause, in contemporary international jurisprudence, probably does not bind the state of the alien from interposing, but does bind the alien from seeking such interposition. These concessions were asserted by Mexican Foreign Minister Saenz, in a note to United States Secretary of State Kellogg on October 7, 1926. Saenz declared:

[9] To avoid repetition, only the general Latin American attitude is presented here. More specific indication of the attitude of the individual states will be found in Chapter IV, *infra*, where the role of the Calvo principles in the various inter-American conferences is traced. It is interesting to note that the Latin American nations did not (with the exception of Chile) reply to the League of Nations Codification Questionnaire (see *infra*, pp. 46ff, 56–57) on the point of the validity of the Calvo Clause. However, as Commissioner MacGregor stated in the *International Fisheries* case (*infra*, pp. 231–240): "With respect to the opinion of the Spanish-American nations . . . it is necessary to bear in mind that they have all maintained the validity of the Calvo Clause and have continued to insert it into all contracts and concessions granted to foreigners, an unquestionable fact which demonstrates that their silence with regard to the inquiry of the League can not be construed as being adverse to the validity of the so often cited Calvo Clause." (*Opinions of Commissioners*, III, p. 211.)

[10] See *supra*, pp. 31–32, for examples. For documentation of the extensive current utilization of the Calvo Clause in Latin America, see the nation-by-nation survey, *infra*, pp. 269–281.

[11] See *infra*, Chapter IV.

[12] See *infra*, Chapter V.

Governmental Attitudes

The Mexican government therefore does not deny that the American government is at liberty to intervene for its nationals; but that does not stand in the way of carrying out an agreement under which the alien agrees not to be the party asking for the diplomatic protection of his government. In case of infringement of any international duty such as a denial of justice would be, the right of the American government to take with the Mexican government appropriate action to seek atonement for injustice or injury which may have been done to its nationals would stand unimpaired. Under these conditions neither would the American government have failed to protect its nationals nor the Mexican government to comply with its laws.[13]

These two major concessions have been accepted by the Latin American nations to reconcile the Clause with the generally accepted rules of international law.[14] While limiting the Calvo Clause in these respects, however, they have not ceased in their efforts to win recognition of the complete validity of the Clause as a bar to diplomatic intervention. The major efforts of recent Latin American diplomacy have been directed toward modifying the existing rules of international law, rather than continuing the debate as to whether the Calvo Clause, in its full sense, is at present legal and valid.[15]

The Attitude of the United States

The United States has been the main protagonist of the opposition to the validity of the Calvo Clause.[16] No other country, outside of Latin America, has had as much opportunity to deal with this vexing concept, and its position in opposition to the Clause has been followed by most of the larger nations of the world.

The United States position on the Calvo Clause, like that of Latin American nations, is tied to its general attitude toward

[13] U.S. Department of State, *American Property Rights in Mexico* (Washington, D.C., 1926), p. 14.

[14] The significance of these qualifications will be discussed in detail, *infra*, pp. 114–116; 259–268.

[15] See *infra*, Chapter IV.

[16] Philip Jessup, *A Modern Law of Nations, An Introduction* (New York, 1948), p. 111.

the institution of diplomatic protection. Although mindful of the many defects and abuses that have characterized diplomatic intervention, the United States has felt that abolishing the right to intervene diplomatically, without substituting an acceptable alternative, would leave its citizens at the mercy of native justice, which often does not measure up to what are considered the international minimum standards. Eliminating, or seriously curtailing, the practice of securing justice for citizens abroad by diplomatic intervention might well result in abuses and inequities far greater than are possible under the present system. While the United States has accepted limitations on this right,[17] and has generally taken the position that simple breach of contract is not an international wrong and thus cannot give rise to the diplomatic interposition of the government unless, after an exhaustion of local remedies, there has been a denial of justice or some flagrant violation of international law,[18] nevertheless, the consistent position of the United States has been that the Calvo Clause cannot serve to prevent the diplomatic interposition by a government which is otherwise justified under the generally recognized rules of international law.[19]

This attitude of the United States is best illustrated by reference to the many diplomatic notes and instructions that have dealt with this problem.

In an early communication, Acting Secretary of State F. W. Seward, on April 15, 1879, expressed the State Department's attitude toward a Calvo Clause: "A stipulation in a contract to be bound by the laws of the country where the money lent is to be employed does not operate where justice is denied in such country, though to make out a claim in such a case such denial of justice must be definitely shown." [20]

---

[17] See *infra*, Chapter IV.

[18] The United States thus distinguishes between contract claims and tort claims. See Borchard, "Contractual Claims in International Law," *Columbia Law Review*, XIII (June 1913), p. 460. The meaning of the term "denial of justice" will be discussed *infra*, pp. 114–116.

[19] Eagleton, *Resp. of States*, p. 172.

[20] Seward to Logan, Moore, *Digest*, VI, p. 293.

Governmental Attitudes

Secretary of State Bayard, in a message to Mr. Scott, minister to Venezuela, June 23, 1887, asserted:

In the 8th article of the contract between the Intercontinental Telephone Company, a New Jersey corporation, and the Venezuelan Government, it was provided that "any doubts or disputes that may arise by reason of this contract shall be decided by the Courts of the Republic in conformity with its laws." With reference to this clause, the Department of State said: "This Department does not concede that this clause constitutes the Venezuelan courts the final arbiters of questions arising under the contract between the corporators and the government of Venezuela, because in the event of a denial of justice by such courts, this Department may under the rules of international law properly intervene." [21]

Secretary of State Bayard reaffirmed this position on February 15, 1888, in a communication directed to Mr. Buck, minister to Peru:

This government can not admit that its citizens can, merely by making contracts with foreign powers, or by other methods not amounting to an act of expatriation or a deliberate abandonment of American citizenship, destroy their dependence upon it or its obligations to protect them in case of a denial of justice.[22]

---

[21] *Ibid.*, p. 294.

[22] *Ibid.* For additional citations of early correspondence supporting this position, see *ibid.*, pp. 293–301. On some occasions, however, interposition has been made dependent on the absence of any renunciation on the part of the citizen of the privilege of appealing to his own government. Secretary of State Fish, in a message to Mr. Butler, consul at Alexandria, Egypt, October 5, 1871, asserted: "It is presumed . . . you are aware that it is a rule of this Department to abstain from officially interfering in matters of contract between citizens of the United States and foreign governments. That interposition is limited to the personal good offices of the agents of this government in behalf of persons who may consider themselves aggrieved. Any interference even to this extent, however, must imply that there should have been no renunciation on the part of the claimant of the privileges of appeal to his own government. When that renunciation has been made a part of the contract itself, as you represent, there would be no ground for interference by this government in behalf of any citizen, whatever may have been his antecedents." *Ibid.*, p. 293. Although some Latin American publicists have made much of this apparent inconsistency (e.g., Esquível Obregón, *México y los Estados Unidos ante el derecho internacional*, pp. 163–164), the position taken by Fish is a distinct exception to the general practice of the Department of State. See Borchard, *Dip. Prot.*, p. 797.

The Calvo Clause

More recently, Secretary of State Kellogg, in a communication directed to the Mexican minister of foreign affairs, on January 28, 1926, spelled out in detail the United States' attitude:

. . . [In] the past this Government has frequently notified the Mexican Government that it does not admit that one of its citizens can contract by declaration or otherwise to bind his own government not to invoke its rights under the rules of international law. Under the rules applicable to intercourse between states, an injury done by one state to a citizen of another state through a denial of justice is an injury done to the state whose national is injured. The right of his state to extend what is known as diplomatic protection can not be waived by the individual. If states by their unilateral acts or citizens by their individual acts were permitted to modify or withhold the application of the principles of international law, the body of rules established by the custom of nations as legally binding upon states would manifestly be gradually broken down.

The right of diplomatic protection is not a personal right, but exists in favor of one state against another. It is a privilege which one state under the rules of international law can extend or withhold in behalf of one of its nationals. Whether or not one of its citizens has agreed not to invoke the protection of his government, nevertheless his government has, because the injury has been inflicted by one state against the other, the right to extend what is termed diplomatic protection.[23]

Secretary of State Stimson reasserted the United States' opposition to the validity of the Calvo Clause in a letter of May 12, 1929, to the Preparatory Committee of the Conference for the Codification of International Law. Stimson wrote:

In general, no contract made by an individual to renounce the diplomatic remedy can have effect if its enforcement would result in any changes or modifications in the ordinary rules of international law. *North American Dredging Co. (U.S.) v. Mexico, Opinions of Commissioners,* September 8th, 1923, page 21.[24]

---

[23] *Rights of American Citizens in Certain Oil Lands in Mexico,* Senate Exec. Doc. No. 96, 69th Congress, 1st Session (1926), pp. 22–23.

[24] League of Nations, Conference for the Codification of International Law, *Bases of Discussion,* Suppl. to Vol. III (C.75(a).M.69(a).1929.V): *Responsibility of States for Damage Caused in Their Territory to the Person or Property of*

Governmental Attitudes

The contemporary attitude of the United States government toward the Calvo Clause is one of continued opposition to its validity. Stanley D. Metzger, assistant legal adviser for economic affairs to the Department of State, in a personal communication dated February 13, 1953, quoted the following passage from a memorandum from Secretary of State Root to the President on March 27, 1908, asserting that this message "represents, as it has since its utterance, the American attitude towards the Calvo Clause." The passage referred to states:

To preclude the claimant in this case from relief, the Calvo Clause — "All the doubts and controversies arising from the interpretation and wording of this contract shall be decided by the courts of the Republic of Venezuela in accordance with its laws, and in no case can they become the foundation for international claims" — is triumphantly invoked. It is true that the claimant company itself waived all rights of diplomatic intervention as far as it was concerned, but an unaccredited agent may not renounce the right or privilege of the Government, and for the purposes of this claim . . . the company is nothing more than a private citizen. A citizen may waive or renounce any private right or claim he possesses; he may not renounce the right or privilege of this Government. It is not merely the right and privilege, it is the duty of the Government to protect its citizens abroad and to see to it that the dignity of this Government does not suffer injury through violence or indignity to the private citizen. Take the case of an act which may at once be a tort and a crime: It is a familiar doctrine that the injured party may waive the tort; he can not waive the crime. The reason is that he may waive a right or privilege which he possesses in his private capacity; he can not waive the right of the public nor the interest of the public, because he is not the agent of the public for such purposes. It therefore follows that this Government may intervene with entire propriety to protect the rights of its citizens, even although such citizens have contracted away the right to diplomatic intervention in so far as it lay in their province.[25]

These quotations accurately reflect the attitude of the Amer-

Foreigners, p. 22. For an analysis of the North American Dredging Company case, see Chapter VII, infra.

[25] The quoted passage may be found in Hackworth, Digest, V, pp. 636–637.

ican government.[26] It should be noted, however, that while the United States considers the Clause ineffective as a bar to its diplomatic intervention, its position, on further examination, does not coincide with that adopted by many leading publicists, i.e., that the Clause is, in its narrow interpretation, superfluous and, in its full meaning, illegal and futile.[27] The United States has not carried its opposition to the Calvo Clause to the extent of attempting actively to discourage its inclusion in concession contracts. The State Department has taken the attitude that it is within the rights of a foreign government to prescribe the terms of concessions which it may grant to American citizens to carry on business within its territories and after a concession in which a certain privilege is denied has been accepted, the United States will not demand the annulment of the provision.[28] Nor will the State Department advise against the acceptance of a Calvo Clause commitment by American citizens. Secretary of State Stimson, in a telegram to the American Embassy at Santiago, on November 26, 1929, stated that "the acceptance of such clauses is a question for the interested companies to decide." [29]

Furthermore, on more than one occasion, the State Department has interpreted a Calvo Clause narrowly, thereby reconciling it to the rules of international law and granting to it a limited degree of validity. Acting Secretary of State Adee, in a communication to Mr. Partridge, minister to Venezuela, described a constitutional requirement that there be inserted in every contract of public interest a clause specifying that doubts and controversies that may arise regarding the meaning and execution

[26] For further documentation of the United States' position, see C. C. Hyde, *International Law Chiefly as Interpreted and Applied by the United States* (Boston, 1947), II, pp. 994–995.

[27] For example, Eagleton, *Resp. of States*, p. 175; Herbert Briggs, *The Law of Nations, Cases, Documents, and Notes* (2nd ed., New York, 1952), pp. 648–649.

[28] Secretary of State Hay maintained this position in a communication to Mr. Powell, minister to Haiti (April 1, 1899), Moore, *Digest*, VI, p. 289. See also Borchard, *Dip. Prot.*, p. 796.

[29] File 810.79611 Pan American Airways /730. Quoted in *The Calvo Clause in American Policy and Practice* (State Department Research Project No. 50, Washington, D.C., 1947), p. 37.

of the contract shall be decided by the Venezuelan tribunals and according to the laws of the republic, "and in no case can such contracts be a cause for international claims." This, he said, was

. . . a gratifying guarantee that, by organic statute, aliens may assert their contractual rights by suit against the state or federal government. The inherent right of an alien to recur to the diplomatic protection of his government in the event of a denial of justice could not be regarded as impaired were the resort thus offered to him withheld or rendered nugatory.[30]

Secretary of State Gresham more specifically accepted the validity of the Calvo Clause in its narrow interpretation. Gresham stated:

As regards the effect of the provision in a contract that "the grantee refuses in all events the diplomatic recourse," the Department prefers not to express a definite opinion in advance of the presentation of a case requiring it. Probably, however, it means only this: That the party claiming under the contract agrees to invoke for the protection of his rights only the authorities, judicial or other, of the country where the contract is made. Until he has done this, and justice is plainly denied him, he can not invoke the diplomatic intervention of his own country for redress. But if his application to the authorities of the country where the contract is made results in a palpable denial of justice, or in a plainly unjust discrimination against the applicant as an American citizen the clause above quoted would hardly be construed to prevent an appeal for diplomatic intervention if such intervention would otherwise be allowable under the rules of international law.[31]

The State Department has also stated that the existence or nonexistence of a Calvo Clause will be influential in determining whether or not it decides to sponsor a claim. Secretary of State Root, in an instruction to the American Legation in Venezuela, noted the existence of a Calvo Clause contractual commitment and suggested "that the company should seek redress for its grievances, if any it has, in the courts of Venezuela." Root de-

---

[30] July 26, 1896. Quoted in Moore, *Digest*, VI, p. 299.

[31] Gresham to Mr. Crawford, September 4, 1893. Quoted in Moore, *Digest*, VI, pp. 299–300.

nied, however, that such a commitment would legally prevent interposition by the United States.[32] In 1908, the solicitor for the State Department, in a memorandum to the secretary of state, approvingly quoted the statement of the British government in regard to the moral weight that should be given to a Calvo Clause commitment. The British, in their statement, asserted:

Although the general international rights of His Majesty's Government are in no wise modified by the provisions of this document [Calvo Clause], to which they were not a party, the fact that the company have so far as lay in their power deliberately contracted themselves out of every remedial recourse in case of dispute, except that which is specified in Article 14 of the contract [Calvo Clause], is undoubtedly an element to be taken into serious consideration when they subsequently appeal for the intervention of His Majesty's Government.[33]

Undoubtedly the most significant qualification of the State Department's position of opposition to the validity of the Calvo Clause is the apparent acceptance of the principle that, although the Calvo Clause does not modify the rights of the state under international law, it does serve to abrogate any rights that are possessed by the individual in this matter. In the statement of Secretary of State Root, recently reaffirmed by Mr. Metzger,[34] it was asserted: "It is true that the claimant company itself waived all rights of diplomatic intervention as far as it was concerned . . ."[35]

This statement would appear to place the United States in agreement with the contentions of Mexican Foreign Minister Saenz that, under the contemporary rules of international law, the Calvo Clause commitment, although not binding upon the state, does bind the individual.[36] The correspondence between

[32] February 28, 1907. Quoted in Hackworth, *Digest*, V, p. 637.
[33] *Correspondence Relating to Wrongs Done to American Citizens by the Government of Venezuela* (Senate Exec. Doc. No. 413, 60th Congress, 1st Session, 1908), p. 79.
[34] *Supra*, p. 41.
[35] Hackworth, *Digest*, V, p. 636. See statement to the same effect, *Wrongs Done to American Citizens by the Government of Venezuela*, p. 116.
[36] *Supra*, pp. 36–37.

the United States and Mexico in relation to the agrarian and petroleum laws promulgated by President Calles in the 1920s has been interpreted by several authorities as having reached agreement on this compromise, i.e., that the Clause binds the individual but not the state.[37] The apparent acceptance of this principle gains greater significance in view of the fact that this is the rule of law laid down in the most recent international arbitral decisions involving the validity and effectiveness of the Calvo Clause.[38]

It will presently be seen that the acceptance of this rule by governments and international tribunals gives recognition to the limited validity of the Calvo Clause, and that its existence or nonexistence in a concession contract is consequently of material importance in arbitral proceedings.[39]

In summation, it may be said the United States has steadfastly denied that the Calvo Clause waiver can prevent interposition that would be otherwise permissible under the generally recognized rules of international law. It bases its position on the Vattelian formula that an injury to a national is an injury to the state of that national, thus giving the state rights of recovery independent of the rights of the individual and not affected by the individual's contractual waiver. It does not consider the insertion of such clauses in concession contracts to be illegal, and will not advise its citizens not to sign such commitments. Nor is it uninfluenced by the existence or nonexistence of such clauses in deciding whether or not to sponsor a national's claim. Finally, the United States is apparently willing to recognize the Calvo Clause as binding on the individual concerned, but not upon his state.

[37] Lionel M. Summers, "The Calvo Clause," *Virginia Law Review*, XIX (March 1933), p. 471; G. H. Stuart, *Latin America and the United States* (New York, 1943), pp. 176–177. No less an authority than Charles C. Hyde, who was solicitor for the State Department when Hughes was secretary of state, supports Saenz in this contention that the Clause is binding on the individual. See "Concerning Attempts by Contract to Restrict Interposition," *AJIL*, XXI (April 1927), pp. 298–301.

[38] *Infra*, Chapters VII and VIII.

[39] *Infra*, pp. 259–268.

The Attitude of Other Leading Powers

Although the Calvo Clause controversy has been rather unique-ly an inter-American dispute, other leading nations have had occasion to express their position in regard to the validity of this concept.

One of the questions submitted to states on the preliminary questionnaire in connection with the League of Nations Confer-ence on the Codification of International Law dealt with the responsibility of states for injuries to aliens when "the individ-ual concerned has contracted not to have recourse to the diplo-matic remedy." [40] In their replies to this question, some nineteen non-American nations took more or less definite positions on the validity of the Calvo Clause.[41]

The Union of South Africa took a definite stand against the validity of the Clause in reply to the questionnaire. In its reply, South Africa asserted:

An agreement between a national of a particular State and a foreign Government not to have recourse to the diplomatic remedy is, as regards his own government, *res inter alios acta* and would therefore not debar his Government from maintain-ing the principles of international law if it felt so inclined. Such an agreement may also be considered void as being against *bonos mores internationales*, seeing that it would tend to relieve the State in question of its duty to live up to the precepts of inter-national law.[42]

Germany, like the United States, has on occasion taken the position that the renunciatory provisions did not bind it, since it was not a party to the contract.[43] Germany's reply to the ques-tionnaire, however, added the qualification that such agreements would affect the rights of the individual, and, under certain cir-

---

[40] *Bases of Discussion*, III (C.75.M.69.1929.V): *Responsibility of States for Damages Caused in Their Territory to the Person or Property of Foreigners*, Question XI (d), p. 133.

[41] The views of nations as evidenced by the arguments of their agents before international tribunals considering the validity of the Calvo Clause will be ex-amined *infra*, Chapters VI, VII, and VIII.

[42] *Bases of Discussion*, III, p. 133.

[43] Moore, *Digest*, VI, p. 300: Beteta and Henríquez, *op. cit.*, p. 44; Borchard, *Dip. Prot.*, p. 799.

cumstances, modify the right of the state to present a claim. Germany replied:

In principle, the answer to the question whether an individual may contract not to have recourse to the aid of his state in defending his interests should be in the negative. In submitting such a claim, the state maintains its own right, of which no private individual can dispose. But it is possible to deduce from agreements of this kind that the individual foregoes his right to regard himself as injured by certain events, so that the State's claim would be devoid of any effective basis.[44]

Australia's reply was brief and positive: "A contract by the individual not to have recourse to the diplomatic remedy in case of denial of justice or violation of international law should be regarded as void." [45] The Right Honorable Richard G. Casey, Australian minister for external affairs, stated in a personal communication dated April 27, 1955, that he saw no reason for altering the view on the Calvo Clause as expressed in this reply. Casey stated:

Should a case involving a Calvo Clause arise the Government would have to consider its attitude to such clause in the light of all the circumstances, and I am not in a position, as you will appreciate, to state in advance what would be its general attitude in relation to such a question. As at present advised, however, I see no reason for altering the views expressed in 1929. I should nevertheless point out that the reply to which you refer was in relation only to Question XI(d) . . . The forms of Calvo Clauses may of course vary from case to case, and the reply to Question XI(d) was not intended as a statement of the Government's views with regard to Calvo Clauses in general.

Austria asserted that a Calvo Clause commitment "on the part of the individual should not in principle, affect the case." [46]

Belgium (in a statement which the Belgium Ministry of Foreign Affairs, in a personal communication dated July 15, 1955, and signed by L. Scheyven, asserted "has still to be considered as being the present position of Belgium") replied: "Renunciation of re-

[44] *Bases of Discussion,* III, p. 133.
[45] *Ibid.*
[46] *Ibid.*

course on the part of the individual concerned does not affect the claim of the state, which he has no power to bind." [47]

Bulgaria's reply, not entirely relevant, was based on the state's right of self-defense: "When a State has acted in self-defense, even when the person concerned has contracted not to have recourse to the diplomatic remedy, the State is entitled to disclaim responsibility." [48]

Denmark, in a lengthy reply, quite properly distinguished between the effect of the Calvo Clause commitment on the individual and the effect on the state, upholding the validity of the Clause as it affects the private rights of the individual, but denying the effectiveness of the Clause in the face of a violation of a treaty or of international law itself. Denmark stated:

If the private person concerned has contracted not to have recourse to diplomatic remedy, this may mean that he has foregone his right in return for consideration or by engaging in procedure. Such an engagement will be binding on him according to the general rules of private law. Just as, in a contract between private individuals, a given court or arbitration tribunal may be selected so that the parties renounce from the outset their right to submit the dispute to the ordinary courts, a private individual may renounce his right to raise a question, through the intermediary of his Government, through the diplomatic channel. But in both cases the rule has its natural limitations. . . . As regards diplomatic protection, it should be remembered that such protection is in many cases the expression of a right or interest possessed by the claimant State rather than by the private person in question. For instance, an individual can not renounce diplomatic protection if it is laid down in a treaty that foreigners shall be exempt from military service, since the Clause has been inserted, not merely on behalf of the private interests of that person, but of the general interests of his country.

In most cases, therefore, the general rule may be upheld that individuals can renounce diplomatic protection — in the sense that the other state may plead such renunciation and oppose diplomatic intervention — only when such renunciation means that the individual foregoes for consideration or by engaging in procedure some right of a private nature. No private individual,

---

[47] *Ibid.*   [48] *Ibid.*

however, can renounce the right of his State, in international law, to plead the violation of treaties or of international law itself.[49]

The Danish Ministry for Foreign Affairs, in a personal communication dated February 23, 1955, and signed by Georg Cohn, stated that "the Danish Government still adheres to the views expressed" in this reply.

Finland upheld the validity of the Calvo Clause, asserting: "Contracting not to have recourse to the diplomatic remedy should be regarded as admissible and valid at law provided the contract has been concluded freely and without constraint." [50] The Finnish Ministry of Foreign Affairs, in a personal communication dated March 16, 1955, stated that there has been no occasion since 1929 for the Finnish government "to precise their attitude towards this question." However, an unofficial memorandum prepared in response to my inquiry by V. J. Ahokas, envoy extraordinary and minister plenipotentiary, legal adviser to the Ministry for Foreign Affairs of Finland, suggests that Finland might not in the future take as positive a stand in favor of the validity of the Calvo Clause. Ahokas, in a statement of his personal opinion, asserted:

. . . I should however doubt very much whether it would be advisable to adopt a point of view so strongly in favour of the Calvo Clause as is contained in the answer mentioned above. . . . For my own part I should consider that the renunciation of diplomatic protection can at the very most have the effect that in certain circumstances the Government of the person interested have to limit their intervention to obvious cases of denial or delay of justice. No private individual however can renounce the right of his State, in international law, to plead the violation of treaties or of international law itself.

Outside of the Americas, Great Britain, more than any other power, has had the greatest opportunity to deal with this controversy. Great Britain has taken the position that its general international right of diplomatic interposition is not modified by

[49] *Ibid.*, pp. 133–134.
[50] *Ibid.*, p. 134.

the renunciatory Clause.[51] However, as seen previously, it has regarded the existence of this contractual provision as an element to be taken into consideration when an appeal for intervention is made. Great Britain has also recognized the restricted validity of the Calvo Clause[52] in accepting it as binding on the individual and agreeing that the Clause would be binding on an international tribunal in the absence of any violation of international law. It is significant that the British, in their reply to the questionnaire, accepted the "complete and exclusive" jurisdiction of local tribunals dealing with disputes over a contract containing the Calvo Clause. The British replied:

His Majesty's Government in Great Britain accept as good law and are content to be guided by the decision of the Claims Commission between the United States of America and Mexico in the case of the North American Dredging Company of Texas of March 31st, 1926, printed in the volume of the *Opinions of the Commissioners*, page 21. It is laid down in this opinion that a stipulation in a contract which purports to bind the claimant not to apply to his Government to intervene diplomatically or otherwise in the event of a denial or delay of justice or in the event of any violation of the rules or principles of international law is void, and that any stipulation which purports to bind the claimant's Government not to intervene in respect of violations of international law is void, but that no rule of international law prevents the inclusion of a stipulation in a contract between a Government and an alien that in all matters pertaining to the contract the jurisdiction of the local tribunals shall be complete and exclusive, nor does it prevent such a stipulation being obligatory, in the absence of any special agreement to the contrary between the two Governments concerned, upon any international tribunal to which may be submitted a claim arising out of the contract in which the stipulation was inserted.[53]

The importance of this definition of Great Britain's attitude toward the validity of the Calvo Clause is greatly enhanced by

---

[51] Borchard, *Dip. Prot.*, pp. 799, 809; Eagleton, *Resp. of States*, pp. 172–173; Moore, *Digest*, VI, p. 300.

[52] Beteta and Henríquez, *op. cit.*, p. 44.

[53] *Bases of Discussion*, III, p. 134. The significance of Britain's explicit approval of the rule of law in the *Dredging* case will be discussed *infra*, pp. 228–229.

the fact that the British Foreign Office, in a personal communication dated September 16, 1954, and signed by E. J. Parsant, stated that the reply of Great Britain to the League of Nations questionnaire still represented its attitude in regard to the Clause. The Foreign Office stated: "Her Majesty's Government have not had occasion to reconsider their view of the Calvo Clause, and should the Clause be invoked in a future case, there is no reason to suppose that the attitude of Her Majesty's Government will have changed."

Hungary, in its reply to the questionnaire, asserted:

In case (d), the individual concerned has only contracted not to enforce his claims by having recourse to a certain remedy — he has not relinquished the right itself; in such circumstances, therefore, he may cause the responsibility of the State to be established through some other channel.[54]

India accepted the reply of Great Britain as expressing its attitude on this controversy, asserting: "The reply submitted on behalf of His Majesty's Government in Great Britain may be taken as covering the position in British India." [55]

Japan denied that the individual's waiver could affect the rights of his state, remarking: "Such 'renunciation of protection' on the part of the individual is deemed to be ineffective in affecting the State's right to diplomatic protection of its citizens or subjects." [56]

Norway likewise denied that the state's right of interposition would be affected:

If the foreigner in question has contracted not to have recourse to action through the diplomatic channel, we presume that the State will nevertheless not be freed from its international responsibility in the cases mentioned in reply to point IV. This applies even if the renunciation expressly includes these cases, since such renunciation can not be regarded as binding on the foreigner's country of origin.[57]

New Zealand accepted the reply of Great Britain as express-

---

[54] *Ibid.*, p. 134.
[55] *Ibid.*   [56] *Ibid.*   [57] *Ibid.*

ing its attitude, stating: "The New Zealand Government desires to associate themselves with the views expressed by His Majesty's Government in Great Britain." [58]

The government of the Netherlands took a firm position in favor of the validity of the Calvo Clause, asserting in its reply: "In this case responsibility may be disclaimed unless the contract was concluded under stress of physical or moral constraint." [59] However, in a personal communication dated May 2, 1955, M. Riphagen, legal adviser to the Netherlands Ministry of Foreign Affairs, asserted that "the Netherlands answer was a short one, and will not appear fully conclusive insofar as it does not indicate what should be understood by 'responsibility'." In a very significant "clarification" of the previous definition of position, Riphagen distinguished between the effect of the Calvo Clause on the rights of the individual and its effect on the rights of the state, thereby modifying the position of the government of the Netherlands in the direction of recognizing the *limited validity* of the Calvo Clause as binding on the individual but not on his state. Riphagen asserted:

Obviously the fact that the individual concerned has contracted not to have recourse to the diplomatic remedy does entitle the other party — provided the contract has not been entered into under stress of physical or moral restraint — to disclaim responsibility *towards the individual* in any procedure before an international Tribunal. Insofar as the State of which the individual is a national, merely asserts a right of this individual, the disclaimer remains applicable.

A different question, however, is the violation by a State of its duties *towards another State* under international law. The resulting responsibility cannot be contracted away otherwise than by agreement between the *States* concerned.

It would seem that the Netherlands position as referred to above is generally in line with the terms of the "Basis of Discussion no. 26" . . .

Poland replied that the Clause was void, stating:

[58] *Ibid.*
[59] *Ibid.*

It is only as regards point (d) (Calvo Clause) that an express reservation should be made — namely, that the renunciation by a private individual of diplomatic protection (both the renunciation and consequent exclusion of settlement by international arbitration of the question whether an international wrong has been committed) is not valid and remains without legal effect as regards the State defending the injured party.[60]

Siam reserved its opinion on the Calvo Clause controversy, as it did with most points of the questionnaire.[61]

Switzerland, quoting Anzilotti, stated:

Renunciation of this kind by an individual would not necessarily bind the State of which he is a national; the latter would always be entitled to hold another State responsible for an act contrary to international law committed in respect of one of its nationals, even if the national in question decides not to complain or has given an understanding not to do so. For, at international law, there is only one injured party, and that party is not the individual, but the State. "In protecting its nationals against foreign States," as Anzilotti very rightly observes, "the State protects its own interests against all unlawful interference, that is to say, against all pretensions of a foreign State not based on international law." In other words, a State is not internationally responsible because an injustice has been committed against an individual, but because such injustice constitutes an act contrary to international law and injures the rights of another State. Conversely, we may agree with Anzilotti that, "as the State in this instance merely exercises its own right, it is never bound to take action against the State which has caused unlawful prejudice to its nationals; it simply possesses the right to do so and it may exercise this right or not as it prefers." [62]

Czechoslovakia, noting the many difficulties involved in this issue, took the position that a waiver of protection is permissible as far as the individual is concerned, but will not operate to bar the interposition of the country itself if it holds that right independently of the desire of the person to be protected. The Czechoslovakian government asserted:

[60] *Ibid.*, p. 135.
[61] *Ibid.*
[62] *Ibid.*

The question whether the person concerned may renounce in advance the right to diplomatic protection by his State has already caused frequent difficulties in practice, and the answers to it have been very varied. In principle, the Czechoslovak Government sees no objection to a previous declaration by the person concerned that in certain circumstances he will have recourse only to the legal remedies afforded him by the national law in question and will not invoke the diplomatic protection of his own country. On the other hand, a renunciation of this kind should in no way prejudice the right of the country itself to intervene, if it holds that right independently of the desire of the person to be protected.[63]

Canada, the last nation to reply, took the position that a Calvo Clause would be binding "only when such a contracting out is allowed by the laws of the state of which the individual is a national." [64] The Canadian Department of External Affairs, in a personal communication dated March 21, 1955, stated that no more recent "occasion has arisen where it has been necessary for this country to reaffirm its position" in regard to the Calvo Clause.

It will be noted that while the replies to the League questionnaire varied a great deal, not all the replies of the non-American powers were unfavorable to the contention of the validity of the Calvo Clause. Only South Africa, Australia, and Austria declared more or less definitely against the Clause. On the other hand, only Finland and the Netherlands came out explicitly in favor of it, and their positions must be considered as basically modified as the result of the statements of key officials of these governments in personal correspondence. In the majority of replies, the position was that a contractual undertaking by a private person not to have recourse to the diplomatic remedy does not bind the state of which he is a national if there is a violation of the generally recognized rules of international law. However, qualifications added by various leading powers, especially in the replies of Great Britain, Denmark, Czechoslovakia, India, and

[63] *Ibid.*
[64] *Bases of Discussion*, Suppl. to Vol. III, p. 4.

New Zealand, and in the personal communication from the Netherlands Ministry of Foreign Affairs, tend toward the mitigation of the strictness and all-inclusiveness of this basic principle, and would appear to indicate a willingness to accept the validity of the Calvo Clause in its restricted or limited form. As Commissioner MacGregor, speaking for the Claims Commission in the *International Fisheries* case, asserted, the replies submitted by a majority of the responding nations "are in practical accord with the opinion expressed in the decision of the *North American Dredging Company of Texas*," [65] a case which affirmed the limited validity of the Calvo Clause.[66] As the British government significantly stated:

. . . no rule of international law prevents the inclusion of a stipulation in a contract between a Government and an alien that in all matters pertaining to the contract the jurisdiction of the local tribunals shall be *complete and exclusive*, nor does it prevent such a stipulation being obligatory, in the absence of any special agreement to the contrary between the two Governments concerned, upon any international tribunal to which may be submitted a claim arising out of the contract in which the stipulation was inserted.[67]

It is also important to note that the League of Nations Basis of Discussion No. 26, which indicated roughly the area of agreement among the replies of the governments on this point, stated:

An undertaking by a party to a contract that he will not have recourse to the diplomatic remedy does not bind the State whose national he is and does not release the State with which the contract is made from its international responsibility.

If in a contract a foreigner makes a valid agreement that the local courts shall alone have jurisdiction, this provision is binding upon any international tribunal to which a claim under the contract is submitted; the State can then only be responsible

---

[65] Claims Commission, United States and Mexico, *Opinions of Commissioners*, III (1931), pp. 209–210.

[66] The rule of law in the *Dredging* case will be analyzed *infra*, pp. 215–223. It is significant that four nations, Great Britain, India, New Zealand, and the United States, specifically cited the *Dredging* case in their replies.

[67] *Bases of Discussion*, III, p. 134. Italics mine.

for damage suffered by the foreigner in the cases contemplated in Bases of Discussion Nos. 5 and 6.[68]

Codification Attempts Involving the Calvo Clause

The Calvo Clause has been the subject of several codification attempts, but, as has been the case with other issues of a similarly controversial nature, little progress has been made.

The most important effort to codify this part of international law, and the only public codification effort that has dealt specifically with the Calvo Clause, was that made under the auspices of the League of Nations. The Assembly of the League, on September 22, 1924, adopted a resolution asking the Council to convene a Committee of Experts with a view toward the "progressive codification" of international law.[69] The Committee of Experts was appointed and, after much deliberation, it drew up reports on seven subjects which it considered "ripe for codification." One of these subjects was the "Responsibility of States for Damage Caused in Their Territory to the Person or Property of Foreigners." The subcommittee delegated to write the preliminary report on this subject consisted of M. Guerrero, *rapporteur*, M. de Visscher, and Mr. Wang Chung-Hui. However, since M. de Visscher and Mr. Wang Chung-Hui were absent, the subcommittee report was written by Guerrero, a citizen of Salvador, and, not surprisingly, it presented the Latin American viewpoint on the general problems involved in the protection of nationals abroad.[70] The report did not specifically deal with the validity

[68] *Ibid.*, p. 135. Bases of Discussion Nos. 5 and 6 (*ibid.*, pp. 48, 51) "refer only to what is properly called denial of justice in its most restricted acceptance" (Commissioner MacGregor, speaking for the commission in the *International Fisheries* case, *Opinions of Commissioners*, III, p. 211). It should be remembered that no Latin American replies were included in the drawing up of this Basis of Discussion. It would be interesting to see what the Basis would have been if the twenty Latin American nations had replied on this point.

[69] League of Nations, *Official Journal*, February 1925, pp. 122–123.

[70] The Guerrero report is reprinted in Eagleton, *Resp. of States*, pp. 233–260, and also in *AJIL*, XX, Spec. Suppl. (1926), pp. 177–203. For a critical analysis of this report, see Borchard, "Responsibility of States for Damage Done in Their Territories to the Person or Property of Foreigners," *AJIL*, XX (October 1926), pp. 738–747.

of the Calvo Clause, but did embrace the "equality of alien with national" formula, which in turn would serve to validate the Clause: "The maximum that may be claimed for a foreigner is civil equality with nationals. . . . In any case, a State owes nothing more than that to foreigners, and any pretension to the contrary would be inadmissible and unjust both morally and juridically." [71]

As a preliminary step to the meeting of an International Conference for the Codification of International Law, the Guerrero report, somewhat modified by the action of the full Committee of Experts, was submitted to a number of governments along with a detailed questionnaire dealing with various elements of the problem of state responsibility for injuries to aliens. Included in the questionnaire, as a Basis of Discussion, was the question of the validity of the Calvo Clause.[72]

The First Conference for the Codification of International Law met at the Hague on March 13, 1930. Some forty-two states, including the United States and eight Latin American nations, were represented. After prolonged discussions, the conference finally adjourned on April 11, 1930, without having discussed the question of the validity of the Calvo Clause.[73] The discussions were characterized by sharp conflicts between the two extremes — "the absolute irresponsibility" advocates and the "absolute responsibility" advocates, and no acceptable basis of negotiation was discovered.[74]

In the Western Hemisphere, the codification of the rules of international law has been one of the chief concerns of the Pan-American movement.[75] In the various sessions of the several

[71] Reprinted in Eagleton, *Resp. of States*, p. 239.

[72] For an analysis of the replies of the governments, see *supra*, pp. 46–56.

[73] For a description of the Hague Conference, see the article by G. Hackworth, the U.S. delegate, "Responsibility of States for Damages Caused in Their Territory to the Person or Property of Foreigners," *AJIL*, XXIV (July 1930), pp. 500–516.

[74] Podestá Costa, *Manual de derecho internacional público*, p. 204; Borchard, "'Responsibility of States' at the Hague Codification Conference," *AJIL*, XXIV (July 1930), pp. 517–540.

[75] John P. Humphrey, *The Inter-American System — A Canadian View* (To-

conferences and committees that have dealt with the problem of codification,[76] the Latin American nations have vigorously attempted to win acceptance of restrictions on the exercise of diplomatic protection. While the Calvo Clause itself has never been formally discussed in these codification conferences, the related Calvo principles of nonintervention and "equality of aliens with nationals" have been frequent topics of debate, with the Latin American nations gradually winning acceptance of their viewpoint on the former and making some headway in their efforts to win acceptance of their viewpoint on the latter.[77]

However, the viewpoint of the United States, on the one hand, and that of the Latin American republics on the other, have not yet become sufficiently reconciled to permit codification of a rule of law on the Calvo Clause.

Here the situation stands at the present time.[78] The results of codification conferences, both in the Americas and in other parts of the world, have not been greatly helpful in our task of determining the rule of law on the Calvo Clause. But these efforts have proved fruitful in that they have given many nations an opportunity to express their positions on the Calvo controversy.

ronto, 1942), p. 219. See "Outline of the Codification of International Law in the Inter-American System with Special Reference to the Methods of Codification," *AJIL*, XLI, Suppl. (1947), pp. 116–138, for a good summary of these efforts.

[76] For a description of the extremely complicated codification machinery, see Edward O. Guerrant, *Roosevelt's Good Neighbor Policy* (Albuquerque, 1950), pp. 76–81.

[77] The role of the Calvo Clause controversy in inter-American relations will be discussed in Chapter IV, *infra*.

[78] The Calvo Clause controversy figured briefly in the discussion over the Draft Declaration of the Rights and Duties of States submitted by Panama to the United Nations International Law Commission. In commenting on Article VIII of the proposed declaration, which dealt with "Diplomatic Intervention," the government of Mexico declared that the draft declaration "should contain a provision expressly stating that diplomatic intervention is out of place in cases where the persons concerned have previously waived it." United Nations International Law Commission, *Preparatory Study Concerning a Draft Declaration of the Rights and Duties of States* (Lake Success, 1948), pp. 74–75. The final draft declaration, approved by the International Law Commission, did not contain an article on diplomatic protection. For a critical evaluation of the importance and influence of this draft declaration, see Hans Kelsen, "The Draft Declaration on Rights and Duties of States," *AJIL*, XLIV (April 1950), pp. 259–276.

This is especially true of the League of Nations' effort, and the documentary evidence contained in the governments' replies to the codification questionnaire is an excellent indication of the attitudes of the leading powers toward the problem of the validity of the Calvo Clause.

One codification effort remains to be considered. A private group, under the auspices of the Harvard Law School faculty, drew up a draft convention on the "Law of Responsibility of States for Damage Done in Their Territory to the Person or Property of Foreigners," Article 17 of which dealt specifically with the validity of the Calvo Clause.[79] While this draft convention does not represent the official viewpoint of any government, it merits special attention because of the quality of the draftsmanship, the prestige of the participating legal scholars, and the fact that it dealt specifically with the Calvo Clause.

Article 17 of the draft convention reads:

A state is not relieved of responsibility as a consequence of any provision in its own law or in an agreement with an alien which attempts to exclude responsibility by making the decisions of its own courts final; nor is it relieved of responsibility by any waiver by the alien of the protection of the state of which he is a national.[80]

The Harvard draft convention thus denies the validity of the Calvo Clause insofar as the responsibility of the concessionaire state is concerned. The reasoning behind this position is indicated by the Comment on Article 17, the concluding paragraphs of which read:

The prevailing view seems to be that the mere stipulation to submit disputes to local courts is confirmatory of the general rule of international law and will be so construed by the national government of the concessionaires. If, however, the renunciation goes so far as to preclude recourse to diplomatic protection in cases of denial of justice, the renunciation of protection will not be considered as binding upon the claimant's government. . . .

The right of the government to submit the claims of its citizens to an international tribunal, is, it may be concluded, supe-

[79] *AJIL*, XXIII, Special Number (1929), pp. 202–215.
[80] *Ibid.*, pp. 202–203.

rior to the right or competency of the individual to contract it away, for whatever the individual's power to renounce a personal right or privilege, he does not represent the government and is, therefore, incompetent to renounce a right, duty, or privilege of the government. On sum total, therefore, the better opinion seems to be that the renunciatory clause is without any effect so far as any changes or modifications in the ordinary rules of international law are concerned.[81]

The opinions expressed in the Harvard draft were representative of the views of the great majority of United States legal scholars at the time it was published, and it probably still represents the prevailing opinion among United States scholars. Although Article 17, on its face, rejects the validity of the Calvo Clause, and is generally so interpreted, it should be noted that, since it refers only to the responsibility of the concessionaire state, it is possible to reconcile this position with the concept of limited validity which, it will be seen, has become the rule of law on this problem as a result of recent international arbitral jurisprudence, the official attitudes taken by the leading nations of the world, and contemporary developments in the field of international law.

Our survey of the official governmental attitudes toward the Calvo Clause would appear to justify certain generalizations.

First, the efforts of the Latin American nations to win acceptance of the complete validity of the Clause as a bar to diplomatic interposition have not met with success. The traditional Vattelian principle that an injury to a national is also an injury to the state of that national gives the state concerned rights of recovery independent of those possessed by the individual and hence unaffected by his contractual waiver. Although the logic and justice of this principle are open to question, it is still generally accepted by most nations as the principle basic to the institution of diplomatic protection. Contemporary developments in the field of international law that tend to give greater emphasis to the role of the individual might well make this principle inoperative. However, at the present time, a majority of states consider

---

[81] *Ibid.*, p. 215. Edwin M. Borchard was the reporter, and Article 17 and the supporting reasoning reflect to a large extent his views on this subject.

it to be valid, and consequently have rejected the complete validity of the Calvo Clause.

Secondly, the rejection of the complete validity of the Calvo Clause does not necessarily result in its complete invalidity, as many publicists contend. On the contrary, recent declarations by a majority of nations that have dealt with this problem would tend to refute the contention that the Clause is invalid, superfluous, and ineffective. It has been suggested that the Clause has not been regarded as ineffective either by the United States or by the leading non-American powers. The nations of the world have indicated an apparent willingness to accord a limited validity to the Calvo Clause, an attitude that finds solid support in recent arbitral jurisprudence that has formulated the rule that the Clause is binding on the individual, although not on the state in the event of a breach of international law.[82]

In later chapters the rule of limited validity will be documented by an analysis of decisions of claims commissions involving the Calvo Clause, and the precise legal significance of this rule will be analyzed.

[82] The question of whether or not this rule of limited validity has any real legal significance will be discussed *infra*, pp. 260–268.

‹ IV ›

The Calvo Clause before Inter-
American Conferences

An important aspect of the Calvo Clause controversy is the major role that the Clause and its underlying principles have played in inter-American diplomacy. As was noted previously, the controversy over the validity of this concept has been rather uniquely American, in that the United States on the one hand and the Latin American republics on the other have been the principal disputants. It is not surprising, then, that the Latin Americans have exerted their greatest efforts through inter-American diplomacy in their struggle to restrict, or if possible eliminate, the institution of diplomatic protection. The Latin American states are, quite obviously, a strong majority in all inter-American conferences, and are thus in a position to exert considerable pressures in these gatherings, something that has not always been possible in the world-wide meetings that have dealt with the rights of aliens.

A relatively large portion of the inter-American conferences held during the past six decades have been devoted, in part at least, to discussion of the institution of diplomatic protection,[1] and the basic principles of the Calvo Doctrine have made substantial progress in these sessions. In the interest of winning Latin American confidence and friendship, as well as for economic and security considerations, the United States, especially since the advent of the Good Neighbor Policy, has made basic

[1] Beteta and Henríquez, *op. cit.*, pp. 35ff.

concessions to the Latin American viewpoints on legal issues. As Edward Guerrant has stated: "Latin America was vital to the security of the United States at the time of the James Monroe Administration. It was vital to the safety of this nation during World War II. The cooperation of the Latin American nations is absolutely essential now in view of the ever-widening gulf separating the United States and the Soviet Union." [2]

Thus, the United States, in an effort to overcome the resentment, suspicion, and bitterness that were the heritage of the Monroe Doctrine and the Roosevelt Corollary, and in order to guarantee hemispheric solidarity in the face of world-wide economic and political stress, has found it expedient to abandon its opposition to some points of the Calvo principles. While this has by no means resulted in total surrender, the story of the inter-American conferences has been one of gradual progress for several of the basic Latin American contentions regarding the practice of governmental intervention in behalf of nationals in foreign countries.

Although inter-American conventions and resolutions do not necessarily make rules of international law, they do furnish material evidence as to what the rules are, and, of course, conventions are binding on the signatory powers. It is therefore highly relevant, in our search for the rule of law on the Calvo Clause, to consider the various debates, resolutions, and conventions that are related to the basic issues involved in the Calvo Clause controversy.[3]

The question of the validity of the Calvo Clause did not formally come before any of the International Conferences of American States until 1938, and then no action was taken on it. However, the basic principles underlying the Calvo Clause have

[2] Guerrant, *op. cit.*, p. 213.

[3] There are a great many difficulties involved in such an investigation. Discussions on the Calvo Clause and the Calvo Doctrine do not appear under these headings, but under such headings as pecuniary claims, arbitration, equality of states, rights and duties of states, rights of aliens, debts and contracts, exhaustion of local remedies, denial of justice, diplomatic protection, intervention, and codification of international law.

been dealt with extensively in all ten International Conferences of American States held to date. Also, debates over the validity of the Clause figured prominently in the sessions of the Eighth American Scientific Conference in 1940, and in the sessions of the Third and Fourth Conferences of the Inter-American Bar Association (an unofficial but influential association of lawyers) in 1944 and 1945.

In the investigation of the diplomacy of the inter-American conferences, attention will be directed toward the evolution of the two main tenets of the Calvo Doctrine — the principle of nonintervention and the principle that the maximum to which aliens resident abroad are entitled is equality with the nationals of the country.[4] Since the Calvo Clause is considered to be a "formalization" of the equality principle, acceptance of the "equality is enough" formula would mean acceptance of the validity of the Calvo Clause, for it would restrict aliens entirely to local redress, the same as nationals.[5]

The Nonintervention Principle before Inter-American Conferences

The basic principle of the Latin American conception of international law is the nonintervention of a state in the affairs of another state.[6] Over the past several decades Latin Americans have striven to win recognition for this principle, first in the Americas, and later in the world. The biggest obstacle to be overcome was the opposition of the United States, which, under the impetus of the Roosevelt Corollary,[7] had not infrequently interfered in the affairs of the Latin American republics, some-

---

[4] See *supra*, pp. 19–20.

[5] See *infra*, pp. 109–110.

[6] The distinguished Latin American legalist J.-M. Yepes asserts that "cette règle est comme l'épine dorsale du droit international au Nouveau Monde." Yepes, "La contribution de l'Amérique Latine au developpement du droit international, public et privé," *Recueil des Cours* (The Hague), XXXII (1930, II), p. 745.

[7] The Roosevelt Corollary has been described as the "classic expression" of the United States policy of intervention. A. P. Whitaker, "A Half-Century of Inter-American Relations, 1889–1940," *Inter-American Affairs* (1941), p. 14.

times with armed forces. The smaller nations of the Western Hemisphere were convinced that their sovereignty and territorial integrity could never be guaranteed as long as the stronger nations of the world could exercise this right of intervention, which, in the eyes of the Latin Americans at least, often amounted to aggression. An international law that sanctioned such intervention was not just, they felt, and consequently should be changed.

The Latin American states made vigorous attempts to accomplish this change by winning United States' acceptance of the principle of nonintervention, but their efforts were of little avail during the early decades of this century, a period of virtually undisputed United States hegemony.[8] In the first five International Conferences of American States, the United States was able to fend off moves by the Latin American republics to draw up a convention or even a resolution on the subject of intervention.[9] The United States suggested instead the use of arbitration conventions, which well might serve as an alternative to intervention in most cases, and a number of such conventions were concluded. But interventions did not cease, and the Latin American states determined to bring their fight for nonintervention out into the open.

The stage for the battle was the Sixth International Conference of American States, held at Havana in 1928. Since the conference met in the midst of actual intervention, and specific justification of that intervention by the United States, it was only natural that intervention should become an important issue.[10]

A resolution of the Fifth International Conference of American States, which had met in Santiago in 1923, called for the Commission of Jurists of Rio de Janeiro to prepare projects of conventions with a view toward codification of public and private

[8] Humphrey, *op. cit.*, pp. 38–39.

[9] It had been the policy of the United States to exclude all controversial matters at the Pan-American conferences. Bemis, *op. cit.*, p. 250.

[10] Carlos Davila, "The Montevideo Conference: Antecedents and Accomplishments," *International Conciliation* (May 1934), p. 137.

international law. These conventions were to be presented to the Havana Conference.[11] The commission met at Rio de Janeiro in 1927 and prepared twelve draft conventions for the codification of public international law, as well as a complete code of private international law.[12] One of these projects, on "States: Existence — Equality — Recognition," contained in Article 3 the following words: "No State has a right to interfere in the internal affairs of another." [13]

The submission of the codification project to the Havana Conference precipitated "the sharpest debates that had ever occurred in the history of the Pan American Conferences." [14] An attempt was made in committee to substitute a less specific, more innocuous statement in place of the nonintervention article, but the majority of Latin American states favored an unqualified condemnation of intervention in any form whatsoever and the article was submitted to the conference without modification. Because no agreement could be reached, the issue was finally postponed to the Montevideo Conference,[15] but only after much bitterness against the interventionist policy of the United States had been exhibited by the Latin American states. The debate was highlighted by an address to the conference by Charles Evans Hughes, the United States secretary of state, in which he defended the intervention policy of the United States and quite frankly attempted to place the responsibility for the interventions on the internal condition of the Latin American countries.[16] In the opinion of one observer, it was "without a doubt" due to to the presence of the distinguished and commanding figure of

[11] *Report of the Delegates of the United States of America to the Fifth International Conference of American States* (Washington, D.C., 1923), p. 131.

[12] For an excellent description of the sessions of the Rio commission, see Bemis, *op. cit.*, pp. 242–255.

[13] International Commission of Jurists, Public International Law Project No. II, reprinted in *AJIL*, XXII, Spec. Suppl. (1928), p. 240.

[14] Bemis, *op. cit.*, p. 251.

[15] *Report of the Delegates of the United States of America to the Sixth International Conference of American States* (Washington, D.C., 1928), p. 12.

[16] *Ibid.*, pp. 14–15.

Mr. Hughes, his prestige, and his skillful diplomacy that this explosive issue was sidetracked and a serious rupture was avoided.[17]

When the question of nonintervention was next taken up by an inter-American conference, the atmosphere of intra-hemispheric relations had definitely changed. By 1933, when the Seventh International Conference of American States met at Montevideo, the United States was actively attempting to win the confidence and friendship of the Latin American states, and was consequently more responsive to the pressures for accepting a nonintervention convention and so demonstrating its "Good Neighborliness." During the Hoover administration a new policy of nonintervention had been slowly taking shape. The Roosevelt administration continued and accelerated the development of this policy toward the Latin American republics. By 1933 the marines had been withdrawn from Nicaragua, and President Roosevelt's decision not to intervene in Cuba appeared to give substance to his promises of a Good Neighbor policy.

Discussion in the Committee on the Problems of International Law saw all states but the United States vigorously and enthusiastically endorse the Convention on Rights and Duties of States, which, in Article 8, asserted: "No state has the right to interfere in the internal or external affairs of another." [18] The committee discussions indicated a strong determination on the part of the Latin American republics not to be put off as they had been at Havana.

Cordell Hull, United States secretary of state, spoke for the "Colossus of the North" at the committee session, and cautiously endorsed the principle of nonintervention.[19] Hull said he felt

. . . safe in undertaking to say that under our support of the general principle of non-intervention as has been suggested, no government need fear any intervention on the part of the United States under the Roosevelt Administration. I think it unfortu-

---

[17] Davila, *op. cit.*, p. 138.

[18] Fifth Session of the Second Committee, *Minutes and Antecedents of the Seventh International Conference of American States* (Montevideo, 1933), pp. 103–128.

[19] *Ibid.*, pp. 121–122.

nate that during the brief period of this Conference there is apparently not time within which to prepare interpretations and definitions of these fundamental terms that are embraced in the report.[20]

Hull went on to add a lengthy reservation, which boiled down to the fact that, in interpreting the words and terms of the convention, the United States would be guided by the public statements of President Roosevelt and "the law of nations as generally recognized and accepted." [21] This reservation was repeated in the final vote of the full committee [22] and as part of the final act of signature at the Plenary Session of December 22, 1933.[23]

Although Montevideo marked a great victory for the Calvo principle of nonintervention, the reservation attached by the United States cast considerable doubt on the precise legal effect of the convention, for, as was seen previously, the law of nations as generally recognized and practiced does sanction intervention under certain circumstances. And it remained for another inter-American conference, meeting at Buenos Aires in 1936, to clarify the situation by emphatically and unqualifiedly incorporating the principle of nonintervention into the body of legal rules that govern relationships among the republics in the Americas. It was at this conference that the United States accepted the Additional Protocol Relative to Non-Intervention with no qualifications, thereby overriding the Montevideo reservation.[24]

The 1936 Non-Intervention Protocol was considerably more explicit than the convention qualifiedly accepted by the United States in 1933. It asserted, in Article I:

The High Contracting Parties declare inadmissible the intervention of any one of them, directly or indirectly, and for whatever reason, in the internal or external affairs of any of the other Parties.

[20] *Ibid.*, p. 121.
[21] *Ibid.*, p. 122.
[22] *Ibid.*, pp. 126–127.
[23] *Ibid.*, pp. 72, 126. This convention was ratified, with the same reservation, by the President on June 29, 1934. 49 U.S. *Stat. L.* 3097 (1935–1936).
[24] *The International Conferences of American States. First Supplement, 1933–1940* (Washington, D.C., 1940), pp. 191–192. See Bemis, *op. cit.*, pp. 289ff, and Humphrey, *op. cit.*, pp. 146ff.

The violation of the provisions of this Article shall give rise to mutual consultation, with the object of exchanging views and seeking methods of peaceful adjustment.[25]

This principle was reaffirmed at Lima by the Eighth International Conference of American States, in a resolution adopted on December 24, 1938; [26] and its importance to intra-American relationships was emphasized by its inclusion in the Charter of the Organization of American States, signed at the Ninth International Conference of American States, held at Bogotá in 1948. Article 15 of Chapter III of the O.A.S. Charter reads:

No State or group of States has the right to intervene, directly or indirectly, for any reason whatever, in the internal or external affairs of any other State. The foregoing principle prohibits not only armed force but also any other form of interference or attempted threat against the personality of the State or against its political, economic and cultural elements.[27]

This statement is more sweeping than the earlier one, for it applies to actions of a "group of states" as well as of one state, and it contains the additional sentence that forbids "any other form of interference" or threats against a state — all of which would appear to make the nonintervention principle "airtight." It has been suggested that the strengthening of the language was a result of the attempt by the United States to influence the 1946 Argentinian election.[28]

[25] Protocol printed in *Report of the Delegation of the United States of America to the Inter-American Conference for the Maintenance of Peace* (Washington, D.C., 1937), Appendix 16, pp. 124–131. The protocol was signed by all 21 delegations, and, as of August 1, 1952, had been ratified by all the republics except Argentina, Bolivia, Panama, Peru, and Uruguay. *Inter-American Juridical Yearbook, 1950–1951*, p. 166. The United States ratified on July 15, 1937. 51 U.S. *Stat. L.* 41 (1937).

[26] Resolution CX, *The International Conferences of American States. First Supplement*, pp. 309–310. This principle was again reaffirmed in Resolution XCV (The Declaration of Caracas) of the Tenth International Conference of American States (1954). See *Final Act* (Washington, D.C., 1954), pp. 96–97.

[27] *Report of the Delegation of the United States of America with Related Documents* (Washington, D.C., 1948), p. 169. The President ratified the Charter for the United States on June 15, 1951. 2 U.S. *Treaties* 2394 (1951).

[28] Arthur Whitaker, "Development of American Regionalism — The Organization of American States," *International Conciliation* (March 1951), pp. 132–133. It should be noted, however, that Article 19 of the Charter provides that measures adopted for the maintenance of peace and security "in accordance with

The acceptance, without reservation, by the United States of the principle of nonintervention has been called "unquestionably the most important decision of the Roosevelt Administration in the creation of the Good Neighbor Policy." [29] The reorientation of United States foreign policy toward the American republics has undoubtedly paid rich dividends in the advancement of the economic and security interests of the Western Hemisphere. Even more important for the purposes of this study, the Good Neighbor policy has resulted in the acceptance of one of the cardinal Calvo principles, nonintervention, as perhaps the basic principle governing international relations in the Americas.

But the mere acceptance of this principle did not end the controversy over this concept, for there remained the question of the interpretation of just what is forbidden by this prohibition of intervention or interference.[30] Since nonintervention in the

existing treaties" do not constitute intervention. See *Report of the Delegation of the United States of America with Related Documents*, p. 38.

[29] Guerrant, *op. cit.*, p. 68. For a Latin American legalist's interpretation of the evolution and importance of the nonintervention principle, see Sepúlveda Gutiérrez, *op. cit.*, pp. 47–50.

[30] The fact that the question of nonintervention is not fully settled is evidenced by the important role that it played in the deliberations of the Tenth International Conference of American States, held in Caracas, Venezuela, on March 1–28, 1954. As Charles Fenwick aptly commented ("Intervention — At the Caracas Conference," *AJIL*, XLVIII (July 1954), p. 451): "It was hardly to be expected that an Inter-American Conference could meet without the issue of intervention, or better, non-intervention, being presented in some form or another." The debate over nonintervention arose in connection with the successful effort of the United States to get a resolution adopted that called for inter-American consultative procedures in the event of the "domination or control of the political institutions of any American state by the international communist movement." Resolution XCIII, *Final Act* (Washington, D.C., 1954), pp. 94–95. Although this resolution created the fear among several Latin American nations that the principle of nonintervention might be endangered, the United States, faced with a serious threat to its security, was insistent. The attitude of the United States was indicated by the statement of John C. Dreier, the United States representative on the Council of the O.A.S., in his article "Organizing Security in the Americas," *Department of State Bulletin*, Vol. XXX, No. 779 (May 31, 1954), p. 835: "We may state it to be an axiom of inter-American relations that non-intervention can only be a reality so long as an adequate collective system of security is available to all states." It is significant that there was no longer any question of unilateral intervention by the United States in the domestic affairs of another American state. The issue was that of collective intervention, prohibited by Article 15 of the O.A.S. Charter, unless it could be brought under Article 19, which makes exception of measures adopted for the maintenance of peace and security in accordance with existing treaties.

Latin American conception means denial of the right of diplomatic protection to foreigners residing in an American republic,[31] some Latin American statesmen and publicists have argued that the Non-Intervention Protocol has banned intervention by diplomacy as well as by arms.[32] Ramón Beteta, assistant secretary of foreign relations of Mexico, argued in a session of the Eighth American Scientific Congress that the "logical consequence" of the 1936 protocol was the "disappearance of the supposed right of protection." [33] The distinguished Mexican lawyer Alfonso García Robles asserted, in a session of the Third Conference of the Inter-American Bar Association, that the Non-Intervention Pact settled the question of "reclamaciones pecuniarias," for these reclamations, "in spite of all the subtle distinctions that can be imagined, always constitute a type of intervention by one state into the affairs of the other." [34]

It is clear, however, that the United States does not consider itself bound by the Non-Intervention Protocol to refrain from intervening diplomatically on behalf of its citizens abroad.[35] While there is some doubt as to the exact meaning of the vague phraseology of the Non-Intervention Protocol, the better opinion holds that the intent was to prohibit armed intervention, i.e., intervention by forceful means.[36] The continuing efforts of

[31] Bemis, *op. cit.*, p. 234.

[32] Calvo used the term to include both armed and diplomatic intervention. See *supra*, p. 18, n. 26. A more recent example of the linking of both armed and diplomatic forms of intervention occurred at the Havana Conference when the Argentine representative stated: "Intervention — diplomatic or armed, permanent or temporary — is an attempt against the independence of nations and can not be justified on the plea of protecting the interests of citizens." Quoted in *Foreign Policy Association Information Service*, iv (April 27, 1928), p. 68.

[33] Beteta and Henríquez, *op. cit.*, p. 30. My translation.

[34] García Robles, *op. cit.*, p. 5. My translation.

[35] See, for example, the statement of the late Edwin Borchard, United States member, Commission of Experts for the Inter-American Codification of International Law, at the Eighth American Scientific Congress: "diplomatic protection has never been regarded as intervention, and the form of intervention against which the United States thinks it is committed is armed intervention." "Remarks by Professor Edwin Borchard . . ." *op. cit.*, p. 71.

[36] A. Freeman, "Recent Aspects of the Calvo Doctrine and the Challenge to International Law," *AJIL*, XL (January 1946), p. 136. Freeman calls any other interpretation "next to incredible." *Ibid.*

the Latin American republics to validate explicitly the Calvo Clause and ban diplomatic intervention would indicate that they also feel that the protocol affects only armed intervention. Nevertheless there can be little doubt that their objective is to win ultimate acceptance of the principle of nonintervention in the sense that Calvo first enunciated it, as applying to "interference of any sort."

The establishment of the principle of nonintervention — even in the limited sense of nonintervention by force — as a rule of law among the American republics has had world-wide implications. It is noteworthy that a similar principle of nonintervention was included in the recent Draft Declaration of the Rights and Duties of States, prepared by the United Nations International Law Commission,[37] which might well presage the adoption of this principle as a rule of international law. In the Western Hemisphere, the substantial victory of Latin America diplomacy in winning the United States to a policy prohibiting armed intervention has greatly encouraged Latin American statesmen and publicists in their fight against the institution of diplomatic protection. Having achieved recognition of one of the Calvo principles, they redoubled their efforts to win acceptance of the second principle, that the maximum protection to which an alien can aspire is equality with nationals.

The Equality Principle before Inter-American Conferences

The concept that aliens are entitled to no better treatment than nationals is closely tied in with the Calvo Clause, for both are directed at restricting the alien to local remedies as the final forum for redress of his grievances. The acceptance of the equality concept as a rule governing intra-American relationships would automatically validate the Calvo Clause, and the accept-

[37] Article 3 reads: "Every State has the duty to refrain from intervention in the internal or external affairs of any other State." The draft declaration and the report of the International Law Commission are reprinted in *AJIL*, Suppl., XLIV (January 1950), pp. 13–21. See also *Preparatory Study Concerning a Draft Declaration of the Rights and Duties of States* (memorandum submitted by the secretary-general, Lake Success, 1948).

ance of the validity of the Calvo Clause would, in large measure, make unnecessary further attempts to win acceptance of the equality rule. Since these two concepts are so closely interrelated, in objective and evolution, they will be discussed jointly.

Although the Latin Americans are able to make a strong logical and moral argument in behalf of the equality principle, the rules of international law as generally recognized and accepted do not hold that a nation fulfills its international obligations by treating aliens as equal to nationals unless such treatment measures up to the so-called international minimum standards.[38] In order to validate the equality principle, the Latin Americans have energetically striven to change the rules of international law and eliminate the minimum standards requirement. As in the case of nonintervention, they have made their greatest efforts to achieve this objective in inter-American conferences, hoping to win over the United States to their viewpoint as the first and very necessary step toward obtaining world-wide recognition of the equality rule. Latin American efforts along this line have figured prominently in the International Conferences of American States, from the First through the Tenth, as well as in other important inter-American conferences, and undoubtedly will continue to play a prominent role in future conferences. Although victory has not crowned their efforts, as it has in their fight for nonintervention, we shall see that they have made considerable progress.

The importance of the equality principle to the Latin Americans is indicated by the fact that it was the first subject considered in any Pan-American deliberation involving the principles that should constitute "American international law."[39] It was one of the major issues before the First International Conference of American States, held in Washington in 1889–1900. The Committee of International Law of this conference, dealing with the problem of claims and diplomatic intervention, issued

---

[38] See *infra*, Chapter V, pp. 112–113.

[39] Bemis, *op. cit.*, p. 234. The problem of whether there is, or should be, an American international law will be discussed *infra*, Chapter V, pp. 117–119.

a majority report that embodied the Latin American viewpoint on the equality principle.[40] The report, in part, read:

The committee gladly recognizes . . . that the foreigner should not be inferior to the native . . . but it cannot understand that the foreigner should enjoy considerations, prerogatives, or privileges denied to the native. . . . [It] repels the pretension that the foreigner should be superior to the native . . .

In a word, in everything touching the exercise of civil rights, natives and foreigners shall be on a perfectly equal footing — equal rights, equal obligations, equal access to the authorities, equal procedure, equal appeals; but in no case shall the foreigner be superior . . . To enjoy all the privileges and all the considerations of natives, to be treated like them, is all to which the foreigner can aspire; and that is what is gladly conceded him.

The foreigner, with all the rights of the native, with no right less, yet with no right more, is the principle which, to the mind of the committee, is the base upon which every theory in the premises should rest — the starting-point for practical conclusions in so interesting a matter. If the Government is responsible to its citizens for infractions of the Constitution or the laws, committed by agents of the public authority in the discharge of the duties, it will be equally responsible to foreigners, and *vice versa*.[41]

This report, clearly expressing the equality principle of Carlos Calvo,[42] was vigorously objected to by the United States delegate on the committee, William Henry Trescot, who submitted a minority report, asserting:

I of course recognize the right of any nation or combination of nations to suggest such amendments and improvements as the progress of civilization renders advisable, but to make such changes a part of international law requires the consent of the civilized world. . . . [Regarding the proposed resolution, I admit] with serious reservations, that the resident foreigner in all contracts with private natives and in relation to violations of municipal law has no right to ask more protection than is given to the native citizen. But even here there is the underlying as-

---

[40] John MacDonell, "South American Republics and the Monroe Doctrine," *Nineteenth Century*, LIII (April 1903), pp. 590–591.

[41] Senate Exec. Doc. No. 183, 51st Congress, 1st Session (1890), pp. 22–24.

[42] Gonzalez, *op. cit.*, pp. 19–21; Humphrey, *op. cit.*, p. 49.

sumption that what is granted by native law and procedure, what is given to the native citizen, is substantial justice. If under any peculiar law, under any absolutism of procedure, under any habit or usage of traditional authority to which natives are accustomed and willing to submit, the native process or judgment does not afford this substantial justice, the right of the foreigner to such substantial justice would be nevertheless complete, and how can it be assured to them? But if this be so in cases of private contention, how is it with the cases where the reclamation of the foreigner is against the Government itself?

Into what court will the Government allow the sovereignty of the nation to be called to answer its responsibilities to the claimant and how is its judgment to be enforced? . . . I can not concur in any opinions which diminish the right or reduces [*sic*] the power of a nation by diplomatic reclamation, which is the manifestation of its moral strength and vitality, to protect the rights and interests of its citizens.[43]

Thus did Trescot counterpose the minimum standards rule which the United States has consistently employed in reply to the equality principle. As would be expected, however, his argument fell on deaf ears, and, over the sole dissenting vote of the United States, the following resolution was adopted:

The International American Conference recommends to the Governments of the countries therein represented the adoption, as principles of American international law, of the following:

(1) Foreigners are entitled to enjoy all the civil rights enjoyed by natives; and they shall be accorded all the benefits of said rights in all that is essential as well as in the form of procedure, and the legal remedies incident thereto, absolutely in like manner as said natives.

(2) A nation has not, nor recognizes in favor of foreigners, any other obligations or responsibilities than those which in favor of the natives are established, in like cases, by the constitution and by the laws.[44]

While this resolution did not modify the rules of international law, it was expressive of the strong sentiment in Latin America

---

[43] Senate Exec. Doc. No. 183, 51st Congress, 1st Session (1890), pp. 26–30.

[44] This resolution, adopted on April 18, 1890, is reprinted in *The International Conferences of American States, 1889–1928* (New York, 1931), p. 45.

on this subject, and it did serve to inspire the incorporation of these principles into many of the constitutions and laws of the Latin American republics.[45]

The Second International Conference of American States, held in Mexico City in 1901–1902, saw the whole question of the status and rights of aliens reopened when a convention was proposed that embodied the controversial principles recommended by the Washington Conference.[46] The United States abstained from the debates and voting on this convention.[47] Delegate William I. Buchanan explained the United States' position:

I think every Delegate here is familiar with the position of the United States Government in the matters treated of in this project, and I arise merely on behalf of the Delegation to say that inasmuch as it will be impossible for us to assent to a very large portion of this report, this Delegation will abstain from taking part in the debate or from voting in whole or in part.[48]

Undeterred by the attitude of the United States, the conference by an affirmative vote of fifteen nations approved the following Convention Relative to the Rights of Aliens on January 29, 1902:

First: Aliens shall enjoy all civil rights pertaining to citizens, and make use thereof in the substance, form or procedure, and in the recourses which result therefrom, under exactly the same terms as the said citizens, except as may be otherwise provided by the Constitution of each country.

Second: The States do not owe to, nor recognize in favor of foreigners, any obligations or responsibilities other than those established by their Constitutions and laws in favor of their citizens.

[45] Beteta and Henríquez, *op. cit.*, p. 35.

[46] See Gonzalez, *op. cit.*, p. 21; Humphrey, *op. cit.*, p. 56; T. Alvarado Garaicoa, *La trascendencia de las reuniones interamericanas* (Guayaquil, 1949), p. 22; J.-M. Yepes, *El panamericanismo y el derecho internacional* (Bogotá, 1930), pp. 109–111.

[47] For a detailed description of the debates and discussions in committee and plenary sessions, see John V. Noel, *The History of the Second Pan-American Congress* (Baltimore, 1902), pp. 195–206.

[48] *Report, with Accompanying Papers, of the Delegates of the United States to the Second International Conference of American States* (Washington, D.C., 1902), p. 23.

Therefore, the States are not responsible for damages sustained by aliens through acts of rebels or individuals, and in general, for damages originating from fortuitous causes of any kind, considering as such the acts of war whether civil or national; except in the case of failure on the part of the constituted authorities to comply with their duties.

Third: Whenever an alien shall have claims or complaints of a civil, criminal or administrative order against a State, or its citizens, he shall present his claims to a competent Court of the country, and such claims shall not be made through diplomatic channels, except in the cases where there shall have been, on the part of the Court, a manifest denial of justice, or unusual delay, or evident violation of the principles of International Law.[49]

Although this convention had no legal force for nonsignatory powers, it should be pointed out again that were Latin Americans to succeed in winning approval of such a convention by the United States, the Calvo Clause would be validated and diplomatic interposition as a whole would be materially restricted.[50]

Although the equality principle figured briefly in discussions concerning arbitration conventions in the Third (Rio de Janeiro, 1906)[51] and Fourth (Buenos Aires, 1910)[52] International Conferences of American States, it did not become a major issue for debate again until the Fifth International Conference of American States held at Santiago in 1923. Topic XIV before the con-

---

[49] *Ibid.*, p. 228. The exception for cases of manifest denial of justice is not as significant as it would at first appear because of the highly restrictive definition given to this term by the Latin Americans. See *infra*, pp. 114–116. The importance of this convention as representative of the Latin American viewpoint is indicated by the statement of the distinguished Latin American international lawyer J.-M. Yepes that this convention is expressive of the true principles of American international law, and that all the nations of this hemisphere should fight to win universal acceptance of these principles. See *El panamericanismo y el derecho internacional*, p. 109. As of August 1, 1952, however, only seven Latin American republics had ratified this convention. *Inter-American Juridical Yearbook, 1950–1951*, p. 156.

[50] Decencière-Ferrandière, *La responsabilité internationale des États à raison des dommages subis par des étrangers* (Paris, 1925), p. 171, n. 1. See *infra*, pp. 109–110.

[51] *Report of the Delegates of the United States to the Third International Conference of the American States* (Washington, D.C., 1906), pp. 41ff, 71–73.

[52] *Report, with Accompanying Papers, Relative to the Fourth International Conference of American States* (Washington, D.C., 1911), pp. 22, 24, 41, 280–282.

ference was "Consideration of the Rights of Aliens Resident within the Jurisdiction of Any of the American Republics," and the discussion of this topic revived the basic issues involved in equality versus minimum standards.

The Colombian delegation brought the issue to a head when it proposed an amendment to the Convention on Pecuniary Claims adopted at the Fourth Conference. This amendment read:

In all cases in which a foreigner may have civil, criminal, or administrative claims or complaints against a State or the nationals thereof he shall bring such claims before the competent court of the country, and he may not present a claim through diplomatic channels except in cases in which there may have been on the part of such court a manifest denial of justice, unusual delay, or evident violation of the principles of international law.[53]

This proposal, very similar to the 1902 convention, was unacceptable to the United States, and, in order to avoid further dissension, the issue, together with the general question of the rights of aliens resident within the jurisdiction of American states, was referred to the Committee of Jurists of Rio de Janeiro who were to study the problem and report back to the next conference.[54]

While the main issue before the Sixth International Conference of American States at Havana in 1928 was the bitter debate over nonintervention,[55] the conference did agree, for the first time, to a Convention on the Status of Aliens that the United States found acceptable. The convention, signed on February 20, 1928, provided:

Article 1. States have the right to establish by means of laws the conditions under which foreigners may enter and reside in their territory.

Article 2. Foreigners are subject as are nationals to local juris-

[53] Quoted in *Report of the Delegates of the United States of America to the Fifth International Conference of American States* (Washington, D.C., 1923), p. 10.

[54] *Ibid.*, pp. 10, 137. See the comments on this conference by Gonzalez, *op. cit.*, pp. 21–22; Beteta and Henríquez, *op. cit.*, pp. 36–37.

[55] *Supra*, pp. 65–67.

diction and laws, due consideration being given to the limitations expressed in conventions and treaties.

. . . .

Article 5. States shall extend to foreigners, domiciled or in transit through their territory, all individual guaranties extended to their own nationals, and the enjoyment of essential civil rights without detriment, as regards foreigners, to equal provisions governing the scope of and the usages for the exercise of said rights and guaranties.[56]

It is apparent that agreement among all the republics was achieved only at the expense of making the phraseology of the convention extremely vague on the equality principle. Since the language of the convention conformed with the general principles of international law,[57] the adoption of the convention cannot be considered a victory for the Latin American viewpoint.

Substantial progress for the equality principle was not, however, long in coming. As we have seen, the period between the Sixth and the Seventh International Conference of American States saw a reorientation of American foreign policy toward Latin America.[58] Under the impetus of the Good Neighbor Policy, the United States was considerably less hostile to the Calvo principles at Montevideo in 1933 than had formerly been the case and it accepted resolutions and conventions on the equality principle that had formerly been rejected.

The issue figured in debates over the Resolution on the International Responsibility of the State and the Convention on Rights and Duties of States, both of which embraced the traditional Calvo view that aliens are entitled only to equality with nationals.

In the Resolution on the International Responsibility of the

---

[56] *The International Conferences of American States, 1889–1928*, p. 415. As of August 1, 1952, this convention, signed by all the republics, had been ratified by all except Argentina, Bolivia, Cuba, El Salvador, Honduras, Paraguay, and Venezuela. *Inter-American Juridical Yearbook, 1950–1951*, p. 159. The United States ratified on May 7, 1930. 46 U.S. *Stat. L.* 2753 (1929–1931).

[57] Francisco José Urrutia, *Le continent américain et le droit international* (Paris, 1928), p. 293.

[58] *Supra*, p. 67.

State, adopted on December 24, 1933, the conference agreed upon the following points:

1. To recommend that the study of the entire problem relating to the international responsibility of the state, with special reference to responsibility for manifest denial or unmotivated delay of justice be handed over to the agencies of codification instituted by the International Conferences of American States and that their studies be coordinated with the work of codification being done under the auspices of the League of Nations.

2. That, notwithstanding this, it reaffirms once more, as a principle of international law, the civil equality of the foreigner with the national as the maximum limit of protection to which he may aspire in the positive legislations of the states.

3. Reaffirms equally that diplomatic protection cannot be initiated in favor of foreigners unless they exhaust all legal measures established by the laws of the country before which the action is begun. There are excepted those cases of manifest denial or unreasonable delay of justice which shall always be interpreted restrictively, that is, in favor of the sovereignty of the State in which the difference may have arisen. Should no agreement on said difference be reached through diplomatic channels, within a reasonable period of time, the matter shall then be referred to arbitration.

4. The Conference recognizes, at the same time, that these general principles may be the subject of definition or limitations and that the agencies charged with planning the codification shall take into account the necessity of definition and limitations in formulating the rules applicable to the various cases which may be provided for.[59]

It should be noted that this resolution explicitly embraced the equality rule "as a principle of international law," and went on to limit diplomatic intervention to cases of "manifest denial or unreasonable delay of justice which shall always be interpreted restrictively."

In sharp contrast to previous debates over the equality rule, there was no United States' opposition to this resolution, either

[59] *Report of the Delegates of the United States of America to the Seventh International Conference of American States* (Washington, D.C., 1934), pp. 270–271.

in subcommittee [60] or committee,[61] and its sole participation was to vote affirmatively, with no reservations, although several other states did enter reservations.[62] While a resolution such as this is not, of course, legally binding on the signatory powers,[63] it is important in that it indicates what the signatories believe the rule of international law to be, and it does offer evidence of the softened attitude of the "Colossus of the North," which had fought so hard against a less explicit resolution in the First Conference.[64] The resolution consequently does represent substantial though not conclusive progress for the Latin American viewpoint.

Encouraged by the acceptance of this resolution, the Latin American republics eagerly awaited the United States' reaction to the Convention on Rights and Duties of States, which came up two days later, on December 26, 1933, and which also contained the equality principle but in the legally binding and enforceable language of a treaty. Article 9 of this convention read:

The jurisdiction of states within the limits of national territory applies to all the inhabitants.

Nationals and foreigners are under the same protection of the law and the national authorities and the foreigners may not claim rights other or more extensive than those of the nationals.[65]

The United States joined the other American republics in signing this convention, but, as had been done with the nonin-

---

[60] *Plenary Sessions, Minutes and Antecedents with General Index* (Montevideo, 1933), pp. 99–159, 169–171.

[61] *Ibid.*, pp. 151–159.

[62] *Ibid.*, p. 158. It may be observed that the United States was gaining something from this resolution in the sense that the institution of diplomatic protection was expressly, if very restrictively, recognized.

[63] Some Latin American authorities have asserted that this resolution is binding on the United States. Sanchez i Sanchez, *op. cit.*, p. 634, asserts that it "withdraws diplomatic protection from aliens." My translation. Charles Fenwick, "The Tenth Inter-American Conference: Some Issues of Inter-American Regional Law," *AJIL*, XLVIII (July 1954), p. 464, commented: "Lawyers may quarrel over the relative legal force of resolutions and treaties; but as a matter of fact the existing practice shows due respect for resolutions . . . treating them as if they had the full force of law."

[64] *Supra*, pp. 73–76.

[65] *International Conferences of American States. First Supplement, 1933–1940*, p. 122. 49 U.S. *Stat. L.* 3097 (1935–1936).

tervention article of the same convention,[66] it added a lengthy reservation which amounted to this: The United States reserved its rights by "the law of nations as generally recognized and accepted." [67] Since international law as generally recognized and accepted does not admit the equality principle, the situation was left in considerable doubt. Nevertheless, the Convention on the Rights and Duties of States represented a sweeping triumph for Latin American jurisprudence and diplomacy on both of the cardinal principles of the Calvo Doctrine,[68] especially in view of the United States' hostile attitude toward a similar convention adopted by the Second Conference at Mexico City.[69]

There immediately arose the question of the precise legal effect of the convention. John P. Humphrey feels that the convention and resolution represented "substantially an acceptance of the Calvo Doctrine," [70] and many Latin American publicists have argued that the equality principle is now part of international law, at least insofar as the relationships among the American republics are concerned.[71] It is interesting to note that several delegates to the Third Inter-American Bar Association Conference argued that the acceptance of Article 9 had given international sanction to the Calvo Clause as part of American international law.[72] However, while there is much debate over the precise effect of this convention on the practice of diplomatic protection, it would

[66] *Supra*, pp. 67–68.

[67] *Supra*, p. 68.

[68] Bemis, *op. cit.*, p. 273.

[69] *Supra*, pp. 76–77. As of August 1, 1952, the Montevideo Convention had been ratified by all the republics except Argentina, Panama, Peru, Uruguay, and Bolivia. *Inter-American Juridical Yearbook, 1950–1951*, p. 161.

[70] *Op. cit.*, p. 123.

[71] Gonzalez, *op. cit.*, pp. 23ff; Beteta and Henríquez, *op. cit.*, p. 37; Sanchez i Sanchez, *op. cit.*, p. 634; Alberto Cruchaga Ossa, "Memorandum sobre el tema de reclamaciones pecuniarias," *Diario de Sessiones* (Eighth International Conference of American States), p. 335, goes so far as to assert "that it is no more appropriate to speak of denial of justice in respect to aliens than in respect to nationals, because it is not possible to have a denial of justice if there exists no right that would be acknowledged." My translation. This convention eliminated that right by adopting the equality rule. *Ibid.*, p. 305.

[72] "Note," *Journal of Comparative Legislation and International Law*, Third Series, XXVI (1944), p. 58. See *infra*, pp. 90–94.

appear that the United States has, by its reservation, maintained its traditional position,[73] and it certainly has not in the intervening years abandoned its advocacy of the minimum standards rule.[74]

This does not nullify the importance of the convention and resolution insofar as the progress of the Calvo principles before inter-American conferences is concerned. The softened attitude of the United States, although dictated, it is true, by political considerations,[75] greatly encouraged Latin American nations in their efforts to win the support of their northern neighbor in the fight to restrict, and if possible eliminate, the institution of diplomatic protection.

The uncertainty connected with the interpretation of the intent and effect of the resolution and convention approved at Montevideo led to the renewal of the debate on the status of aliens and the general problem of diplomatic protection at the Inter-American Conference for the Maintenance of Peace which was held at Buenos Aires in 1936. Subject No. 6 on the agenda was the "Formulation of principles with respect to the elimination of force and of diplomatic intervention in cases of pecuniary claims and other private actions," and this topic was referred for discussion to Committee IV on Judicial Problems.

In the committee discussions, three drafts for a proposed Convention Relative to the Collection of Public and Contractual Debts, and to Diplomatic Protection were submitted for debate. One of these drafts, proposed by Argentina, Chile, and Peru, and endorsed by a majority of the republics, specifically prohibited diplomatic intervention. It read: "The High Contracting Parties bind themselves, without any reservation, not to use armed force nor to have recourse to diplomatic intervention, nor to accept

[73] See Borchard, "The 'Minimum Standard' of the Treatment of Aliens," *Proceedings of the American Society of International Law* (1939), p. 69.

[74] The United States still considers its reservation operative as far as Article 9 is concerned, although the 1936 Protocol on Non-Intervention overrode the reservation insofar as nonintervention is concerned. See *Report of the Delegation of the United States of America to the Ninth International Conference of American States* (Washington, D.C., 1948), p. 37. See also Bemis, *op. cit.*, p. 289.

[75] Humphrey, *op. cit.*, p. 123.

it, for the collection of public or contractual debts, or for the support of claims the origin of which is exclusively pecuniary." [76]

The United States opposed this draft, and in the ensuing discussion it became apparent that "it was not possible to secure such unanimity of opinion as might serve as the basis for a Convention between the American Republics." [77] Consequently, at the suggestion of the United States, the conference decided to refer the matter to the Committee of Experts created by an agreement of the conference at Montevideo and directed this body to prepare a project of convention to be submitted to the Eighth International Conference. [78]

The Committee of Experts met at Washington in April 1937 and again at Lima in November and December of 1938. [79] The sessions of this committee demonstrated once again the fundamental disagreement among the American republics on the issues of the status of aliens and the right of diplomatic protection. The committee, after lengthy and sometimes bitter discussion, finally agreed on a compromise report, [80] signed by all members of the committee present, [81] which indicated "substantial unanimity" against the use of force or diplomatic intervention for the collection of debts, provided arbitration could be invoked to settle cases of alleged denial of justice. [82] The draft conven-

[76] *International Conferences of American States. First Supplement, 1933–1940*, pp. 165–166. The United States has traditionally taken the position that there are specific rules regarding contractual claims differing from those applicable to tort claims, although both types are included in the Latin American expression "pecuniary claims." See Borchard, *Dip. Prot.*, pp. 284ff.

[77] *International Conferences of American States, First Supplement*, pp. 165–166.

[78] Resolution XXXV, adopted December 21, 1936, *Report of the Delegation of the United States of America to the Inter-American Conference for the Maintenance of Peace* (Washington, D.C., 1937), pp. 27, 232–234.

[79] For an excellent account of the committee sessions as well as of the debate at Lima, see Borchard, "The 'Committee of Experts' at the Lima Conference," *AJIL*, XXXIII (April 1939), pp. 269–282. See also, by the same author, "Committee of Experts, Pan American Codification of International Law," *AJIL*, XXXI (July 1937), pp. 471–473.

[80] Humphrey, *op. cit.*, p. 155; Beteta and Henríquez, *op. cit.*, p. 38.

[81] Alfranio de Mello Franco, Luis Anderson Morúa, Edwin M. Borchard, and Alberto Cruchaga Ossa, who signed with a reservation. *Diario de Sessiones*, p. 295.

[82] *Report of the Delegation of the United States of America to the Eighth International Conference of American States* (Washington, D.C., 1941), p. 19.

tion on pecuniary claims recommended by the Committee of Experts to the Eighth International Conference of American States (Lima, 1938) provided:

1. The High Contracting Parties pledge themselves, without any reservation, not to employ armed force for the collection of public debts or contractual debts.

2. The High Contracting Parties agree not to intervene diplomatically in support of claims arising out of contract, unless there has been a denial of justice or infraction of a generally recognized international duty.

3. In the event of unjustified repudiation or breach of the terms of a contract and the failure to settle the claim by resort to local remedies and diplomatic negotiation, either creditor or debtor may demand and obtain the arbitration of the issue of unjustified repudiation or violation, denial of justice or infraction of a generally recognized international duty.[83]

In memorandums accompanying the report and the draft convention, Alberto Cruchaga Ossa argued for equal treatment of aliens and nationals, and maintained that, if the treatment were equal, no diplomatic claim could be justified. Edwin Borchard, representing the United States on the committee, rejected this argument, and painstakingly and convincingly documented the position of the United States that equality is adequate only if it meets the internationally recognized minimum standards of treatment; if these standards are not obtained, an international obligation arises which limits national sovereignty. Furthermore, even if a state does deprive its own citizens of their rights, this does not justify depriving foreigners of the same rights.[84]

The issue was referred to the Second Commission, which dealt with problems of international law, and which, after lengthy

[83] Translation by Borchard, "The 'Committee of Experts' at the Lima Conference," *AJIL*, XXXIII (April 1939), p. 274. The original Spanish text may be found in *Diario de Sessiones*, p. 295.

[84] See this excellent series of memorandums for a classic discussion of the issues involved in the equality vs. the minimum standards rule: Cruchaga Ossa, "Memoranda sobre el tema de reclamaciones pecuniarias," *Diario de Sessiones*, pp. 301–311, 325–331, 332–333, 334–335; Borchard, *ibid.*, pp. 311–325, 331–332, 333–334. Borchard's arguments, from the standpoint of the generally recognized rules of international law, would appear to be the sounder of the two analyses. These arguments will be examined in more detail, *infra*, Chapter V, pp. 107–113.

discussion, found that it was unable to resolve the differences of opinion. The United States, further modifying its traditional position in an effort to reach an acceptable compromise, was apparently willing to commit itself against the use of force or diplomatic intervention for the collection of pecuniary claims, provided arbitration were available in cases of denial of justice. But the majority of the American republics, under the leadership of Argentina and Mexico, were against the use of force or diplomatic intervention under any circumstances, their point of view being the traditional Latin American one that foreigners are entitled to no better treatment than citizens.[85] After it became apparent that no agreement could be reached, the conference, upon the Second Commission's recommendation, referred the entire matter to the Committee of Experts for further study and directed it to report back to the Ninth International Conference.[86]

Thus ended the discussions of this issue for the time being. It is interesting to note that the Calvo Clause itself figured in the Cruchaga Ossa–Borchard debates. Cruchaga Ossa argued that the Calvo Clause would be valid under the new principles of American international law, since it is based on the equality formula which would operate to restrict foreigners to local redress, the same as nationals.[87] Borchard replied that the Calvo Clause in its extreme form can be abused, just like diplomatic protection in its extreme form could be abused.[88] Although Borchard originally favored inclusion of an article that would specifically deny the full validity of the Calvo Clause, he later changed his mind, because of the impossibility of reaching any agreement, and recommended that all reference to the Clause be omitted in any draft convention.[89]

---

[85] Humphrey, *op. cit.*, p. 155.

[86] Resolution XIX on Pecuniary Claims, December 21, 1938, *Report of the Delegation of the United States of America to the Eighth International Conference of American States*, pp. 127–128. The matter was not, however, taken up at the Ninth Conference, which did not meet until 1948 because of World War II.

[87] *Diario de Sessiones*, pp. 302–303.

[88] *Ibid.*, p. 315.   [89] *Ibid.*, p. 318.

The Lima Conference is noteworthy, from the standpoint of this study, for another reason. At this conference, for the first time, a formal convention was submitted by the delegation from Mexico that specifically recognized the integral validity of the Calvo Clause.[90]

Mexico, in submitting the Project of Convention on the Effects of the Renunciation by the Nationals of a State of the Diplomatic Protection of Their Government, argued that any action for peace of this continent should include, in addition to provisions for peacefully resolving conflicts among American republics, an effort to suppress the causes from which the conflicts originate.[91] Among these causes, the Mexicans argued, special attention should be given to the problem of nationals in a foreign country, who often wish to accept the benefits but none of the drawbacks of living and investing in foreign lands.[92] This leads to intervention, strained relations, exaggerated reclamations, "and differences which jeopardize the very sovereignty of the state." [93] This danger had led Calvo to assert that in order to end the intrusion of governments into the internal affairs of other states, all foreigners, on entering the territory of a foreign country, "ought to become subject to the legislation and jurisdiction of the authorities under identical conditions with nationals." [94]

Mexico went on to assert that in view of the fact that the acceptance of this principle of absolute equality was at the moment meeting with obstacles, principally of a traditional character, and in view of the fact that the requirement of renunciation of diplomatic protection appeared in the national legislation of the majority of states of this continent, "an expression of a

[90] Sepúlveda Gutiérrez, *op. cit.*, p. 76, asserts that this convention was submitted only to clarify the situation, since the resolutions and conventions of the International Conferences of American States have already impliedly accepted the validity of the Calvo Clause. See also García Robles, *op. cit.*, p. 23.

[91] *Diario de Sessiones*, p. 291.

[92] *Ibid.*

[93] *Ibid.* My translation.

[94] *Ibid.* My translation.

nearly unanimous agreement," [95] and, finally, in view of the fact that the validity of this renunciation was disputed by some countries, who maintained that protection of nationals abroad is a right of the state and that the renunciation does not obligate the state, it was felt necessary to clarify the situation by submitting the following draft convention: "The High Contracting Parties recognize as valid the renunciation of the diplomatic protection by their governments which their nationals make, and agree not to initiate or demand this protection in such cases." [96]

No action was taken by the Lima Conference on this draft convention, nor do the records of the conference reveal any formal discussion of the Mexican proposal, although Edwin Borchard, writing in 1939, commented in regard to the Lima discussions: "These various efforts, not yet concerted, would seem to indicate a wide spread Latin American desire for a policy which would either narrow greatly or abolish the institution of diplomatic protection." [97] The draft convention is significant, however, because of the apparent admission by Mexico that the Calvo Clause, in its full sense as a complete bar to interposition, is not recognized as valid under the present rules of international law and that therefore the rules must be changed to validate the Clause in the same manner in which they were changed to validate nonintervention. Such a validation of the Calvo Clause by inter-American convention is by no means impossible. The Clause was formally brought up for the first time at Lima, and it will remain for history to determine whether this is but the beginning of concentrated efforts by the Latin Americans to win recognition for this principle, as they have done with the other Calvo principle.

Although the next formal International Conference of American States was not held until ten years later, in 1948, the controversy over the Calvo Clause and its underlying principles

[95] *Ibid.*, p. 292. My translation.

[96] *Ibid.* My translation.

[97] "The 'Committee of Experts' at the Lima Conference," *AJIL*, XXXIII (April 1939), p. 279.

was by no means dormant during the intervening decade. Quite to the contrary, the discussion and argumentation seemed to reach its crest during the war years.

Antonio Gómez Robledo, professor of international law at the National University of Mexico, demanded in 1940 the acceleration of the fight to eliminate diplomatic intervention, urging his fellow scholars to accept ". . . the duty of fundamenting [establishing?] with tenacious investigations the international validity of the Calvo Clause as one of the possible bulwarks that the future offers against the pertinacious invasion of claims brought up against us." [98]

Mexican publicists and statesmen were not long in answering this call to action, and, in succeeding years, most of the battle for validating the Calvo Clause and restricting diplomatic protection was carried on under their leadership, particularly in inter-American conferences, public and private. Their first opportunity came at the Eighth American Scientific Congress, held at Washington, D.C., in 1940. Ramón Beteta, subsecretary of foreign relations of Mexico, and Ernesto Henríquez of the Juridical Department, Office of the Secretary of Foreign Relations of Mexico, submitted a paper to the sessions of the Conference on International Law, Public Law, and Jurisprudence. This paper ably presented the Latin American viewpoint on the Calvo Clause and diplomatic protection, arguing that inter-American resolutions and conventions, reinforced by considerations of justice and equity, had abolished both armed and diplomatic intervention, and had impliedly accepted the validity of the Calvo Clause.[99] Edwin Borchard, probably the outstanding United States authority on this branch of international jurisprudence, was in attendance at the conference, and, setting aside his prepared address, rose to answer the Mexicans' arguments.[1] While

---

[98] *The Bucareli Agreements and International Law*, translated by S. de la Selva (Mexico, 1940), p. 177. The Preface of the book describes the author as one "who speaks authoritatively for a large sector of Mexican opinion." *Ibid.*, p. v.

[99] "La protección diplomática de los intereses pecuniarios extranjeros en los estados de América," *Proceedings*, pp. 27–48.

[1] *Ibid.*, pp. 69–75. The arguments advanced will be examined *infra*, Chapter V, pp. 107–114.

no action was taken at this conference, the unrelenting efforts of the Latin Americans to demonstrate the acceptability of the Calvo Clause under the rules of international law indicated a strong determination to continue the fight against diplomatic intervention whenever and wherever the opportunity to do so arose.

Perhaps the most determined effort by Latin Americans in recent years to win support specifically for the acceptance of the validity of the Calvo Clause was that made during the Third and Fourth Conferences of the Inter-American Bar Association (1944 and 1945).[2] At these conferences, several delegates from Mexico led an impassioned and effective attack on diplomatic protection and presented strong arguments in favor of the validity of the Calvo Clause. To be sure, the Inter-American Bar Association is not an official organization, but victory for the Latin American efforts here would have added great weight to their arguments before subsequent International Conferences of American States.

Toribio Esquível Obregón opened the assault in a paper to the Third Inter-American Bar Association Conference in which he carefully documented a stinging criticism of the institution of diplomatic protection, citing many examples of the abuses of this practice both in the Western Hemisphere and in the world as a whole.[3] After a lengthy analysis of the historical facts surrounding the practice of diplomatic protection, Esquível Obregón concluded that while a nation has the right and obligation to protect the commercial relations of its citizens with other states, it definitely does not have the right or obligation to protect the wealth acquired by its citizens while resident in other countries, especially if the citizens, in order to enjoy the fruits and posses-

[2] A. Freeman, in his article "Recent Aspects of the Calvo Doctrine and the Challenge to International Law," *AJIL*, XL (January 1946), p. 122, asserts that the Latin American effort made at these conferences was in reality "the final and logical phase of a determined campaign against one of the most fundamental pillars of international law," i.e., diplomatic protection.

[3] "Protección diplomática de los ciudadanos en el extranjero," *Memoria de la Tercera Conferencia de la Federación Interamericana de Abogados* (Mexico, 1944), III, pp. 218–236.

sion of these riches, have expressly renounced the right to invoke such protection.[4]

Alfonso García Robles, in what is perhaps the best presentation of the legal arguments for the Latin American viewpoint on diplomatic protection and the Calvo Clause, then delivered a brilliant appeal to the conference to go on record as favoring the abolition of the institution of diplomatic protection and the sanctioning of the validity of the Calvo Clause.[5] García Robles argued that the logical implication of the action of the American republics in condemning all intervention was the prohibiting of diplomatic intervention as well. However, since in international affairs the dictates of logic are not always followed, it is necessary to take positive steps to abolish this "product of Hegelian influence" which is an outgrowth of the expansionism of the nineteenth century and which is "in flagrant contradiction with the modern-day democratic tendencies." This institution, he said, is juridically, morally, and pragmatically bad. In its place should be substituted an International Protection of the Rights of Man, which would operate without regard to nationality or political considerations, and would guarantee basic rights for all men.[6]

Dealing with the validity of the Calvo Clause as such, the Mexican lawyer asserted that the arguments adduced against its validity lack all juridical and moral basis. To deny the validity of the Clause is, he insisted, an affront to the other state and is equivalent to implying that the state has not achieved a reasonable standard of civilized justice, contrary to the many conventions, resolutions, and declarations in which are proclaimed, with sober insistency, the excellence and the similarity of the democratic institutions of this continent.[7] The ultimate objec-

[4] *Ibid.*, p. 236. The legal arguments contained in Esquível Obregón's analysis will be examined *infra*, Chapter V, pp. 107–114.

[5] "La protección diplomática, la Cláusula Calvo y la salvaguardia de los derechos internacionales del hombre," *Memoria*, III, Apéndice, pp. 5–25.

[6] This summation of García Robles' argument is based on his own summary, *ibid.*, pp. 23–24. The important legal issues raised will be examined *infra*, Chapter V, pp. 107–114.

[7] *Memoria*, III, Apéndice, pp. 23–24.

tive, therefore, should be the substitution of an international system of protection of the basic rights of man in place of the present unilateral system whereby each state is responsible for protecting its own citizens. In the meantime, García Robles urged, the conference should go on record as favoring inter-American conventions that would recognize the integral validity of the Calvo Clause and also would establish that states are not responsible for damages caused to aliens as a result of civil wars.[8]

These suggestions were referred to a subcommittee of the Committee on Post-War Problems. So effective were the arguments advanced by the Mexican lawyer that they won the support of no less a personage than Frederic R. Coudert, then president of the American Society of International Law. A draft resolution, embodying García Robles' proposals, was drawn up by Coudert, García Robles, and Dr. Riesco, members of the special subcommittee.[9] This resolution, known as the Riesco-Coudert-García Robles resolution, stated:

The Third Conference of the Inter-American Bar Association Resolves:

1. To strive that, in the world order, the so-called "Diplomatic Protection of Nationals Abroad" be replaced with the "International Protection of the Rights of Man," permitting the first to be maintained temporarily, while an international system appropriate for the application of the second is organized, only for those well-defined cases of denial of justice, restrictively interpreted, that are found expressly anticipated in treaties or conventions, to which not only the claimant state but also the state which is the object of the reclamation are parties.

2. To declare, in what refers especially to America, that the nations of this continent, due to the similarity of their republican institutions, their irrevocable desire for peace, their profound sense of humanity and tolerance and their absolute adherence to the principles of international law, of the sovereign equality of the states, and of individual liberty without religious or racial prejudice, have attained an analogous "reasonable stand-

[8] *Ibid.*, p. 24.
[9] Freeman, "Recent Aspects of the Calvo Doctrine and the Challenge to International Law," *AJIL*, XL (January 1946), p. 121; *Cuarta Conferencia, Federación Interamericana de Abogados* (Santiago, 1946), III, pp. 1411, 1460.

ard of civilized justice," which makes diplomatic protection unnecessary in their case, since among states which fulfill this condition, it is a principle universally accepted, without a single
discrepancy, that equality of rights with the national is the maximum limit to which a foreigner may aspire.

3. To work in order that the American republics, as the first
step toward the goal of the total and explicit abolition, by treaty,
of diplomatic protection, subscribe to two continental conventions, which later can be transformed into world-wide agreements, recognizing respectively the integral validity of the Calvo
Clause — which is nothing more than a legal formula to obtain
the practical application of the principle of the equality of rights
mentioned in the previous clause—and the irresponsibility of
the state for damages caused to foreign residents as a result of or
during civil wars.[10]

Although there was a good deal of support initially for the
approval of this attractively phrased resolution, the conference
finally decided to postpone a decision until its next meeting.
Resolution 71 of the Third Conference of the Inter-American
Bar Association directed that the studies of Esquível Obregón
and García Robles, along with the Riesco-Coudert-García Robles
draft resolution, be sent to affiliated organizations for study and
recommendations that would be submitted to the Fourth Conference.[11]

In the intervening months, the draft resolution was given
careful scrutiny. At first glance, it appeared to be aiming at the
desirable, albeit somewhat revolutionary, objective of elevating
and improving the position of the individual in international
law. Closer study by legal scholars, however, convinced many
that the objective accomplished might be entirely different. Although strong support could be found for modifications and improvements in the present system of the protection of the rights
of aliens abroad,[12] many of the scholars realized that the complete abolition of this system, while the world awaited the devel-

[10] My translation. The special subcommittee submitted this resolution on
August 7, 1944. The resolution is nearly identical with that originally recommended by García Robles. See *Memoria*, III, Apéndice, pp. 24–25.

[11] *Memoria*, I, p. 65.

[12] See *supra*, pp. 11–13.

opment of an international system of protection that perhaps would never materialize, might well result in abuses and injustices far exceeding those connected with the present system.[13]

By the time of the Fourth Conference of the Inter-American Bar Association, which met at Santiago in October 1945, strong opposition had developed against the draft resolution, not only from United States sources, but even from some Latin Americans, who, while favoring the validation of the Calvo Clause, did not agree that all diplomatic protection should be immediately abolished without the existence of a suitable alternative. There also existed a great deal of doubt as to whether the association should become involved in a controversy that was actually as much political as legal.

The Riesco-Coudert-García Robles draft resolution was referred to the Committee on Post-War Problems for its study and recommendation. It was immediately apparent that committee members were, if possible, going to avoid taking a stand on the draft resolution. The president of the committee, John Bullington, stated that in spite of the fact that the resolution "would receive the nearly unanimous approval of the members of the association," there was little hope that it would receive the "universal acceptance of the governments of the American republics," and therefore no action should be taken by the association. He recommended that the association endorse the compulsory jurisdiction of the newly formed International Court of Justice as a means to settle such disputes.[14]

It appeared that a majority of delegates at the conference were in favor of postponing any action on the controversial resolution for fear that any action taken might seriously hinder the progress of the association. None of the studies submitted to the

[13] See Freeman, "Recent Aspects of the Calvo Doctrine and the Challenge to International Law," *AJIL*, XL (January 1946), pp. 121–147. García Robles' views on the Calvo Clause were, however, well received in Latin America. His book, *La Cláusula Calvo ante el derecho internacional* (Mexico, 1939), in which he set forth many of his ideas later presented to this conference, was warmly reviewed by Clara Romero Estrada in *Revista de derecho internacional*, XLIII (1943), pp. 353–358.

[14] "Informe," *Cuarta Conferencia*, III, pp. 1387–1396. My translation.

conference, with the exception of that of García Robles, favored taking action on the resolution.[15] The conference, after considerable debate, and over the strong opposition of the Mexican delegates, finally decided that this matter "although legal in form, is so mixed with political subjects that no resolution should be adopted."[16]

The issue was brought up again during the Inter-American Conference on the Problems of War and Peace, which met at Mexico City in 1945 and adopted a Resolution on the International Protection of the Essential Rights of Man. Mexico, in submitting the draft resolution for the consideration of the conference, repeated many of the arguments offered by García Robles to the Inter-American Bar Association conferences. Mexico pointed out that an international protection of the rights of man

. . . would offer the tremendous advantage of permitting the replacement by a collective international protection of diplomatic protection, the objections to which have been pointed out by numerous writers, and the abuses of which a majority of the Republics of the New World have so bitterly experienced, especially with respect to financial claims. . . . When the system in question is functioning efficiently, there will disappear the only valid objection made by the most ardent proponents of the said diplomatic protection which, in the final analysis, is incompatible with the principle of individual non-intervention of States and makes futile in practice that principle of juridical equality between the citizen and alien by placing the latter, when he is a

[15] Studies were submitted by Osvaldo de Castro Larraín of Chile (*Cuarta Conferencia*, III, pp. 1396–1407), Alwyn V. Freeman of the United States (*ibid.*, pp. 1436–1457), Alfonso García Robles of Mexico (*ibid.*, pp. 1458–1466), Amos J. Peaslee of the United States (*ibid.*, pp. 1408–1414), Hector Ríos Igualt of Chile (*ibid.*, pp. 1424–1436), and Alfredo Campanella of Mexico (*ibid.*, pp. 1414–1423). Frederic Coudert, in a letter to the conference, withdrew his support from the resolution, recommending further study, in spite of the fact that "there is much that can be said in favor of its acceptance" (my translation, *ibid.*, pp. 1412–1413). The legal analyses contained in these various studies will be examined *infra*, Chapter V, pp. 107–114.

[16] Resolution No. 48, *Cuarta Conferencia*, III, p. 1604. My translation. A footnote to this resolution indicates that an agreement was made that this matter would be taken up again at the next conference, but it has not to date been formally discussed in any of the association's conferences.

national of a powerful country, in a privileged position, or one in which, in order that it may be possible to accept without any restriction whatever the principle of equality of rights between the national and alien as the maximum limit to which the latter may aspire in the country of his residence, it is necessary to guarantee him a "minimum standard of civilized justice."

Through the international protection of the "Essential Rights of Man," that standard would be fully assured and its guarantee would henceforth be a collective international guarantee and not one dependent upon the desires of the Government of the State of origin, as has occurred to date; the protection that would be given to the individual would be granted him in his capacity as a human being and would no longer have anything to do with the power of the said State.[17]

The conference, with no opposition from the United States, resolved that the Inter-American Juridical Committee prepare a Draft Declaration of the International Rights and Duties of Man for the consideration of the Ninth International Conference of American States. The resolution stated, in part:

The Declaration of the United Nations has proclaimed the need for establishing international protection of essential rights of man;

In order to make such protection effective it is necessary to define these rights, as well as the correlative duties in a declaration to be adopted as a convention by the States;

International protection of the essential rights of man would eliminate the misuse of diplomatic protection of citizens abroad, the exercise of which has more than once led to the violation of the principles of non-intervention and of equality between nationals and aliens, with respect to the essential rights of man.[18]

This action at Mexico City appeared to indicate an important new approach to the fight on diplomatic protection by Latin Americans. Unsuccessful in their efforts to win acceptance either of the absolute equality principle over the minimum standards rule or of the full validity of the Calvo Clause as a by-pass to

---

[17] Quoted in *Report of the Delegation of the United States of America to the Inter-American Conference on Problems of War and Peace* (Washington, D.C., 1946), pp. 158–159.

[18] Resolution XL, March 7, 1945, *ibid.*, pp. 108–109.

the minimum standards rule,[19] the Latin American republics, under the leadership of Mexico, are now attempting to establish that minimum standards of civilized justice actually do exist in the Western Hemisphere, and so therefore that this legal obstacle to the complete equality rule has disappeared. To accomplish this, they first must win agreement on what basic rights are included in the minimum standards. Resolution XL was a step in this direction, for a Declaration of the International Rights and Duties of Man would create definite international standards, to be enforced through international action, in contrast to the vague standards that now exist, enforced unilaterally by diplomatic interposition. An international agency to enforce these inter-American standards was envisioned in another resolution by this same conference calling for the study of an Inter-American Peace System which would include an Inter-American Court of Justice.[20] Enforcement of individual rights through this method would clearly involve intervention, but it would be international or multilateral and not the hated unilateral intervention. Latin Americans apparently would be willing to accept such a limitation on their sovereignty in order to eliminate the institution of diplomatic protection.[21]

This new approach to the objective of eliminating diplomatic protection was destined to prove considerably more difficult to handle than past efforts. The ideal of basic human rights proclaimed and protected by an international agency had great appeal.[22] The United States, however, has adopted the attitude that the time is not yet ripe for such action and has attempted in recent years to delay any positive action, on either a binding Covenant of Human Rights or an Inter-American Court to which individuals could directly appeal violations of these basic

---

[19] See *infra*, pp. 112–114.

[20] Resolution XXXIX, *Report of the Delegation of the United States of America to the Inter-American Conference on Problems of War and Peace*, pp. 107–108.

[21] See A. P. Whitaker, "Pan America in Politics and Diplomacy," *Inter-American Affairs* (1945), p. 14.

[22] See Borchard, *Dip. Prot.*, pp. 861–864.

rights. This attitude, difficult for Latin Americans to understand, has been subjected to strong criticisms.

The idea of an Inter-American Court, as distinct from the present International Court, has great attraction for Latin Americans. As Mexico stated in a Code for an Inter-American Court which was submitted to the Buenos Aires Peace Conference of 1936:

American legal controversies should be decided by American judges . . . [and] a correct understanding of facts pertaining to the Americas is more readily to be obtained by Americans themselves. . . . An organization of American justice would save us from the errors attendant upon the defective empirical system of the Claims Commissions, providing stronger guaranties of objectivity in the awards, of expedition in procedure, and of economy in expenditures.[23]

Indeed, the first permanent court in the world for the settlement of international disputes was the Central American Court established in 1907.[24] While this court has ceased to function, the ideal which it represented remains and has figured prominently in recent inter-American conferences. Not the least motivation for an inter-American court is the fact that such a tribunal, on which Latin Americans would be in a strong majority, would quite naturally be much more sympathetic to Latin American legal doctrines than would a world court.[25] It is not surprising, therefore, that the United States has not shown any intense desire to see such an inter-American tribunal set up.

The new approach of Latin America in attempting to restrict or eliminate the institution of diplomatic protection was quite evident during the sessions of the Ninth International Confer-

---

[23] Quoted by James Brown Scott (ed.), *Inter-American Tribunal of International Justice* (Washington, D.C., 1937), p. xiii. This is an excellent survey of the efforts made up to 1937 to establish such a tribunal.

[24] For a discussion of the ten cases brought before the court in its ten-year history, see M. O. Hudson, "The Central American Court of Justice," *AJIL*, XXVI (October 1932), pp. 759–786. Individuals, who had access to the court after exhausting local remedies, brought five of these cases before the tribunal.

[25] Bemis, *op. cit.*, p. 254, asserts that with a tribunal dominated by Latin American jurists "there is no doubt how such a court would interpret a Calvo Clause."

ence of American States which met at Bogotá in 1948.[26] Although
the advance agenda of the conference did not contain any items
on the Calvo Clause, the Calvo Doctrine, pecuniary claims, or
related matters, the controversy actually played a prominent
role in conference deliberations.

In accordance with the resolution of the 1945 conference, the
Inter-American Juridical Committee formulated, in 1946, a draft
Declaration of the International Rights and Duties of Man.
After submission of this draft to the states for their comments,
a definitive project was presented by the Juridical Committee
for the consideration of the Ninth Conference.[27] After lengthy
discussion, it was decided that the Declaration of the International Rights and Duties of Man would be approved in the form
of a resolution rather than a treaty.[28] While the Latin American
states, especially Mexico, were disappointed in not getting a
treaty, nevertheless, they felt, the declaration would clarify somewhat what is included in the term "minimum standards" as it
applies to the rights of man in the Americas.

The conference also approved a resolution which called for the
creation of an Inter-American Court.[29] This was another distinct
achievement for Latin American diplomacy, for the United States
felt that the creation of such a tribunal was premature and
would involve drafting a treaty guaranteeing human rights; in
addition, the United Nations was engaged in similar work.[30]

[26] The Ninth Conference was scheduled to meet in 1943, but because of the
wartime emergency and the frequent meetings of the foreign ministers of the
American states, the meeting was postponed to 1948.

[27] *Report of the Delegation of the United States of America to the Ninth
International Conference of American States* (Washington, D.C., 1948), p. 80.

[28] *Ibid.*, p. 81. Resolution XXX, the contents of which are not relevant to
this study, can be found in *ibid.*, pp. 260–266.

[29] Resolution XXXI, *ibid.*, p. 266. The Inter-American Council of Jurists was
charged with the responsibility of drawing up a statute for such a court for the
consideration of the Tenth Conference.

[30] *Ibid.*, p. 82. The view of the United States apparently won out before the
Inter-American Juridical Committee, which on September 26, 1949, recommended to the Inter-American Council of Jurists that action on Resolution
XXXI be postponed pending approval of an inter-American convention calling
for the establishment of such a court. The delegate from Mexico dissented. Report printed in *Inter-American Juridical Yearbook, 1949*, pp. 298–300. On May

The Calvo Clause

The Calvo controversy also figured in the Charter of the Organization of American States, which was approved at this conference. Chapter III of the Charter dealt with the "Fundamental Rights and Duties of States." In the committee of the conference charged with drafting this chapter, the United States delegation took the view that in such a document as the Charter only the most fundamental and generally acceptable statement of the rights and duties of states should be included, and that to attempt to go further would not only create major drafting difficulties, in view of the highly technical and in some cases controversial issues involved, but "might prejudice prompt ratification." [31] However, the view that prevailed in the committee was that the American states had already in the Montevideo Convention on the Rights and Duties of States, ratified by nineteen republics, reached agreement on extensive statements of the basic rights and duties, and that therefore the drafting of this chapter of the Charter was principally one of phrasing already accepted statements in a manner appropriate for Charter provisions. As a result "Chapter III is principally an incorporation of the provisions of the 1933 Convention with some additions and rephrasing." [32]

The greatest controversy before this committee regarded the language and intent of Article 12 of Chapter III, which dealt with the rights of aliens and brought to the fore once again the

22, 1950, the Inter-American Council of Jurists, by majority vote, approved this report, urging postponement of the creation of the tribunal. See *Handbook, First Meeting of the Inter-American Council of Jurists* (Washington, D.C., 1950), pp. 89–102. This report and recommendation were presented to the Tenth Conference, which after lengthy discussion passed Resolution C instructing the Council of the Organization to ascertain the position of each of the member states with respect to the proposed Inter-American Court. If the majority of the member states are in favor of doing so, the subject is to be referred to the Inter-American Juridical Committee for the preparation of a draft which would then be submitted to the Eleventh Conference by the council. *Final Act* (Washington, D.C., 1954), pp. 100–101. See also Resolution XXIX, *ibid.*, pp. 36–37.

[31] *Report of the Delegation of the United States of America to the Ninth International Conference of American States*, p. 36.

[32] *Ibid.*; see also C. C. Fenwick, "The Ninth International Conference of American States," *AJIL*, XLII (July 1948), p. 556.

Calvo controversy.[33] The working committee originally had voted to include the following provisions, based on the 1933 convention: "The jurisdiction of States within the limits of national territory applies to all inhabitants. Nationals and aliens are under the same protection and owe the same obedience to the laws and authorities of the country." [34] A question over the interpretation of this article immediately arose. It appeared that by declaring aliens and nationals to be subject to the "same jurisdiction," the right of appeal to diplomatic protection would be eliminated. The United States delegation objected to this second sentence, explaining that while it has accepted the proposition "as sound international law" that nationals and aliens are subject to the jurisdiction of the state in which they reside, "it has consistently not accepted as correct the principle that both are necessarily under the *same* protection." [35] The United States maintained its traditional position that, if the treatment accorded the alien falls below generally recognized standards, the government of the state of which the alien is a national may properly bring the matter to the attention of the authorities of the other state. "The sentence referred to would contravene this right, and the United States position in this regard is consistent with its reservation to the 1933 Convention." [36]

At the instance of the United States, the second sentence was dropped, and it was decided to add the words "whether nationals or aliens" to the first sentence. Article 12, as finally agreed upon, read: "The jurisdiction of States within the limits of their national territory is exercised equally over all the inhabitants, whether nationals or aliens." [37] The delegation of Mexico insisted

[33] *Ibid.*

[34] Quoted in *Report of the Delegation of the United States of America to the Ninth International Conference of American States*, p. 36.

[35] *Ibid.*, p. 37.

[36] *Ibid.*

[37] *Charter of the Organization of American States* (Washington, D.C., 1948), p. 26. As of August 1, 1952, the Charter had been ratified by all the republics except Argentina, Chile, and Uruguay. *Inter-American Juridical Yearbook, 1950–1951*, p. 162. The President ratified the Charter for the United States on June 15, 1951. 2 U.S. *Treaties* 2394 (1951). The Latin American states were unsuc-

that the substance of the second sentence was contained in the terms of Article 12 as it remained,[38] and a statement was made for the record by the delegation of Mexico and Ecuador to the effect that approval of Article 12 does not modify or reduce the scope of Article 9 of the Montevideo Convention on the Rights and Duties of States with respect to those countries that have signed and ratified that convention.[39]

The Latin American republics were to make yet another attempt to eliminate diplomatic protection, and this time their efforts were somewhat more successful. The Pact of Bogotá, a treaty on pacific settlement of disputes approved by the Ninth Conference, included one article on substantive law although the treaty was concerned basically with procedures.[40] This article dealt directly with the problem of diplomatic protection and provided:

Article VII. The High Contracting Parties bind themselves not to make diplomatic representations in order to protect their nationals, or to refer a controversy to a court of international jurisdiction for that purpose, when the said nationals have had available the means to place their case before competent domestic courts of the respective state.[41]

Although the proponents of this article contended that it represented nothing more than the established rule of the constitutions of all their countries,[42] the United States felt that "this Article appears to have the effect of abolishing the internation-

cessful in an attempt to get an article on diplomatic protection included in the United Nations International Law Commission's Draft Declaration on the Rights and Duties of States. See *supra*, p. 58, n. 78.

[38] Fenwick, "The Ninth International Conference of American States," *AJIL*, XLII (July 1948), p. 556.

[39] *Report of the Delegation of the United States of America to the Ninth International Conference of American States*, p. 37.

[40] Fenwick, "The Ninth International Conference of American States," *AJIL*, XLII (July 1948), p. 560.

[41] *American Treaty on Pacific Settlement. The Pact of Bogotá* (Washington, D.C., 1948), p. 16. As of 1954, the pact had been ratified by only Costa Rica, El Salvador, Haiti, Honduras, Mexico, Nicaragua, Panama, and the Dominican Republic. See Dreier, *op. cit.*, p. 833.

[42] Fenwick, "The Ninth International Conference of American States," *AJIL*, XLII (July 1948), p. 560.

ally recognized right of protection of nationals in the cases described." [43] It was further asserted:

While fully recognizing the duty of aliens to be bound by the laws of any state in whose jurisdiction they find themselves, the Delegation did not feel that a useful purpose was to be served in doing away with the international legal requirement that states maintain certain minimum standards in their treatment of such persons or their property.[44]

The United States, although it signed the treaty, entered the following reservation to Article VII:

The Government of the United States can not accept Article VII relating to diplomatic protection and the exhaustion of remedies. For its part, the Government of the United States maintains the rules of diplomatic protection, including the rule of exhaustion of local remedies by aliens, as provided by international law.[45]

Thus the controversy stands at the present time. The inclusion of the Latin American viewpoint on diplomatic protection in the Pact of Bogotá, and its partial inclusion in the O.A.S. Charter, give evidence of the continuing determination of the Latin American states to work through the inter-American conferences in order to achieve victory for the Calvo principles.

The Tenth International Conference of American States (March 1954), meeting in what could well be described as an atmosphere of crisis, did not directly renew the controversy over the question of diplomatic protection, although the Calvo principle of nonintervention figured prominently in the debates over the major topic on the agenda, the problem of Communistic in-

---

[43] *Report of the Delegation of the United States of America to the Ninth International Conference of American States*, p. 50.

[44] *Ibid.*, p. 51.

[45] *American Treaty on Pacific Settlement. The Pact of Bogotá*, p. 27. Because of rather widespread dissatisfaction with the pact, there was strong sentiment at the Tenth Conference to revise it. No agreement could be reached, however, and Resolution XCIX was adopted, calling for member nations to ratify the pact if they wished, or to submit revision suggestions to the council of the organization which, with the aid of its technical agencies, could prepare drafts for the consideration of the Eleventh Conference. *Final Act* (Washington, D.C., 1954), pp. 99–100.

filtration of a government in the Western Hemisphere.[46] In keeping with what appears to be the new approach to this problem, the conference did, however, move closer to the eventual establishment of an Inter-American Court,[47] and, as has been indicated before, such a court, dominated by Latin Americans, would be quite naturally very sympathetic toward the traditional Latin American aspirations on the question of diplomatic protection and the Calvo Clause. In view of the recent history of the Calvo principles before inter-American conferences, it would seem quite likely that these issues will again arise at the Eleventh International Conference of American States (scheduled to be held during 1959 at Quito, Ecuador), if not before.

This survey of the diplomacy of the various inter-American conferences suggests that the two basic Calvo principles, both of which have as their ultimate objective the curtailment or elimination of diplomatic protection, have not fared as badly as has, at times, been suggested. The first of these principles, nonintervention, has been accepted as perhaps the basic rule governing the relations among states in the Americas. The second, equality, has made considerable progress since the First Conference and has actually won partial acceptance, although the United States refuses to accept it in its full and intended sense as barring diplomatic interposition. The issue is by no means settled, however, and the Latin Americans are continuing in their efforts to win total victory. They are still hopeful of obtaining recognition of the absolute equality principle through inter-American conventions, as is evidenced by their inclusion of such a provision in the Pact of Bogotá. Recent trends indicate a new approach: to overcome the minimum standards obstacle to the equality rule, Latin Americans have suggested setting up minimum standards by inter-American convention with a Latin American–dominated court to supervise and enforce these standards. The notable suc-

[46] See *supra*, p. 70, n. 30.
[47] See *supra*, p. 99, n. 30.

cesses achieved in the past would suggest that these recent efforts are by no means doomed to failure.[48]

We have seen how the Good Neighbor policy of the United States has been the greatest facilitating element in the progress of the Calvo principles in inter-American diplomacy. The continuation and perhaps augmentation of that policy under the Eisenhower administration may result in further concessions to the Latin American legal theories in order to solidify the economic and security structure of the Western Hemisphere. Global security commitments of the United States have, in recent years, resulted in less attention to inter-American problems, which long had a number one priority. A lessening of world tension, or, on the other hand, sharp reversals in the existing *status quo*, might increase the United States' interest in Latin America and encourage a greater sensitivity to her aspirations on the subject of diplomatic interposition.

The Calvo Clause, as has been shown, is closely related to these issues. Acceptance of the equality rule in its full sense would automatically validate, and make unnecessary, the Clause. While this survey of the diplomacy of the inter-American conferences has not produced a great deal of evidence that will aid us in the precise task of determining the rule of law on the Calvo Clause, it has been valuable in that it places the Clause in its proper setting, i.e., as a device to curb diplomatic interposition, and it supplies valuable insight into the nature of the legal issues involved in the Calvo Clause controversy. It is to an examination of these legal issues that attention will be directed in the next chapter.

[48] In a somewhat related problem, the Latin Americans achieved a notable success when the United Nations General Assembly, by a vote of 36–4, adopted a resolution on December 21, 1952, which endorsed substantially the Latin American view on the right of a state to nationalize properties and undertakings. See Edward D. Re, "Nationalization and the Investment of Capital Abroad," *Georgetown Law Journal*, XLII (November 1953), pp. 44–68.

The Legal Issues Involved

THE present status of the Calvo Clause and its underlying principles in inter-American diplomacy has been detailed in the previous chapter. There remains the task of determining the precise status of the Calvo Clause under the rules of international law as generally recognized and practiced. In this investigation, primary attention will be devoted to an analysis of the international decisional law that has involved this concept. However, in order properly to understand and interpret the complex role that the Clause has played in international jurisprudence, it is necessary first to examine briefly the legal issues involved in this controversy.

Charles Fenwick has stated that "in no field of international law have more highly controversial questions arisen than in that which involves the relations between the state and citizens of foreign states." [1] Certainly, in this highly controversial field, the question of the Calvo Clause could well be considered one of the most controversial. A major authority in this field has commented privately that the matter of diplomatic claims is one of the most exasperating topics that can be discussed with a Latin American, and Latin Americans would wholeheartedly concur insofar as United States publicists are concerned.

In regard to the argumentation over the Calvo Clause, it is, as Professor Dunn has pointed out, "quite possible to erect a logically sound argument on either side of the case, so far as abstract theory is concerned, and to support it by an impressive

---

[1] *International Law* (3rd ed., New York, 1948), p. 275.

106

amount of precedents." [2] The complexity of the controversy stems in large part from the fact that it involves a conflict between two widely recognized sovereign rights of a state — the right to protect its nationals abroad, and the right to have jurisdiction over all inhabitants within its territory.[3]

It should be noted once again that the arguments over the validity of the Calvo Clause are closely tied in with the general question of the institution of diplomatic protection. The objective of the Calvo Clause is to eliminate the interposition of states to secure protection for their nationals, which in the past has not infrequently been abused. Strictly from a legal standpoint, the Clause is perhaps the only means of protection available to the underdeveloped regions.[4]

Although the legal arguments for and against the validity of the Calvo Clause have been largely developed in the appraisal of the institution of diplomatic protection and in the examination of the official positions of the various governments, it is desirable to deal with these issues more specifically in their legal frame of reference, emphasizing in this connection the pro and con positions and theories of the leading publicists of the world, as the necessary preliminary to an examination of the decisional law.

There are two basic arguments that are put forth in behalf of the validity of the Calvo Clause.[5] The first is that if the alien is accorded equality of treatment with the nationals of a state, he has no right, under the rules of international law, to demand more. The Calvo Clause, by waiving the right to the special privilege of diplomatic protection, merely formalizes this rule of equality into a contractual commitment. The second argument advanced in behalf of the Clause is that there is no sound logical or juridical reason not to hold the individual to his voluntarily

---

[2] Dunn, *Prot. of Nat.*, p. 169. See also De Beus, *op. cit.*, p. 31.

[3] This conflict is emphasized by most Latin American scholars. See Gonzalez, *op. cit.*, pp. 7–9; Esquível Obregón, *op. cit.*, pp. 235–236. The commission in the *North American Dredging* case also pointed up this conflict. *Opinions of Commissioners*, I, p. 26. See *supra*, pp. 3–4.

[4] Feller, *Mex. Claims Com.*, p. 198.

[5] See Beteta and Henríquez, *op. cit.*, pp. 33–34.

accepted contractual promise not to seek redress for grievances by any other means than the local remedies available, a contractual promise that presumably would not have been made if it were not warranted by the expectation of handsome profits.

Before the Latin American arguments in behalf of the Calvo Clause are presented in more detail, we should observe that it is virtually impossible to separate the legal from the political. A careful reading of the various Latin American publicists who have dealt with this problem will indicate that most of the arguments advanced in support of the full validity of the Clause are mainly based on theoretical, moralistic, and political considerations. It will be seen that international law, as evidenced by the rulings of courts, the declarations of governments, and the writings of publicists, does not recognize either of the two basic Latin American arguments as valid law, whatever their appeal might be on the basis of logic or equity. Consequently, Latin American scholars have, by and large, ignored case law in developing their arguments. In seeking legal support for their position, they have relied chiefly on the conventions and resolutions of the various International Conferences of American States which have embraced these Calvo principles. Most of the Latin American arguments in recent years have been devoted to buttressing their contention that the rules of international law should be changed, at least insofar as the Americas are concerned.[6] These considerations should be kept in mind in the examination of the Latin American viewpoint.

The first of the basic arguments on the validity of the Calvo Clause is generally prefaced with a strong criticism of the institution of diplomatic protection. As has been indicated previously, the Latin Americans feel strongly that diplomatic protection — inherently unjust, ineffective, and subject to serious abuse — is essentially a weapon of the strong to coerce the weak, and constitutes a form of intervention in the internal affairs of another state. It is disruptive of the harmonious relations among nations, they believe, and it actually works against the person

[6] These efforts were detailed *supra*, Chapter IV.

who is allegedly injured, because his rights of recovery are dependent to a large extent on the strength of his nation rather than on the intrinsic merit of his claim.[7]

At one time in the history of the world, Latin Americans say, it might have been true that foreigners often found themselves in a condition of manifest inferiority to the citizens of the nation. In their exercise of civil rights, they were perhaps subjected to restrictions which constituted real disadvantages to their persons and property, and, moreover, they were probably often regarded with suspicion and treated with disfavor. But today the situation has been reversed, for aliens, who have available the right of diplomatic appeal, actually have greater rights than citizens.[8] This privileged position for foreigners is entirely unjust, Latin Americans insist. A nation discharges all responsibility toward an alien when it accords him equality with its citizens. No alien has a right to demand more.[9] To insist upon the special privilege of diplomatic appeal is an affront to the nations of Latin America, since it is equivalent to denying that they have achieved a reasonable standard of civilized justice.[10] There is no need for this special privilege of diplomatic appeal among states that have similar republican institutions and a common heritage of justice and democracy, the existence of which has been confirmed by frequent inter-American conventions and resolutions.[11]

According to Latin Americans the validity of the Calvo Clause is derived from this principle of equality.[12] The Calvo Clause is

[7] Esquível Obregón, *op. cit.*, pp. 218–236; García Robles, *op. cit.*, pp. 20–23. See also *supra*, pp. 34–36.

[8] Gonzalez, *op. cit.*, pp. 11–12.

[9] *Ibid.*, pp. 33–37; García Robles, *op. cit.*, p. 14; Gómez Robledo, *op. cit.*, pp. 59–64; Sanchez i Sanchez, *op. cit.*, p. 632; Sepúlveda Gutiérrez, *op. cit.*, p. 79; Beteta and Henríquez, *op. cit.*, p. 35; Esquível Obregón, *op. cit.*, pp. 154–155; Yepes, *op. cit.*, p. 109; Antokoletz, *op. cit.*, I, pp. 413–414. These publicists will generally admit state responsibility if equality is not accorded. See Borchard, "The 'Minimum Standard' of the Treatment of Aliens," *Proceedings of the American Society of International Law* (1939), p. 68. Nearly all the American constitutions concede to foreigners basic rights similar to nationals. See Campanella, *op. cit.*, p. 1422.

[10] García Robles, *op. cit.*, p. 19.

[11] *Ibid.*, p. 18; Beteta and Henríquez, *op. cit.*, p. 34.

[12] Sanchez i Sanchez, *op. cit.*, p. 634; Yepes, "Les problèmes fondamentaux

The Calvo Clause

nothing more than a legal formula to achieve equality between aliens and nationals, for it simply denies to the alien any special rights of diplomatic appeal while he is engaging in business in the state, provided always that he has full and free access to the local tribunals on the same basis as nationals.[13] Equality being a legitimate formula for governing the status of aliens abroad, the formalization of this formula via the Calvo Clause has full validity under the rules of international law.

The second argument for the validity of the Calvo Clause reinforces the first. Certainly the logic and justice of granting the alien equality as the maximum to which he can aspire is greatly enhanced if the individual voluntarily agrees to this condition and by contractual commitment waives any rights to diplomatic intervention.[14] In expectation of compensatory profits, the individual has, without any coercion, waived his right of diplomatic appeal, the *sine qua non* of the contract.[15] Therefore he has none. Since the right of the state is based necessarily on the right of its national, and cannot exceed that right, its right to intervene evaporates with the contractual waiver of the individual's right.

To hold that it is actually the state of the national that is injured, Latin Americans say, is a logical and judicial fiction, based on a Vattelian formula that has long since proved itself inappropriate to the realities of international intercourse.[16] If the individual who received the injury were an agent or emissary of the state, then an injury to the agent, such as an ambassador or a

du droit des gens en Amérique," *Recueil des Cours* (The Hague), XLVII (1934), pp. 105–107.

[13] García Robles, *op. cit.*, pp. 17, 19.

[14] Sanchez i Sanchez, *op. cit.*, p. 634.

[15] Podestá Costa, "La responsabilidad internacional del estado," *Cursos Monográficos*, II (1952), p. 215–216.

[16] Esquível Obregón, *op. cit.*, pp. 233–234; Beteta and Henríquez, *op. cit.*, pp. 34, 45–46. A. S. de Bustamante y Sirven, *Derecho internacional público* (Havana, 1933–1938), III, pp. 505–506, asserts: "It is easy to illustrate graphically the weakness of this reasoning when it is considered that the government does not put in a claim for itself, and that it makes it solely through and for the national, to the extreme that when it obtains a reparation it would be inconceivable that it profit by it and thus augment the revenue of its budget, instead of handing it to the victim on whose behalf it acted . . . And it will result that this victim, contrary to the contract, profits by the results of a reclamation which he had renounced beforehand." My translation.

consul, could be an injury to the state itself, giving it rights of recovery independent of any action by the individual. However, in the average case there is no injury to the state of that alien.

It is no longer true that the individual is a mere cipher under the law of international claims. The position of the individual claimant is taken into account, in spite of the fact that theoretically the state is the sole claimant.[17] Particularly in view of the growing recognition of the individual as a subject of international law, the old Vattelian theory is unacceptable.[18] It is the individual who is freely choosing the forum for the adjudication of any disputes, it is within his competence to waive the right of diplomatic appeal, and that waiver binds the state.

This, in essence, is the Latin American argument in behalf of the validity of the Calvo Clause.[19] But however logical and morally sound the argument may be,[20] it is not necessarily the law.

[17] See Feller, *Mex. Claims Com.*, p. 199; Tan Shao-Hwa, "Spontaneous Renunciation of Governmental Protection by Certain Missionaries in China," *China Weekly Review*, XLVII (January 26, 1929), p. 366.

[18] Gonzalez, *op. cit.*, pp. 25–31, is one of the very few Latin American lawyers to note this very significant relationship between the validity of the Calvo Clause and the emergence of the individual as a subject of international law. This point will be discussed in detail, *infra*, pp. 223–226, 282–286.

[19] An additional argument is occasionally advanced. This view would hold that if an individual can break his ties of nationality through expatriation, he can therefore lessen those ties by contractual waiver of his state's protection. See Gonzalez, *op. cit.*, p. 36; García Robles, *op. cit.*, p. 18. This view was accepted by Commissioner van Vollenhoven in the *North American Dredging Company of Texas* case. See *infra*, pp. 201–202. For critical comment on this thesis, see De Beus, *op. cit.*, pp. 70–72.

[20] The attractiveness of the Latin American view has won many supporters. Simeon E. Baldwin, in an address before the 24th Conference of the International Law Association (1907), stated: "[It] . . . seems reasonable to hold parties consenting to an express contract, which confines them in case of a breach to such remedies as the forum of the defendant may offer, to have waived any other, providing always that such remedies are to be had in tribunals fairly and justly administered. While the nation to which the creditor claiming under such a contract may belong could not be disabled by his act from pressing his claim through diplomatic channels or otherwise, it would not be likely to do so, nor should it be, in consequence of its action, referred to an international tribunal for examination, would that tribunal fail to give the proviso great weight in determining whether the claimant was entitled to relief." *Report*, pp. 184–185. Professor Borchard calls the Latin American viewpoint "very logical." "Remarks by Professor Edwin Borchard on Papers of Dr. Beteta and Dr. Cruchaga Ossa," *Proceedings of the Eighth American Scientific Congress*, X, p. 74. See also Feller, *Mex. Claims Com.*, pp. 198–199.

The majority of publicists outside of Latin America, reflecting to a large extent the viewpoints of their respective foreign offices, have held the Calvo Clause cannot by itself bar a state from intervening diplomatically, if such intervention is otherwise permissible under the rules of international law.

To each of the two basic arguments advanced in behalf of the full validity of the Calvo Clause, international lawyers have generally counterposed two rebuttals. To the first point, that an individual can aspire only to equality of treatment with nationals and the Calvo Clause is a mere contractual formalization of this equality rule, publicists answer with the minimum standards doctrine. To the second point, that the individual's voluntary waiver of the diplomatic remedy should be respected, publicists reply with the rule formalized by Vattel that an injury to a national is an injury to the state of that national, and this therefore gives the state rights of recovery independent of the rights of the individual and hence unaffected by his waiver.

The leading publicists of Europe and North America readily admit that there have been, in the past, abuses of the right of diplomatic protection.[21] But, they maintain, the cure proposed — to abolish diplomatic protection without substituting a satisfactory alternative method of safeguarding the rights of citizens abroad — might well result in abuses and discriminations far exceeding those that exist today.[22] Diplomatic protection is not intervention but is merely the advancing of a claim in diplomatic form without the exertion of any force or coercion behind it. It simply asks the defendant country to submit to the processes of law. Why should any country object to that?[23]

In general, the publicists say, equality is all to which aliens have a right to aspire, provided that the basic minimum standards as dictated by the practice of international law are preserved. If a state keeps its nationals in a condition of abject

[21] Peaslee, *op. cit.*, p. 1409.

[22] Borchard, "Memorandum sobre el tema de reclamaciones pecuniarias," *Diario de Sessiones*, p. 315.

[23] Borchard, "Remarks by Professor Edwin Borchard . . ." *Proceedings of the Eighth American Scientific Congress*, X, p. 71.

slavery, this does not automatically give it the right to accord
the same treatment to aliens, who are protected by international
as well as municipal law. If minimum standards are not met,
there exists a valid justification for diplomatic interposition to
secure justice for aliens.[24] This does not constitute a privileged
position for foreigners, since nationals have the local political
processes through which to combat unjust governmental acts,
something which is normally denied to aliens.[25] Since equality
is not the rule accepted by the generally recognized principles of
international law as governing the relations between alien and
national, the formalization of the equality rule via the Calvo
Clause is consequently not valid as an impediment to diplomatic
intervention.

Further, international law as generally recognized and practiced holds that diplomatic interposition is a right of the state;
hence the citizen, who is not an agent of the state, cannot sign
away the right of his country to intervene.[26] The Calvo Clause
which purports to accomplish this waiver of a right of the state
by an unaccredited agent is actually, says one publicist, "an im-
pertinent usurpation of the sovereign prerogatives of another
state," and hence is void under the rules of international law.[27]
The conclusions of the Harvard Research on this point of inter-

[24] For a classic documentation of the minimum standards rule with generous
references to court decisions, state practice, and the writings of publicists, see
Borchard, "Memorandum . . ." *Diario de Sessiones*, pp. 318–322. See also
Dunn, "International Law and Private Property Rights," *Columbia Law Re-
view*, XXVIII (February 1928), p. 175; Alexander Fachiri, "Expropriation and
International Law," *BYIL* (1925), p. 159; Eagleton, *Resp. of States*, p. 110;
Fred K. Nielsen, *International Law Applied to Reclamations Mainly in Cases
between the United States and Mexico* (Washington, D.C., 1933), p. 8.

[25] Bullington, *op. cit.*, p. 1389.

[26] Borchard, "Remarks by Professor Edwin Borchard . . ." *Eighth American
Scientific Congress*, X, p. 74; Peaslee, *op. cit.*, 1409. This rule is stated by
Freeman, *Denial of Justice*, pp. 470–471, as "*jus publicum privatorum pactis
mutari non potest.*" See also Nielsen, *op. cit.*, p. 8; Schwarzenberger, *op. cit.*,
I, pp. 73–75. L. Oppenheim, *International Law*, I (7th ed. by H. Lauterpacht,
London, 1948), p. 312.

[27] Freeman, "Recent Aspects of the Calvo Doctrine and the Challenge to
International Law," *AJIL*, XL (January 1946), p. 132. Foreign offices, by and
large, consider diplomatic intervention a right of the state rather than a right
of the individual. See *supra*, pp. 37–41, 46–54.

national law accurately reflect the prevailing opinion among the publicists of the United States and Europe: "In sum total, therefore, the better opinion seems to be that the renunciatory clause is without any effect so far as any changes or modifications in the ordinary rules of international law are concerned." [28]

In view of this failure to win acceptance of the complete validity of the Calvo Clause,[29] some Latin Americans, as we have seen, have indicated a willingness to narrow down the scope of the Clause in order to make it more compatible with the present rules of international law. Although the language of the Clause remains as inclusive as ever, a number of Latin American international lawyers have admitted that it would not bar an international claim in the event of an unjustifiable delay or a manifest denial of justice.[30] But this concession is more apparent than real, for there is a great deal of confusion and uncertainty among publicists over the precise meaning of the term "denial of justice." [31] This confusion and uncertainty has led some authorities

---

[28] *AJIL*, XXIII, Special Number, p. 215. See *supra*, pp. 59–60. The majority of European publicists share this view. See A. Decencière-Ferrandière, *La responsabilité internationale des États à raison des dommages subis par des étrangers* (Paris, 1925), p. 169; A. de Lapradelle and N. Politis, *Recueil des arbitrages internationaux* (Paris, 1905, 1923), II, p. 595; Georges Scelle, "Règles générales du droit de la paix," *Recueil des Cours* (The Hague), XLVI (1933), p. 662.

[29] Several prominent Latin American jurists have conceded the invalidity of the Clause under the present rules of international law. See, for example, Alejandro Alvarez, *Le droit international américain* (Paris, 1910), pp. 121–122, who asserts: "Cette clause, de même que les dispositions législatives dont nous venons de parler, est d'une valeur très douteuse, étant donné que la réclamation diplomatique, par sa nature même, doit être exclusivement régie, à défaut de convention entre les États, par les principes du droit international." See also Gómez Robledo, *op. cit.*, pp. 173–174; Lucio M. Moreno Quintana and Carlos M. Bollini Shaw, *Derecho internacional público* (Buenos Aires, 1950), p. 169.

[30] Antokoletz, *op. cit.*, III, p. 139; Andres Bello, *Principios de derecho internacional* (2nd ed., Paris, 1864), pp. 81–82; Yepes, "Les problèmes fondamentaux du droit des gens en Amérique," *Recueil des Cours* (The Hague), XLVII (1934), p. 106; Ríos Iqualt, *op. cit.*, p. 1428; H. Accioly, "Memorandum sobre el tema de reclamaciones pecuniarias," *Diario de Sessiones*, p. 339; Alberto Ulloa, "Memorandum sobre el tema de reclamaciones pecuniarias," *ibid.*, p. 338. Some Latin American publicists would distinguish between resident aliens and transients or aliens temporarily residing in a state. See Bello, *op. cit.*, p. 82; Ríos Iqualt, *op. cit.*, pp. 1427–1430.

[31] Germany, in its reply to the League of Nations Codification Questionnaire, *Bases of Discussion*, III, p. 41, pointed up this disagreement, stating: ". . . As

to assert that the term cannot be defined,[32] and others to suggest the discontinuance of the use of the term in international jurisprudence.[33] The Latin American countries have generally taken a very narrow view of what constitutes a denial of justice. They have tried to define the term unilaterally so as to cover only outrageous derelictions by the courts when they refuse access to the judicial remedies, when they refuse to render a decision, or when they flagrantly deny due process of law.[34] This restricted procedural definition of the term, which would virtually exclude interposition, has not won wide acceptance by foreign offices, courts, or the leading publicists of the world.[35] Although there is a great deal of confusion as to the precise meaning of

to the exact nature of a 'denial of justice' opinions again vary widely. Some take it to mean an actual refusal to do justice; others hold that it is an unconscionable delay in procedure which may amount to an absolute refusal of justice; while others say that it consists in any clear violation of the law to the detriment of foreigners as a whole or certain nationals in particular."

[32] John Bassett Moore believed it not to be "practicable to lay down in advance precise and unyielding formulas by which the question of a denial of justice may in every instance be determined." See *Report, with Accompanying Papers, relative to the Fourth International Conference of American States*, p. 24.

[33] Oliver J. Lissitzyn, *op. cit.*, pp. 645–646, states: "The foregoing examination of the meanings attached to the term 'denial of justice' by writers and of its use in diplomatic practice and in international adjudications clearly shows that no agreement, or even predominance of opinion, exists on this question. . . . In short, it is believed that the use of the term is to be avoided as much as possible . . . There is no necessity for its use, since the particular acts or omissions meant to be covered by it can be enumerated and defined expressly. The development of international law as a body of definite legal principles and rules will not be facilitated by the use of vague terms." For further discussion of the controversy surrounding the meaning of this term, see Freeman, *Denial of Justice*, pp. 84–183; G. G. Fitzmaurice, "The Meaning of the Term 'Denial of Justice'," *BYIL* (1932), pp. 93–114; Victor M. Maúrtua and James Brown Scott, *Responsibility of States for Damages Caused in Their Territory to the Person or Property of Foreigners* (New York, 1930), pp. 36–42.

[34] For example, Gómez Robledo, *op. cit.*, pp. 162–163, gives the following definition: "By this expression what is meant is the flagrant, patent denial of justice, beyond any doubt that a clear mind might entertain, to the injury of an alien demanding justice, whether by hindering his access to the courts, or by depriving him of the aids essential in the procedures involved, or, in fine, by applying the law, in the sentence given, with notorious bad faith and the desire to injure the said alien because of his condition as such." See also Antokoletz, *op. cit.*, III, pp. 58–59; Sepúlveda Gutiérrez, *op. cit.*, pp. 27–38.

[35] Nielsen, *op. cit.*, p. 11; Eagleton, *Resp. of States*, p. 175, n. 44; Borchard, "Remarks by Professor Edwin Borchard . . ." *Proceedings of the Eighth American Scientific Congress*, X, p. 74.

this term, there seems to be near unanimity in rejecting the Latin American version.[36]

It is thus seen that the Calvo Clause may be interpreted in two ways, i.e., as a complete renunciation of diplomatic protection or as a promise to be satisfied with local redress unless there is a denial of justice.[37] As was indicated previously, the Calvo Clause in its complete sense has been rejected by the majority of publicists. The Clause in its limited sense is considered by the majority of publicists to be legal but superfluous in view of the fact that it is already a well-established rule of international law that local remedies must normally be exhausted and a denial of justice, in the more widely accepted sense of the term, suffered before there are grounds for recourse to diplomatic intervention.[38] Herbert Briggs, in a representative analysis, has stated:

To the extent that a Calvo Clause requires resort to local remedies it is merely confirmatory of the rule of international law which ordinarily requires the exhaustion of local remedies with a consequent denial of justice prior to the presentation of an international claim. However, to the extent that it pretends to cause a surrender of the rights of the claimant's State under international law or to oust the jurisdiction of an international tribunal, the Calvo Clause is legally without effect. Thus the clause is either superfluous or irrelevant on the point of international law.[39]

---

[36] The Harvard Research defined denial of justice as "a denial, unwarranted delay or obstruction of access to courts, gross deficiency in the administration of judicial or remedial process, failure to provide those guaranties which are generally considered indispensable to the proper administration of justice, or a manifestly unjust judgement. An error of a national court which does not produce a manifest injustice is not a denial of justice." *Op. cit.*, p. 173.

[37] See Sepúlveda Gutiérrez, *op. cit.*, pp. 59–60.

[38] Borchard asserts that this rule that diplomatic interposition is proper only if local redress is sought in vain and a denial of justice suffered "is so thoroughly established that the detailed citation of authorities seems hardly necessary." See *Dip. Prot.*, p. 818, n. 1.

[39] *The Law of Nations, Cases, Documents, and Notes* (2nd ed., New York, 1952), pp. 648–649. For nearly identical statements, see Eagleton, *Resp. of States*, p. 175; Borchard, *Dip. Prot.*, pp. 809–810; Lipstein, *op. cit.*, p. 145; Alf Ross, *A Textbook of International Law* (New York, 1947), p. 265. Some publicists have asserted that the limited Clause would perhaps have utility in that it would serve to emphasize this rule of international law. See Borchard, "The Calvo and Drago Doctrines," *Encyclopaedia of the Social Sciences*, III, p. 155; Eagleton, *Resp. of States*, p. 171.

The Legal Issues Involved

Although the Latin Americans have narrowed down the scope of the Calvo Clause to this limited version, they have increased their efforts to validate the Calvo Clause in its full sense by achieving recognition of the equality principle through inter-American conventions.[40]

In addition, the Latin Americans have attempted to establish the existence of an American international law which would be distinct from the general principles of international law, many of which they consider to be inappropriate to intra-hemispheric relations. The leader in this effort is the distinguished Latin American jurist Alejandro Alvarez, who has devoted a great deal of study and effort to documenting his contention that this special species of international law is, in fact, arising to meet the special needs and circumstances of inter-American relationships.[41]

The cornerstone of this new international law would be exemption from diplomatic interference,[42] and it would sanction the Calvo Doctrine. T. Esquível Obregón has written:

The Calvo Doctrine should have a prominent place in American international law, for, apart from its intrinsic justice, and the great authority of the man who formulated it, it forms part of the political constitutions of some American countries that have incorporated in them the "Calvo Clause" so-called, the con-

[40] See *supra*, pp. 72–104. Beteta and Henríquez, *op. cit.*, p. 38, suggest these efforts might soon bring victory, asserting: "It is not reckless to suppose that, as the knowledge of our American countries among themselves improves, as commercial interchange increases, and with the situation, accepted each day more clearly by the United States, of the friendship and confidence of the Latin American countries being more compatible to her interests than maintaining their fear through continued diplomatic pressure, there will come about in the near future the definite triumph of the thesis of the equality between nationals and foreigners and the disappearance in American international law of the supposed right of diplomatic protection." My translation.

[41] *Le droit international américain* (Paris, 1910). See also, by the same author, "Latin America and International Law," *AJIL*, III (April 1909), pp. 269–353. Judge Alvarez, in his dissenting opinion in the *Colombian-Peruvian Asylum* case, I.C.J. *Reports* 1950, p. 293, defined American international law as follows: "This expression does not mean, as may appear at first sight and as many would have us believe, an international law which is peculiar to the New World and entirely distinct from universal international law, but rather the complex of principles, conventions, customs, practices, institutions and doctrines which are peculiar to the Republics of the New World."

[42] John MacDonell, *op. cit.*, p. 592.

tractual renouncement, that is, of diplomatic protection demanded by foreigners. To this date the only impediment to the prevalence of the Calvo Doctrine among the peoples of America — which doctrine has no object other than to introduce in America principles of justice accepted in Europe — is the overwhelming power of the United States.[43]

Although the advocacy of an American international law, as distinct from the law of nations, has won some support,[44] the weight of opinion would still hold that international law must have the attribute of universality to be effective and would generally deny that there is or should be such a thing as an American international law.[45] It cannot be denied that there is a body

[43] Quoted by Gómez Robledo, *op. cit.*, pp. 175–176. Cruchaga Ossa, *op. cit.*, pp. 302–303, asserts that the Calvo Clause would be acceptable under an American international law which would include the equality formula.

[44] For example, Homero Henríquez, *Origen y evolucion del derecho internacional americano* (Ciudad Trujillo, 1948); Yepes, *El panamericanismo y el derecho internacional*, p. vii.

[45] Borchard, "Memorandum sobre el tema de reclamaciones pecuniarias," *Diario de Sessiones*, p. 315. A substantial number of Latin American publicists would share this view. See, for example, Sepúlveda Gutiérrez, *op. cit.*, pp. 75–76; Podestá Costa, *Manual de derecho internacional público*, pp. 24–25; Alberto Ulloa y Sotomayer, *Derecho internacional público* (Lima, 1938), I, pp. 70–75. The judgment of the International Court of Justice in the *Colombian-Peruvian Asylum* case (Judgment of November 20, 1950: I.C.J. *Reports* 1950, p. 266), in rejecting the contention of Colombia that "American international law in general" justified her, as the state granting asylum, to qualify the offense by a unilateral and definitive decision, binding on Peru, did not display too much sympathy for the concept of American international law in spite of the fact that Alvarez was one of the judges. Alona E. Evans, "The Colombian-Peruvian Asylum Case: Termination of the Judicial Phase," *AJIL*, XLV (October 1951), p. 761, stated: "A reading of the first judgment would suggest that the Court was more concerned with a strict interpretation of the Havana Convention than with exploring the limits of regional international law . . ." Judge Alvarez dissented from the judgment of the court, taking the position that there is an American international law, and that the majority failed to take into consideration that there are special rules governing asylum in America different from those in other parts of the world. I.C.J. *Reports* 1950, pp. 290–302. As a result of this decision, Latin American circles have been strongly critical of the court for "not understanding regional customs and psychology and for being too strongly influenced by European or Anglo-Saxon conceptions." See Laurent Jully, "Arbitration and Judicial Settlement — Recent Trends," *AJIL*, XLVIII (July 1954), p. 394. This decision might well have the effect of discouraging Latin Americans from further submission of disputes to the court, and of increasing their determination to set up an Inter-American Court. The Latin American states reaffirmed their traditional concept of asylum at the Tenth

of principles of distinctly American origin and evolution whose application is confined to the Western Hemisphere.[46] But the possibility of establishing an American international law, acceptable to the United States, that would validate the Calvo Clause must be considered as remote.[47] If the Calvo Clause is to win acceptance, it probably will come by other methods.[48]

One other method of achieving recognition of the Calvo Clause that appears to have escaped the attention of the majority of Latin American publicists would be the augmentation of the trend toward recognition of the individual as a true subject of international law.[49] If the individual were recognized as a subject of international law this would validate the Calvo Clause, for it would overcome the principal obstacle, the Vattelian rule.[50] The exact status of the individual under the contemporary rules of international law is the subject of a great deal of discussion and disagreement and will be discussed in detail in a later chapter.[51]

This brief examination of the legal issues involved in the Calvo Clause controversy reveals the complexity of the problem. There are two viewpoints, basically in conflict, and it is possible to say much for each, at least insofar as theory is concerned. It has been seen that the large majority of publicists outside of Latin America are of the opinion that the Calvo Clause is, in its broad and true sense, void and illegal, and in its narrower or limited sense, superfluous and without any effect on the rules of interna-

International Conference of American States. See Resolution CVII, *Final Act* (Washington, D.C., 1954), pp. 104–105.

[46] Nonintervention would be an example. See Bemis, *op. cit.*, p. 252; M. M. L. Savelberg, *Le problème du droit international américain* (The Hague, 1946), pp. 306–321.

[47] For a good summary of the various facets of the controversy over the existence of an American international law, see H. B. Jacobini, *A Study of the Philosophy of International Law As Seen in Works of Latin American Writers* (The Hague, 1954), pp. 127–136.

[48] It should be noted that the recent efforts of the Latin Americans to create an Inter-American Court would, if successful, augment considerably the body of rules that are confined, in application, to the New World.

[49] An exception would be Gonzalez, *op. cit.*, pp. 25–31.

[50] Gómez Robledo, *op cit.*, pp. 173–174; Philip Jessup, *op. cit.*, p. 111.

[51] *Infra*, pp. 282–286.

tional law. But it should be remembered that complete reliance on the opinions of the publicists, however learned, is apt to be misleading.[52]

To discover and document the true rule of law on the Calvo Clause, it is necessary to turn now to international jurisprudence. The analysis of this decisional law will be divided into three chapters. Chapter VI will examine the cases involving the Calvo Clause before 1926. Chapter VII will deal with the landmark decision of the United States–Mexican Claims Commission in the *North American Dredging Company of Texas* case. Chapter VIII will analyze the decisional law since 1926. This particular division was made for several reasons. First, the Calvo Clause per se played no real role in determining the outcome of the decisions in any of the cases before 1926. Second, in the *Dredging* case, and those that followed it, there was a special provision in the *compromis* that waived the necessity of exhausting local remedies. Third, in the *Dredging* and subsequent cases, the validity of the Calvo Clause as such was examined in detail for the first time by an international tribunal. Finally, it is necessary to interpret international law, and the decisions of the tribunals that apply it, in the light of the conditions of the world today. Recent arbitral rulings on the Calvo Clause must be examined against the background of the growing integration of the world community and correlative developments in the field of international law. In subsequent chapters the importance of these considerations and their impact on the jurisprudence involving the Calvo Clause will be discussed in detail.

[52] An interesting example of the fact that it is dangerous to rely solely on the writings of publicists in seeking evidence as to what is a rule of international law was the controversy in 1953 in the United States Senate over the NATO Status of Forces Agreement. This agreement, providing that member nations would have jurisdiction over offenses committed by foreign troops while off duty, was attacked by a number of senators on the ground that international law forbade such jurisdiction. In support of this contention, several standard treatises were quoted. The Department of Justice, however, was able to demonstrate that the principles as enunciated by the publicists (based on *dicta*) were at variance with the practice of nations, and hence were not representative of the true rule of international law. The Senate then consented to ratification. See Murray L. Schwartz, "International Law and the NATO Status of Forces Agreement," *Columbia Law Review*, LIII (December 1953), pp. 1091–1113.

‹ VI ›

Arbitral Decisions Involving the
Calvo Clause up to 1926

ALTHOUGH the international law governing the responsibility of
states for injuries to aliens is one of the most highly developed
branches of that law,[1] neither the Permanent Court of International Justice, nor the International Court of Justice has had occasion to rule on the validity of the Calvo Clause.[2] However, the
practice of setting up mixed claims commissions for the adjudication of claims presented by states for injuries to their
nationals in other states — a practice that has become very frequent in the course of the last century and a half — has provided
an abundant body of case law.[3] It is to the decisional law of

---

[1] Jessup, *op. cit.*, p. 94.

[2] Schwarzenberger, *op. cit.*, p. 64. Cf. Permanent Court of International Justice (Series A, Nos. 1–24; Series B, Nos. 1–18; Series A/B, Nos. 40–80; Series C,
Nos. 1–19, 52–88. Leyden, Holland). Manley O. Hudson, *World Court Reports*
(4 vols., Washington, D.C., 1934–1943). International Court of Justice, *Reports
of Judgments, Advisory Opinions and Orders* (annual vols. since 1947, Leyden,
Holland).

[3] An excellent survey of international arbitrations through 1938 is contained
in A. M. Stuyt, *Survey of International Arbitrations, 1894-1938* (The Hague,
1939), hereinafter referred to as Stuyt, *Survey*. There are three standard collec-
tions which contain the arbitral jurisprudence from 1794 to 1902. These are
H. La Fontaine, *Pasicrisie internationale. Histoire documentaire des arbitrages
internationaux* (Berne, 1902); John Bassett Moore, *History and Digest of the
International Arbitrations to Which the United States Has Been a Party* (6
vols., Washington, D.C., 1898), hereinafter referred to as Moore, *Int. Arb.*; A.
de Lapradelle and N. Politis, *Recueil des arbitrages internationaux* (2 vols.,
Paris, 1905 and 1923. Vol. I covers the judgments and treaties before 1855 and
Vol. II covers the years through 1872. A third volume, covering an additional
four years and prepared by A. de Lapradelle, Jacques Politis, and André Salomon, was published in 1954. A fourth volume is in preparation.). From 1902

these mixed claims commissions that we must now turn in order to determine the rule of law on the Calvo Clause. In the period covered by this chapter, the years up to 1926, arbitral jurisprudence reflects to a large degree the confusion and controversy that have characterized the evolution of the Clause in diplomacy and in the writings of the publicists.

The Calvo Clause has been more or less directly at issue in more than thirty international arbitrations.[4] Edwin Borchard has asserted that up to 1926, nineteen cases involved the problem of the Clause, with eight cases upholding its validity and thus prohibiting an international claim, and with eleven cases denying its efficacy to bar the jurisdiction of a claims commission.[5] The leading publicists of Latin America and the United States are in agreement with Borchard's summation.[6]

to the present day, this jurisprudence is to be found only in divers documents, books, and papers. However, several recent surveys are extremely useful: Hackworth, *Digest*; H. Lauterpacht (and others), *Annual Digest and Reports of Public International Law Cases, 1919–* (London, 1932–), hereinafter referred to as *Annual Digest*; Jackson H. Ralston, *The Law and Procedure of International Tribunals* (Stanford, Calif., 1926), hereinafter referred to as Ralston, *Int. Trib.* Special mention should be made of the recent United Nations' *Reports of International Arbitral Awards* (5 vols. to date, 1948–1953, Leyden, Holland). This excellent series, containing the reports of the various arbitrations since World War I, promises to fill a regrettable gap in the documentation of arbitration, and is welcomed by students of the law of international claims.

[4] Latin American states have been frequent participants in international arbitration proceedings. A perusal of Stuyt, *Survey*, indicates that Latin American states were parties to 193 of the 408 arbitrations reported, or about 47.3 per cent. Up until 1919, when there occurred a great many World War I claims, Latin American states had participated in 54 per cent of the arbitrations reported. Of all these arbitrations in which Latin American states were parties along with the Great Powers, and in which awards were made, the Latin Americans, I have calculated, lost 82 per cent. This has not served to alleviate Latin American suspicion and distrust of this method of settling disputes.

[5] "Decisions of the Claims Commissions, United States and Mexico," *AJIL*, XX (July 1926), p. 538. See, to the same effect, Borchard, "The Calvo and Drago Doctrines," *Encyclopaedia of the Social Sciences*, III, pp. 153–156; Borchard, *Dip. Prot.*, pp. 800–801.

[6] Beteta and Henríquez, *op. cit.*, p. 44; Sepúlveda Gutiérrez, *op. cit.*, p. 69; Gonzalez, *op. cit.*, p. 44; Briggs, *op. cit.* (1st ed., 1938), p. 541; Feller, *Mex. Claims Com.*, pp. 185–186. This chapter will discuss four additional cases not usually cited by publicists, but in which the Calvo Clause figured to a sufficient extent to warrant brief treatment. Occasionally the same case is cited by a different name, as when Feller, *op. cit.*, p. 185, n. 3, cites the *Day and Garrison* case, *infra*, pp. 133–136, as the *Beales, Nobles, and Garrison* case. Sometimes

Arbitral Decisions up to 1926

It is clear that the thread of arbitral decisions on the validity of the Clause up to 1926 is anything but uniform, with the validity of the Clause apparently being upheld nearly as often as it has been denied.[7] This inconsistency of the arbitral jurisprudence as evidenced by the eleven to eight split would seem to indicate an irreconcilable controversy. This is particularly remarkable in view of the near unanimity among publicists in regarding the Clause as either void or superfluous. It is my belief, however, that such listings of the pro and con Calvo Clause decisions are without value, for a careful examination of early arbitral jurisprudence shows that the Clause was not the determining factor in any of the cases commonly cited as upholding the validity of this principle.[8] Further, the existence or non-existence of the Calvo Clause did not materially alter the decisions of any of the tribunals that dealt with this problem up to 1926. To properly cite a case as one which accorded the Clause

publicists have included citations which are not judicial arbitrations but are diplomatic settlements, as was the case of the *United States (Thurston) v. the Dominican Republic, U.S. For. Rel.* (1898), pp. 274–291. In addition, some cases have been cited in which the Calvo Clause figured in the pleadings but was not dealt with by the commission, as was the situation in the *United States (Salvador Commercial Company) v. Salvador* (sometimes cited as the *El Triunfo Company* case), *U.S. For. Rel.* (1902), pp. 838–873. A. M. Stuyt, in his volume on *The General Principles of Law* (The Hague, 1946), p. 118, n. 47, refers the reader to a number of additional cases in regard to the Calvo Clause. However, these cases do not in fact involve the Clause but deal only with the local remedies rule. This study will examine only arbitral rulings in which the Clause actually was at issue.

[7] Freeman, *Denial of Justice*, p. 473. Five cases that came before the Mixed Claims Commissions set up after World War I involved the effectiveness of private arbitration agreements which were somewhat analogous in principle to the Calvo Clause. The commissions took jurisdiction, ruling that jurisdiction in the matter of contracts before the war was of a public nature and could not be excluded by a clause of arbitration inserted in the contract, and that the grantor state had wished to substitute an international for a national forum thus absolving the claimant from his pledge. See *Brixhe et Deblon v. Wurtembergische Transport Versicherungs Gesellschaft, Tribunaux Arbitraux Mixtes,* II (1923), pp. 395–401; *Baumblatt v. Merck, ibid.,* pp. 919–924; *Goulley v. Société anonyme "Bosphore," ibid.,* V (1926), pp. 410–415; *Gouvernement hellénique v. Vulkan Werke, ibid.,* pp. 887–899; *Ciocci Gaetano v. Gesellschaft für den Bau von Eisenbahnen in der Türkei, ibid.,* pp. 907–912. See Summers, *op. cit.,* p. 481, n. 62; Ralston, *Int. Trib.,* p. 72.

[8] It is noteworthy that Briggs, *op. cit.,* quite wisely refrained from including this "arbitral scoreboard" in the second edition of his book.

any *legally meaningful* validity or effectiveness, it must be demonstrated that the Clause per se actually served to bar a claim that would have been otherwise admissible under the generally recognized rules of international law. If it is found that the claim would, at any event, have been dismissed in accordance with sound principles of international law, then the Clause must be considered as superfluous and the support of its validity must be considered superficial and undeterminative. It does not necessarily follow merely because a Calvo Clause existed in the contract, and the case was dismissed, that one resulted in the other, as is so often assumed.

In the present analysis of the decisional law, the approach in each case will be to determine precisely what role, if any, the Calvo Clause actually played in *determining* a final decision that would have been to the contrary in its absence. Careful analysis of the international arbitral jurisprudence up to 1926 will demonstrate that there have not been any decisions that can properly be cited as upholding the validity of the Clause, and therefore this early decisional law would tend to support the contention that the Calvo Clause cannot, by itself, operate to bar diplomatic intervention if such intervention is otherwise justified under the rules of international law.[9]

In the analysis of this early arbitral jurisprudence, care will be taken to distinguish between the actual rule of law in each case and the dicta. It should not be forgotten that claims commissions, especially in the early period, were political as well as legal bodies, and since sovereign states were the parties before the tribunal, there was a strong temptation to soften the blow of an adverse decision by couching the opinion in the language of the diplomat rather than the jurist.[10] It is not unusual to find superfluous statements designed to placate one of the parties,

---

[9] It will be seen, however, that beginning with the *North American Dredging Company of Texas* case, decided in 1926, the existence of the Clause did, for the first time, actually and materially affect the decision reached regarding the presentation of international claims, and thus for the first time realized a degree of validity in international arbitral jurisprudence. See *infra*, Chapter VII.

[10] At least one commission considered its function to be conciliation rather than adjudication. See *infra*, pp. 127–128.

especially if such superfluities did not serve to alter the final judgment.

Cases will be grouped together by commissions, rather than by pro and con rulings, the more common practice. Each group will be examined separately, for this method will reveal any possible inconsistent or contradictory opinions by the same commission. This, of course, would be of material importance in determining the value of the judgments as precedents.

The Calvo Clause before the United States and Peruvian Claims Commission

The earliest instance in which the Calvo Clause figured in an international arbitral award was a case that came before the United States and Peruvian Claims Commission set up under the Convention of December 4, 1868, for the purpose of bringing to a "speedy and equitable settlement" the claims of American citizens that arose against Peru during a period of internal strife and war with Spain.[11] The case was that of the *United States (H. Milligan) v. Peru* and was decided February 11, 1870.[12] The claim was for the sum of 327,000 soles as damages for alleged arbitrary revocation by the Peruvian government of a contract granted to an American company, represented by the claimant, to build and own for a number of years a macadamized tramway between Callao and Lima and a horse railroad on several streets of the latter city.[13] The Peruvian special commissioner, Dr. Manuel Pino, took the position that the original grantees, having transferred their rights to other parties, in violation of an

[11] Moore, *Int. Arb.*, II, p. 1639. See also Stuyt, *Survey*, p. 88. For an excellent account of the early history of the relations between the United States and Peru with regard to international claims, see Louis Clinton Nolan, "The Relations of the United States and Peru with Respect to Claims, 1822–1870," *Hispanic American Historical Review*, XVII (February 1937), pp. 30–66.

[12] The opinions rendered by the commission in the *H. Milligan* case have never been published, but they are available in manuscript form in the United States National Archives in a volume entitled *Libro de Minutas*, pp. 444–448. The opinions are also abstracted in Moore, *Int. Arb.*, II, pp. 1643–1644, and in Lapradelle and Politis, *op. cit.*, II, pp. 594–595.

[13] *Libro de Minutas*, *op. cit.*, p. 444; Moore, *Int. Arb.*, II, p. 1643; Lapradelle and Politis, *op. cit.*, II, p. 594.

article of the contract, before the road was completed, lost their right to sue the government; he also maintained that, by virtue of a Calvo Clause provision in the contract, they had bound themselves to refer all matters of difference between themselves and other parties to the courts of Peru and therefore had no right of appeal to the Mixed Commission.[14] The American commissioner, M. Vidal, held that the article of the contract in regard to the transfer of the road was inoperative insofar as Milligan was concerned because the claimant became a stockholder under a provision of the contract which authorized the grantees to issue stock in order to raise funds, and also that, in regard to the Calvo Clause, the Peruvian government by declaring the contract null and void had deprived itself of the benefits of the article by which the company was bound to refer all differences with other parties to the Peruvian courts. In regard to the Calvo Clause, Commissioner Vidal stated:

It is said in the contract that in case of any disagreement or misunderstanding between the grantees and other parties, the former shall refer the matter to the Courts of the country, and to no others. That article would have done very well, had the Company been in working order, and the road constructed or in the course of construction. Of course the Government of Peru could not allow any other Government to interfere between Peruvians and a Peruvian railroad company.

Should, for instance, a mob have destroyed a section of a road, or should a party have sued the company for the loss of property or limb, on account of the carelessness of the employees of the road, it is natural that those cases should have been decided upon by the Courts of the country. But the actual case is quite different.

What does the Company complain of? They complain of the loss of a lawful contract, through the arbitrary *dictum* of the

[14] *Libro de Minutas*, pp. 446–448; Moore, *Int. Arb.*, II, p. 1643; Lapradelle and Politis, *op. cit.*, II, p. 594. The Calvo Clause normally comes before the various commissions in the form of a preliminary objection to the jurisdiction of the commission in view of the claimant's waiver of the diplomatic remedy. A number of authorities have taken the position that the Calvo Clause defense against an international reclamation does not have any bearing on the question of jurisdiction but goes to the merits of the claim. See *infra*, p. 238, n. 21. Precedent would appear to hold it to be a jurisdictional question, however.

Peruvian Executive. Can the Peruvian Government say that the contract is null and void; and that, nevertheless, the company shall abide by all its articles? I would like to know from the Government of Peru what is the position they choose to take in regard to that contract; for really I do not understand what they mean.

Is the contract still good? Very well, then let the Company build the road, instead of preventing them by a decree from going to work.

On the other hand is a contract null and void by virtue of a decree; in other words is there no longer any contract between the Government of Peru and the company? In that case those professions about the enforcement of the articles of the contract are quite meaningless and inopportune.

The company sues the Government of Peru, before our Commission for the violent and arbitrary deprivation of their legitimate property. Considering the importance of the enterprise and the great profit which they would have realized for a number of years, I am not surprised to see at such a high figure, the amount of the award, which they claim from this Commission, as an indemnification for the loss of what they legitimately owned. Therefore I am in favour of awarding H. Milligan . . . the sum mentioned in the memorial on this claim.[15]

The commission, thus failing to agree, was prepared to refer the issue to one of the umpires in accordance with Article I of the convention.[16] However, Commissioner Vidal "again urged upon Dr. Pino the principle of conciliation," arguing "the desirableness of departing in the decision of cases from strict rules of law, and of acting upon the principle of conciliation."[17] Commissioner Vidal asserted that the commission "was not a severe tribunal of justice" and that by the convention its decisions were not to be regarded as obligatory precedents.[18]

Article VIII of the convention read: "The High Contracting Parties declare that this Convention shall not be considered as a precedent obligatory upon them, and that they remain in perfect liberty to proceed in the manner that may be deemed most

---

[15] *Libro de Minutas*, pp. 445–446.
[16] Stuyt, *Survey*, p. 88.
[17] Moore, *Int. Arb.*, II, pp. 1643, 1644.
[18] *Ibid.*, p. 1644.

convenient regarding the diplomatic claims that may arise in the future." [19]

As a result of Mr. Vidal's arguments for conciliation, the commissioners agreed to make an award in favor of the claimant for the sum of 75,000 soles, in lieu of the 327,000 originally requested.[20]

In spite of the fact that this case has been widely cited as denying the validity of the Calvo Clause,[21] it seems apparent that the question of the validity of the Clause as such was not discussed and actually played very little role in determining the outcome of the decision, which, in the words of the American commissioner, was based on principles of conciliation rather than on the basis of law. The precedential value of the case, by the admission of the American commissioner, is nil, for it seems clear that the final decision and award were based on a suggested compromise rather than on the principles of international law, and, furthermore, it is erroneous to translate the argument of Mr. Vidal into a ruling by the commission.[22]

[19] *Ibid.*, p. 1643.

[20] *Ibid.*, p. 1644; *Libro de Minutas*, p. 448; Lapradelle and Politis, *op. cit.*, II, p. 595.

[21] E.g., Eagleton, *Resp. of States*, p. 173, n. 40; Borchard, *Dip. Prot.*, p. 807; Feller, *Mex. Claims Com.*, p. 186, n. 9.

[22] It should be noted that the reasoning of Mr. Vidal that the cancellation of the contract canceled the Calvo Clause did not actually deal with the validity of the Clause as such. This reasoning, moreover, has been strongly criticized by several authorities. See Summers, *op. cit.*, p. 476. Lapradelle and Politis, *op. cit.*, II, p. 595, assert: "L'argumentation du commissaire américain ne semble pas admissible, car la question de savoir si le Pérou avait eu le droit de révoquer son contrat était précisément une question d'interprétation de ce contrat, qui devait, d'après ses propres termes, être soumise aux tribunaux du Pérou." In the *Anglo-Iranian Oil* case before the International Court of Justice (Judgment of July 22, 1952, I.C.J. *Reports* 1952, p. 93), the contract between the government of Iran and the Anglo-Iranian Oil Company, Limited, contained an arbitration agreement (Article 22) which provided that "any differences between the Parties of any nature whatever, and in particular any differences arising out of the interpretation of this Agreement and of the rights and obligations therein contained . . . shall be settled by arbitration." The Iranian government, taking a position similar to that of Mr. Vidal, refused to comply with this obligation of the contract on the grounds that the nullification of the contract also nullified the arbitration commitment. Great Britain strongly contested this position. The court never ruled on this point, since it rejected the case for want of jurisdiction. However, Judge Levi Carneiro, in his dissenting opinion, stated:

It would appear, then, that the *Milligan* case does not carry much weight in the determination of the rule of law on the Calvo Clause, and its citation by publicists as denying the validity of the Clause would seem to be a misrepresentation of the proceedings and decision of the commission.

The Calvo Clause before the United States and Mexican Claims Commission

Another early case commonly cited as upholding the validity of the Calvo Clause [23] came before the United States and Mexi-

"Even if the annulment of the contract could have been decreed . . . it would not follow that this act would exclude the jurisdiction of the arbitral tribunal provided for in . . . this contract. It could be argued that that tribunal would retain jurisdiction to decide as to the effects and the questions resulting from this act and to assess the compensation payable, and also to decide whether it considers such compensation to be legitimate" (*ibid.*, p. 164). A somewhat similar issue figured in the *Lena Goldfields* arbitration (September 2, 1930). The Concession Agreement between the company and the Russian Soviet government for the development of mineral resources in the Soviet Union contained the following provision: "All disputes and misunderstandings in regard to the construing or fulfilment of this Agreement and of all schedules thereto, on the declaration of either of the parties, are examined and settled by the Court of Arbitration." The court was to consist of one member to be chosen by each of the parties, and a super-arbitrator to be selected by mutual agreement. Failing such agreement, the government was to appoint six candidates from a Stockholm mining academy, from which the company would select the super-arbitrator. The court was duly selected, and proceeded to hear the complaint of the company that the government, by its conduct in breach of the contract, had made the performance of the agreement impossible. The government challenged the jurisdiction of the court, withdrew its arbitrator, and failed to appear to answer the company's claim. The government charged that the company "by stating that it took no further responsibilities, by refusing further financing, and by withdrawing the powers of attorney from its representatives, had dissolved the Concession Agreement," and that therefore under "these circumstances the Arbitration Court had ceased to function." The court held, in regard to this contention of the government, that the company had been relieved from further obligations under the contract because the conduct of the government on numerous occasions had constituted "a breach of the contract going to the root of it." Furthermore, even though the contract had been breached, and certain obligations under it thus dissolved, the remedial or procedural elements of the contract were still in effect and hence the government's challenge of the competence of the court was not well taken. See the complete opinion of the court, printed in the London *Times* of September 3, 1930. Brief abstracts from the opinion will be found in *Annual Digest* (1929–1930), pp. 3–4, 426–428.

[23] Borchard, *Dip. Prot.*, p. 804; Feller, *Mex. Claims Com.*, p. 185, n. 3; Eagleton, *Resp. of States*, p. 173, n. 39.

The Calvo Clause

can Mixed Claims Commission set up under the Convention of July 4, 1868.[24] This convention was entered into for the purpose of adjusting the claims of citizens of the United States against the Mexican Republic, and the claims of the citizens of Mexico against the United States, arising out of transactions of a date after February 2, 1848, and before February 1, 1869. The jurisdiction of the commission extended to all claims on the part of corporations, companies, or private individuals, citizens of the United States, upon the government of Mexico, arising from injuries to their persons or property by authorities of Mexico, and of all claims on the part of corporations, companies, or private individuals, citizens of Mexico, upon the United States, arising from injuries to their persons or property by the authorities of the United States.[25]

The case before this commission which involved the Calvo Clause was that of the *United States (Tehuantepec Ship-Canal, and Mexican and Pacific Railroad Company) v. Mexico.*[26] The claim was for the sum of $546,315,038.66, interest included, for damages sustained by reason of the failure of the Mexican government to comply with the terms of a contract of May 15, 1865. The contract contained the following stipulation:

Also, that all questions that may arise under this arrangement, between the General and State Governments aforesaid, and the said second party, shall be adjusted by private arbitration — the

[24] Stuyt, *Survey*, p. 85.

[25] *Claims on the Part of Citizens of the United States and Mexico under the Convention of July 4, 1868, between the United States and Mexico* (Washington, D.C., 1877), p. 12. The history of Mexico has been marked by the frequent presentation of international claims. Gómez Robledo, *op. cit.*, p. 145, has stated: ". . . Our history is the history of the foreign claims brought against our country, so that there is no moment during the national period of Mexico when it was not subject to some mixed claims commission of one sort or another, or when at least it did not have to bear with some compromise on the question of claims pending." For an account of Mexico's early experiences with foreign claims, see C. C. Hyde, "Mexico and the Claims of Foreigners," *Illinois Law Review*, VIII (January 1914), pp. 355–372.

[26] Docket No. 491, decided November 27, 1873. The opinion of the commission in this case has never been published but is available in manuscript form in the United States National Archives in a volume entitled *United States and Mexican Claims Commission, Opinions*, II, pp. 545–547. It is also abstracted in Moore, *Int. Arb.*, III, pp. 3132–3133.

arbitrators, two in number, to be chosen one by each of the parties interested, and in the event of their disagreement the question or questions in dispute shall be referred to some court of justice of lawful jurisdiction in the United States of Mexico.[27]

The American and Mexican commissioners were in agreement as to the disposition of the case, so there was no need to refer it to the umpire. William Henry Wadsworth of Kentucky, the American commissioner, declared in the brief opinion:

Admitting all that memorialist claims; the authority of Carvajal, the breaches of the contract by the government of Mexico, the willingness and readiness of memorialist fully to comply on its part, and the offer to do so; etc., etc., etc., (and we give no opinion on these points) nevertheless this Commission ought not to take jurisdiction of the controversy, but leave the memorialist to that method of adjustment expressly provided for by the contract.

There is nothing in the record to show that memorialist has made any effort to settle the questions of difference by private arbitration, or by an appeal to the Courts of Justice specially indicated by the contract. This must first be shown before we can venture to decide upon the complaint, as one referred to us by the Convention. Whether the authority of Carvajal to make such a contract be affirmed or denied, it was but the dictate of ordinary prudence on his part to reserve the adjustment of all controversies which might grow out of such enormous and unprecedented engagements to the courts of Mexico, [since] private arbitration might prove unavailing.

There we leave for adjustment, when the interested parties please to present them, the appalling claims of memorialist.[28]

The commission concluded by stating that other objections might be taken to the jurisdiction of the tribunal, but "that which has been stated seems to us sufficient for the rejection of the claim." [29]

[27] *Opinions*, II, p. 546. Moore, *Int. Arb.*, III, pp. 3132–3133, probably through typographical error, reported the concluding phrase of the Calvo Clause as reading: ". . . shall be referred to some court of justice of lawful jurisdiction in the United States *or* Mexico." Italics mine. The actual language of the Clause is, of course, much more restrictive and more in the nature of the usual renunciatory provision.

[28] *Opinions*, II, pp. 546–547.

[29] *Ibid.*, p. 547.

In this case, while attention was called to the Calvo Clause by Commissioner Wadsworth, the actual basis for dismissal was the generally recognized rule of international law that local remedies must normally be exhausted before the commission could take jurisdiction. The Clause emphasized but did not modify this rule. If the Clause had not been included in the contract, this rule would still have been applicable, and therefore it must be concluded that existence of the Calvo Clause per se did not serve to bar an international claim otherwise admissible under the rules of international law. The conclusion, therefore, would appear to be that the *Tehuantepec Ship-Canal Company* case is not properly included in any listing of cases upholding the validity of the Calvo Clause.

The Calvo Clause before the United States and Venezuelan Claims Commission

The Calvo Clause next became an issue in several cases decided by the United States and Venezuelan Mixed Claims Commission set up under the Conventions of December 5, 1885, March 15, 1888, and October 5, 1888, to adjudicate all claims on the part of corporations, companies, or individuals, citizens of the United States, upon the government of Venezuela, which might have been presented before August 1, 1868, and which by the terms of the convention were proper to be submitted to its jurisdiction.[30]

[30] Article 2, Convention of 1885, quoted in Stuyt, *Survey*, p. 150. This present commission succeeded an earlier United States–Venezuelan Commission, set up by the Convention of April 25, 1866, which met at Caracas, Venezuela. It is interesting to note that the earlier commission was the only one to have arbitral proceedings to which the United States was a party impeached for alleged fraud on the part of the tribunal. Charges of irregularity and conspiracy to defraud involved the American commissioner, David M. Talmage, the umpire, Juan N. Machado, Jr., the United States minister at Caracas, Thomas N. Stilwell, and Stilwell's brother-in-law, William P. Murray. They allegedly conspired to defraud claimants by exacting huge attorney fees (40 to 60 per cent of the award), payable to Murray who would represent them. It was then arranged for the clients of Murray to get very generous awards, while many meritorious claims of non-clients were dismissed. Because of these revelations, the new commission was set up to rehear the Caracas claims and to hear a few new ones subsequently submitted. See Moore, *Int. Arb.*, II, pp. 1659–1676.

The Calvo Clause figured in the case of the *United States (Melville E. Day and David E. Garrison) v. the United States of Venezuela*,[31] the case of the *United States (Henry Woodruff) v. the United States of Venezuela*, and the case of the *United States (Flannagan, Bradley, Clark and Co.) v. the United States of Venezuela*, the latter two decided together.[32]

The *Day and Garrison* case came before the commission on July 14, 1890. It involved a claim for the arbitrary annulling of two contracts for immigration and steam communication in the amount of $487,500.00 including interest. The claimants had been awarded $250,000.00 by the old Caracas Commission.[33] The agent of Venezuela based his defense to the claim on several different grounds, one of which was that the contracts had never been legally entered into and were hence invalid, and a second of which was that Article 18 of the contract provided for the submission to arbitration at Caracas of

. . . any doubts, differences, difficulties, or misunderstandings that may arise from, or have any connection with, or in any manner relate to this contract, directly or indirectly. . . . The opinion of the two arbitrators or the decision of the Umpire should there be one, shall be considered as a judgment . . . and therefore, this contract shall never, under any pretext or reason whatever, be cause for any international claims or demands.[34]

The case was dismissed and the claim disallowed on the ground that the original contract was invalid.[35] However, the umpire, J. V. L. Findlay of Baltimore, Maryland, and the Venezuelan commissioner, J. Andrade, expressed the opinion that, even if the claim had been admissible on other grounds, it should be

[31] Docket No. 38, *United States and Venezuelan Claims Commission, 1889–1890. Opinions Delivered by the Commission in the Principal Cases* (Washington, D.C., 1890), pp. 247–273. Generous excerpts from the opinions are contained in Moore, *Int. Arb.*, IV, pp. 3548–3564. This case was known as the *Beales, Nobles, and Garrison* case before the old Caracas Commission, and is sometimes cited as such.

[32] Docket Nos. 20, 25, *Opinions* . . . (1890), pp. 425–456. The majority and minority opinions are abstracted in Moore, *Int. Arb.*, IV, pp. 3564–3567.

[33] *Opinions* . . . (1890), p. 247.

[34] *Ibid.*, p. 255.

[35] *Ibid.*, pp. 271–272. The reasons why the commission unanimously ruled the contract invalid are not germane to this investigation.

dismissed in view of Article 18. Findlay, speaking for the commission, asserted:

But, passing this, it is further to be observed that the clause in both of the contracts, providing for arbitration at Caracas, clearly shows that neither of them, on any pretext, was ever to be made cause for an international claim. It is true that it has been urged in answer to this, that both contracts were struck down by the decrees annulling them, and that the arbitral clause fell with them. But that argument is more specious than real. It is conceded, of course, that one party to a contract can not break it at his pleasure, and without the consent of the other, but when both parties agree, as in this case, that any doubts, differences, difficulties, or misunderstandings of any class or nature whatever that may arise from, or have any connection with, or in any manner relate to the contract, shall be referred to arbitration, and one of the parties declares that he is not bound by the contract and attempts to annul it, then the attempt to revoke, of necessity, if language has any meaning, being a "difficulty" relative to the contract, must be one of the questions agreed to be submitted. If these contracts had been good and valid in other respects, and the Messrs. Beales and Nobles had demanded that the "difficulty" growing out of their annulment should be referred to arbitration as provided, and the Government at Caracas had refused its assent to the submission, then a question might have arisen whether there was not such a denial of justice on the part of that government as would have warranted the interposition of the good offices of the United States in behalf of the injured parties. No such demand appears to have been made, but the case was submitted to the old Commission under the Convention of 1866, and was decided by the Umpire upon the assumption just stated, that the decrees annulled the provision as to arbitration, and thus produced the very result of converting into cause for an international claim, a difficulty relating to the contract which by its terms expressed in the most solemn manner was never to be made such on any *pretext* whatever. A distinction was made in argument between a reference of differences or misunderstandings arising out of the construction of the contracts, and a difficulty as to the existence of the contract itself, it being admitted that a controversy of the first kind was legitimate matter for arbitration, but the second was not, or rather could not be made so, because when the contract was annulled there was no longer any provision for arbitration. But that assumes the right to annul without making the revocation a subject of arbitral decision, and such assumption can not be made without the further assumption that a difficulty *relative* to the contract does not and was not intended to include a question as to whether there was such a contract. The case seems to us too clear for doubt, and on this ground alone, if there was no other, we should reject the claim.[36]

The American commissioner, J. Little, while agreeing that the claim should be dismissed, dissented on the Calvo Clause issue. Little stated:

I am constrained, with high respect, to dissent from . . . [the conclusions on the effect of the Calvo Clause.] The declaration of annulment of the contracts by the Venezuelan Executive was tantamount to a refusal to arbitrate. Declaring the *whole* of the contract at an end, it, the company had a right to assume, would not countenance action under *any* of their provisions. The Government under the contracts had a voice in the selection of arbitrators. Its action closed the door, therefore, to arbitration; and the failure to resort to that means of adjustment can not, in my judgment, be rightfully set up as a defense here in its behalf. Still, the contracts being invalid (if for no other reason, because in excess of Camacho's authority, which, being of so high and extraordinary a character, should have been strictly construed, and action confined clearly within its terms), neither the arbitration clauses nor the decrees of annulment are of moment; and I join in the decision.[37]

Although this case is commonly cited as one of the eight upholding the validity of the Calvo Clause,[38] it would seem apparent that the validity of the Clause as such was not a decisive issue. The existence of the Clause did not determine the outcome, for if the Clause had not been included in the contract, the case would still have been dismissed on the ground that the original contract was not valid. Support for the Clause was in the nature of dictum only, and this support was qualified by the apparent failure of the claimant to exhaust local remedies.[39]

[36] *Ibid.*, pp. 270–271.
[37] *Ibid.*, p. 273.
[38] Borchard, *Dip. Prot.*, p. 801; Feller, *Mex. Claims Com.*, p. 185, n. 3; Eagleton, *Resp. of States*, p. 173, n. 39.
[39] *Opinions* . . . (1890), pp. 270–271.

Therefore, even this dictum support of the Clause is not complete, for the commission admits that a refusal of Venezuela to arbitrate might give rise to the question of whether or not there had been a denial of justice. Since local remedies had not been exhausted, the dictum support of the Clause was actually only support of the well-recognized rule of international law that local remedies must normally be exhausted before the presentation of an international claim.

This same commission had a second opportunity to examine the validity or effectiveness of a Calvo Clause. On August 26, 1890, the commission delivered its opinion in the *Woodruff* and *Flannagan, Bradley, Clark and Co.* cases, which were consolidated at the argument, and were disposed of together.[40] In this case a claim was made against Venezuela for the payment of certain bonds issued to the claimants by the Company of the Railway of the East, which company subsequently came into possession of the Venezuelan government. The bonds on which the claim was based belonged to Flannagan, Bradley, Clark and Co., to whom, together with certain Venezuelans, a concession had been granted by the Venezuelan government in 1859 for the construction of the railway.[41]

In a long and rather involved opinion, the commission refused to take jurisdiction of the claim, holding "that the cause of the action had been misconceived, and proofs therefore not supplied that otherwise might have been forthcoming . . ."[42] and, more importantly, that a diplomatic claim was in any case inadmissible because of Article 20 of the concession, which provided: "Doubts and controversies which at any time may occur in virtue of the present agreement shall be decided by the common law and ordinary tribunals of Venezuela, and they shall never be, neither the decision which shall be pronounced upon them, nor anything relating to the agreement, the subject of international reclamation."[43] The majority of the commission asserted:

---

[40] *Ibid.*, p. 425. These cases are normally referred to as the *Flannagan* case.
[41] *Ibid.*, pp. 425–428; Moore, *Digest*, VI, p. 302.
[42] *Opinions* . . . (1890), p. 450.
[43] *Ibid.*, p. 426; Moore, *Digest*, VI, p. 302.

The concession or charter was granted on the distinct condition, as clearly expressed as language could make it, that nothing relative to it or any decision upon matters growing out of it, would ever be made the subject of an international reclamation; but on the contrary, all doubts and controversies of whatever kind affecting the agreement, should be referred to the judicial tribunals of Venezuela, and be there determined in the ordinary course of the law.

The failure to pay the stock subscription, in our opinion, was a clear violation of the terms of the concession, but it is equally clear that Venezuela, either from experience or forecast, realized the importance of referring all questions which might arise in the prosecution of the enterprise, to the jurisdiction of her own tribunals, and expressly excluded them from the sphere of international reclamations.

Nothing could be clearer, more comprehensive or specific than the language of the concession upon this point. . . . This she certainly had a right to do, and the concessionaries, if we may adopt that term, had an equal right to decline the concession on such terms. When they made their contract they knew exactly what they were doing and with whom they were contracting. . . .

Have they any standing before this Commission? A majority of its members answered this question in the negative in the case of *Beales, Nobles, and Garrison,* and they have learned nothing since which induces them to think that they were wrong in that conclusion.

We have no right to make a contract which the parties themselves did not make, and we would be surely doing so, if we undertook to make that the subject of an international claim, to be adjudicated by this Commission, in spite of their own voluntary undertaking, that it was never to be made such, and should be determined in the municipal tribunals of the country with respect to which the controversy arose . . .

Recurring to the concession, if it be said, as it has been said before, that Venezuela has waived her right to have questions arising under it determined by her own courts, and has submitted herself to the jurisdiction of this tribunal by the terms of the Convention of 1885, we can only repeat that there is no evidence of such an intention; that no inference of this kind can be drawn from the general submission of "all claims"; that these where contractual in their nature necessarily come before us in the textual form in which the agreement has been embodied, and that when we look to that and see that jurisdiction is not only not given but expressly denied, we should be breaking the contract instead of enforcing it, if we adopted any other construction . . .[44]

The American commissioner, J. Little, dissented. Mr. Little asserted:

An agreement, in my judgment, between the United States and Venezuela to submit these claims to a Mixed Commission for decision according to justice, superseded and took the place of any previous understanding between the latter and the claimants, if any binding one existed, to submit them to any other tribunal for determination. . . . I do not believe a contract between a sovereign and a citizen of a foreign country not to make matters of difference or dispute, arising out of an agreement between them or out of anything else, the subject of an international claim, is consonant with sound public policy, or within their competence.

It would involve *pro tanto* a modification or suspension of the public law, and enable the sovereign in that instance to disregard his duty towards the citizen's own Government. If a state may do so in a single instance, it may in all cases. By this means it could easily avoid a most important part of its international obligations. It would only have to provide by law that all contracts made within its jurisdiction should be subject to such inhibitory condition. For such a law, if valid, would form the part of every contract therein made as fully as if expressed in terms upon its face. Thus we should have the spectacle of a state modifying the international law relative to itself! The statement of the proposition is its own refutation. The consent of the foreign citizens concerned can, in my belief, make no difference — confer no such authority. Such language as is employed in Article 20, contemplates the potential doing of that by the sovereign towards the foreign citizen for which an international reclamation may rightfully be made under ordinary circumstances. Whenever that situation arises, that is, whenever a wrong occurs of such a character as to justify diplomatic interference, the Government of the citizen at once becomes a party concerned. Its rights and obligations in the premises can not be affected by any precedent agreement to which it is not a party. Its obliga-

[44] *Opinions* . . . (1890), pp. 434–437.

tion to protect its own citizen is inalienable. He, in my judgment, can no more contract against it than he can against municipal protection.[45]

It would appear that here is surely a decision that upheld the validity of the Calvo Clause, and many authorities have so cited it.[46] However, it is necessary to point out that there had not been any attempt to obtain redress in the courts of Venezuela and the commission expressed grave doubts that the Clause would be effective in case of a denial of justice. In important passages of the opinion, the commission asserted:

. . . Even when such questions were transferred for adjudication by her courts, such was her anxiety to avoid any possible international entanglement, that she resorted to the *doubtful* expedient, perhaps, of providing that the decision of her courts should not be drawn in question by foreign intervention. Whether a decision so made in palpable violation of the rights of the parties could be allowed to stand, on a claim of denial of justice, is a question not necessary for the decision of this case, *but we should think it more than doubtful*. . . . Had the claimants resorted to the courts of Venezuela for relief, and been refused in a case clearly showing that there was a denial of justice, a difficult question, as before observed, would have been presented as to how far a Commission of this kind could afford redress, when the claimants had not only submitted themselves to the exclusive jurisdiction of another tribunal, but had also agreed that any decision of that tribunal should not be made the basis or occasion of an international claim. *In point of fact no effort appears to have been made to invoke the aid of the Venezuelan courts*, but the claimants made their appeal directly to the Executive Department of the Government. Whatever may have been the practical outcome of a resort to the courts for assistance, however abortive such an attempt may have proved, we have no right to assume the folly or futility of such a course, in

[45] *Ibid.*, pp. 451–452. Professor Borchard has stated that Commissioner Little's dissenting opinion "has since become the starting point for the decisions of subsequent commissions denying the binding character of the Clause in case of a subsequent agreement by the two nations to submit the question to arbitration." See Borchard, *Dip. Prot.*, pp. 801–802.

[46] E.g., Feller, *Mex. Claims Com.*, p. 185, n. 3; Borchard, *Dip. Prot.*, p. 801; Eagleton, *Resp. of States*, p. 173, n. 39.

the face of the solemn stipulation of the parties, that they will look to that quarter for relief, and no other.[47]

It would appear that once again the support for the Calvo Clause is more superficial than real. The commission was not actually recognizing the validity of the Clause except to the extent that it conformed to the local remedies rule. Support for the Clause was then support for this well-recognized rule of international law.[48]

In conclusion, we may say that these cases before the United States and Venezuelan Claims Commission did not really test the validity or effectiveness of the Calvo Clause. In neither the *Day and Garrison* case nor the *Flannagan* case can it be said that the Clause as such determined the final outcome of the decisions. Since the jurisprudence of this commission does not materially clarify the rule of law in regard to the validity of the Calvo Clause, it would appear that the frequent citation of these cases as upholding the validity of the Clause is actually a misrepresentation of the real bases for the judgments rendered.

The Calvo Clause before the United States and Chilean Claims Commission

The Calvo Clause next came up in the jurisprudence of the United States and Chilean Claims Commission, set up under the Convention of August 7, 1892, for the adjustment of claims of either country against the government of the other growing out of acts committed by civil or military authorities.[49]

[47] *Opinions* . . . (1890), pp. 434–436. Italics mine. The commission stated (*ibid.*, p. 436) that there was no evidence that Venezuela, in the Convention of 1885, showed any intent to waive the Calvo Clause provision. If she had, or if the convention had been interpreted as implying that she had, perhaps the commission would have accepted jurisdiction as several subsequent commissions did.

[48] It is interesting to note that when the claimants, after the adjournment of the commission, again invoked the intervention of the United States, Secretary of State Hay, in a communication to Mr. Woodruff dated November 28, 1900, refused to present the claim again to the Venezuelan government "until there has been a compliance with the aforesaid stipulation [i.e., to exhaust local remedies], resulting in a denial of justice." See Moore, *Digest*, VI, pp. 300–301.

[49] Article 1 of the convention. See Stuyt, *Survey*, p. 182; Ralston, *International Arbitrations from Athens to Locarno* (Stanford, Calif., 1929), p. 209. The

In the case of the *United States (North and South American Construction Company) v. the Republic of Chile*,[50] the commission had occasion to rule on the effect of a Calvo Clause provision in a contract entered into by a United States corporation with the government of Chile for the construction and equipment of certain lines of railroad in that country. In 1890 the Chilean government abrogated the contract, and, taking possession of all the company's works and materials, proceeded to construct the road itself. Because of this action, the claimant demanded damages to the amount of £1,303,334 5s. 3d.[51]

To this claim the respondent government invited the commission to assent to the following propositions:

1st. That the claimant corporation by its contract with the Government of Chile agreed that in all matters and things relating to the contract the company was to be treated as a citizen of Chile, and that in relation to such things and matters it would neither invoke nor accept the mediation or protection of the United States.

2nd. That it does not appear that the company has attempted to secure its rights under the contract, as those rights are set forth in the memorial, by the aid of the constituted authorities of Chile.[52]

The commission examined the relevant articles of the concession which determined the legal relationship between the government of Chile on the one hand and the claimant company on the other. The following articles of the General Conditions for the construction of railways (Chilean law of October 16, 1888) were deemed pertinent:

Article 18. The contractor or contractors will be considered for the ends of the contract as Chilean citizens. In consequence they renounce the protection which they might ask of their re-

convention is reprinted in *The Final Report of George H. Shields, Agent and Counsel of the United States before the United States and Chilean Claims Commission* (Washington, D.C., 1894), Appendix, pp. 1–8.

[50] *United States and Chilean Claims Commission. Minutes of Proceedings and Decisions* (Washington, D.C., 1894), pp. 21–39.

[51] *The Final Report of George H. Shields*, pp. 54–55.

[52] *Minutes of Proceedings and Decisions*, p. 21.

spective Governments, or which these might officiously lend them in support of their pretensions.

Article 48. Any difficulty or dispute which may occur between any of the resident State engineers and any other engineer, appointed as representative of the contractor, as to the construction of any work, quality of material, and in general in the practical execution of the contract, will be decided by the engineer or engineers the Government may name, with appeal to the Ministry of Industry and Public Works, who will decide finally.

Article 49. The difficulties or disputes of any nature which may arise in the interpretation and extension of the contract will be decided summarily and without other appeal by the arbitrating arbitrators named, one by the Ministry of Industry and Public Works, another by the Supreme Court of Justice, and the third by the contractor.[53]

In addition to these statutory provisions, Article 20 of the contract with the claimant company, concluded October 18, 1888, provided:

The difficulties or disagreements of every nature which may arise in the interpretation or execution of the contract will be decided summarily and without appeal by three arbitrating arbitrators named, one by the Minister of Industry and Public Works, another by the Supreme Court of Justice, and the third by the contractors.[54]

The majority of the commission, consisting of the American commissioner, John Goode, and the umpire, A. de Claparède, a citizen of the Swiss Confederation, interpreted these statutory provisions and the Calvo Clause in the contract as meaning

. . . that all questions arising out of the contract itself, such as the proper construction to be placed on any of its provisions, the amount of payment due, the annihilation of the contract in the case provided for by the contract itself, shall be decided summarily and without appeal by the tribunal of arbitrators, and that any dispute as to the practical execution of the con-

---

[53] *Ibid.,* pp. 22–23.

[54] *Ibid.,* p. 23. This contract had obtained the sanction of a law in Chile by an act of the two houses of the Chilean Congress and had been signed by the president of Chile.

tract, such as the proper execution of any particular work, the selection of the material, shall be decided by the engineers named by the Government of Chile with the right of appeal to the Ministry of Industry and Public Works. In regard to all these purposes of the contract, the contractor agrees to be considered as a Chilean citizen and to be treated in all respects as a Chilean citizen who might enter into a similar contract for similar purposes. To this extent, and to this extent only, has the claimant agreed to renounce the protection which as a citizen of the United States it had a right to demand from its own Government.[55]

The majority opinion went on to assert that, in return for the commitment to be considered as a Chilean citizen for the ends of the contract, the memorialist had been assured access to the special arbitration tribunal. This last provision

. . . must be looked upon as one of the considerations of the contract; it should have the effect to exempt the memorialist from the jurisdiction of the regular courts of Chile and to subject it to the competence and to the decision of the Tribunal of Arbitration provided for by Article 49 of the General Conditions.[56]

The Tribunal of Arbitration would have been competent to decide whether the company was entitled to damages for the loss of its property, but the decree of September 11, 1891, suppressing the tribunal also suppressed the rights of the claimant. The commission stated:

It is not to be doubted that in view of the suppression of one of the principal considerations of the contract, concerning jurisdiction by the Chilean Government, the memorialist can not be further considered bound by the corresponding obligation concerning jurisdiction, according to which it renounces the protection of its Government; seeing that by renouncing this protection for the ends of the contract it has placed itself under the protection of that tribunal . . . suppressed by decree of the Government of Chile of September 11, 1891. . . . By the suppression of this Tribunal of Arbitration the memorialist *has recovered* its entire right to invoke or accept the mediation or protection of the Government of the United States.[57]

[55] *Ibid.*, p. 24.　　[56] *Ibid.*
[57] *Ibid.*, p. 25. Italics mine.

The majority of the commission then proceeded to reject the second proposition of the demurrer, stating:

. . . the claimant was not bound after the suppression of the Tribunal of Arbitration, despite the accepted contract, to resort to the aid of the regular courts of Chile, inasmuch as, recurring to the latter, it seems to have sanctioned the suppression of the aforesaid Tribunal or recognized the jurisdiction of those courts, which conjecture has been set aside by Article 49 of the General Conditions for the benefit of the contracting parties.[58]

In addition, the majority, echoing the words of Mr. Little in the *Flannagan* case,[59] held that the convention had substituted the Arbitration Commission for the Chilean courts in the cases under its jurisdiction, and consequently exhaustion of local remedies was not necessary.[60]

The Chilean commissioner, Domingo Gana, submitted a vigorous dissent,[61] arguing that the claim was not one subject to the jurisdiction of the commission. The claimant company had voluntarily accepted the obligation to consider itself as a Chilean citizen for the ends of the contract and to renounce the protection of its government. The question of the propriety of the suppression of the Tribunal of Arbitration should have been submitted to the Chilean courts, as other citizens of Chile would do under the same circumstances. To hold otherwise would be to

. . . wrest the cognizance of this matter from the jurisdiction of Chile and submit it to this Commission . . . [which would] cast into forgetfulness the stipulations legitimately contracted and appeal to a course which, if it be accepted, would essentially change the contract, compelling the Republic of Chile to answer before a tribunal from whose jurisdiction it was exempt.[62]

Mr. Gana concluded by asserting:

It is not to be presumed that the Republic of Chile or the

---

[58] *Ibid.* It would appear that Lapradelle and Politis' criticism of the argument of Commissioner Vidal in the *Milligan* case, *supra*, p. 128, n. 22, would also apply here.

[59] *Supra*, pp. 138–139.

[60] *Minutes of Proceedings and Decisions*, pp. 25–26.

[61] *Ibid.*, pp. 27–39.

[62] *Ibid.*, p. 39.

United States on signing the existing Convention had in view the annulling or varying of a contract which the parties signed with sufficient legal capacity and in accordance with public law.[63]

While this case is widely cited by authorities as one denying the validity of the Calvo Clause,[64] it should be noted that the ruling of the commission did not deny the validity of the Calvo Clause, or, for that matter, even discuss its validity as such. The majority of the commission ruled that the Clause was no longer operative due to the suppression of the special arbitration tribunal. By the suppression of this tribunal, the commission held, the claimant *recovered* its right to invoke the diplomatic protection of its government. If the tribunal had not been suppressed, presumably recourse would have had to be made to it before the presentation of an international claim, Calvo Clause or no Calvo Clause, by virtue of the local remedies rule.

The Calvo Clause before the Great Britain and Chilean Claims Commission

On September 26, 1893, a convention was signed by Great Britain and Chile for the creation of a mixed tribunal in order to decide all claims for which the government of Chile might be held responsible because of the acts and operations executed by the land and sea forces of the republic during the civil war which began on January 7, 1891, and ended on August 28, 1891, and also those claims which were caused by subsequent events, for which the government might be held responsible.[65]

Three cases involving the Calvo Clause came before this commission. The first was the case of *Great Britain (Robert Stirling) v. the Republic of Chile,* which was decided on September 30, 1895.[66]

[63] *Ibid.*

[64] E.g., Eagleton, *Resp. of States,* p. 173, n. 40; Feller, *Mex. Claims Com.,* p. 186, n. 9; Borchard, *Dip. Prot.,* p. 807.

[65] Article 1 of the convention. See Stuyt, *Survey,* p. 185. The convention is reprinted in La Fontaine, *op. cit.,* pp. 451–453. For a brief historical background of the commission, see *Reclamaciones presentados al Tribunal Anglo-Chileno, 1894–1896* (5 vols., Santiago, 1896), I, pp. v–viii.

[66] *Reclamaciones* . . . I, pp. 128–187.

Robert Stirling, representing a British corporation, the Anglo-Chilean Nitrate and Railway Company, submitted a claim in excess of 2000 pounds sterling in compensation for requisitions and damages suffered by the concern during the civil war.[67] The Chilean agent, in his argument before the commission,[68] petitioned that the tribunal declare itself incompetent to take jurisdiction of the claim, and therefore to reject it, on two grounds: first, that a stock company could not possess the requisite British nationality as prescribed by the convention, and second, that the company, through its predecessor (a Señor Eduardo Squire), had agreed to be governed by the Chilean law of August 28, 1886, which provided that the concessionaires be subject to the laws of Chile, as if they were Chileans, for the resolution of all questions that might arise over the execution of the concession.[69]

The majority of the commission, consisting of the British commissioner, Alfred St. John, and the umpire, Camille Janssen, a citizen of Belgium, accepted jurisdiction. The commission rejected the first contention of the Chilean agent with little difficulty, holding that a stock company of British origin and ownership was considered to be a "British subject" within the meaning of the term as used in the convention.[70]

In regard to the Calvo Clause commitment, the majority rejected the petition of the Chilean agent on several different grounds. First, that the law of August 28, 1886, properly interpreted, does nothing but restate the principle, "universally admitted," that foreigners must submit to local remedies all disputes and controversies that arise over contracts with the state. The commission asserted that it is not possible to give to

[67] *Ibid.*, p. 152. [68] *Ibid.*, pp. 129–134.
[69] *Ibid.* The law, quoted *ibid.*, p. 160, provided: "Artículo único. — Siempre que se otorguen permisos o concesiones para la construccion de una obra o trabajo público, o para el goce de algun derecho a una persona o empresa particular, ella o quienes sus derechos representen, aun cuando sean estranjeros i no residan en Chile, se considerarán domiciliadas en la República, i quedarán sujetas a las leyes del país, como si fueran chilenas, para la resolucion de todas las cuestiones que se susciten con motivo de la obra para la cual se otorgan el permiso o las concesiones."
[70] *Ibid.*, pp. 158–160.

this law, which assimilates the foreign concessionaires with the Chilean citizens "for the resolution of all questions relative to the concession or the profits agreed upon," a broader interpretation than that which it implies, "and pretend that the individuals or companies, in a positive way, have abdicated their foreign nationality for the exercise of their rights in Chile." [71] Secondly, even if the law could be interpreted more broadly as requiring the foreigner to abdicate his nationality for the exercise of these rights in Chile, this law would be superseded at least temporarily by the solemn convention concluded between the two states, which was enacted into law by Chile on May 11, 1894. The rights of recovery of the British subjects would therefore properly be based on this later law.[72] Thirdly, in their key argument against the applicability of the Calvo Clause provision, the majority of the commission held that this claim "did not have any relation to the execution of the contract of concession," but rather was based on damages resulting from the civil war, and therefore would not, in any case, fall within the terms of the Calvo Clause stipulation.[73]

The Chilean commissioner, L. Aldunate, entered a long and vigorous dissent,[74] claiming that a stock company was a fictitious person, and hence not a British subject who would have standing to present a claim.[75] The greater part of the dissent, however, contended that the claimants had undertaken a voluntary obligation to remain subject to the local law and jurisdiction "as if they were Chileans." [76] This obligation precluded the commission from properly taking jurisdiction of the claim.[77]

Here once again, in a case frequently cited as denying the efficacy of the Calvo Clause,[78] the validity of the Clause as

---

[71] *Ibid.*, pp. 160–161. My translation.
[72] *Ibid.*, p. 161.
[73] *Ibid.*, pp. 161–162.
[74] *Ibid.*, pp. 163–187.
[75] *Ibid.*, pp. 166–167.
[76] *Ibid.*, p. 181.
[77] *Ibid.*, pp. 181–182, 187.
[78] E.g., Borchard, *Dip. Prot.*, p. 808, n. 2; Feller, *Mex. Claims Com.*, p. 186, n. 9.

such was not actually discussed. The case involved a somewhat vaguely worded Calvo Clause stipulation, the intent and meaning of which were not entirely clear to the commission. The commission, in dealing with the case as a tort claim based on revolutionary damages and not as a contract claim, held the Clause inapplicable, not void.

This same commission had another opportunity to deal with the Calvo Clause in the case of *Great Britain (The Nitrate Railways Company Limited) v. the Republic of Chile*, decided on November 15, 1895.[79] In this case, the Nitrate Railway Company, incorporated in England and duly recognized by Chile, sought from Chile a sum in excess of 48,000 pounds sterling, plus interest, for the damages and injuries caused by the fighting forces during the Chilean civil war.[80]

It appeared that the Nitrate Company had succeeded to a railroad concession originally granted by Peru to the Ramon Monteroi i Hermanos Company. Articles 12 and 15 of the original concession permitted this transfer of rights to third persons with the consent of the government, provided, however, that "if the transfer is made in favor of foreigners, they should remain subject to the laws of the country, without power to exercise any diplomatic recourse." [81] The Nitrate Company, substituting for the first concessionaire, accepted the obligations of this contract. Chile had been substituted for Peru as a party to the contract by its annexation of the territory of Tarapaca, the site of the railroad concession.

The memorial of the company alleged that the claimant had applied several times to the government without success, and that this commission was its sole remaining recourse. In further arguments, the British agent asserted that recourse to this Claims Commission did not constitute diplomatic recourse, for this was not a diplomatic body. Even if it were, the renunciatory clause was not applicable, for it only pertained to matters relat-

[79] *Reclamaciones* . . . II, pp. 220–327.
[80] *Ibid.*, p. 320.
[81] *Ibid.*, p. 323. My translation.

ing to the execution of the contract, and not to the abuses and injuries which were the cause of the reclamation.[82]

The Chilean agent, in his series of replies, contested the claim on several grounds, but his main argument was that the tribunal was incompetent to entertain this reclamation, for, according to certain clauses of the contract of concession, the concessionaires had renounced for themselves and their successors all diplomatic recourse in connection with the construction or exploitation of these railways. Submission of the claim to the commission was obviously one of the forms of diplomatic recourse that the contract had intended to prohibit. In addition, the contract had established a special tribunal of arbitration to resolve any differences which, for any reason, might arise between the company and the government. This tribunal was not utilized by the claimant.[83]

The majority of the commission, consisting of Señor Aldunate and Mr. Janssen, ruled that the commission could not take jurisdiction of the claim, stating:

Considering that private individuals or associations can, for the purpose of obtaining from a foreign government privileges and concessions of public works, of mines or of exploitation of ways of communication, and to accommodate thus their own interests, renounce the protection of their governments, and agree by contract not to resort to diplomatic action in the case of difficulties arising between themselves and the ceding government; that as every government possesses the right not to give such concessions, except to its nationals, it can, if it consents to grant such concessions to foreigners, require them to place themselves upon a footing of equality with nationals, and that they should promise not only to submit themselves to the laws of the country, but also not to invoke the intervention of the governments to which they belong in the solution of contentious questions which may arise from contracts freely entered into; that no principle of international law forbids citizens to agree personally to such contracts, which furthermore do not obligate foreign governments . . . [84]

[82] *Ibid.*, pp. 220–231, 251–274.
[83] *Ibid.*, pp. 231–251, 274–320.
[84] *Ibid.*, p. 322. My translation.

149

Further, the majority argued, while the commission was a tribunal of justice, it was also set up by diplomatic agreement, and submitting a claim to it would, in fact, constitute diplomatic recourse. Therefore

. . . the individuals or companies which have obligated themselves by contract freely consummated not to have recourse personally to diplomatic action, likewise cannot invoke, directly or personally, the intervention of the British Legation, or seek the jurisdiction of this tribunal, for the resolution of questions which may arise between them and the government with which they have contracted and with which they have made express agreements . . .[85]

The majority opinion goes on to assert that since the Nitrate Company took over the original concession, it accepted its obligations as well as its privileges, one of which was to submit to the laws of the country "without power to exercise any diplomatic recourse." [86] This obligation was accepted freely and in anticipation of compensatory profits. The commission furthermore stated that "it cannot be sustained that this clause in the contract . . . applies only to the direct and immediate effects of the concession"; it refers to "all the acts of the company, while the concession is in force," and it specifically refers "all litigious matters that might arise between the government and the concessionaires" to the special arbitration tribunal set up, and this special tribunal's jurisdiction would logically comprise all claims which the Nitrate Company is now presenting.[87]

In view of these facts, the majority of the commission declared itself incompetent to take jurisdiction, and directed the Nitrate Company to seek redress through the proper channels.[88]

Commissioner St. John of Great Britain dissented. He felt that the commission should take jurisdiction, arguing that the claims presented did not arise out of the execution of the contract, but from the civil war, and so consequently the Calvo Clause would

[85] *Ibid.*, pp. 322–323. My translation.
[86] *Ibid.*, p. 323. My translation.
[87] *Ibid.*, pp. 324–325. My translation.
[88] *Ibid.*, p. 325.

not apply. Mr. St. John also disagreed with the commission's interpretation of the clauses in question, and denied that the presentation of this claim constituted diplomatic recourse, even if such were actually forbidden.[89]

The majority of the commission thus held that there is no principle of international law that forbids an alien from entering into a contract containing the Calvo Clause and thereby renouncing his right to the diplomatic intervention of his own government in case of difficulties arising over the execution of the contract. This renunciation was also held to apply to appeals to an international claims tribunal. The commission held the Calvo Clause binding on the individual but not on his state.[90] This rule of limited validity laid down by the commission has been accepted, in large part, by recent international claims commissions, and has become, as we shall see, the rule of law on this concept in contemporary international jurisprudence.[91]

In spite of the fact that the *Nitrate* decision was a forerunner of the recent rulings on the validity of the Calvo Clause, there remains the task of determining the precise role that the Calvo Clause played in the final disposition of this case. Although this case is widely cited as upholding the validity of the Calvo Clause,[92] it should be noted that the commission ruled that the Clause was not binding upon the state, and also that there apparently had not been any attempt to exhaust the local remedies by seeking redress in the special arbitration tribunal provided for in the contract.[93] Consequently, even if the Calvo Clause renunciation had not been in the contract, the commission would

[89] *Ibid.*, pp. 325–327.

[90] See Borchard, *Dip. Prot.*, p. 804. However, it should be noted that the state was in fact barred from submitting the claim.

[91] The existence and significance of this rule of law will be documented in Chapters VII and VIII, *infra*.

[92] E.g., Feller, *Mex. Claims Com.*, pp. 185–186, n. 3; Eagleton, *Resp. of States*, p. 173, n. 39; Borchard, *Dip. Prot.*, p. 804.

[93] The British agent argued that the jurisdiction of this special tribunal did not apply to all operations under the contract (*Reclamaciones* . . . II, pp. 251–274). The Chilean agent denied this (*ibid.*, pp. 231–251); the commission apparently agreed with the Chilean agent and directed the claimant to seek redress through proper channels (*ibid.*, p. 325).

presumably have rejected jurisdiction. In other words, this case did not really furnish a test for a meaningful application of the commission's limited validity rule.

The authority of the *Nitrate* case as supporting the rule of limited validity of the Calvo Clause was further weakened by the action of this same commission in the last of three decisions it handed down that involved this concept. This case was *Great Britain (Antofagasta and Bolivia Railway Company, Ltd.) v. the Republic of Chile*, decided on March 23, 1896.[94]

The *Antofagasta* case presented the commission with a factual situation very similar to the *Nitrate* case. The Antofagasta and Bolivia Railway Company claimed from the republic of Chile the sum of 200,000 pesos for compensation and indemnification for losses suffered during the occupation of their railway by the authorities of Chile during the Civil War of 1891.[95]

The central issue in the case was whether the commission could take jurisdiction over the claim in view of Article 10 of the concession contract, originally awarded to a Chilean company but later transferred to the present claimant. The article read: "The Company and the persons or societies to whom they may transfer their rights to the railway, shall remain in every case subject exclusively to the authorities and laws of the Republic." [96]

The majority of the commission, consisting of Mr. St. John and Mr. Janssen, asserted that this contractual stipulation did not hinder in any manner the right of the company to invoke the jurisdiction of the commission which was set up to adjudicate these types of claims by the solemn treaty agreement of the two countries, subsequently enacted into law by the republic of Chile.[97] As their grounds for taking jurisdiction in spite of the Calvo Clause, the majority cited "the principles enunciated" in the *Stirling* case, stating that there was, in the present case, no new element to change their previous decision.[98]

[94] *Reclamaciones* . . . III, pp. 699–816.
[95] *Ibid.*, p. 788.
[96] *Ibid.*, pp. 799, 805. My translation.
[97] *Ibid.*, p. 799.
[98] *Ibid.*, pp. 798, 799. My translation.

The majority, in choosing to follow the *Stirling* case rather than the *Nitrate* case, added considerable confusion to the actual position of the commission on the effect of a Calvo Clause commitment. The Clause was held inapplicable, even though the origin of the claim, the nature of the damages, and the renunciatory provision involved were very similar to those presented to the commission in the *Nitrate* case. Although the wording of the stipulations varied slightly, agreeing to remain "subject exclusively to the authority and the laws of the republic" and agreeing to remain "subject to the laws of the country, without power to exercise any diplomatic recourse" would appear to involve substantially the same commitment. Especially in view of the failure of the commission even to mention their ruling in the *Nitrate* case, its decision in the instant case considerably weakens the precedential value of the rule formulated in its previous decision.

Commissioner Aldunate of Chile entered a long and vigorous dissent, arguing that "it would be difficult to express in terms more energetic and categorical a more explicit renunciation on the part of the concessionaires of all diplomatic protection." [99] Aldunate quite properly criticizes the commission for conveniently ignoring its own precedent in the *Nitrate* case. Since this claim was nearly identical to that involved in the *Nitrate* case, the same rule should apply, he insisted. The Convention of 1893 no more superseded the instant contract-law between the government and the claimant than it had the similar contract-law in the *Nitrate* case.[1]

The rule set forth in the *Antofagasta* case is that a convention will serve to supersede a Calvo Clause stipulation if that is the intent of the parties. The commission, by citing the principles enunciated in the *Stirling* case as the grounds for its decision in the instant case, apparently also reaffirmed their previous ruling that the Clause was inapplicable because of the origin of the claim in civil war damages rather than in doubts and contro-

[99] *Ibid.*, p. 805. My translation.
[1] *Ibid.*, pp. 809–815.

versies over the contract. Actually, although this case is included in listings of cases that have denied the validity of the Clause,[2] it did not deal with the issue of the validity of the Clause as such but merely held it inapplicable under the given circumstances.

In evaluating the precedential value of these three decisions by the Anglo-Chilean Claims Commission or in estimating their contribution to the determination of the rule of law on the Calvo Clause, it is important to note the seemingly inconsistent and contradictory rulings of the commission in similar situations. The fact that the commission ruled one way in the *Nitrate* case and another way in the *Stirling* and *Antofagasta* cases weakens the impact of this jurisprudence on the problem under investigation. But it does serve to exemplify the confusion and uncertainty that surrounded the Calvo Clause during this early period of international arbitration and to emphasize the impossibility of detecting a consistent and meaningful rule of law. And, of course, the ruling in the *Nitrate* case, granting the Clause a limited validity by holding that it was binding on the individual though not on his state, is significant as the rule of law accepted in later international arbitral judgments.

The Calvo Clause before the United States and Portuguese Claims Commission

Several states outside of the American continents became involved in the Calvo Clause controversy when the Clause figured briefly in the creation of the Mixed Claims Commission between the United States and Great Britain, on the one hand, and Portugal, on the other, which was set up under the Convention of June 13, 1891, to adjudicate the case of the *United States (McMurdo) v. Portugal*.[3]

---

[2] E.g., Borchard, *Dip. Prot.*, p. 808, n. 2; Feller, *Mex. Claims Com.*, p. 186, n. 9.

[3] The convention is printed in Moore, *Int. Arb.*, II, pp. 1874–1875; La Fontaine, *op. cit.*, pp. 397–398. For a description of the events and diplomacy involved in the creation of the tribunal, see Moore, *Int. Arb.*, II, pp. 1865–1899; Marjorie M. Whiteman, *Damages in International Law* (3 vols., Washington, D.C., 1937–1943), III, pp. 1694–1703.

On December 14, 1883, the Portuguese government granted to Edward McMurdo, a citizen of the United States, a concession for the construction of a railway from Lourenca Marques to the Transvaal frontier. The concession provided for the private arbitration of all differences that might arise between the two parties over the execution of the contract. In 1889, the Portuguese government canceled the concession and took possession of the railway,[4] which, with the aid of a group of British investors, had then been completed. The United States and Great Britain intervened, and the Portuguese government offered to arbitrate the dispute with the concessionaire under the private arbitration clause of the contract. The United States, however, refused this offer, stating:

. . . The offer of arbitration now held out to the Portuguese company, which has practically ceased to exist, is not the offer of arbitration contemplated by the concession to Colonel McMurdo. That concession provided for the arbitration of any difficulties which might arise between Colonel McMurdo and the company which he was to form, on the one hand, and the Portuguese Government on the other. Such a difficulty having arisen in consequence of the action of the Portuguese Government, that Government, instead of offering to submit it to arbitration, makes it a ground for the annulment of the concession and the seizure of the property acquired thereunder. But, having thus annulled the concession, the Portuguese Government now appeals to its provisions as governing the rights of the contractors and investors. If the terms of the concession still bind those persons to the arbitration therein provided, they must also be held likewise to bind the Portuguese Government, and hence to require the rescinding of the order of annulment and the restoration of the property to its owners in order that such arbitration may take place. It is scarcely necessary to say that it is not within the power of one of the parties to an agreement first to annul it, and then to hold the other party to the observance of its conditions as if it were a subsisting engagement.[5]

Negotiations continued, and finally Portugal agreed to the

---

[4] The grounds for the cancellation and seizure are not germane to this study.

[5] James G. Blaine, secretary of state, to Mr. Loring, minister to Portugal, November 30, 1889. See Moore, *Int. Arb.*, II, pp. 1870–1871.

demands for indemnity to the heir of McMurdo and the British investors, and the above-mentioned convention was drawn up to create an arbitration commission to fix "the amount of the indemnity due by Portugal to the claimants of the other two countries." [6] An arbitration tribunal was, in due course, appointed by the president of Switzerland, and, after lengthy hearings, handed down its decision on March 29, 1900, awarding the claimants 15,314,000 francs (Swiss), with interest, in addition to 28,000 pounds paid on account in 1890.[7]

Although the *McMurdo* case is widely cited in listings of cases that have denied the validity of the Calvo Clause,[8] it should be noted that the validity of the Clause per se was not at issue in this case, and, what is more important, the effect of the Clause figured only in the diplomacy that led to the creation of the arbitration tribunal, not in the actual deliberations of the tribunal itself, which was set up with the express stipulation that it was not to determine whether or not there should be damages awarded but only to determine what the amount of these damages should be. Consequently, it was not within the competence of the tribunal to determine whether the private arbitration clause would exclude its jurisdiction, for its jurisdiction over this specific claim was explicitly authorized by the parties to the convention. While the attitude of the United States, as expressed in the Blaine communication, is, of course, important, it is erroneous to cite this statement as representing the ruling of an international claims commission.[9]

[6] Convention of June 13, 1891. See *ibid.*, p. 1874. The United States had insisted that the arbitration would not review the merits of the case, but would be constituted solely to determine the amount of reparation due. See *ibid.*, pp. 1871–1872.

[7] *U.S. For. Rel.* (1900), pp. 903–904. The commissioners were Joseph Blaesi, Andreas Heusler, and Charles Soldan.

[8] E.g., Eagleton, *Resp. of States*, p. 173, n. 40; Feller, *Mex. Claims Com.*, p. 186, n. 9.

[9] It is interesting to note that both Feller and Eagleton, *ibid.*, refer to Moore, *Int. Arb.*, II, p. 1865, as the authority for their citation of this case as being one that has denied the validity of the Clause. But Moore's volumes were printed in 1898, two years before the commission delivered its opinion. It would appear that these authorities have perhaps confused diplomatic negotiation with arbitral jurisprudence. The decision of the commission, *Sentence finale du Tri-*

Arbitral Decisions up to 1926

The Calvo Clause before the French and Venezuelan Claims Commission

The sundry decisions of the various Venezuelan claims commissions organized in the early years of this century produced a considerable share of the international jurisprudence involving the validity of the Calvo Clause. Dealing more or less directly with this issue were no fewer than twelve cases among the decisions handed down by the mixed tribunals set up to arbitrate the claims of Germany, Britain, Italy, the United States, Belgium, France, the Netherlands, Spain, Mexico, and Sweden-Norway against Venezuela.

Venezuela, at the turn of the century, was beset with internal strife and economic chaos which resulted in a great many petitions by resident aliens to their home governments for intervention to compel Venezuela to make reparations for alleged damages to their persons or property. Venezuela, as a result of strong pressures from the claimant states, especially Germany, Britain, and Italy, agreed to submit all these claims to arbitration and to set aside, for their settlement, a certain percentage of the customs revenues of two of her principal ports of entry. Protocols were negotiated with the various claimant states, and commissions were set up for this purpose.[10]

The first of the tribunals to be set up was the French and Venezuelan Claims Commission, created by the Convention of February 19, 1902.[11] This commission had occasion to deal with

bunal arbitral du Delagoa (March 29, 1900), is reprinted in La Fontaine, op. cit., pp. 398–410. In its opinion, the commission restricted its deliberations to its predetermined function, i.e., the determination of the amount of damages due to the claimant. Portugal had already, in the convention, admitted its liability, thus making an inquiry into the effect of the Calvo Clause superfluous. Neither the memorial of the United States nor the reply of Portugal dealt with the issue of the private arbitration proviso, which indicated that it was not a real issue in the adjudication. See Moore, Int. Arb., II, pp. 1878–1891.

[10] For a brief description of the events that led to the creation of these tribunals, see Ralston, International Arbitrations from Athens to Locarno, pp. 221–224. The United States, invoking the Monroe Doctrine, was instrumental in getting a settlement by arbitration rather than by use of force. Latin Americans tend to forget incidents like this, in which the intervention of the United States was of great benefit to them.

[11] The convention is reprinted in the Report of French-Venezuelan Mixed Claims Commission of 1902 (prepared by J. H. Ralston and W. T. S. Doyle,

the Calvo Clause in the case of *France (French Company of Venezuelan Railroads) v. the United States of Venezuela.*[12] The claim presented in behalf of the French Company of Venezuelan Railroads sought 18,483,000 francs in compensation for the fact that Venezuela was allegedly responsible for the company's ruination, as consideration for the offer of the company to renounce its railroad concession to the respondent government, including all its properties, and, furthermore, as reparation for damages suffered because of the requisition of some of the claimant's property during the civil war.[13]

The French company, due to a series of disastrous mishaps including floods, earthquakes, and involvement in civil wars, had decided to abandon its concession in Venezuela. They were seeking damages from the respondent government, allegedly for the nonexecution of contractual obligations and the nonpayment of sums due to the claimant. Venezuela had continued to make interest payments, but, because of the state of her finances, was unable to meet all her obligations to the company. The claimant was willing to accept cancellation of its contract-concession, and to abandon its property, provided that the damages claimed were awarded in full. Venezuela was apparently unwilling to cancel the contract, and denied liability for the losses associated with its abandonment by the claimant. The portion of the claim arising out of the damage to the claimant's property while in the use of the government during the civil war was not contested in principle but only as to the amount of compensation.[14]

The French commissioner, Count E. de Peretti de la Rocca, ruled in favor of the claimant,[15] and the Venezuelan commissioner, Dr. José de Jesús Paúl, denied damages other than those resulting directly from the civil war.[16] In view of this disagree-

Washington, D.C., 1906), pp. 1–3. See also Stuyt, *Survey*, p. 253. For comment on the jurisprudence of this tribunal, see *Journal du droit international* (Clunet), XXXII (1905), p. 1196.

[12] *Report of French-Venezuelan Mixed Claims Commission of 1902*, pp. 367–452.

[13] *Ibid.*, p. 443.

[14] *Ibid.*, pp. 428–440.

[15] *Ibid.*, pp. 405–409, 425–428.

[16] *Ibid.*, pp. 369–405, 409–425.

ment, the claim was referred to the umpire, Frank Plumley of Northfield, Vermont, for final disposition.[17] The umpire held, in agreement with the Venezuelan commissioner, that the government was not the sole cause of the ruin of the claimant company and was therefore not liable for the damages demanded for this reason.[18] In regard to the request by the company for the rescission of the contract with the consequent payment of compensation to the claimant for the properties abandoned to the government, the umpire ruled that the convention had not given the commission the power to rescind or revoke a contract without the consent of both parties. Its jurisdiction was limited to providing indemnities for damages suffered by Frenchmen in Venezuela. For the commission to order such a rescission would be contrary to the convention and would actually "require a payment by Venezuela to the claimant company for damages in fact suffered in the United States of America at the hands of the umpire."[19]

In support of this ruling, Plumley called attention to the existence of a Calvo Clause in the contract, the presence of which had not figured in the opinions of either the French or the Venezuelan commissioner. Plumley stated:

The umpire can not entirely ignore the restrictive features of the contract between the claimant company and the respondent Government, which in terms and in fact strictly required and still requires that all doubts and controversies arising from that contract should be resolved by the competent tribunals of the respondent Government.[20] Certainly to consider and determine the question of its rescission is the most serious doubt, the most important controversy, which could grow out of or arise from the contract in question. A claim for damage may be regarded as ulterior to the contract, especially where the damage has accrued from the operation of the parties under the contract, but the question of its rescission is an entirely different proposition. The unrestricted

---

[17] *Ibid.*, pp. 428–452.

[18] *Ibid.*, p. 449.

[19] *Ibid.*, p. 445.

[20] A modification of the contract on April 16, 1891, had added the additional proviso that "in no case were these doubts and controversies to give place to international claims." *Ibid.*, p. 430.

agreement to submit to an arbitral tribunal the question of damages suffered by Frenchmen in Venezuela may properly be considered, if necessary, as equivalent to a suspension of the provision in the contract, were the damages claimed to be such as arose or grew out of the contract; but the agreement to submit a question of damages arising through operations performed under a contract, in no sense suggests a purpose to arm that tribunal with plenary power to consider and settle the question involved in the rescission of a contract, and therefore does not suggest an intent on the part of the High Contracting Powers to ask on the one hand or to grant on the other the suspension of the restrictive features referred to, which are contained in said contract. What is here said concerning the matter of rescission applies with equal force to the matter of abandonment. It is therefore the deliberate and settled judgment of the Umpire that he can not determine this claim on the basis of a declared and directed rescission or of abandonment, and can only decide the amount of the award, this to depend upon the ordinary bases of damages which have been suffered in Venezuela by the French Company of Venezuelan Railroads at the hands of those for whom the respondent Government is responsible.[21]

The amount of indemnity finally awarded for damages resulting from the civil war, and for which the respondent government was held responsible, was set at 387,875.70 francs.[22]

Although the Calvo Clause figured in the opinion of the umpire to the extent that it could not be "entirely ignored," this case does not contribute much toward determining the rule of law on the Calvo Clause.[23] The effect of the Clause was not discussed by either the French or the Venezuelan commissioner, which indicated that they felt it to be of little relevance to the issue at hand. The Clause also did not arise in the usual manner as a preliminary objection to the jurisdiction of the commission, but appeared only as a consideration supplemental to the umpire's basic reason for denying the claimant's petition to rescind the contract. His main reasoning was that while the convention did give the commission authority to adjudicate doubts and

[21] *Ibid.*, pp. 445–446.

[22] *Ibid.*, p. 452.

[23] This case is not included in the usual listings of cases that have upheld or denied the validity of the Calvo Clause.

controversies arising out of the contract, and thus rendered the Clause inoperative in this respect, it did not confer upon the commission the power to authorize abandonment or rescission. Umpire Plumley further stated that the unrestricted agreement to submit to an arbitral tribunal the question of damages suffered by Frenchmen in Venezuela "may properly be considered, if necessary, as equivalent to a suspension of the provision in the contract . . ." [24] The decision therefore was based upon an interpretation of the *compromis*, and it must be assumed that the decision of the umpire would have been the same whether there had been a Calvo Clause in the contract or not.

The Calvo Clause before the Italian and Venezuelan Claims Commission

The Calvo Clause controversy figured briefly in the jurisprudence of the Italian and Venezuelan Claims Commission, set up under the Convention of February 13, 1903,[25] in the case of *Italy (Martini) v. the United States of Venezuela.*[26]

Martini submitted a claim for the sum of 9,064,965.34 bolivars for damages resulting from various events and activities associated with the civil strife in Venezuela.[27] The Venezuelan commissioner, Nicomedes Zuloaga, submitted a preliminary question objecting to the jurisdiction of the commission in view of Article 16 of the contract, which provided: "The doubts or controversies which may arise in the interpretation and execution of the present contract will be resolved by the tribunals of the republic in conformity with its laws, and in no case will be the ground for international reclamation." [28]

When the Italian and Venezuelan commissioners disagreed, Umpire Jackson H. Ralston, a citizen of the United States, ad-

---

[24] *Report of French-Venezuelan Mixed Claims Commission*, p. 209. See James W. Garner, "Decisions of the American Mexican Mixed Claims Commissions," *BYIL* (1927), p. 183, n. 1.

[25] The convention is printed in *Venezuelan Arbitrations of 1903* (prepared by Jackson H. Ralston, Washington, D.C., 1904), pp. 643–647. See also Stuyt, *Survey*, p. 269.

[26] *Venezuelan Arbitrations of 1903*, pp. 819–846.

[27] *Ibid.*, p. 839.

[28] *Ibid.*, p. 841. My translation.

judicated the claim,[29] and held that this contractual commitment of the claimant would not serve to oust the jurisdiction of the commission, stating:

Even if the dispute now presented to the Umpire could be considered as embraced within the terms "Las dudas ó contraversias que puedan suscitarse en la inteligencia y ejecución del presente contrato," in the judgment of the Umpire the objection may be disposed of by reference to a single consideration.

Italy and Venezuela, by their respective Governments, have agreed to submit to the determination of this Mixed Commission the claims of Italian citizens against Venezuela. The right of a sovereign power to enter into an agreement of this kind is entirely superior to that of the subject to contract it away. It was, in the judgment of the Umpire, entirely beyond the power of an Italian subject to extinguish the superior right of his nation, and it is not to be presumed that Venezuela understood that he had done so. But aside from this, Venezuela and Italy have agreed that there shall be substituted for national forums, which, with or without contract between the parties, may have had jurisdiction over the subject-matter, an international forum, to whose determination they fully agree to bow. To say now that this claim must be rejected for lack of jurisdiction in the Mixed Commission would be equivalent to claiming that not all Italian claims were referred to it, but only such Italian claims as have not been contracted about previously, and in this manner and to this extent only the protocol could be maintained. The Umpire can not accept an interpretation that by indirection would change the plain language of the protocol under which he acts and cause him to reject claims legally well founded.[30]

The umpire, having denied that the Calvo Clause affected the commission's jurisdiction, proceeded to review the merits of the claim and found for Martini to the extent of 439,673.16 bolivars, plus interest.[31]

The *Martini* case is considered to be one of the clearest rulings among the decisions of this period regarding the effectiveness of the Calvo Clause.[32] Ralston ruled that the individual's waiver

---

[29] *Ibid.*, pp. 820–837.
[30] *Ibid.*, p. 841.
[31] *Ibid.*, p. 846.
[32] Freeman, *Denial of Justice*, p. 479, describes Ralston's opinion as being

was superseded by the convention, that the right of a nation to enter into such an agreement is entirely superior to that of the subject to contract it away, and that it was entirely beyond the power of an Italian subject to extinguish the superior right of his nation. These statements of Ralston accurately reflect the predominant attitude of publicists on the efficacy of the Clause.[33]

It should be noted, however, that Ralston actually ruled that damages were due because of the closing of a port in violation of the contract and that the dispute was not within the term "doubts and controversies which may arise in the interpretation or execution of the contract." Therefore his opinion on the Calvo Clause would appear to be only dictum.[34] Furthermore, Ralston did not deal with the validity of the Clause as such in his much-publicized dictum, but only ruled that it would be inoperative in the face of the plain language of the convention agreement between the states which, in the opinion of the umpire, showed that both governments intended that it should supersede the Calvo Clause. It is not entirely clear from the opinion how Ralston would have ruled if the convention had not been "clear" on this point.[35]

The Calvo Clause before the Great Britain and Venezuelan Claims Commission

The Calvo Clause also figured in the deliberations of the British-Venezuelan Claims Commission, set up by the Convention of February 13, 1903,[36] in the case of *Great Britain (Selwyn) v. the United States of Venezuela.*[37]

"free from the obliqueness frequently characterizing other awards." Borchard, *Dip. Prot.*, p. 805, calls this decision "good law."

[33] Freeman, *Denial of Justice*, p. 479.

[34] See Borchard, *Dip. Prot.*, p. 805, n. 1.

[35] The *Martini* award figured in a later adjudication of an Italian-Venezuelan Commission on May 3, 1930. The case arose over alleged nonperformance of the Ralston award and other controversies. Ralston's ruling on the Calvo Clause was not at issue in this later decision. See the United Nations' *Reports of International Arbitral Awards*, II, pp. 977–1008; *AJIL*, XXV (July 1931), pp. 554–592.

[36] The convention is reprinted in *Venezuelan Arbitrations of 1903*, pp. 292–295. See also Stuyt, *Survey*, p. 266.

[37] *Venezuelan Arbitrations of 1903*, pp. 322–327.

The Calvo Clause

The umpire, Frank Plumley, rendered the decision because of the disagreement between the British and Venezuelan commissioners over the question of jurisdiction. The Venezuelan agent had raised three objections to the commission's jurisdiction:

(1) That, if this claim is admissible otherwise, it is barred by the fact that a suit is now pending in the local courts, wherein the claimant is the plaintiff and Venezuela is the defendant, based upon the same right of action; and having elected to pursue his remedy there he can not change the forum of his own selection and present his claim to this Commission, especially since there has been no delay in court except through his own inaction.

(2) A certain provision of the contract between the Government and the claimant, because of which contract this claim exists, the language of which provision follows: "Any doubts and controversies that may arise regarding the spirit or execution of this present contract will be settled by the tribunals of the Republic and according to their laws without their being in any case a matter for an international claim."

(3) That this is a claim under a contract and that controversies of a contractual character, excepting the railway claims, are not submitted to this Commission, but instead, injuries to property of British subjects and matters akin thereto, as is to be seen by inspection of the protocol, which by specifically including the railway contractual claims inferentially and impliedly excludes all other contract claims.[38]

Umpire Plumley, in regard to the first objection, ruled that the jurisdiction of the commission, under the terms of the convention, was not affected by the pendency of the suit in the local courts.[39] Concerning the second and third objection, the umpire ruled:

. . . the claim before him has in no particular to deal with "any doubts and controversies . . . regarding the spirit or execution of" the contract in which such terms appear. . . . The fundamental ground of this claim as presented is that the claimant was deprived of valuable rights, of moneys, properties, property,

[38] *Ibid.*, pp. 322–323.

[39] *Ibid.*, pp. 323–325. Plumley stated that "within the limits prescribed by the convention constituting it the parties have created a tribunal superior to the local courts." (*Ibid.*)

and rights of property by an act of the Government which he was powerless to prevent and for which he claims reimbursement. . . . How much of the claim comes under this head it is not necessary to consider. The question of jurisdiction is determined if in any part the case falls within this class. The Umpire has above stated that such is the fundamental feature of this claim, and hence that it is not a matter of contract, and is open to neither of the last two objections of Venezuela.[40]

The opinion of Umpire Plumley illustrates the reluctance of these early commissions to rule directly on the validity of the Calvo Clause. As in this case, most of the tribunals did not go into the question of the validity of the Clause as such, but ruled that it was inoperative in the given situation. In the *Selwyn* case, it was held that the claim did not arise out of doubts or controversies as envisioned in the Clause, and hence the Clause was not applicable. It would not appear that the citation of this case as one that denied the validity of the Calvo Clause [41] is fully in accord with the ruling of the commission, since the umpire ruled the Clause inapplicable, not invalid. This case would not, however, serve to modify the basic contention of the ineffectiveness of the Calvo Clause in the determination of the final judgments of the court.

The Calvo Clause before the United States and Venezuelan Claims Commission

The Calvo Clause figured in no fewer than nine decisions of the United States–Venezuelan Claims Commission, set up by the Convention of February 17, 1903.[42] The brief opinions which were delivered by one or both of the commissioners without the necessity of referring the cases to the umpire will be analyzed first, with the five claims arbitrated by the umpire given more extensive treatment in view of their more detailed examination of the problem under investigation.

In the case of the *United States (Coro and La Vela Railway*

---

[40] *Ibid.*, pp. 325–326.

[41] E.g., Feller, *Mex. Claims Com.*, p. 186, n. 9.

[42] The convention is reprinted in *Venezuelan Arbitrations of 1903*, pp. 1–4. See also Stuyt, *Survey*, p. 270.

and Improvement Company) v. the Republic of Venezuela,[43] the concession contained the following provision: "Any doubt or controversy that may arise in the interpretation or execution of this contract will be decided by the ordinary tribunals of the Republic, and in no case or for any motive will any international claims be admitted on account of this concession." [44]

In a brief, two-page opinion, Dr. Paúl, the Venezuelan commissioner, speaking for the commission, ruled that the claim was based on a breach of contract by the government. He accepted jurisdiction and awarded the sum of $61,104.70 to the claimant.[45] The Clause did not figure in the opinion, its existence not even being mentioned by the Venezuelan commissioner.[46] The fact that there had been a governmental breach of contract relieved the commission from directly construing the effect of the renunciatory provision. Although this case does not, in view of the failure of the commission even to mention the Clause, contribute much toward determining the rule of law on the Calvo Clause,[47] the decision would imply that the commission considered the Clause inoperative, under the terms of the protocol, in case of governmental breach of contract.

The same action was taken by Dr. Paúl, speaking for the commission, in the case of the *United States (del Genovese) v. the Republic of Venezuela*,[48] in which a nearly identical Calvo Clause provision appeared in the concession.[49] The Venezuelan commissioner ruled that the claim was based on a breach of contract by the government [50] and, in a four-page opinion, did not even mention the existence of the Clause, much less analyze its valid-

---

[43] *Report of Robert C. Morris, Agent of the United States, before the United States and Venezuelan Claims Commission* (Washington, D.C., 1904), pp. 68–70.

[44] Moore, *Digest*, VI, p. 307; Ralston, *Int. Trib.*, p. 65.

[45] *Report of Robert C. Morris*, p. 70.

[46] *Ibid.*, pp. 69–70.

[47] It is, however, frequently included in listings of cases that have denied the validity of the Clause — for example, Feller, *Mex. Claims Com.*, p. 186, n. 9; Borchard, *Dip. Prot.*, p. 808, n. 2.

[48] *Venezuelan Arbitrations of 1903*, pp. 174–178; *Report of Robert C. Morris*, pp. 396–401.

[49] Moore, *Digest*, VI, p. 307; Ralston, *Int. Trib.*, p. 65.

[50] *Venezuelan Arbitrations of 1903*, p. 174.

ity,[51] although it has been cited as a case that denies the validity of the Calvo Clause.[52] Presumably, here again the commission felt the Clause to be inoperative in the face of a breach of contract by the Venezuelan government under the terms of the convention.

The situation was the same in the case of the *United States (La Guaira Electric Light and Power Co.).*[53] The American commissioner, William E. Bainbridge, speaking for the commission, dismissed without prejudice a claim made against Venezuela on account of a breach of contract by a municipal corporation, ruling that the claim was against the corporation and not the government, and so it should properly be pursued in the local courts.[54] Commissioner Bainbridge added, however, that this case ". . . is very different from one in which the Government itself has violated a contract to which it is a party. In such a case the jurisdiction of the Commission under the terms of the protocol is beyond question." [55]

It would once again appear that this case cannot properly be included in listings of cases in which the validity of the Calvo Clause was either upheld or denied,[56] since the Clause was not mentioned in the opinion,[57] or even in the briefs presented by the respective agents.[58] Indeed, as Professor Borchard has pointed out, there is no evidence from the case, as reported, that the contract actually contained the renunciatory Clause.[59]

In the case of the *United States (Kunhardt) v. the Republic of Venezuela,*[60] both the American commissioner and the Venezuelan commissioner agreed in the judgment to dismiss the major portion of the claim without prejudice, although for different

[51] *Ibid.*, pp. 174–178.
[52] E.g., Feller, *Mex. Claims Com.*, p. 186, n. 9.
[53] *Venezuelan Arbitrations of 1903*, pp. 178–182.
[54] *Ibid.*, p. 182.
[55] *Ibid.* This passage would appear to confirm the suggested reason for the two previous rulings.
[56] The case is so included in Ralston, *Int. Trib.*, p. 65.
[57] *Venezuelan Arbitrations of 1903*, pp. 178–182.
[58] See *Report of Robert C. Morris*, pp. 401–405.
[59] Borchard, *Dip. Prot.*, p. 807, n. 3.
[60] *Venezuelan Arbitrations of 1903*, pp. 63–72.

reasons. Commissioner Paúl, in his concurring opinion, called attention to the existence of a Calvo Clause provision in the contract which read: "That any doubt or dispute arising from the interpretation of this contract should be decided by the courts of the Republic according to its laws, and they could not in any case be a motive for an international claim." [61] The bare citation of the Clause is, however, the full extent to which it figured in Paúl's opinion. He did not elaborate on its impact, and it did not materially influence his final judgment, which was reached on the ground that the American shareholders of a Venezuelan corporation did not have sufficient interest, barring dissolution or liquidation of the corporation, to appear before the tribunal as claimants.[62] Bainbridge held that there did exist a sufficient interest, but because the extent of the interest of the claimants was not ascertainable due to the want of proof of the amount of liabilities, he agreed to the dismissal of the claim without prejudice.[63]

Although Paúl's citation of the Clause perhaps could be considered as an implied sanctioning of its provisions,[64] his statement did not represent the view of the commission, and it did not even determine his own final judgment. Under these circumstances, it would not seem warrantable to classify this case as even supporting the validity of the Clause in dictum, and it appears certain that the existence of the Clause did not alter or affect the final decision of the two commissioners.[65]

These four cases support the contention that the Calvo Clause per se did not, in any of the arbitral rulings up to 1926, actually determine the judgment in any case. This same observation will

[61] *Ibid.*, p. 70.

[62] *Ibid.*, pp. 70–72.

[63] *Ibid.*, pp. 63–70.

[64] Borchard, *Dip. Prot.*, p. 804, states that Paúl "upheld the validity of the Clause although his conclusion to this effect was not involved in the final judgment."

[65] An indication of the extreme degree of confusion that surrounds these early arbitral rulings involving the Calvo Clause is evidenced by the fact that Feller, *Mex. Claims Com.*, pp. 185–186, n. 3, includes the *Kunhardt* case in his listing of those which have upheld the validity of the Calvo Clause, and Eagleton, *Resp. of States*, p. 173, n. 40, includes this same case in his listing of those that have denied its binding force.

be further illustrated by an examination of the five decisions of this commission involving the Calvo Clause which, because of the disagreement between the United States and Venezuelan commissioners, were submitted to the umpire for final adjudication.

The first of these was the case of the *United States (Woodruff) v. the Republic of Venezuela.*[66] This case was in the form of a reopening of the *Woodruff* and *Flannagan, Bradley, Clark and Co.* claim which had been dismissed without prejudice by the United States–Venezuelan Claims Commission set up by the Convention of 1885.[67] The facts of the case, previously described, remained the same.[68] The American and Venezuelan commissioners disagreed, with the American commissioner endorsing the position that Commissioner Little had maintained in the previous hearing of the claim.[69] The controversy was consequently referred to the umpire, Charles Augustinus Henri Barge, of Holland, for final adjudication.

Article 20 of the contract between the claimant and the Venezuelan government for the organization of the Eastern Railroad Company had contained the following Calvo Clause:

Doubts and controversies which at any time might occur in virtue of the present agreement shall be decided by the common laws and ordinary tribunals of Venezuela, and they shall never be, as well as neither the decision which shall be pronounced upon them, nor anything relating to the agreement, the subject of international reclamation.[70]

Umpire Barge ruled that the present claim must be considered within the "doubts and controversies" included in the renunciatory Clause.[71] Barge went on to assert:

Furthermore, whereas certainly a contract between a sov-

---

[66] *Venezuelan Arbitrations of 1903*, pp. 151–161; *Report of Robert C. Morris*, pp. 307–324.

[67] See *supra*, pp. 136–140. A separate appeal to reopen the *Flannagan, Bradley, Clark and Co.* case was denied by the commission. See *Report of Robert C. Morris*, pp. 540–543.

[68] *Supra*, p. 136.

[69] *Venezuelan Arbitrations of 1903*, pp. 151–158.

[70] *Ibid.*, p. 159.

[71] *Ibid.*

ereign and a citizen of a foreign country can never impede the right of the Government of that citizen to make international reclamation, wherever according to international law it has the right or even the duty to do so, as its rights and obligations can not be affected by any precedent agreement to which it is not a party;

But whereas this does not interfere with the right of a citizen to pledge to any other party that he, the contractor, in disputes upon certain matters will never appeal to other judges than to those designated by the agreement, nor with his obligation to keep this promise when pledged, leaving untouched the rights of his Government to make his case an object of international claim whenever it thinks proper to do so and not impeaching his own right to look to his Government for protection of his rights in case of denial or unjust delay of justice by the contractually designated judges;

Whereas therefore the application of the first part of Article 20 of the aforesaid agreement is not in conflict with the principles of international law nor with the inalienable right of the citizen to appeal to his Government for the protection of his rights if it is in any way denied to him, equity makes it a duty to consider that part of Article 20 just as well as all other not unlawful agreements and conditions of said contract wherever that contract is called upon as a source of those rights and duties whereon a claim may be based.[72]

Barge, dealing next with the possible objection that Venezuela had waived this contractual commitment by agreeing to the convention, asserted:

. . . [It] is to be considered that even in the case of this claim as a claim against the Venezuelan Government, owned by an American citizen, being a claim that is entitled to be brought before this Commission, the judge, having to deal with a claim fundamentally based on a contract, has to consider the rights and duties arising from that contract, and may not construe a contract that the parties themselves did not make, and he would be doing so if he gave a decision in this case and thus absolved from the pledged duty of first recurring for rights to the Venezuelan courts, thus giving a right, which by this same contract was renounced, and absolve claimant from a duty that he took upon himself by his own voluntary action . . .[73]

[72] *Ibid.*, p. 160.   [73] *Ibid.*

While it might at first appear that Umpire Barge, in refusing to take jurisdiction of the claim, was according validity to the Calvo Clause,[74] and that its existence actually did determine the outcome of the decision, closer examination reveals that the Clause was not, in fact, the determinant basis of the ruling. As in the previous adjudication, no attempt had been made to secure local redress. Umpire Barge himself pointed out the significance of this fact: "Whereas, it does not appear that any appeal of that kind was ever made to the Venezuelan courts, it must be concluded that claimant failed as to one of the conditions that would have entitled him to look on his claim as on one on which a decisive judgment might be given by this Commission." [75]

Barge therefore construed the Calvo Clause as constituting, until an application had been made to the Venezuelan court, a waiver of the right to appeal to other judges, "except naturally in case of denial or unjust delay of justice, which was not only not proven, but not even alleged." [76]

The fact situation in the *Woodruff* case once again did not provide any real test of the validity or effectiveness of a Calvo Clause, for, as has been suggested before, the test of any meaningful validity would be whether the existence of a Calvo Clause actually determined a judgment of a tribunal that would have been contrary in its absence. In view of the well-recognized local remedies rule, it must be assumed that jurisdiction would have been declined with or without the Calvo Clause stipulation. In addition, the value of this case in determining the rule of law on the concept under examination is further weakened by the reluctance of the umpire to adhere to his own ruling in subsequent decisions.

The umpire next had occasion to rule on a claim that involved the Calvo Clause in the case of the *United States (Rudloff) v.*

[74] This case is widely included in listings of cases that have upheld the validity of the Calvo Clause. See, for example, Feller, *Mex. Claims Com.*, p. 185, n. 3; Podestá Costa, "La responsabilidad internacional del estado," *Cursos Monográficos*, II (1952), p. 215.

[75] *Venezuelan Arbitrations of 1903*, p. 160.

[76] *Ibid.*, p. 161.

the Republic of Venezuela.[77] The claim was for damages for the breach by the Venezuelan government of a contract for the construction by the claimants of a market house at Caracas, and it was referred to Umpire Barge as a result of the disagreement between the American and Venezuelan commissioners on the preliminary question of jurisdiction. The jurisdiction of the commission was challenged on the grounds that the suit was at present pending before the local courts and that the contract involved contained the following provision: "Article 12. The doubts and controversies that may arise on account of this contract shall be decided by the competent tribunals of the Republic in conformity with the laws and shall not give reason for any international reclamations."[78]

Commissioner Bainbridge had ruled that these two facts did not bar the jurisdiction of the commission.[79] In regard to the Calvo Clause, the American commissioner, in an opinion closely following Little's dissent in the *Flannagan* case,[80] which he quoted, held that "in regard to that portion of Article 12 of the contract inhibiting international reclamation, it is perfectly obvious that under the established principles of the law of nations such a clause is wholly invalid."[81] In regard to the portion of Article 12 that required the settlement of doubts and controversies by resort to the local tribunals, Bainbridge ruled that this obligation was removed by the abrogation of the contract by Venezuela.[82]

Commissioner Paúl had ruled that the two objections to jurisdiction were well taken and the claim could not therefore be entertained by the commission, especially since local remedies had not been exhausted and there was no allegation of a denial of justice.[83]

Umpire Barge, in an interlocutory decision on the question of

[77] *Ibid.*, pp. 182–200; *Report of Robert C. Morris*, pp. 415–440.
[78] *Venezuelan Arbitrations of 1903*, p. 183.
[79] *Ibid.*, pp. 183–189.
[80] *Supra*, pp. 138–139.
[81] *Venezuelan Arbitrations of 1903*, p. 186.
[82] *Ibid.*, p. 187.
[83] *Ibid.*, pp. 189–192.

jurisdiction, ruled that the claim was admissible.[84] Barge, in an opinion that would appear to be inconsistent with his earlier views on the Calvo Clause, asserted that Article 12, by itself,

. . . does not withdraw the claims based on such a contract from the jurisdiction of this Commission, because it does not deprive them of any of the essential qualities that constitute the character which gives the right to appeal to this Commission; but that in such cases it has to be investigated as to every claim, whether the fact of not fulfilling this condition and of claiming in another way, without first going to the tribunals of the Republic, does not infect the claim with a *vitium proprium,* in consequence of which the absolute equity (which, according to the same protocol, has to be the only basis of the decisions of this Commission) [85] prohibits this Commission from giving the benefit of its jurisdiction (for as such it is regarded by the claimant) to a claim based on a contract by which this benefit was renounced and thus absolving claimants from their obligations, whilst the enforcing of the obligations of the other party based on that same contract is precisely the aim of their claim; and

Whereas the evidence of such a *vitium proprium* can only be the result of an examination of the claim in its details, the jurisdiction of the Commission as to the examination of the case is not impeached by the above-mentioned clause, leaving open for the decision of the Commission the question whether this clause, under circumstances sufficiently evidenced after investigation, forbids the Commission in absolute equity to give claimants the benefit of this jurisdiction as to the decision;

Wherefore this argument does not seem conclusive against the jurisdiction of this Commission.[86]

The ruling of Umpire Barge in the instant case would appear to mean that the Calvo Clause cannot, of itself, serve to bar jurisdiction, even if local remedies have not been exhausted.[87]

---

[84] *Ibid.,* pp. 192–194.

[85] The convention, *ibid.,* p. 2, provided in Article 1 that "the Commissioners, or, in case of their disagreement, the Umpire, shall decide all claims upon a basis of absolute equity, without regard to objections of a technical nature, or of the provisions of local legislation."

[86] *Ibid.,* p. 193. Sepúlveda Gutiérrez, *op. cit.,* p. 69, apparently misinterpreting the rule of this case, cites it as one in which jurisdiction was denied because of the Calvo Clause.

[87] Barge's ruling on this point is similar to that of Umpire Plumley in the *Selwyn* case. See *supra,* p. 164.

This would seem to be in conflict with his earlier ruling in the *Woodruff* case.

The question as to the effect of the Calvo Clause was next presented to Umpire Barge in the case of the *United States (American Electric and Manufacturing Co.) v. the Republic of Venezuela.*[88] The contract between the claimant and the Venezuelan government to build telephone communications in Venezuela contained the following provision: "Doubts and controversies that may arise in consequence of this contract shall be settled by the courts of the Republic in conformity with its laws."[89] The agent of Venezuela had opposed the commission's jurisdiction over the claim on the basis of this commitment. But Umpire Barge ruled that the commission did have jurisdiction. The claim actually arose not out of "doubts and controversies" but because of the failure of the government to honor an alleged independent promise to abrogate a prior and inconsistent concession given to another company.[90] Barge asserted:

Whereas, therefore, not the contract, but the pretended promise from which the contract had to deduce its value, shows itself as cause of this claim, no article of the contract seems apt to interfere with the question of jurisdiction about a claim originated in the nonfulfillment of a promise by which only that contract would obtain its full force and proper value;

Wherefore the fact that the claimant company did not first go to judges chosen by itself in this contract does not disable it to come to this Commission for decision in a claim, originated in pretended promises whereon the force of the contract depended.[91]

Therefore, since the claims arose from actions not included in contractual "doubts and controversies," the commission would take jurisdiction, the umpire ruled, and hear the claim on its merits.[92] The commission's action in taking jurisdiction in spite of the fact that local remedies had not been exhausted was ap-

[88] *Venezuelan Arbitrations of 1903*, pp. 246–250; *Report of Robert C. Morris*, pp. 511–520.
[89] *Venezuelan Arbitrations of 1903*, p. 248.
[90] *Ibid.*
[91] *Ibid.*
[92] *Ibid.*

parently based on the default of the government on its previous promise.

The umpire, in the next case to come before him that involved the Calvo Clause, made still more uncertain his actual attitude toward the validity and effectiveness of the renunciatory provision. In the case of the *United States (Orinoco Steamship Company) v. the Republic of Venezuela*[93] Barge disallowed the greater part of the 7,288,007.16 bolivar claim which arose over the alleged abrogation by Venezuela of a contract concession which purportedly gave the Orinoco Company exclusive navigational rights on certain streams, overdue payments from the respondent government, and damages and losses sustained during the revolution.[94]

The concession, in Article 14, had the following provision:

Disputes and controversies which may arise with regard to the interpretation or execution of this contract shall be resolved by the tribunals of the Republic in accordance with the laws of the nation, and shall not in any case be considered as a motive for international reclamations.[95]

Umpire Barge did not deal with this article as one which would affect the preliminary question of jurisdiction and did not even mention it in ruling that the Orinoco claim was one which could be adjudicated by the commission.[96] The umpire stated that the "main question to be examined" was whether Venezuela had in fact by the contract granted to the company exclusive navigational rights on two channels of the Orinoco River, and whether the decree that had reopened the channels to free navigation had abrogated this contract. The Orinoco Company had based the bulk of the damages claimed on this point. Barge, basing his ruling on an interpretation of the contract, held that Venezuela had not violated any alleged monopolistic privileges and hence was not liable for the damages claimed as a result of

[93] *Ibid.*, pp. 72–141; *Report of Robert C. Morris*, pp. 213–280.

[94] *Venezuelan Arbitrations of 1903*, p. 97.

[95] *Ibid.*, pp. 86–87.

[96] *Ibid.*, pp. 84–85. The Calvo Clause almost invariably arises as a preliminary question of jurisdiction, and it was so treated by Barge in his previous rulings on the Clause.

the reopening of the channels to free navigation; therefore this was not a proper ground on which to base a claim.[97]

Barge then referred to the Calvo Clause as a supplementary consideration in disallowing this part of the claim.[98] The umpire asserted:

. . . even when it might be admitted that the reopening of the channels to free navigation might furnish a ground to base a claim on (*quod non*), whilst investigating the right of claimant and the liability of the Venezuelan Government, it has not to be forgotten that, besides the already-mentioned articles, the contract has another article, *viz*, Article 14, by which the concessionary pledged himself not to submit any dispute or controversies which might arise with regard to the interpretation or execution of this contract to any other tribunal but to the tribunals of the Republic, and in no case to consider these disputes and controversies a motive for international reclamation, which article, as the evidence shows, was repeatedly disregarded and trespassed upon by asking and urging the intervention of the English and United States Governments without ever going for a decision to the tribunals of Venezuela. . . .[99]

Barge went on in his opinion to point out that the British government, upon being requested to intervene on behalf of the claimant, made the following replies on two different occasions:

Although the general international rights of His Majesty's Government are in no wise modified by the provisions of this document to which they were not a party, the fact that the company, so far as lay in their power, deliberately contracted themselves out of every remedial recourse in case of dispute, except that which is specified in Article 14 of the contract, is undoubtedly an element to be taken into serious consideration when they subsequently appeal for the intervention of His Majesty's Government.

The company does not appear to have exhausted the legal

[97] *Ibid.*, pp. 87–89.

[98] Barge also held that this portion of the claim should be disallowed because the transfer of the contract to American interests was illegal since no prior notice of the transfer was given to Venezuela as required in the contract (*ibid.*, p. 91).

[99] *Ibid.*, p. 90.

remedies at their disposal before the ordinary tribunals of the country, and it would be contrary to the international practice for His Majesty's Government formally to intervene in their behalf through the diplomatic channel unless and until they should be in a position to show that they had exhausted their ordinary legal remedies with a result that a *prima facie* case of failure or denial of justice remained.[1]

In view of this attitude expressed by the British government, Barge stated that

. . . if in general this is the only just standpoint from which to view the right to ask and to grant the means of diplomatic intervention and in consequence *casu quo* of arbitration, how much the more where the recourse to the tribunals of the country was formally pledged and the right to ask for intervention solemnly renounced by contract, and where this breach of promise was formally pointed to by the Government whose intervention was asked . . .[2]

Barge held that the issue involved did originate from "doubts and controversies" over the interpretation of the contract,[3] and "absolute equity" would not permit "that a contract be willingly and purposely trespassed upon by one party in view to force its binding power on the other party" nor would it permit "making the same contract a chain for one party and a screw press for the other."[4] Therefore, Barge stated, "It must be concluded that Article 14 of the contract disables the contracting parties to base a claim on this contract before any other tribunal than that which they have freely and deliberately chosen . . ."[5]

Although this case has been included in listings of cases that have upheld the validity of the Calvo Clause,[6] it should be noted

[1] *Ibid.*

[2] *Ibid.*, p. 91. The company, originally controlled by British interests, had first appealed to Great Britain for intervention.

[3] *Ibid.*, p. 90.

[4] *Ibid.*, p. 91. Barge's repeated references to "absolute equity" suggest that this requirement might have led the umpire to a view of the Clause that he would otherwise not have held.

[5] *Ibid.* Although here Barge seems to speak of the Clause as affecting jurisdiction, he apparently, as previously pointed out, considered it as affecting the merits of the case, for he had explicitly accepted jurisdiction.

[6] E.g., Feller, *Mex. Claims Com.*, p. 185, n. 3; Podestá Costa, "La responsabilidad internacional del estado," *Cursos Monográficos*, II (1952), p. 215.

that the Clause was not the sole or even the main ground for the decision. Since Barge had rejected the claim on the basis that the reopening of the channels to free navigation was not a proper ground on which to base a claim, his opinion on the Calvo Clause would appear to be only dictum. Furthermore, even this dictum support of the Clause is qualified since local remedies had not been exhausted. It would appear, then, that the case did not actually test the validity of the Clause, for even in its absence the claim would have been rejected on several grounds, including the local remedies rule. In view of the manner in which this opinion has been so soundly criticized,[7] and especially in view of the inconsistencies of the Barge rulings considered as a

[7] The United States vigorously protested the Barge award in this case and demanded a rehearing on the grounds that the award disregarded the terms of the protocol and contained essential errors of law and fact which would invalidate it in accordance with the principles of international law. The Memorandum of the Law Officer of the Department of State "In the Matter of the *Orinoco Steamship Company v. Venezuela,*" *Correspondence Relating to Wrongs Done to American Citizens by the Government of Venezuela* (Senate Exec. Doc. No. 413, 60th Cong., 1st Session, 1908), pp. 78–84, concluded that the decision to uphold the Calvo Clause "is, under the circumstances of the case, and bearing in mind the condition of the administration of justice in Venezuela, in absolute disregard of the terms of the protocol, opposed to the plain principle of justice that he who seeks equity must do equity, and inconsistent not only with the decisions arrived at by other judges before the mixed commissions but absolutely inconsistent with the various opinions expressed by the learned Umpire himself on the other occasions when the question arose before him." Diplomatic correspondence ensued between the two governments, and the United States finally severed diplomatic relations. After a change of regimes in Venezuela, the two governments finally agreed to the Protocol of February 13, 1909, which, in part, agreed to submit the *Orinoco* case to the Hague Permanent Court of Arbitration. In due course, the Hague Court heard the case and did declare the Barge award void on a number of points, but held that the award was severable and on some points not open to the objection of the United States. These points, which constituted the largest items of the claim, financially speaking, the court declined to re-examine on their merits. But as a result of the court's re-examination of the points upon which it held the Barge award void, it allowed a recovery, including interest, of $92,637.52 against the $28,224.93 originally allowed by Dr. Barge. In regard to Barge's ruling on the Calvo Clause, the court did not discuss the validity of the Clause as such, but held that Venezuela, by the Conventions of 1903 and 1909, had renounced invoking the Calvo Clause, and so overruled Barge's opinion on this point. See George G. Wilson, *The Hague Arbitration Cases* (Boston, 1915), pp. 217–229; Whiteman, *op. cit.,* III, p. 1687; William C. Dennis, "The Orinoco Steamship Company Case before the Hague Tribunal," *AJIL,* V (January 1911), pp. 35–64. This was the first time that a decision of an international tribunal had been annulled and revised by another international tribunal. See Dennis, *op. cit.,* p. 36.

whole, this case does not actually weaken the basic contention
that the Calvo Clause did not enjoy any meaningful legal significance in the period under examination.

Umpire Barge's "vacillating adventures in the wonderland of
the Calvo Clause," to use Freeman's apt description,[8] were
brought to a remarkable climax in the *United States (Turnbull)
v. the Republic of Venezuela* case.[9] The Turnbull claim actually
involved several claims heard as one, all originating out of the
propriety of the alleged nullification of contracts for the exploitation of the resources of Venezuela.[10] The contracts involved in
the various claims contained the following clause: "Article 11.
Any questions or controversies which may arise out of this contract shall be decided in conformity with the laws of the Republic and by the competent tribunals of the Republic." [11]

Although the umpire admitted that there might well be grounds
for a claim of breach of contract against the respondent government, he asserted:

> It has not to be forgotten that the contract in question has an
> Article 11 . . . which article forms part of the contract just as
> well as any of the other articles, and which article has to be
> regarded just as well as any of the other articles, as the declara-
> tion of the will of the contracting parties, which expressed will
> must be respected as the supreme law between parties, according
> to the immutable law of justice and equity: *pacta servanda*,
> without which law a contract would have no more worth than
> a treaty, and civil law would, as international law, have no other
> sanction than the cunning of the most astute or the brutal force
> of the physically strongest.[12]

Barge went on to examine what the parties intended by the
introduction of this article into the contract, and to what extent
it interfered with the claims being examined by the commission:

> Now, whereas it is clear that in the ordinary course of affairs,
> when nothing especially was stipulated thereupon, all questions

[8] *Denial of Justice*, p. 476.
[9] *Venezuelan Arbitrations of 1903*, pp. 200–246; *Report of Robert C. Morris*,
pp. 451–508.
[10] *Venezuelan Arbitrations of 1903*, pp. 239–244.
[11] *Ibid.*, pp. 241–244.
[12] *Ibid.*, p. 244.

and controversies arising for reason of the contract would have to be decided by the competent tribunals and in conformity with the laws. There must be looked for some special reason to make this stipulation, and to induce parties to pledge themselves expressly to a course of action they would without this special pledge be obliged to follow just as well.[13]

The umpire, stating that there must be a meaning in the article that "makes the judges by law the judges by contract as well," asserted:

. . . this meaning can be no other but that parties agreed that the questions and controversies that might arise for reason of the contract should be decided only by the competent tribunals of the Republic, and therefore not by the judges of the country of the other party, if he be a foreigner, nor by arbitration either national or international . . .[14]

Umpire Barge was not content to stop here in his interpretation of the intent and effectiveness of the Calvo Clause. In the most sweeping phraseology ever used by an international tribunal in regard to this concept, Barge went on to state:

. . . it is not to be overlooked that it is not said in the contract that *the claims* of one party against the other should be judged (that is to say, allowed or disallowed) by the mentioned judge only, but that only these judges should decide about the *questions and controversies* that might arise; which decision of course implies the decision about the question whether the interpretation of the contract by one of the parties, or that party's appreciation of facts in relation to the contract were right, and therefore could be a good reason for a claim for damages, so that properly speaking there could be no basis for a claim for damages, but the decision of expressly indicated judges about this question or controversy.[15]

"Consequently," the umpire stated,

. . . if one of the parties claims for damages sustained for reason of breach of contract on the part of the other party, these damages can, according to the contract itself, only be declared due in case the expressly designed judges had decided that the

[13] *Ibid.*, pp. 244–245.
[14] *Ibid.*, p. 245.
[15] *Ibid.*

fact, which according to the demanding party constituted such a breach of contract, really constituted such a breach, and therefore formed a good basis whereon to build a claim for damages. Parties have deliberately contracted themselves out of any interpretation of the contract and out of any judgment about the ground for damages for reason of the contract, except by the judges designed by the contract; and where there is no decision of these judges that the alleged reasons for a claim for damages really exist as such, parties, according to the contract itself, have no right to these damages, and a claim for damages which parties have no right to claim can not be accepted. Parties' expressly expressed will, and their formal pledge that for reason of the contract no damages should be regarded as due by [but?] those declared due by the indicated judges, must be respected by this Commission, when judging about a claimed [claim?] based on such a contract, just as well as all the other stipulations of that contract, and therefore it can not declare due damages that parties in that contract solemnly themselves declared not to be due.[16]

Umpire Barge held that the claims actually were "based on points that are questions and controversies" in the sense of those terms as used in the contract,[17] and, in view of the fact that

. . . not one decision of the competent tribunals of Venezuela about these questions and controversies that would make these damages due was laid before this Commission, while according to the contract itself between parties only such damages should be due which were asked on such grounds as would have been declared good grounds by these tribunals, the Commission can not declare due the damages claimed which the parties, by contract, declared not to be due.[18]

It would appear that here at last a case has been uncovered that can with propriety be cited as one that has upheld the validity of the Calvo Clause.[19] But, if the actual basis of the decision is separated from the excessively broad language of the

[16] *Ibid.*

[17] *Ibid.*

[18] *Ibid.*

[19] It has been so cited in most of the listings of pro and con cases. See, for example, Feller, *Mex. Claims Com.*, pp. 185–186, n. 3; Podestá Costa, "La responsabilidad internacional del estado," *Cursos Monográficos*, II (1952), p. 215.

umpire, we see that no attempt has been made at exhausting local remedies, nor has there been any allegation of a denial of justice. Consequently, while Barge based his rejection of jurisdiction on the Calvo Clause commitment, it must be assumed that the umpire would have ruled the same way even if the Calvo Clause had not been present in the contract.

In addition, this opinion of Umpire Barge has been subjected to vigorous criticism by the leading publicists, partly because of its inconsistency with his earlier rulings, especially in the *Rudloff* case,[20] and partly because of the sweeping language of the opinion with which he supported his decision. The famed international lawyer John Bassett Moore aptly made the following comment on the dictum of the decision:

It may be superfluous to remark that, according to this view, there can be no room whatever for international action, in diplomatic, arbitral, or other form, where the renunciatory clause exists, unless indeed to secure the execution of the judgment of a local court favorable to the claimant; for, if the parties have "no right to claim" damages which the local courts have not found to be due, it is obvious that international action of any kind would be as inadmissible where there had been an adverse judgment, no matter how unjust it might be, as where there had been no judgment whatever.[21]

Barge's much criticized dictum that an international reclamation is permissible only if the municipal court has given a judgment in favor of the claimant, would, of course, if accepted, give the Clause meaningful validity. But, if we consider the nearly universal rejection of his views by the diplomats, publicists, and jurists,[22] and the fact that his views were not actually determinative in the final *Turnbull* decision itself, this pretended recognition of the meaning and effect of the Clause does not serve to modify the contention that the Clause, by itself, did not enjoy any meaningful legal significance in the period up to 1926.

It might be well at this point to summarize briefly this examination of the role of the Calvo Clause before the United States–

[20] *Supra*, pp. 171–174.
[21] *Digest*, VI, p. 307.
[22] See Lipstein, *op. cit.*, p. 138; Freeman, *Denial of Justice*, pp. 476–477.

Venezuelan Claims Commission of 1903. The Clause was involved in more decisions (nine) before this tribunal than before any other, and its treatment by the commission is indicative of the role it played in international arbitral jurisprudence as a whole in this early period.

In the four cases decided by one or both of the commissioners, without referring the issue to the umpire, three of the opinions did not discuss the Clause, or even mention its existence.[23] In the fourth, the Clause was mentioned but not discussed in any way by the Venezuelan commissioner, and at best could be considered dictum in a concurring opinion, without any effect whatsoever on the final judgment rendered by both the commissioners.[24] Certainly, therefore, these four decisions cannot properly be included in any listings of cases that have either upheld or denied the validity of the Clause. The Clause existed,[25] but did not materially influence the judgment of the commission.

In the five decisions rendered by Umpire Barge, no evidence is found of any real legal effectiveness of the Clause in determining judgments that would have been decided to the contrary in its absence. In the *Woodruff*, *Orinoco*, and *Turnbull* cases, commonly cited as upholding the validity of the Calvo Clause, there had been no exhaustion of local remedies, which fact, by itself, even in the absence of the Calvo Clause, would normally serve to bar the presentation of an international claim. As has been indicated previously, it is erroneous to assume that because a Calvo Clause existed, and jurisdiction was denied, one caused the other to happen. Only if there had been exhaustion of local remedies, and a denial of justice suffered, would these cases have tested the validity and effectiveness of the Calvo Clause.

Also relevant to the evaluation of the significance of the rulings that involved the Calvo Clause handed down by Umpire Barge is the fact that his decisions, taken as a whole, have been subject to criticism seldom equaled in the history of interna-

---

[23] *Coro and La Vela Railway, del Genovese*, and the *La Guaira Electric Light and Power Co.* cases.

[24] *Kunhardt* case.

[25] Except in the *La Guaira* case where there is some doubt that a Calvo Clause was even in the contract.

tional arbitration. Alwyn Freeman's statement that "it would require considerable intellectual prestidigitation to reconcile Barge's hopelessly inconsistent stands in these cases" accurately reflects the attitude of the leading publicists.[26] The analysis of the law officer of the United States State Department is worth quoting:

As will be seen from this analysis, Doctor Barge assumed no less than four distinct and inconsistent positions in regard to the question of the validity and effect of the Clause under consideration: First, in the *Woodruff* case, October 2, 1903, he held that the Clause in question was binding except in the case of denial of justice and dismissed a claim where no attempt had been made to appeal to the local courts, but without prejudice as to the merits of the case. Second, November 4, 1903, he held in the *Rudloff* case, where a suit had been already brought by the claimants against the Government and was at the time actually pending in the courts, that "absolute equity" permitted the Commission to give relief, notwithstanding the Clause in the contract binding the parties to appeal to the local courts, and he did actually make an award in favor of the claimants for $75,745. Third, February 20, 1904, in the present [*Orinoco*] case, he refused to allow the claim in great part, giving as one of his reasons that the claimant had bound itself by contract to appeal to the local courts, and that "absolute equity" forbade that a contract should be made a chain for one party and a screw press for the other. And fourth, and lastly, in the *Turnbull* case, April

[26] *Denial of Justice*, p. 477. Eagleton, *Resp. of States*, p. 173, n. 39, states that "the decisions of Umpire Barge . . . are too inconsistent to be of value as precedents." Borchard, *Dip. Prot.*, p. 808, n. 2, asserts that "no two of Umpire Barge's decisions construing the renunciatory clause seem to be consistent with each other." R. Floyd Clarke, "Intervention for Breach of Contract or Tort Committed by a Sovereignty," *Proceedings of the American Society of International Law* (1910), p. 162, made the following comment on Barge's decisions: "These contradictory decisions, absurdly reasoned, and resulting in mutually destructive conclusions, fit only for *opéra bouffe*, would afford material for the gaiety of nations, were it not that the ripple of laughter dies on the lips when we consider the gross injustice thus perpetrated on private claimants. Decisions such as these have retarded the cause of international arbitration as a solvent for the disputes of nations beyond any possibility of computation. They deserve to be set in a special pillory of their own, so that international arbitrators shall know that however absolute their authority may be in the case in hand, there is a body of public opinion which will fearlessly criticize and condemn such absurd and despotic rulings, and so that at least the possibility of a just criticism shall have its full effect as a deterrent cause in preventing the repetition of such offenses."

12, 1904, he held that the Clause precluded the success of any claimant who had not actually sued in the local courts and recovered a verdict, and he therefore made final disposition of the case, the sweeping language of his opinion making no provision for any exception whatsoever, even in the case of the plainest denial of justice. . . . The opinions of the learned Umpire are absolutely irreconcilable and do not even show a consistent progression. It was at one time thought that equity varied with the length of the chancellor's foot. It is perhaps not entirely unfair to suggest that in this case "absolute equity" seems to have varied with the seasons of the year.[27]

It would appear, then, in view of the negligible and often nonexistent role played by the Calvo Clause in some of these decisions, the failure to exhaust local remedies in cases that superficially, at least, seemed to accord to the Clause some degree of validity, the inconsistent and conflicting positions taken by the commission in the various cases, and the over-all criticism that has been leveled at the rulings of this tribunal, that the jurisprudence of the United States–Venezuelan Claims Commission of 1903 would support the basic contention that the Calvo Clause did not, by itself, serve to bar a claim otherwise receivable under the rules of international law, and hence, in the period under consideration, did not enjoy any legally significant validity.

The Calvo Clause before the Brazilian and Bolivian Claims Commission

The Brazilian-Bolivian Claims Commission, set up under the Treaty of Petropolis, February 6, 1907, to adjudicate claims arising from administrative acts and from events happening in the territories exchanged in the "Acre" affair,[28] had occasion to rule on the validity and effectiveness of a form of the Calvo Clause in the case of *Bolivia (Rogerio and Co.) v. Brazil.*[29] Although this case is not one of the nineteen usually cited by

---

[27] *Correspondence Relating to Wrongs Done to American Citizens by the Government of Venezuela,* pp. 83–84.

[28] See Stuyt, *Survey,* p. 278. For the background of the controversy that led to the organization of the tribunal, see H. A. Moulin, "L'affaire du territoire d'Acre," *RGDIP,* XI (1904), pp. 150–191.

[29] Claim No. 21, decision rendered on January 29, 1909, *O Tribunal Arbitral*

authorities as involving the Calvo Clause during the period under consideration, it merits at least brief attention because the Clause played as much, or as little, role in this case as in the eight usually listed as having denied the validity of the Calvo Clause.

The concession-contract involved contained a clause which set up a system of arbitration for all questions concerning its scope and interpretation, "as well as any questions that might arise" under the contract, by a specially designated arbitrator, whose decision would be final.[30]

The Claims Commission refused to take jurisdiction of the instant claim, directing that the claimant prosecute his rights before the proper court, which he had failed to do.[31] The commission asserted:

Considering that the said contract formally establishes that all questions concerning its scope and interpretation, as well as any questions that might arise under it, would be submitted to arbitration . . .

Considering that the most characteristic difference that might arise under a contract is that of discussing its very existence and validity . . .

Considering that the arbitral jurisdiction is essentially voluntary and is based on the explicit trust of the parties in each other;

Considering therefore that the contractual commitment . . . only can be altered in an express manner by the concording will of both parties;

Considering that the Government of Bolivia has manifested an intention not to alter the contractual commitment contained in Article 17 of the contract [the Calvo Clause] of March 12, 1900 . . .

Brasileiro-Boliviano (prepared by Helio Lobo, Rio de Janeiro, 1910), pp. 69–74. The commission, as of the date of this decision, consisted of Dr. Claudio Pinilla (Bolivia); Dr. Ubaldino do Amaral (Brazil); Mgr. Alessandro (umpire).

[30] *Ibid.*, p. 71. The clause read: "Toda cuestión sobre la inteligencia ó alcances del presente contrato, así como sobre cualquiera emergencia de el, será sometida á arbitraje designándose, desde luego, para el caso, como á arbitro, para que falle sin ulterior recurso, al presidente de la Corte Federal de la República Argentina, y por escusa ó impedimiento de éste, á cualquiera de los miembros de aquél alto Tribunal, por el order de antiquedad."

[31] *Ibid.*, p. 73.

Considering that the claimant considering himself damaged . . . demanded payment of his indemnity in the form and currency agreed upon in the same contract, which shows that the claimant affirmed the existence and the obligation of the conventional disposition of the contract;

Considering that it is not proper to divide the unity of a juridical act, sustaining the efficacy of some of its clauses and the nonefficacy of others;

The Tribunal declares itself incompetent to take cognizance of the present claim, directing that these documents be returned to the claimant so that he might prosecute his rights before the proper court.[32]

It is interesting to note that even in this arbitration between Latin American states, there was not complete agreement as to the effect of a Calvo Clause commitment. The Brazilian commissioner, Dr. Ubaldino do Amaral, dissented. While he admitted that the specially designated arbitrator would have jurisdiction over the claim "by virtue of the arbitration clause," he argued that the Brazilian-Bolivian Arbitral Tribunal also had jurisdiction by virtue of the Treaty of Petropolis which set up this tribunal. He stated that while the *compromis* did not create a *superior* jurisdiction, it had created a *concurrent* jurisdiction over this type of claim, and hence the tribunal should hear the case on its merits since it had been submitted to the tribunal first.[33]

In the *Rogerio* case, as in the previously considered decisions which purportedly recognized the efficacy of the Calvo Clause, there was no real test of the validity of the Clause; here again local remedies had not been exhausted by the claimant.

The Calvo Clause before the Great Britain and Costa Rican Claims Commission

There remains to be considered the jurisprudence of one more commission that dealt with the Calvo Clause in the period under consideration. A claims commission was set up by Great Britain

---

[32] *Ibid.*, pp. 72–73. My translation.
[33] *Ibid.*, p. 73. My translation.

and Costa Rica under the convention of January 12, 1922,[34] to arbitrate the cases of *Great Britain (Royal Bank of Canada) v. Costa Rica* and *Great Britain (Central Costa Rica Petroleum Co.) v. Costa Rica*.[35] The decisions were rendered by United States Chief Justice William Howard Taft, sole arbitrator, on October 18, 1923.

The claims were based on a concession and debt that depended on the acts of the Tinoco government, which was in power in Costa Rica from early 1917 until September 1919. The Costa Rican government that was a party to this arbitration represented the restoration of the government which had been overthrown by Tinoco, a former secretary of war. After the demise of the Tinoco government, the Costa Rican Congress, on August 22, 1922, passed a Law of Nullities, invalidating all contracts made, with or without legislative approval, between the executive power and private persons during the period of the Tinoco regime. Costa Rica claimed that the act removed her liability in this matter. Britain denied it, and asserted that the case should be heard on its merits.[36]

The main issue in the cases was whether the Law of Nullities of 1922 served to relieve Costa Rica of liability under the contracts. Justice Taft said no, holding that the Tinoco government was actually sovereign and must be considered "a link in the continuity of the Government of Costa Rica," and so the present government was responsible for its official acts.[37]

The Calvo Clause became an issue in the arbitration because of one of the preliminary objections of the Costa Rican agent to the jurisdiction of the commission. It was asserted that both the

[34] See Stuyt, *Survey*, p. 355.

[35] The opinion and award in these two cases were first published in pamphlet form, but were later reprinted in *AJIL*, XVIII (January 1924), pp. 147–174, and are also reprinted in the United Nations' *Reports of International Arbitral Awards*, I, pp. 370–399. These cases are commonly referred to as the Tinoco Arbitration.

[36] *AJIL*, XVIII (January 1924), pp. 148–149. For a description of the events that led up to this arbitration, as well as for an analysis of these claims, see M. O. Hudson, "Arbitration between Great Britain and Costa Rica," *American Bar Association Journal*, X (July 1924), pp. 486–487.

[37] *AJIL*, XVIII (January 1924), pp. 150–154.

claimants were bound by their own contractual obligation entered into with the government of Costa Rica, or by the laws of Costa Rica, to which they had subscribed, not to present their claims by way of the diplomatic intervention of their home government, but to submit their claims to the courts of Costa Rica.[38]

The concession of the Petroleum Company contained the following provisions:

Article XIX. The present contract shall elapse and the Government may so declare by an Executive Order, in the following cases only . . .

6. If the contractor has recourse to diplomatic action in connection with any dispute or litigation as to the rights and privileges granted by this contract, but the forfeiture of this concession shall not be pronounced by the Government without having given to the concessionaire the opportunity to defend himself nor without having submitted the point to arbitration.

Article XXI. Any dispute arising between the parties in respect to the interpretation or execution of this contract which can not be compromised, shall be submitted to arbitration and decided according to the laws of Costa Rica. If the parties fail to agree on one arbitrator, each shall appoint one, and the two arbitrators in case of disagreement shall choose a third as umpire.[39]

In regard to whether these two clauses affected the right of the Petroleum Company to pursue its claim before the commission, Mr. Taft stated:

These two limitations do not seem to include within their scope such a question as the power of the Tinoco Government to grant the concession, or the obligation of the present Government of Costa Rica to recognize it. They cover the interpretation and construction of the contract rather than the fundamental question of its existence.[40]

With respect to the Royal Bank, however, the facts were somewhat different. The establishment of a branch of the Royal

[38] *Ibid.*, p. 157.
[39] *Ibid.*, pp. 157–158.
[40] *Ibid.*, p. 158.

Bank of Canada in Costa Rica was only authorized on condition
that the limitations of the National Banking Law be accepted
in full.[41] Relevant provisions of this law read:

Article 11. Companies organized abroad for the establishment
of banks of any kind within the Republic shall subject themselves for effective organization to the provisions of this law and
the banks, as well as their shareholders, shall be impressed with
the character of Costa Rica citizenship to the extent of being
denied the power to invoke the laws of any foreign country in
matters relating to the affairs or operations of such banks; such
matters must be decided by the tribunals of Costa Rica and in
entire conformity with the laws of the Republic.

Article 12. Banks established in the country as branches of
foreign banks shall be equally subject to the provisions of the
preceding article.[42]

Taft, in rejecting these provisions as limitations on the commission's jurisdiction, asserted:

It is doubtful whether these restrictions upon the bank by
their terms go so far as to forbid its appeal for diplomatic intervention in protection of its rights. They show clearly that the
powers conferred by the Government of its origin can not en-
large its banking powers in Costa Rica and that its rights are
to be decided by Costa Rican courts and according to Costa
Rican law. But to carry this to a denial of the right to a diplomatic intervention by its own Government to avoid legislative
nullification of its rights without a hearing would be going far.[43]

However, whatever might be the intent or effectiveness of
these provisions, Taft asserted, these restrictions

. . . upon each claimant would seem to be inapplicable to a case
like the present where is involved the obligation of a restored
government for the acts or contracts of a usurping government.
. . . In view of the Law of Nullities the restored Government
must be held to have waived the enforcement of any limitation
upon the right of the bank to invoke the protection of its home
Government under the circumstances.[44]

[41] *Ibid.*
[42] *Ibid.*, pp. 158–159.
[43] *Ibid.*, p. 159.
[44] *Ibid.*, p. 160.

After thus ruling on the issues of jurisdiction, the arbitrator heard the case on its merits, and, holding that the claims were lacking in merit, denied any awards to the claimant.[45]

These cases, although not included in publicists' listings of the nineteen decisions that involved the validity of the Calvo Clause, conform to the pattern of the previously considered arbitrations. The validity of the Clause itself was not discussed by the commission. Mr. Taft held that the Clause was "inapplicable" to the instant case and hence it was unnecessary to determine its validity under the rules of international law.

Conclusions Regarding the Influence of the Calvo Clause in International Arbitral Jurisprudence up to 1926

This survey of the arbitral jurisprudence that has involved the Calvo Clause before 1926 would appear to support several general conclusions.

The main emphasis in this examination has been to determine the precise effect of the Calvo Clause in each case. In other words, attention has been primarily directed at discovering whether the Calvo Clause served to bar an international claim that would have been otherwise admissible under the generally recognized rules of international law.

Nineteen cases are cited by authorities as having involved the Clause up to 1926.[46] In the eight cases listed as having upheld the validity of the Clause,[47] the decisions do not, in fact, actually support the validity of the clause. In seven of these cases, there had been no exhaustion of local remedies[48] and jurisdiction would presumably have been declined even without the renunciatory waiver in accordance with the local remedies rule. Consequently, the Clause did not determine any decision that would

---

[45] *Ibid.*, pp. 161–174.

[46] Borchard, "Decisions of the Claims Commissions, United States and Mexico," *AJIL*, XX (July 1926), p. 538; Beteta and Henríquez, *op. cit.*, p. 44; Sepúlveda Gutiérrez, *op. cit.*, p. 69; Gonzalez, *op. cit.*, p. 44; Feller, *Mex. Claims Com.*, pp. 185–186; Briggs, *op. cit.*, (1st ed., 1938), p. 541.

[47] These eight are *Day and Garrison; Flannagan; Tehuantepec; Woodruff; Orinoco; Turnbull; Kunhardt;* and *Nitrate Railway Co.*

[48] *Tehuantepec, Day and Garrison, Flannagan, Nitrate Railway Co., Woodruff, Orinoco,* and *Turnbull.*

have been to the contrary in its absence. In the eighth case,[49] the existence of the Clause was mentioned, without elaboration, in a concurring opinion, but the case was actually determined on other grounds.

If we sort out the actual rule of these cases from the dicta and extraneous statements, it would appear that not one of these cases actually can be cited with propriety in any listings of decisions that have upheld the validity of the Calvo Clause. This does not mean that the Clause served no purpose at all, for it undoubtedly re-emphasized the local remedies rule; the failure of the claimant to abide by his contractual commitment perhaps tended to reinforce the determination of the commissions to apply the international law principle that requires a claimant to first seek redress in the local courts. However, as far as the jurisdictional question of the admissibility of a claim is concerned, the Calvo Clause accomplished nothing that would not have been accomplished by the application of the well-recognized local remedies rule. It is important to keep in mind that *only if local remedies had been exhausted, and jurisdiction still had been declined because of the Clause*, would these cases be significant in demonstrating an application of the Calvo Clause.

It should be noted, also, that the eleven cases normally cited as having denied the validity of the Clause[50] did not actually deal with the validity of this concept as such. It is not to be overlooked that in one of these cases the decision was explicitly based on the principle of conciliation rather than adjudication, and the denial of the effectiveness of the Clause was found only in the opinion of one of the commissioners and not in the decision of the commission.[51] In two others, the Calvo Clause was not even mentioned in the opinion of the commission.[52] In the remaining eight, the commissions showed a great reluctance to deal directly with the validity of the Clause, and chose rather to

---

[49] *Kunhardt.*

[50] *Milligan, North and South American Construction Co., Stirling, Antofagasta, McMurdo, Martini, Selwyn, Coro and La Vela Railway, del Genovese, Rudloff,* and *American Electric Company.*

[51] *Milligan* case.

[52] *Coro and La Vela Railway* and *del Genovese* cases.

find that the Clause was inapplicable to the given fact situations, usually because either the claim did not arise out of "doubts or controversies," or the convention that set up the special jurisdiction of the commission served to supersede the contractual renunciation by the claimant.[53]

It would appear that this analysis of the decisional law in the period under consideration would justify the conclusion that in no decision was the validity of the Calvo Clause actually tested, and, consequently, in no instance did the Calvo Clause realize legally meaningful validity in the sense that its existence actually determined final disposition of a case that would have been adjudicated to the contrary in its absence. Moreover, it is impossible to discover a consistent strain of reasoning that would constitute a rule of law on this concept, either confirming or denying the validity of the Clause. There is, as has been seen above, a glaring lack of consistency in this decisional law, even in the jurisprudence of the same commission, as was the case with the Anglo-Chilean and the United States–Venezuelan (1903) commissions. To be sure, the Clause did serve as a convenient "hook" on which to hang a decision, and it undoubtedly did serve to emphasize the local remedies rule. However, the fact that the Calvo Clause per se did not determine a decision, plus the inconsistency and confusion that have characterized the treatment of this concept, would tend to substantiate the conclusion that the Clause did not play a determinative role in international arbitral jurisprudence up to 1926 and inclusion of these early cases in any pro and con listings of decisions on the Calvo Clause is actually without any real value.

---

[53] The four additional cases surveyed (*French Company of Venezuelan Railroads, Rogerio, Central Costa Rica Petroleum Co.* and *Royal Bank of Canada,* and *La Guaira*), although not included in these nineteen, do not serve to modify these conclusions.

‹ VII ›

The North American Dredging
Company Case

THE period between 1923 and 1934 saw the creation and functioning of the various Mexican claims commissions. The creation
of these commissions between Mexico and some six other nations
represented, in a way, the climax of Mexico's long history of
being involved in international reclamations. The history of
Mexico is, in the words of a famous Mexican scholar, "the history
of the foreign claims brought against our country." [1]

A. H. Feller, who has given special study to this subject, has
stated:

The subject of the claims of foreign nationals plays a more important part in the history of the foreign relations of Mexico
than in that of any other country. Indeed, it might almost be
possible to write that history in terms of international claims.
The primary reason for the inordinate importance of this subject
in Mexican foreign relations is undoubtedly to be found in the
troubled history of Mexico. Where revolution followed upon revolution and governments were sometimes as transitory as the
seasons of the year, the lives and property of aliens were subjected to peril in a greater degree than in countries with a more
stable political system. On the other hand, the claims which revolutionary disturbances created were sometimes seized upon by
foreign states as a pretext for furthering territorial ambitions
and economic imperialism. The undeveloped riches of Mexico's
natural resources attracted hordes of adventurers to whom the
opportunity of collecting on a large claim against the government was an attractive alternative to slower methods of making

[1] Gómez Robledo, *op. cit.*, p. 145.

profits. The military inferiority of Mexico and the subserviency to foreign interests of some transitory government occasionally led to the acknowledgment of fraudulent or inflated claims. Such acquiescence would embitter Mexican public opinion and lead to further antagonism to aliens. The chronic difficulties of the Mexican treasury would make it difficult to liquidate the claims, and the net result would be an increase of ill-feeling between the two countries.[2]

The immediate cause for the Mexican claims commissions to be set up was the decade of turbulence and violence which followed the revolution aimed at the regime of Porfirio Diaz in 1910. The succeeding revolutions and chaotic conditions produced a large number of claims on behalf of aliens for alleged injuries to their persons and property. After several unsuccessful efforts, the governments of these aliens, led by the United States, finally won Mexican acceptance of a series of conventions that agreed to the submission of these claims against Mexico to international arbitration. The agreement between the United States and Mexico was signed September 8, 1923,[3] with separate conventions later being signed by France, Germany, Great Britain, Italy, Spain, and Belgium.[4]

The jurisprudence of these commissions includes some highly significant rulings on points of international law. Perhaps the most important of these rulings were those that dealt with the Calvo Clause.

Sir John H. Percival, the distinguished British commissioner on the British-Mexican Claims Commission, has stated that the problem of the validity of the Calvo Clause was ". . . the most important problem with which the Commissions had to deal, both from the point of view of the amount of the claims, which

[2] *Mex. Claims Com.*, p. 1.

[3] This convention, sometimes called the Bucareli Agreement, is reprinted with later revisions in Feller, *Mex. Claims Com.*, pp. 321–384. See also Stuyt, *Survey*, pp. 372–373. For a discussion of this convention, and the events leading up to it, see Dunn, *The Diplomatic Protection of Americans in Mexico* (New York, 1933), pp. 401–406. For a highly critical treatment of this same subject, see Gómez Robledo, *op. cit., passim*; Salvador Diego-Fernandez, *Los Pactos de Bucareli* (Mexico, 1937), pp. 12–31.

[4] See Feller, *Mex. Claims Com.*, pp. 23–28.

in several cases amounted to over a million pounds, and the effect of the decisions on future international disputes . . ." [5]

Of these highly significant decisions that dealt with the Clause, unquestionably the most important was that rendered by the United States–Mexican General Claims Commission in the case of the *United States (North American Dredging Company of Texas) v. the United Mexican States.*[6] This case, a landmark in the evolution of the Calvo Clause in international arbitral jurisprudence, is of such importance in determining the rule of law on the Clause that it merits separate and extensive treatment.

It should be noted that the importance of this case has been recognized by governments, courts, and publicists, the three chief law-determining agencies. Great Britain, India, New Zealand, and the United States, in their replies to the League Codification Questionnaire on the validity of the Calvo Clause, specifically cited the ruling of the commission in the *Dredging* case.[7] As the commission stated in the *International Fisheries* case, the replies of Germany, Bulgaria, Denmark, Hungary, Norway, and the Netherlands were "in practical accord" with the decision in the *Dredging* case.[8] The recognition by international tribunals of the importance of the *Dredging* decision is evidenced by the fact that both the United States–Mexican and British-Mexican commissions specifically cited and followed the *Dredging* rule in adjudicating later claims that involved the Calvo Clause.[9] Publicists, even though they may be critical of the rule laid down by the commission, recognize it as the key case in the jurisprudence involving the Clause.[10]

[5] "International Arbitral Tribunals and the Mexican Claims Commission," *Journal of Comparative Legislation and International Law*, XIX (3rd Series, 1937), p. 102.

[6] March 31, 1926, *Opinions of Commissioners*, I, pp. 21–34. Dunn, *The Diplomatic Protection of Americans in Mexico*, p. 406, agrees that "of the decisions rendered by the Commission, perhaps the most important from the standpoint of international law and the future of diplomatic protection was that given in the *North American Dredging Company* case."

[7] *Supra*, pp. 40, 50–52.

[8] *Opinions of Commissioners*, III, p. 210. See *supra*, pp. 46–56.

[9] *Infra*, Chapter VIII.

[10] E.g., Eagleton, *Resp. of States*, p. 175, n. 43, states that "the opinion seems to offer the most complete exposition of the Calvo Clause in contracts which

The North American Dredging Company Case

Before we begin the summation and analysis of the *Dredging* opinion, it may be well to point out several differences between the instant case and previous arbitral rulings on the validity of the Calvo Clause. In the *Dredging* case, the commission, recognizing the inconsistency, contradiction, and confusion that had characterized earlier arbitral rulings on the validity of the Calvo Clause, made no reference to any precedents on the subject, but examined the question *de novo*.[11] Also, in the *Dredging* case, for the first time, a commission dealt extensively and directly with the issue of the validity of the Calvo Clause in a case that turned directly on the effectiveness of the renunciatory provision in contracts.[12] Furthermore, and perhaps the most important distinction between this case and previous arbitral rulings, there was in the *compromis* a special provision that *waived the necessity of exhausting local remedies* before the presentation of an international claim.

This waiver of the local remedies rule was explicitly contained in Article V of the convention, which read:

The High Contracting Parties, being desirous of effecting an equitable settlement of the claims of their respective citizens thereby affording them just and adequate compensation for their losses or damages, agree that no claim shall be disallowed or rejected by the Commission by the application of the general principle of international law that the legal remedies must be exhausted as a condition precedent to the validity or allowance of any claim.[13]

The importance of this provision cannot be overemphasized, for, if the Calvo Clause is, as many authorities assert, merely a restatement of the local remedies rule, then the waiving of the rule would make the Clause of no effect. If, however, in spite of the waiver of the local remedies rule, the existence of the Calvo Clause still is held to be legally meaningful, then it would appear

has yet been made." Feller speaks of the "important influence" this case has had. See *Mex. Claims Com.*, p. 192. See also De Beus, *op. cit.*, pp. 84–85, and p. 49 where he speaks of this decision as "very elaborate and valuable."

[11] Borchard, "Decisions of the Claims Commissions, United States and Mexico," *AJIL*, XX (July 1926), p. 538.

[12] Dunn, *Diplomatic Protection of Americans in Mexico*, p. 406.

[13] Stuyt, *Survey*, p. 372.

that it must be something more than a superfluous restatement of this generally recognized rule. The existence of Article V must be kept foremost in mind in any evaluation of the rule of the *Dredging* case.[14]

The Decision of the Commission

In previous examinations of cases that have involved the Calvo Clause, the opinions were quoted only to the extent necessary to present accurately the part of the decision that actually dealt with the Clause. But in the instant case the entire opinion dealt with the question of the validity of the Calvo Clause and it will be necessary to quote rather extensively from the decision of the commission.

The *Dredging* case came before the commission, which at this time was composed of C. van Vollenhoven of Holland (umpire), Edwin B. Parker (United States commissioner), and Fernandez MacGregor (Mexican commissioner), on the motion of the Mexican agent to dismiss a claim for the recovery of the sum of $233,523.30 with interest thereon, which was the amount of losses and damages alleged to have been suffered by the claimant for "breaches of a contract for dredging at the port of Salina Cruz." [15]

[14] Similar articles providing for the waiver of the local remedies rule were included in the conventions signed by Mexico with France, Germany, Great Britain, Italy, and Spain. See Feller, *Mex. Claims Com.*, p. 34. Article III of the "Terms of Submission" of the Pecuniary Claims Arbitration Agreement between the United States and Great Britain, signed on August 18, 1910, also had waived the local remedies rule by providing that ". . . no claim shall be disallowed or rejected by the application of the general principle of international law that the legal remedies must be exhausted as a condition precedent to the validity of the claim." 37 U.S. *Stat. L.* 1625 (1911–1913) at p. 1629. In the Claims Convention between the United States and Panama, signed July 28, 1926, Article V contained an essentially similar waiver. 47 U.S. *Stat. L.* 1915 (1931–1933) at p. 1920. Needless to say, this provision in the various Mexican claims conventions has been the object of strong criticism by Latin American publicists. See, for example, Gómez Robledo, *op. cit.*, p. 162. Several United States scholars have also criticized this provision as being unwise. See Briggs, "The Settlement of Mexican Claims Act of 1942," *AJIL*, XXXVII (April 1943), p. 231; Eagleton, "L'epuisement des recours internes et le déni de justice, d'après certaines décisions récentes," *RDILC*, XVI (3rd Series, 1935), pp. 504–526.

[15] *Opinions of Commissioners*, I, p. 21. The commission, in holding that the claim arose out of "breaches of a contract," did not discuss the physical facts or conditions on which the claim was based, nor did it deal with the

The North American Dredging Company Case

The jurisdiction of the commission had been challenged on two grounds. The first of these, that "claims based on an alleged non-performance of contract obligations are outside the jurisdiction of this Commission," was summarily rejected by the commis-

allegations of the American agent that the losses sustained by the claimant were the result of violations of the rules and principles of international law by the Mexican government and its officials, which, it was argued, obviated the necessity to resort to the local courts for relief. The memorial stated that in pursuance of the contract entered into on November 23, 1912, the corporation brought its equipment to the port of Salina Cruz and began extensive dredging operations. The Madero government, with which the contract had been signed, at first made regular payments. However, following the outbreak of the Huerta revolution, no payments were made for the work done under the contract. Because of this default, the company finally stopped its dredging operations and removed its equipment. For the balance due for the completed dredging, the claimant sought the sum of $121,427.77. In addition, the company demanded compensation in the amount of $19,834.74 for the stopping of work "by arbitrary orders of the Inspector of the Mexican Federal Government," and compensation in the amount of $92,260.79 for the illegal detention of a dredge and some scows. Although the first part of the claim could properly be considered breach of contract, the second part of the claim was based on the alleged tortious conduct of Mexican officials. The interruption and interference with the dredging work by the inspector for the government, one Señor Ocampo, had resulted in a complete stoppage of work for a total of eighteen days in May and July of 1913. Evidence submitted in the memorial to support this contention of arbitrary and wrongful stoppage of work included an affidavit by Erick E. Mattson, the superintendent in charge of the dredge, who asserted that there was no cause for this arbitrary interference with the execution of the contract. The memorial cited several attempts by the company to obtain redress from the administrative branch of the Mexican government, although no steps were taken to sue the government in court. This failure was allegedly due to the fact that the administrative officials to whom the company had appealed had informed the claimant that the Mexican government did not have the money to pay the claims, that when money was available a settlement would be reached, and that in the meantime a suit against the government would be considered an unfriendly act. Furthermore, owing to revolutionary conditions, such a suit would be fruitless, and the company was not financially able to undertake litigation because the losses sustained had forced it into liquidation. See the *Memorial* of the agent of the United States (available in the National Archives: Records of Boundary and Claims Commissions and Arbitrations, Record Group 76), and see Petition to Rehear filed by the agent for the United States, referred to in Dunn, *Diplomatic Protection of Americans in Mexico*, p. 408, n. 5. While these allegations of tortious conduct were not established by judicial determination, it should be noted that Mexico did not challenge them, but merely moved to dismiss the case on jurisdictional grounds, which, according to Feller, *Mex. Claims Com.*, pp. 191–192, means that "all the allegations of the Memorial must be taken as confessed." The failure of the commission to examine these allegations to determine whether an immediate denial of justice existed has been quite properly criticized by authorities. See, for example, Hyde, *International Law*, II, pp. 995–996. See also *infra*, pp. 211–212.

sion.[16] The second was that a contract containing the so-called Calvo Clause "deprives the party subscribing said Clause of the right to submit any claims connected with his contract to an international commission." [17] The commission unanimously sustained the motion of the Mexican agent to dismiss the claim on this second count.[18]

The Calvo Clause involved in this case stipulated:

> The contractor and all persons who, as employees or in any other capacity, may be engaged in the execution of the work under this contract either directly or indirectly, shall be considered as Mexicans in all matters, within the Republic of Mexico, concerning the execution of such work and the fulfillment of this contract. They shall not claim, nor shall they have, with regard to the interests and the business connected with this contract, any other rights or means to enforce the same than those granted by the laws of the Republic to Mexicans, nor shall they enjoy any other rights than those established in favor of Mexicans. They are consequently deprived of any rights as aliens, and under no conditions shall the intervention of foreign diplomatic agents be permitted, in any matter related to this contract.[19]

The commission asserted that it was "fully sensible of the importance of any judicial decision either sustaining in whole or in part, or rejecting in whole or in part, or construing the so-called Calvo Clause" in contracts between nations and aliens, and that it appreciated the "legitimate desire" on the part of nations to deal with persons and property within their own jurisdictions according to their own laws and to apply remedies provided by their own authorities and tribunals, which laws and remedies "in no wise restrict or limit their international obligations, or restrict or limit or in any wise impinge upon the correlative rights of other nations protected under rules of international law." It went on to pose the central issue of the case as being whether "such legitimate desire" may be accomplished through "appropriate and carefully phrased contracts"; what form such a contract might take; what its scope and its limitations would be; and

---

[16] *Opinions of Commissioners*, p. 22.
[17] *Ibid.*
[18] *Ibid.*, pp. 33–34. [19] *Ibid.*, p. 22.

whether clause 18 of the contract involved would "fall within the field where the parties are free to contract without violating any rule of international law." [20]

The commission took the position that it is not necessary to choose between the extremes of either upholding the Calvo Clause altogether, or denying its efficacy completely, stating:

The Commission does not feel impressed by arguments either in favor of or in opposition to the Calvo Clause, in so far as these arguments go to extremes. The Calvo Clause is neither upheld by all outstanding international authorities and by the soundest among international awards nor is it universally rejected. The Calvo Clause in a specific contract is neither a clause which must be sustained to its full length because of its contractual nature nor can it be discretionarily separated from the rest of the contract as if it were just an accidental postscript. The problem is not solved by saying yes or no; the affirmative answer exposing the rights of foreigners to undeniable dangers, the negative answer leaving to the nations involved no alternative except that of exclusion of foreigners from business. The present stage of international law imposes upon every international tribunal the solemn duty of seeking for a proper and adequate balance between the sovereign right of national jurisdiction, on the one hand, and the sovereign right of national protection of citizens on the other. No international tribunal should or may evade the task of finding such limitations of both rights as will render them compatible within the general rules and principles of international law. By merely ignoring worldwide abuses either of the right of national protection or of the right of national jurisdiction no solution compatible with the requirements of modern international law can be reached. [21]

The commission went on to assert that "it is quite possible to recognize as valid some forms of waiving the right of foreign protection without thereby recognizing as valid and lawful every form of doing so," and consequently upholding the Clause in the present case need not mean that all nations may lawfully bind foreigners to relinquish all rights of protection. [22]

The commission, in two very significant yet generally over-

[20] *Ibid.*, pp. 22–23.
[21] *Ibid.*, p. 23.
[22] *Ibid.*

looked passages of this decision, next dealt with the relation of the Calvo Clause to the emerging role of the individual under international law:

The Commission also denies that the rules of international public law apply only to nations and that individuals can not under any circumstances have a personal standing under it. As illustrating the antiquated character of this thesis it may suffice to point out that in article 4 of the unratified International Prize Court Convention adopted at the Hague in 1907 and signed by both the United States and Mexico and by 29 other nations this conception, so far as ever held, was repudiated.

It is well known how largely the increase of civilization, intercourse, and interdependence as between nations has influenced and moderated the exaggerated conception of national sovereignty. As civilization has progressed individualism has increased; and so has the right of the individual citizen to decide upon the ties between himself and his native country. There was a time when governments and not individuals decided if a man was allowed to change his nationality or his residence, and when even if he had changed either of them his government sought to lay burdens on him for having done so. To acknowledge that under the existing laws of progressive, enlightened civilization a person may voluntarily expatriate himself but that short of expatriation he may not by contract, in what he conceives to be his own interest, to any extent loosen the ties which bind him to his country is neither consistent with the facts of modern international intercourse nor with corresponding developments in the field of international law and does not tend to promote good will among nations.[23]

In a series of five paragraphs dealing with the "Lawfulness of the Calvo Clause," the commission asserted that the Clause can be rejected only if it is clearly repugnant to a generally recognized rule of international law; that there exists no such rule prohibiting all limitation of the right of protection; that the meaning of the present Calvo Clause is only a promise not to ignore local remedies; that such a promise is not illegal insofar as it only limits the right of protection, and does not destroy it; and, finally, that the Clause is not inconsistent with the law of

[23] *Ibid.*, pp. 23–24.

nature. This summation of the attitude of the commission toward the "lawfulness" of the Calvo Clause does not, however, do justice to either the reasoning of the tribunal or the importance of the theory presented. It seems desirable, therefore, to quote these five paragraphs in full:

The contested provision, in this case, is part of a contract and must be upheld unless it be repugnant to a recognized rule of international law. What must be established is not that the Calvo Clause is universally accepted or universally recognized, but that there exists a generally accepted rule of international law condemning the Calvo Clause and denying to an individual the right to relinquish to any extent, large or small, and under any circumstances or conditions, the protection of the government to which he owes allegiance. Only in case a provision of this or any similar tendency were established could a parallel be drawn between the illegality of the Calvo Clause in the present contract and the illegality of a similar clause in the Arkansas contract declared void in 1922 by the Supreme Court of the United States [*Terral v. Burke Construction Co.*, 257 U.S. 529, 42 S. Ct. 188], because of its repugnance to American statute provisions. It is as little doubtful nowadays as it was in the day of the Geneva Arbitration that international law is paramount to decrees of nations and to municipal law; but the task before this Commission precisely is to ascertain whether international law really contains a rule prohibiting contract provisions attempting to accomplish the purpose of the Calvo Clause.

The Commission does not hesitate to declare that there exists no international rule prohibiting the sovereign right of a nation to protect its citizens abroad from being subject to any limitation whatsoever under any circumstances. The right of protection has been limited by treaties between nations in provisions related to the Calvo Clause. While it is true that Latin-American countries — which are important members of the family of nations and which have played for many years an important and honorable part in the development of international law — are parties to most of these treaties, still such countries as France, Germany, Great Britain, Sweden, Norway, and Belgium, and in one case at least even the United States of America (Treaty between the United States and Peru, dated September 6, 1870, Volume 2, Malloy's *United States Treaties*, at page 1426; article 37) have been parties to treaties containing such provisions.

The Calvo Clause

What Mexico has asked of the North American Dredging Company of Texas as a condition for awarding it the contract which it sought is, "If all of the means of enforcing your rights under this contract afforded by Mexican law, even against the Mexican Government itself, are wide open to you, as they are wide open to our own citizens, will you promise not to ignore them and not to call directly upon your own Government to intervene in your behalf in connection with any controversy, small or large, but seek redress under the laws of Mexico through the authorities and tribunals furnished by Mexico for your protection?" and the claimant, by subscribing to this contract and seeking the benefits which were to accrue to him thereunder, has answered, "I promise."

Under the rules of international law may an alien lawfully make such a promise? The Commission holds that he may, but at the same time holds that he can not deprive the government of his nation of its undoubted right of applying international remedies to violations of international law committed to his damage. Such government frequently has a larger interest in maintaining the principles of international law than in recovering damage for one of its citizens in a particular case, and manifestly such citizen can not by contract tie in this respect the hands of his government. But while any attempt to so bind his government is void, the Commission has not found any generally recognized rule of positive international law which would give to his government the right to intervene to strike down a lawful contract, in the terms set forth in the preceding paragraph 10, entered into by its citizen. The obvious purpose of such a contract is to prevent abuses of the right to protection, not to destroy the right itself — abuses which are intolerable to any self-respecting nation and are prolific breeders of international friction. The purpose of such a contract is to draw a reasonable and practical line between Mexico's sovereign right of jurisdiction within its own territory, on the one hand, and the sovereign right of protection of the government of an alien whose person or property is within such territory, on the other hand. Unless such line is drawn and if these two coexisting rights are permitted constantly to overlap, continual friction is inevitable.

It being impossible to prove the illegality of the said provision, under the limitations indicated, by adducing generally recognized rules of positive international law, it apparently can only be contested by invoking its incongruity to the law of nature

(natural rights) and its inconsistency with inalienable, inde-
structible, unprescriptible, uncurtailable rights of nations. The
law of nature may have been helpful, some three centuries ago,
to build up a new law of nations, and the conception of inalienable rights of men and nations may have exercised a salutary
influence, some one hundred and fifty years ago, on the development of modern democracy on both sides of the ocean; but they
have failed as a durable foundation of either municipal or international law and can not be used in the present day as substi-
tutes for positive municipal law, on the one hand, and for positive international law, as recognized by nations and governments
through their acts and statements, on the other hand. Inalienable rights have been the cornerstones of policies like those of
the Holy Alliance and of Lord Palmerston; instead of bringing
to the world the benefit of mutual understanding, they are to
weak or less fortunate nations an unrestrained menace.[24]

The commission, having found the Calvo Clause to be lawful,
next took up the problem of what was "the true meaning of Article 18 of the present contract." The meaning of Article 18 was
not to prohibit all diplomatic recourse, but

Reading this article as a whole, it is evident that its purpose
was to bind the claimant to be governed by the laws of Mexico
and to use the remedies existing under such laws. The closing
words "in any matter connected with this contract" must be
read in connection with the preceding phrase "in everything connected with the execution of such work and the fulfillment of
this contract" and also in connection with the phrase "regarding
the interests or business connected with this contract." In other
words, in executing the contract, in fulfilling the contract, or in
putting forth any claim "regarding the interests or business connected with this contract," the claimant should be governed by
those laws and remedies which Mexico had provided for the protection of its own citizens. But this provision did not, and could
not, deprive the claimant of his American citizenship and all that
that implies. It did not take from him his undoubted right to
apply to his own Government for protection if his resort to the
Mexican tribunals or other authorities available to him resulted
in a denial or delay of justice as that term is used in international
law. In such a case the claimant's complaint would be not that
his contract was violated but that he had been denied justice.

[24] *Ibid.*, pp. 24–26.

The basis of his appeal would be not a construction of his contract, save perchance in an incidental way, but rather an internationally illegal act.

What, therefore, are the rights which claimant waived and those which he did not waive in subscribing to article 18 of the contract? (a) He waived his right to conduct himself as if no competent authorities existed in Mexico; as if he were engaged in fulfilling a contract in an inferior country subject to a system of capitulations; and as if the only real remedies available to him in the fulfillment, construction, and enforcement of this contract were international remedies. All these he waived and had a right to waive. (b) He did not waive any right which he possessed as an American citizen as to any matter not connected with the fulfillment, execution, or enforcement of this contract as such. (c) He did not waive his undoubted right as an American citizen to apply to his Government for protection against the violation of international law (internationally illegal acts) whether growing out of this contract or out of other situations. (d) He did not and could not affect the right of his Government to extend to him its protection in general or to extend to him its protection against breaches of international law. But he did frankly and unreservedly agree that in consideration of the Government of Mexico awarding him this contract, he did not need and would not invoke or accept the assistance of his Government with respect to the fulfillment and interpretation of his contract and the execution of his work thereunder. The conception that a citizen in doing so impinges upon a sovereign, inalienable, unlimited right of his government belongs to those ages and countries which prohibited the giving up of his citizenship by a citizen or allowed him to relinquish it only with the special permission of his government.

It is quite true that this construction of article 18 of the contract does not effect complete equality between the foreigner subscribing the contract on the one hand and Mexicans on the other hand. Apart from the fact that equality of legal status between citizens and foreigners is by no means a requisite of international law — in some respects the citizen has greater rights and larger duties, in other respects the foreigner has — article 18 only purposes equality between the foreigner and Mexicans with respect to the execution, fulfillment, and interpretation of this contract and such limited equality is properly obtained.[25]

[25] *Ibid.*, pp. 27–28.

The commission then pointed out how the claimant had entirely ignored its legal obligation under the contract:

If it were necessary to demonstrate how legitimate are the fears of certain nations with respect to abuses of the right of protection and how seriously the sovereignty of those nations within their own boundaries would be impaired if some extreme conceptions of this right were recognized and enforced, the present case would furnish an illuminating example. The claimant, after having solemnly promised in writing that it would not ignore the local laws, remedies, and authorities, behaved from the very beginning as if article 18 of its contract had no existence in fact. It used the article to procure the contract, but this was the extent of its use. It has never sought any redress by application to the local authorities and remedies which article 18 liberally granted it and which, according to Mexican law, are available to it, even against the Government, without restrictions, both in matter of civil and of public law. It has gone so far as to declare itself freed from its contract obligations by its *ipse dixit* instead of having resort to the local tribunals to construe its contract and its rights thereunder. And it has gone so far as to declare that it was not bound by article 7 of the contract and to forcibly remove a dredge to which, under that article, the Government of Mexico considered itself entitled as security for the proper fulfillment of its contract with claimant. While its behavior during the spring and summer of 1914, the latter part of the Huerta administration, may be in part explained by the unhappy conditions of friction then existing between the two countries in connection with the military occupation of Veracruz by the United States, this explanation can not be extended from the year 1917 to the date of the filing of its claim before this Commission, during all of which time it has ignored the open doors of Mexican tribunals. The record before this Commission strongly suggests that the claimant used article 18 to procure the contract with no intention of ever observing its provisions.[26]

The commission next dealt with the very difficult problem of reconciling the upholding of the Calvo Clause obligation with the waiver of the local remedies rule in the convention:

Under article 18 of the contract declared upon the present claimant is precluded from presenting to its Government any

[26] *Ibid.*, p. 29.

claim relative to the interpretation or fulfillment of this contract. If it had a claim for denial of justice, for delay of justice or gross injustice, or for any other violation of international law committed by Mexico to its damage, it might have presented such a claim to its Government, which in turn could have espoused it and presented it here. Although the claim as presented falls within the first clause of Article I of the Treaty, describing claims coming within this Commission's jurisdiction, it is not a claim that may be rightfully presented by the claimant to its Government for espousal and hence is not cognizable here, pursuant to the latter part of paragraph 1 of the same Article I.

It is urged that the claim may be presented by claimant to its Government for espousal in view of the provision of Article V of the Treaty, to the effect "that no claim shall be disallowed or rejected by the Commission by the application of the general principle of international law that the legal remedies must be exhausted as a condition precedent to the validity or allowance of any claim." This provision is limited to the application of a general principle of international law to claims that may be presented to the Commission falling within the terms of Article I of the Treaty, and if under the terms of Article I the private claimant can not rightfully present its claim to its Government and the claim therefore can not become cognizable here, Article V does not apply to it, nor can it render the claim cognizable, nor does it entitle either Government to set aside an express valid contract between one of its citizens and the other Government.[27]

The commission then returned to the general effects of its interpretation of the Calvo Clause:

Manifestly it is impossible for this Commission to announce an all-embracing formula to determine the validity of all clauses partaking of the nature of the Calvo Clause, which may be found in contracts, decrees, statutes, or constitutions, and under widely varying conditions. Whenever such a provision is so phrased as to seek to preclude a Government from intervening, diplomatically or otherwise, to protect its citizen whose rights of any nature have been invaded by another Government in violation of the rules and principles of international law, the Commission will have no hesitation in pronouncing the provision void. Nor does this decision in any way apply to claims not based on

[27] *Ibid.*, pp. 30–31.

express contract provisions in writing and signed by the claimant or by one through whom the claimant has deraigned title to the particular claim. Nor will any provision in any constitution, statute, law, or decree, whatever its form, to which the claimant has not in some form expressly subscribed in writing, howsoever it may operate or affect his claim, preclude him from presenting his claim to his Government or the Government from espousing it and presenting it to this Commission for decision under the terms of the Treaty.

Even so, each case involving application of a valid clause partaking of the nature of the Calvo Clause will be considered and decided on its merits. Where a claim is based on an alleged violation of any rule or principle of international law, the Commission will take jurisdiction notwithstanding the existence of such a Clause in a contract subscribed by such claimant. But where a claimant has expressly agreed in writing, attested by his signature, that in all matters pertaining to the execution, fulfillment, and interpretation of the contract he will have resort to local tribunals, remedies, and authorities, and then wilfully ignores them by applying in such matters to his Government, he will be held bound by his contract and the Commission will not take jurisdiction of such claim.[28]

In conclusion, the commission summarized its considerations on the Calvo Clause as follows:

(a) The Treaty between the two Governments under which this Commission is constituted requires that a claim accruing before September 8, 1923, to fall within its jurisdiction must be that of a citizen of one Government against the other Government and must not only be espoused by the first Government and put forward by it before this Commission but, as a condition precedent to such espousal, must have been presented to it for its interposition by the private claimant.

(b) The question then arises, Has the private claimant in this case put itself in a position where it has the right to present its claim to the Government of the United States for its interposition? The answer to this question depends upon the construction to be given to article 18 of the contract on which the claim rests.

(c) In article 18 of the contract the claimant expressly agreed that in all matters connected with the execution of the work covered by the contract and the fulfillment of its contract obli-

[28] *Ibid.*, pp. 31–32.

gations and the enforcement of its contract rights it would be bound and governed by the laws of Mexico administered by the authorities and courts of Mexico and would not invoke or accept the assistance of his Government. Further than this it did not bind itself. Under the rules of international law the claimant (as well as the Government of Mexico) was without power to agree, and did not in fact agree, that the claimant would not request the Government of the United States, of which it was a citizen, to intervene in its behalf in the event of internationally illegal acts done to the claimant by the Mexican authorities.

(d) The contract declared upon, which was sought by claimant, would not have been awarded it without incorporating the substance of article 18 therein. The claimant does not pretend that it has made any attempt to comply with the terms of that article, which as here construed is binding on it. Therefore the claimant has not put itself in a position where it may rightfully present this claim to the Government of the United States for its interposition.

(e) While it is true that under Article V of the Treaty the two Governments have agreed "that no claim shall be disallowed or rejected by the Commission by the application of the general principle of international law that the legal remedies must be exhausted as a condition precedent to the validity or allowance of any claim," this provision is limited to claims falling under Article I and therefore rightfully presented by the claimant.

(f) If it were necessary to so construe article 18 of the contract as to bind the claimant not to apply to its Government to intervene diplomatically or otherwise in the event of a denial of justice to the claimant growing out of the contract declared upon or out of any other situation, then this Commission would have no hesitation in holding such a clause void *ab initio* and not binding on the claimant.

(g) The foregoing pertains to the power of the claimant to bind itself by contract. It is clear that the claimant could not under any circumstances bind its Government with respect to remedies for violations of international law.

(h) As the claimant voluntarily entered into a legal contract binding itself not to call as to this contract upon its Government to intervene in its behalf, and as all of its claim relates to this contract, and as therefore it can not present its claim to its Government for interposition or espousal before this Commission, the second ground of the motion to dismiss is sustained.[29]

[29] *Ibid.*, pp. 32–33.

Commissioner Parker, in a brief concurring opinion, accepted "as correct my fellow Commissioners' construction of Article 18 of the contract," and therefore concurred in the disposition of claim.[30] But Mr. Parker re-emphasized that the Calvo Clause thus interpreted would not prevent interposition in case of a denial of justice or violation of international law, pointing out that any attempt by contract to do this would be "void *ab initio* as repugnant to the rules and principles of international law." [31]

This is the essence of the opinion of the commission in the *North American Dredging* case. While, in my opinion, the *Dredging* case is by far the most important decision in the jurisprudence that has involved the Calvo Clause, and while it enjoys great authority because of its acceptance by statesmen and jurists, it is nevertheless not a well-reasoned or logically consistent decision. It represents an excellent example of the fact that technical weaknesses and logical inconsistencies do not necessarily destroy or even lessen the impact or influence of a decision.

One major weakness of the decision is the fact that the tribunal did not give sufficient attention to the precise nature of the acts of the Mexican government of which the company complained. The commission took the position that the claim was based on a breach of contract, an assumption that had an important bearing on its entire decision. Although the commission flatly stated that a Calvo Clause would not be effective in barring a claim based on a denial of justice, delay of justice, or any other violation of international law, it did not even discuss the documented allegations in the memorial that specifically charged that the losses sustained by the claimant were the result of violations of rules and principles of international law by the government of Mexico and its officials. Since these allegations were not challenged by Mexico in the pleadings, it would appear reasonable to expect the commission at least to examine them in its decision. It is, of course, the prerogative of the commission to determine the exact basis of the claim, but in the face of these uncontested allegations of internationally illegal acts, a more ex-

[30] *Ibid.*, p. 34.
[31] *Ibid.*

plicit determination was perhaps in order.[32] One may infer from
the language of the opinion that, in the viewpoint of the commission, the acts complained of, being related to the contract,
could not of themselves be regarded as international delinquen-
cies giving rise to a claim when a Calvo Clause is involved. They
could become such only in the event of a denial of justice in the
courts.[33] It would appear highly improper, however, to deal with
such an important point by implication. If the physical facts as
to the breach of contract as set forth in the uncontested memorial are taken at face value, there is impressive evidence of an
immediate denial of justice that might serve to obviate the
necessity to have recourse to the local courts. The commission
was definitely wrong in not dealing directly with this point.

A careful reading of the opinion of the commission will indicate various logical inconsistencies and instances in which the
commission undermined or contradicted its own reasoning.[34] The
commission had special trouble with its interpretation of the
Calvo Clause involved, and with reconciling this interpretation
with the explicit waiver of the local remedies rule in the *compromis*.

In regard to the interpretation of the Calvo Clause in the con-

[32] Several authorities have charged that the commission misinterpreted the
facts of the case in holding that the claim was based on breach of contract.
See, for example, Feller, *Mex. Claims Com.*, pp. 191–192; Hyde, *International
Law*, II, pp. 995–996.

[33] This interpretation is suggested by Dunn, *Diplomatic Protection of Americans in Mexico*, p. 410. This inference is borne out by the following statement
of the Mexican commissioner in the *International Fisheries* case, *Opinions of
Commissioners*, III, p. 220: "It is worthy of note that in this case as in that of
the *North American Dredging Company*, the American Agency maintained that
the question was not one of non-fulfillment of contract, but one of international delinquency incurred directly by the State, of a denial of justice, of a
wrongful act, and thus the Memorial of said claim spoke of interruptions to
the work owing to *arbitrary orders* given by Mexican Government officials, of
the *wrongful detention* of a dredge and its accessories, and of two launches
which were a total loss. Notwithstanding the aspect given to them by the
American Agency, the facts were held by this Commission to be matters relating to the contract to which the North American Dredging Company of Texas
was a party."

[34] For a scholarly criticism of the commission's logical consistency, see Feller,
Mex. Claims Com., pp. 187–192; Dunn, *Diplomatic Protection of Americans in
Mexico*, pp. 407–412.

tract, it must be remembered that the ultimate purpose of the Clause is to prohibit completely diplomatic interposition. An objective reading of Article 18 would certainly indicate that the language employed was designed to accomplish this purpose. The commission erroneously interpreted the language of the Clause very narrowly, holding that it merely required the claimant to seek redress in the courts of Mexico for any doubts or controversies arising out of the contract, and did not, and could not, ban interposition in case of internationally illegal acts.[35] This narrow interpretation of the broad phraseology of the Calvo Clause in question has been justifiably subjected to sharp criticism by publicists and jurists.[36]

From the language of the opinion it is apparent that the failure of the claimant to seek redress in the local courts weighed very heavily in the determination of the final outcome of the case. But the *compromis* explicitly relieved claimants of this obligation, and the commission experienced considerable difficulty in overcoming this hurdle. The commission ruled that while Article V waived the general principle of international law that requires the exhaustion of local remedies, this did not relieve the individual from his obligations under the Calvo Clause, and therefore he could not "rightfully" present his claim to his government until he had fulfilled his contractual commitment.[37]

[35] *Opinions of Commissioners*, I, p. 32.

[36] The American commissioner who served on the United States–Mexican Claims Commission when it later decided the *International Fisheries* case, Fred K. Nielsen, criticized in strong terms the construction of the Calvo Clause in the *Dredging* case. Mr. Nielsen, *ibid.*, III, p. 226, stated: "I consider that the Commission construed the language of the contractual provisions involved in that case in such a way as to give them a meaning entirely different from that which their language clearly reveals — a meaning not even contended for by Mexico. In order to do that the Commission resorted to both elimination, substitution and rearrangement of language of the contractual provisions." Feller, *Mex. Claims Com.*, pp. 188–189, calls the commission's interpretation of Article 18 "a rather disingenuous construction" and a "perversion of language." See also Dunn, *Diplomatic Protection of Americans in Mexico*, pp. 409–412; De Beus, *op. cit.*, pp. 68–69.

[37] In the case of *Rep. française (Georges Pinson) v. Etats-Unis mexicains, Jurisprudence de la Commission Franco-Mexicaine des Réclamations, 1924–1932* (Paris, 1933), pp. 1–40, at p. 24, the commission president, J. H. W. Verzijl, speaking for the commission, ruled, by way of *obiter*, that a similar provision

Legal scholars are in general agreement that this is not the proper interpretation of Article V.[38]

We see, then, that the decision in the *North American Dredging Company of Texas* case is not free from the defects that have so often characterized the treatment of the problem of the Calvo Clause by international tribunals. The decision taken as a whole suffers from inconsistent and illogical reasoning and from the loose treatment of the facts and of Article V. These features of the case have attracted the critical attention of the publicists, who, on the whole, have tended to discount the authority of the case because of the technical weaknesses. However, the practical significance of these criticisms is lessened because of the acceptance of the case as "good law" by a number of states and by succeeding arbitral commissions.[39] As has been pointed out before, approval or rejection of a judicial ruling by the publicists, however learned, is not nearly so useful in determining the rule of law on a given concept as the attitude of governments and of international tribunals. Consequently, the most important task in analyzing the *Dredging* case is not a detailed review of these scholarly criticisms, but rather the determination of the precise rule set forth by the commission, and the impact of this rule on the problem under consideration.

in the French-Mexican Convention explicitly excluded the principle of the Calvo Clause, asserting: "La contexte dans lequel l'équité figure à l'article VI est tout autre, à savoir la stipulation qui exclut expressément, pour le jugement des présentes réclamations, le principe de la nommée 'clause Calvo' aux termes suivants: 'Le Gouvernement du Mexique étant désireux d'arriver à un règlement équitable des réclamations définies à l'article III ci-dessus, et d'accorder aux intéresés une indemnité juste, qui corresponde aux pertes et dommages subis, il est convenu que la Commission ne devra écarter ou rejeter aucune réclamation pour le motif que les recours légaux n'auraient pas été épuisés avant présentation de ladite réclamation.' "

[38] E.g., Lipstein, *op. cit.*, p. 145; Feller, *Mex. Claims Com.*, pp. 189–191; Borchard, "Decisions of the Claims Commissions, United States and Mexico," *AJIL*, XX (July 1926), p. 540; Dunn, *Diplomatic Protection of Americans in Mexico*, p. 411. Nielsen in *International Fisheries* case, *Opinions of Commissioners*, III, pp. 227–228, 267–269, points out that jurisdiction is determined only by the *compromis*, and not by the rules of international law. Consequently, the express terms of the *compromis* should be determinative in dealing with a Calvo Clause if it comes before the commission as a question of jurisdiction.

[39] *Infra*, pp. 228–229, 231–255.

The North American Dredging Company Case

The Rule of Law of the *Dredging* Case

In the examination of the decisional law that has involved the Calvo Clause, the main objective has been to determine precisely what role, if any, the Clause played in the final disposition of each case. To accomplish this, we have asked in each case whether the Calvo Clause itself served to bar a claim that would have been otherwise admissible in its absence. In the arbitral jurisprudence before 1926 we discovered no decision in which the Clause per se actually barred a claim, and hence we concluded that the Clause did not have any legally meaningful validity in the international arbitral jurisprudence of this period.

In the *Dredging* case, however, by this same criterion, the Clause, for the first time, is found to have played a legally significant role in determining the final outcome of the case. In the absence of the Calvo Clause, jurisdiction would have been accepted. The Calvo Clause, and only the Calvo Clause, was the basis on which the commission unanimously held that the claim was not admissible. To be sure, local remedies had not been exhausted, and perhaps it might be asserted that this failure, and not the contractual stipulation, actually barred the claim. But it must not be overlooked that the convention, in Article V, had explicitly provided that claims were not to be rejected because of the failure to exhaust local remedies. Furthermore, this same commission had readily taken jurisdiction of claims based on contract and made awards on them without regard to whether local remedies had been pursued or not.[40] Consequently, it would appear that the Clause did actually serve to bar a claim that would have been otherwise receivable, and therefore, did realize a degree of validity in international decisional law.

The difficulty is to determine just what this degree of validity is, and what rule the commission formulated in order to support its recognition of the limited validity of the Calvo Clause.

It might be well to repeat for emphasis that the commission

---

[40] See the opinion of the commission in the *Illinois Central Railroad* case, *Opinions of Commissioners*, I, p. 20, where it was asserted: "The Commission has no hesitation in rejecting the contention that while under Article V the legal remedies need not be 'exhausted' some resort must nevertheless be had

rejected in no uncertain terms the full validity of the Calvo Clause as a complete bar to diplomatic interposition under all circumstances. The commission, probably erroneously,[41] interpreted the Calvo Clause narrowly, as a promise to seek redress for grievances in the local courts, and explicitly stated that the renunciatory provision would not bind the state from intervening in case of a denial of justice or breach of some generally recognized rule of international law. Although some Latin American lawyers have argued that this case did uphold the complete validity of the Calvo Clause,[42] the language of the decision definitely does not support this contention.[43]

It is equally clear that the rule of the *Dredging* case does not support the contention of many publicists that the Clause is illegal, futile, or superfluous.[44] The Clause, according to the commission, is not opposed to any rule of international law, and it certainly cannot be considered superfluous or futile if it actually served to bar a claim that would have been admissible in its absence.

Consequently, the rule of law in the instant case would appear to be somewhere in between the two extreme views. The Clause

to the local tribunals before the claim can be so impressed with an international character as to confer jurisdiction on this Commission."

[41] *Supra*, pp. 212–213. See also Freeman, *Denial of Justice*, pp. 488–489.

[42] Several Latin American delegates took this position at the Third Inter-American Bar Association meeting. See *supra*, pp. 90–93; "Note," *Journal of Comparative Legislation and International Law* (3rd Series, XXV, 1944), p. 58. Podestá Costa, "La responsabilidad internacional del estado," *Cursos Monográficos*, II (1952), p. 215, asserts that this case was one in which the commission pronounced for the validity of the Calvo Clause.

[43] Commissioner van Vollenhoven, "La jurisprudence de la Commission générale de réclamations entre les États-Unis d'Amérique et le Mexique, en 1926," *Bulletin de L'Institut intermédiaire international*, XVI (1927), p. 238, emphatically states this point. See also G. Godfrey Phillips, "The Anglo-Mexican Special Claims Commission," *Law Quarterly Review* (April 1933), p. 235. Many Latin American publicists have strongly criticized the commission for its failure to take a forthright stand in favor of the full validity of the Clause. See, for example, Gómez Robledo, *op. cit.*, p. 176; Beteta and Henríquez, *op. cit.*, pp. 44–45; Sepúlveda Gutiérrez, *op. cit.*, pp. 69–71.

[44] For example, Briggs, *The Law of Nations* (2nd ed., 1952), pp. 648–649, declared that the Clause is still either "superfluous" or "irrelevant." For nearly identical statements, see Eagleton, *Resp. of States*, p. 175; Borchard, *Dip. Prot.*, pp. 809–810; Lipstein, *op. cit.*, p. 145; Alf Ross, *op. cit.*, p. 265.

was held to be neither completely valid nor completely invalid. The commission formulated the rule of the limited validity for the Calvo Clause which served as somewhat of a compromise on the issue of the validity of the contractual renunciation of diplomatic protection.[45]

A great many of the leading authorities have interpreted the rule of the *Dredging* case very narrowly as being merely a restatement of the local remedies rule, arguing that the Clause had validity and effect only to the extent that it coincided with the usual requirement of international law that local remedies must be exhausted before seeking diplomatic intervention or submitting a claim to an international tribunal.[46] To these observers, the instant case did nothing to change their opinion about the superfluity of the Clause as interpreted by this commission.[47] But this appraisal of the *Dredging* case does not give sufficient attention to the specific waiver of the local remedies rule in the convention. If, in the opinion of the commission, the Clause had been merely a restatement of the local remedies rule, then Article V of the convention should certainly have been determinative and have operated to nullify the Calvo Clause. It would therefore appear clear that the rule of the *Dredging* case is considerably more than that the Calvo Clause merely restates the local remedies rule. The true importance of the case lies in the fact that the commission held that the Clause was binding on the individual in that it precluded him from presenting to

[45] This desire to reach a compromise between the two extreme views is suggested by the following quotation, *Opinions of Commissioners*, I, p. 23: "The Commission does not feel impressed by arguments either in favor of or in opposition to the Calvo Clause, in so far as these arguments go to extremes." H. F. Alfaro, presiding commissioner when this same commission decided the *International Fisheries* case, stated (*Opinions of Commissioners*, III, p. 223): "The decision mentioned [*Dredging*], establishes therefore a just and reasonable middle ground."

[46] Borchard, "Decisions of the Claims Commissions, United States and Mexico," *AJIL*, XX (July 1926), p. 539, asserts: "Whether this decision on the Calvo Clause does anything more than state a commonly acknowledged rule of international law seems doubtful." Feller, *Mex. Claims Com.*, p. 192, states that the *Dredging* case, "in effect, is nothing more than a restatement of the well-settled rule that local remedies must be exhausted."

[47] E.g., Eagleton, *Resp. of States*, pp. 168, 175.

his government any claim connected with the contract, but not binding on his state in that it would not prevent his government from espousing a claim based on the violation of international law. This is the rule which, because of its acceptance (and extension) by later tribunals and because it is compatible with the attitude of many of the leading nations, is, in my opinion, the rule of law on the Calvo Clause.

That this is actually the rule of law of the *Dredging* case can be substantiated by reference to the opinion itself, by the way in which the *Dredging* rule was interpreted and applied by later tribunals, and by reference to the analyses of authorities who have studied this problem recently.

The previously quoted passages from the commission's opinion clearly show that the rule formulated was that the Clause was binding on the individual but not on his state in the event of a violation of international law. It might be well at this point, however, to repeat some of the salient passages to document this contention.

The commission, having declared that it "denies that the rules of international public law apply only to nations and that individuals can not under any circumstances have a personal standing under it," [48] stated that, to declare the Clause void, it must be proven that there exists a generally accepted rule of international law that condemns the Calvo Clause and denies "to an individual the right to relinquish to any extent, large or small, and under any circumstances or conditions, the protection of the government to which he owes allegiance." [49] Having declared that no such rule exists,[50] the commission held that by the Calvo Clause commitment "the *present claimant is precluded from presenting to its Government* any claim relative to the interpretation or fulfillment of this contract." [51] The claimant, because it violated its contractual renunciatory provision, "has not put

[48] *Opinions of Commissioners,* I, pp. 23–24.
[49] *Ibid.,* p. 24.
[50] *Ibid.,* p. 25.
[51] *Ibid.,* p. 30. Italics mine. The commission distinguished between "(1) the presentation by the citizen of a claim to his Government and (2) the espousal of such claim by that Government." *Ibid.*

itself in a position where it may *rightfully* present this claim to the Government of the United States for its interposition." [52] The commission, in concluding its decision, once again enunciated this principle, stating:

As the claimant voluntarily entered into a legal contract binding itself not to call as to this contract upon its Government to intervene in its behalf, and as all of its claim relates to this contract, and as therefore *it can not present its claim to its Government* for interposition or espousal before this Commission, the second ground of the motion to dismiss [the Calvo Clause] is sustained. [53]

It would appear clear that the rule of the case, as evidenced by these quotations, is that an individual is legally bound by his Calvo Clause commitment. But the commission made it equally clear that the state would not be bound by this contractual agreement to which it was not a party. The commission stated: "The foregoing pertains to the power of the claimant to bind itself by contract. It is clear that the claimant could not under any circumstances bind its Government with respect to remedies for violations of international law." [54]

The fact that this is the actual rule of the case is further evidenced by the interpretation and application of the *Dredging* rule by later tribunals. While these decisions will be analyzed in detail in the next chapter, it is desirable to illustrate this point here by reference to the decision of the Anglo-Mexican Claims Commission in the *Mexican Union Railway* case. [55] In this case, the commission, specifically asserting that it concurred in the analyses of the *Dredging* case, "not thinking it necessary to repeat them, or possible to express them better," [56] applied this limited validity formula and held the Calvo Clause binding on the individual, thus barring him from presenting the claim to his government, [57] although not binding on his state with respect to

---

[52] *Ibid.*, pp. 32–33. Italics mine.
[53] *Ibid.*, p. 33. Italics mine.
[54] *Ibid.*
[55] *Decisions and Opinions of the Commissioners*, pp. 157–175.
[56] *Ibid.*, p. 160.
[57] *Ibid.*, pp. 162–163.

remedies for violations of international law.[58] One passage of the opinion [59] illustrates how the commission, applying what in its opinion was the real rule of the *Dredging* case, held that the Clause was binding on the individual who signed it. The commission asserted:

By this contract the claimant has solemnly promised *not to apply* to his Government for diplomatic intervention but to resort to the municipal courts. He has waived the right upon which the claim is now presented. *He has precluded himself* by his contract *from taking the initiative,* without which his claim can have no standing before this Commission and can not be recognizable. *Quite apart from the right of the British Government, his claim is such that it can not be pursued before . . . this Commission . . .*[60]

If there is still some doubt that this is in fact the rule of the *Dredging* decision, reference should be made to the analysis of the United Nations Secretariat's Legal Department which compiled the recently published fourth volume of the United Nations' *Reports of International Arbitral Awards.* In reporting the commission's decision in the *Dredging* case, the Legal Department summarized the rule of this case as follows:

A Calvo Clause *held* to bar claimant from presenting to his Government any claim connected with the contract in which it appeared and hence to place any such claim beyond the jurisdiction of the tribunal. The Clause will not preclude his Government from espousing, or the tribunal from considering, other claims based on the violation of international law. Article V of the *compromis held* not to prevent the foregoing result.[61]

---

[58] *Ibid.,* p. 164.

[59] This decision is discussed in detail, *infra,* pp. 240–247.

[60] *Decisions and Opinions of the Commissioners,* p. 163. Italics mine. Analysis of the other cases that have followed the *Dredging* rule will further indicate that this is the rule of law of the *Dredging* case. See *infra,* Chapter VIII.

[61] United Nations, *Reports of International Arbitral Awards,* IV (1952), p. 26. A very few publicists have recognized this to be the rule of law of the instant case. Summers, *op. cit.,* pp. 472–473, summarized the rule: "Briefly, it is that the individual can renounce the right to invoke diplomatic protection in so far as he himself is concerned (except in the case of denial of justice) but this renunciation will not have any effect on his Government which will always have the right to intervene if it deems it to be to its best interests to do so." See the interpretation of the *Dredging* rule by Great Britain, *supra,* p. 50.

The North American Dredging Company Case

This then is the rule of the *Dredging* case. It should be noted that this formula is not particularly new, having been enunciated in two former arbitrations that involved the Calvo Clause. Although the commission decided the case *de novo*, and did not refer to precedent, it might well have cited the *Nitrate* case [62] and the *Woodruff* case [63] as authority for its ruling. In both these cases, the respective commissions had ruled that no principle of international law prevented an alien from legally committing himself to seek redress for his grievances in the local courts, which promise would preclude him from seeking the interposition of his government in violation of this contractual obligation. As in the instant case, the commissions asserted that such an agreement would not, of course, bind the government itself from intervening in the event of some internationally illegal action such as a denial of justice. The main difference between the *Dredging* case and these previous rulings is that in the instant case the application of this rule actually served to bar a claim that would have been otherwise receivable, which was not the case in the earlier arbitrations.[64] Thus this rule, although not new, received vitality and meaningful legal significance for the first time in the *Dredging* decision.

It should also be noted that this rule of limited validity is compatible with the attitudes taken by many of the leading nations of the world toward the Calvo Clause. While the actual attitudes of the nations toward the *Dredging* case itself will be considered below,[65] it is relevant to point out here that the United States, Great Britain, Mexico, and other nations have, in their official declarations, apparently indicated a willingness to accept the Clause as binding on the individual (except in case of denial of justice) though not upon his state.[66]

[62] *Supra*, pp. 148–152.
[63] *Supra*, pp. 169–171.
[64] *Supra*, pp. 151–152, 171.
[65] Pp. 228–229.
[66] The attitude of the nations of the world toward the Calvo Clause, with special reference to their position on this rule of limited validity that holds the Clause binding on the individual but not upon his state, was detailed *supra*, Chapters III and IV. See especially pp. 44–45, 54–55. G. H. Stuart, *op. cit.*,

The commission in the *Dredging* case, in formulating this rule, distinguished between the right of the state to intervene, which is unaffected by the Calvo Clause, and the right of the individual to seek the intervention of his state, which the Clause prohibits except where there is a violation of international law. This clearly indicates that the commission had to look behind the actual presentation of the claim to see whether it had been "rightfully" presented by the claimant to his government. The commission did so in the instant case, stating:

. . . But it is urged that when a Government espouses and presents a claim here, the private interest in the claim is merged in the Nation in the sense that the private interest is entirely eliminated and the claim is a national claim, and that therefore this Commission can not look behind the act of the Government espousing it to discover the private interest therein or to ascertain whether or not the private claimant has presented or may rightfully present the claim to his Government for interposition. This view is rejected by the Commission . . .[67]

There is no doubt that this rule of limited validity is difficult to apply, and in one way at least, would appear to be contradictory. If it does not bind the state, does it actually have any real meaning? On the other hand, if it binds the individual not to seek redress from his government, does not the Clause in turn actually serve to bind the state in the sense that it prevents the state from sponsoring a claim that was "wrongfully" presented

pp. 176–177, asserts that "a compromise seems to have been reached" in the correspondence between the United States and Mexico in relation to the agrarian and petroleum laws promulgated by President Calles that involved the validity of the Calvo Clause when Mexico admitted the right of the United States to intervene diplomatically but denied to the individual, who had signed the Clause, the right to invoke such protection on his own initiative. See *supra*, pp. 44–45. The message of the secretary of state to the president on March 27, 1908 (quoted as the official position of the State Department toward the validity of the Calvo Clause in a letter to me, dated February 13, 1953) asserted: "It is true that the claimant company itself waived all rights of diplomatic intervention as far as it was concerned, but an unaccredited agent may not renounce the right or privilege of the Government . . ." See *supra*, pp. 41–42. This would appear to put the United States in agreement with the rule of the *Dredging* case. The acceptance of this principle by the leading nations of the world is, of course, of great significance in determining whether the rule of the instant case is actually the rule of law on the Calvo Clause.

[67] *Opinions of Commissioners*, I, p. 30.

in violation of the Calvo Clause stipulation? The apparent inconsistency and contradiction involved in the rule led the Harvard Research study to comment: "While some arbitrators . . . seem to have evolved the rule that the Clause is binding upon the claimant, but not on his Government, it is difficult to see how such an inconsistent rule can be applied . . ." [68]

The precise content and effect of the rule of the *Dredging* case will be analyzed in a later chapter.[69] It suffices to state at this point that this rule is by no means ineffective as evidenced by the fact that its application has served to bar claims in five recent cases that would have been receivable in its absence.[70]

The Commission's Discussion of the Role of the Individual in International Law

An extremely important part of the commission's opinion in the *Dredging* case dealt with the emerging role of the individual in international law. It is highly significant that the first tribunal to accord any real degree of validity to the Calvo Clause was also the first tribunal, in the words of Lionel Summers, "to pronounce itself in favor of the individual." [71]

Although the significance of the commission's reference to the role of the individual has escaped the attention of nearly all United States, European, and even Latin American publicists,[72] it is noteworthy that the commission prefaced its entire treatment of the "Lawfulness of the Calvo Clause" [73] with a strong assertion that an individual does have a personal standing under international law and with a brief discussion of the changing nature of international intercourse and the corresponding developments in international law. The following key passage of the opinion is worth repeating:

[68] *AJIL*, XXIII, Special Number (1929), p. 215.
[69] *Infra*, Chapter IX.
[70] *Infra*, Chapter VIII.
[71] *Op. cit.*, p. 474.
[72] The exceptions would be Summers, *op. cit.*, pp. 473–474, and Schwarzenberger, *op. cit.*, p. 65. This part of the *Dredging* opinion was reprinted in *Annual Digest* (1925–1926), pp. 261–262, under the section entitled "Position of Individual in International Law."
[73] *Opinions of Commissioners*, I, pp. 24–26.

The Commission also denies that the rules of international public law apply only to nations and that individuals can not under any circumstances have a personal standing under it. As illustrating the antiquated character of this thesis it may suffice to point out that in Article 4 of the unratified International Prize Court Convention adopted at the Hague in 1907 and signed by both the United States and Mexico and by 29 other nations this conception, so far as was ever held, was repudiated.

It is well known how largely the increase of civilization, intercourse, and interdependence as between nations has influenced and moderated the exaggerated conception of national sovereignty. As civilization has progressed individualism has increased; and so has the right of the individual citizen to decide upon the ties between himself and his native country. There was a time when governments and not individuals decided if a man was allowed to change his nationality or his residence, and when even if he had changed either of them his government sought to lay burdens on him for having done so. To acknowledge that under the existing laws of progressive, enlightened civilization a person may voluntarily expatriate himself but that short of expatriation he may not by contract, in what he conceives to be his own interest, to any extent loosen the ties which bind him to his country is neither consistent with the facts of modern international intercourse *nor with corresponding developments in the field of international law* and does not tend to promote good will among nations.[74]

The fact that the commission prefaced its recognition of the limited validity of the Calvo Clause with its recognition of the limited emergence of the individual as a subject of international law indicates the close correlation between these two important developments in the minds of the commissioners. The evidence of the role of the individual as a subject of international law was

[74] *Ibid.*, pp. 23–24. Italics mine. Article 4 of the Convention Relative to the Creation of an International Prize Court read: "An appeal may be brought — (1) By a neutral Power . . . (2) By a neutral individual, if the judgment of the national court injuriously affects his property, subject, however, to the reservation that the Power to which he belongs may forbid him to bring the case before the Court, or may itself undertake the proceedings in his place. (3) By an individual subject or citizen of an enemy Power, if the judgment of the national court injuriously affects his property in the cases referred . . ." See Scott, *The Hague Conventions and Declarations of 1889 and 1907*, p. 189.

scanty and perhaps even questionable in 1926.[75] However, such evidence is much more impressive today, and one is led to wonder whether the rather hesitant and qualified statements of the commission would not be much more positive, detailed, and documented if written in 1955.[76]

It should be noted that the commission not only theorized about the possible role of the individual under international law, but actually used its belief in the status of the individual as one of the grounds for upholding the limited validity of the Calvo Clause. The action of the individual in agreeing to seek redress for his grievances in the local courts was held to be determinative in spite of the action of the states in waiving this requirement in the convention.[77] Although theoretically the state is the only claimant, the commission, acting on the premise that the state is not the only subject of international law, took into consideration the fact that the individual does have status under this law and does possess rights and duties, and thus can be held to the obligation of his contractual commitment by an interna-

[75] Although the argument of the commission that since an individual can break his ties of nationality he can consequently loosen them in his own interests has been supported by Latin American authorities (e.g., García Robles, *op. cit.*, p. 18; Gonzalez, *op. cit.*, p. 36), it has been generally criticized by publicists. De Beus, *op. cit.*, p. 70, states that "even if the individual *should* have the right to expatriate himself, thereby destroying entirely the ties linking him to his State, it does not necessarily follow that he would also have the right to *loosen those ties to a certain extent*. Nationality implies a number of mutual rights and obligations between the State and the national, and even if the latter would be entitled to throw off the whole complex of these rights and obligations in its entirety, this would not necessarily imply his right to diminish certain of these rights and obligations as he would please." In regard to the commission's reliance on the International Prize Court Convention, Nielsen quite soundly questioned the importance of an unratified treaty as *proof* of the adoption of a rule. Nielsen also questioned the commission's interpretation of this convention. See his dissent in the *International Fisheries* case, *Opinions of Commissioners*, III, pp. 252–253.

[76] See *infra*, pp. 284–286.

[77] Borchard, *Encyclopaedia of the Social Sciences*, III (1930), p. 155, stated that the Calvo Clause had the effect of "canceling in these cases the waiver of the treaty." Thus it would appear that the action of the individual in the Calvo Clause is in a sense superior to the action of the state in the treaty. See Freeman, *Denial of Justice*, pp. 481–482. The commission would have been faced with a different and difficult situation if the waiver in the *compromis* had included a specific reference to the Calvo Clause. It is extremely doubtful, however, that Latin American states would ever agree to such a provision.

tional tribunal.[78] The action of the individual was actually held to circumvent the action of the states in the convention, which certainly would appear to give great emphasis and weight to the position of the individual in international law.

The commission's recognition of the limited role of the individual in international law materially contributed to the basis for its recognition of the limited validity of the Calvo Clause as binding on the individual though not on his state. It should not be forgotten that full recognition of the individual as a subject of international law, and not a mere object, would in turn win recognition of the full validity of the Calvo Clause.[79] This close relationship between the Calvo Clause and the role of the individual in international law will be discussed in greater detail in Chapter IX when the present status and the future of the Clause is considered.[80]

Impact and Influence of the *Dredging* Case

On the whole, as was indicated previously, the leading publicists of the United States and Europe have been quite critical of the commission's decision in the *Dredging* case. Most of the criticisms are directed at more or less technical considerations of the case,[81] although some authorities have condemned the opinion

---

[78] Feller, *Mex. Claims Com.*, p. 199, asserts that "the law of international claims is replete with inherent contradictions, rules which do take into account the position of the individual claimant in spite of the fact that the state is theoretically the only claimant." If a claim before an international tribunal were exclusively a public claim presented by the government, then, of course, the individual's contractual waiver would be of no import whatsoever, and the Calvo Clause would be dead. See also Summers, *op. cit.*, p. 475; Ralston, *Int. Trib.*, p. 138.

[79] Gómez Robledo, *op. cit.*, pp. 173–174; Jessup, *op. cit.*, p. 111. It is interesting to note that the *Dredging* opinion roughly coincided with the first pioneer studies regarding the true role of the individual under international law. See H. Lauterpacht, *International Law and Human Rights* (New York, 1950), pp. 6–7.

[80] *Infra*, pp. 282–286.

[81] Most of these criticisms have been noted in our discussion of the case. However, a brief résumé might be appropriate at this point. C. C. Hyde, *International Law*, II, pp. 995–996, criticized the commission for failure to take heed of the precise acts on which the claim was based and failure to interpret the *compromis* correctly. The first of these criticisms is echoed by Feller, *Mex. Claims Com.*, pp. 191–192. The latter criticism is endorsed by Borchard, "De-

The North American Dredging Company Case

en toto.[82] Even Latin American publicists have been critical of the commission's ruling, although they consider it a step in the right direction.[83] But it should be noted that not all authorities are critical of the case, and many, especially those who have studied this problem recently, have accepted the decision as good law.[84]

cisions of the Claims Commissions, United States and Mexico," *AJIL*, XX (July 1926), pp. 539–540, who states that the conclusion of the commission on Article V "is not altogether convincing," and by Freeman, *Denial of Justice*, pp. 481–482. In regard to this first objection, while the commission is properly subject to criticism for not examining the facts more closely, its action would suggest that a denial of justice must be flagrant and patent in order to overcome a Calvo Clause commitment to seek redress in the local courts. In regard to the second objection, it should be noted that the publicists who are most critical of the commission's interpretation and application of the convention have not, it would appear, recognized the true rule of the case, nor have they given sufficient attention to the fact that the commission was basing its decision at least partly on what it understood to be the "new" developments in international law which, in the eyes of the commissioners, permitted them to give greater weight and influence to the actions of the individual.

[82] Dunn, *Diplomatic Protection of Americans in Mexico*, p. 408, describes the opinion as a "long and involved course of reasoning . . . marked by various logical inconsistencies and can not be said to have clarified the situation in regard to Calvo Clauses to any great extent." The most vigorous and unrestrained criticism of the case was made by Commissioner Nielsen in his dissent in the *International Fisheries Company* case, *Opinions of Commissioners*, III, pp. 225–286. Mr. Nielsen, at times becoming excessively vitriolic, asserted: "I am constrained to say that the opinion contains nothing of any consequence with which I agree" (p. 226) and referred to "the utter lack of any basis in law for any conclusion submitted in the former opinion" (p. 226). Furthermore, Mr. Nielsen stated, "the most casual examination into abundantly available evidence of the law disproves those conclusions [i.e., of the *Dredging* opinion]. The Commission did not concern itself with any such evidence" (p. 227). The essence of this dissent will be examined *infra*, pp. 236–239.

[83] See Gómez Robledo, *op. cit.*, p. 176, who calls the decision "awkward," "timid," and a "political solution." Sepúlveda Gutiérrez, *op cit.*, pp. 69–71, criticizes the long and complicated reasoning of the commission and its failure to enunciate a general rule upholding the full validity of the Calvo Clause. See also Beteta and Henríquez, *op. cit.*, p. 45.

[84] Thus J. W. Garner, "Decisions of the American Mexican Mixed Claims Commissions," *BYIL* (1927), p. 182, comments that the *Dredging* decision "is in accord with the general jurisprudence of arbitral commissions . . ." Sir John H. Percival, *op. cit.*, p. 103, describes the opinion in the instant case as "careful and learned." Schwarzenberger, *op. cit.*, p. 66, asserts that this decision is "fully in accordance with the . . . general principles enunciated by the Permanent Court of International Justice, and fills a gap in international jurisprudence in the important topic of international economic law." De Beus, *op. cit.*, p. 83, states his agreement with the decision of the commission in upholding the limited validity of the Calvo Clause, although he takes issue with several points of the commission's

While the critics of the *Dredging* opinion have argued that its technical weaknesses greatly lessen its impact and influence,[85] these criticisms, even if warrantable and taken at face value, do not necessarily weaken the importance of the case or of its rule. This would not be the first time a bad case has become good law.

Furthermore, the *Dredging* opinion was specifically cited and followed in all subsequent Calvo Clause cases that came before the United States–Mexican and British-Mexican Claims commissions, thus giving the decision and its rule of law a prestige and precedential impact hitherto entirely lacking in the jurisprudence involving the Calvo Clause.[86] As has been pointed out before, the *Dredging* decision was specifically cited by Great Britain, India, and New Zealand as the basis for their replies to the League Codification Questionnaire on the validity of the Calvo Clause. The United States also cited this decision in its reply to the same questionnaire.[87] Great Britain's reply is worth repeating:

His Majesty's Government in Great Britain *accepts as good law and are content to be guided by* the decision of the Claims Commission between the United States of America and Mexico in the case of the *North American Dredging Company of Texas* . . . It is laid down in this opinion that a stipulation in a contract which purports to bind the claimant not to apply to his Government to intervene diplomatically or otherwise in the event of a denial or delay of justice or in the event of any violation of the rules or principles of international law is void, and that any stipulation which purports to bind the claimant's Government not to intervene in respect of violations of international law is void, but that *no rule of international law prevents the inclusion* of a stipulation in a contract between a Government and

reasoning. Summers, *op. cit.*, p. 473, asserts that "in theory it is hard to object to the decision."

[85] Feller, "Some Observations on the Calvo Clause," *AJIL*, XXVII (July 1933), p. 461, asserts that a critique of the *Dredging* case in its own terms and on the basis of the reasoning behind it, "results in a substantial diminution of . . . [its] value for the development of international law." Hyde, *International Law*, II, p. 996, n. 7, states that the misinterpretation of the facts and the *compromis* will "lessen the importance of the decision which was not responsive to what the record adduced."

[86] See *infra*, Chapter VIII.

[87] *Supra*, pp. 40, 50–52.

an alien that in all matters pertaining to the contract *the jurisdiction of the local tribunals shall be complete and exclusive,*
nor does it prevent such a stipulation *being obligatory,* in the
absence of any special agreement to the contrary between the
two Governments concerned, *upon any international tribunal* to
which may be submitted a claim arising out of the contract in
which the stipulation was inserted.[88]

Thus did Great Britain explicitly accept not only the case itself
but also the interpretation of its rule as holding the Clause binding on the individual although not on his state in case of a violation of the rules of international law.

It is clear that the *Dredging* case, though criticized by publicists, has won acceptance before judicial tribunals and in foreign offices. It is definitely the landmark case in the international
arbitral jurisprudence that has involved the Calvo Clause. The
commission formulated the rule of the limited validity of the
Calvo Clause as binding on the individual in that it precluded
him from presenting to his government any claim connected
with the contract though not binding on his state, and, moreover,
gave this rule vitality and legally meaningful significance by applying it to the instant case with the result that it actually served
to bar a claim that would have been admissible if the Clause had
not existed.

No case before the *Dredging* opinion really tested the validity
of the Calvo Clause, for in no case was its validity either denied
as such or upheld as such in the sense that it, and it alone, prevented the submission of an international claim. Consequently,
the search for the rule of law on the Calvo Clause must be restricted to the *Dredging* case and after, and this rule of limited
validity formulated by this commission and accepted by subsequent tribunals and by a representative number of governments
must be recognized as the rule of law on the Calvo Clause.[89]

[88] *Bases of Discussion,* p. 134. Italics mine. India and New Zealand associated
themselves with this reply. The replies of a majority of the states to this questionnaire would appear to be in accord with the *Dredging* rule. See *supra,* pp.
54–56.

[89] It is interesting to note, in the form of a postscript to this chapter, that

The Calvo Clause

It is now necessary to turn attention to the arbitrations that have involved the validity of the Calvo Clause after the *Dredging* case and then to determine as precisely as possible the full content and legal significance of this rule of law on the Calvo Clause, as well as the present status and possible future evolution of this concept in international diplomacy and jurisprudence.

the North American Dredging Company finally did win an award of $128,627.77 for damages claimed in the present litigation. The United States national commission set up under the "Settlement of Mexican Claims Act of 1942" to settle claims and disperse the forty million dollars paid by Mexico as a lump sum settlement of all claims of American citizens against Mexico up to 1940, "reheard" the Dredging Company claim in 1947 and held: "[With] all due deference to the learned members of said [United States–Mexican] Commission, we are unable to agree with the position thus taken. In our view, Article V of the Convention of September 8, 1923, is controlling as to the right of the United States Government; that pursuant thereto said Government may present this claim on behalf of the claimant, and that this Commission has jurisdiction to decide the claim. . . . After a careful consideration of the facts involved herein and the authorities applicable thereto, we are led to conclude that the provisions of clause 18 of the contract did not curtail the right of the General Claims Commission to pass upon the merits of the claim presented . . . The right to present this claim is controlled by the provisions of Article V . . . [and therefore] there exists no reason for considering the question as to whether the claimant has exhausted legal remedies, since said Article specifically provides that no claim shall be disallowed or rejected by the Commission for failure to exhaust such legal remedies." See *American Mexican Claims Commission. Report to the Secretary of State* (Washington, D.C., 1948), pp. 298–305; Briggs, "The Settlement of Mexican Claims Act of 1942," *AJIL*, XXXVII (April 1943), pp. 222–232. Although, from the purely financial viewpoint of the claimant, this might be considered a reversal of the previous ruling on the claim, it would be erroneous to assume that this action by a purely national commission could, in any manner whatsoever, overrule or even weaken the decision or rule of the *Dredging* case in international jurisprudence. From the viewpoint of this study, the action of the domestic commission is of interest but of no determinative import to our task of determining the rule of law on the Calvo Clause.

Arbitral Decisions Involving the
Calvo Clause since 1926

THE true significance and impact of the *Dredging* case is evidenced by the marked influence that it has had on subsequent adjudications that have involved the Calvo Clause. The Clause has figured in seven international arbitrations since the 1926 decision, all coming before the various Mexican claims commissions in the second and third decades of this century.

The approach in analyzing this decisional law will be the same method used previously. In each case, the objective will be to determine the precise degree of effectiveness accorded to the Calvo Clause, and also the rule formulated as the basis for the decision. The same criterion of meaningful validity will be employed — did the Clause actually serve to bar an international claim that would have been admissible in its absence.

Further Opinions of the United States
and Mexican Claims Commission

The United States and Mexican Claims Commission that handed down the momentous decision in the *Dredging* case had another opportunity five years later to construe the effect of a Calvo Clause commitment on the submission of an international reclamation in the case of the *United States (International Fisheries Company) v. the United Mexican States*.[1] The personnel of the commission had changed over the half-decade, with H. F.

[1] Docket No. 625, opinion rendered in July 1931, *Opinions of Commissioners*, III, pp. 207–286.

Alfaro of Panama selected by mutual agreement of the two governments to be presiding commissioner in place of C. van Vollenhoven, and Fred K. Nielsen the American commissioner in place of Edwin B. Parker. Fernández MacGregor remained as Mexican commissioner. Despite this change of personnel, the decision in the instant case closely followed that in the *Dredging* case.

The claim of the International Fisheries Company was based on damages resulting from the alleged arbitrary and wrongful cancellation of a concession granted by Mexico to a Mexican company called "La Pescadora, S. A.," the stock of which was almost entirely owned by the North American corporation.[2] The concession contained the following Calvo Clause, essentially similar to that contained in the *Dredging* case:

Article 32. The Concessionary Company or whosoever shall succeed it in its rights, even though all or some of its members may be aliens, shall be subject to the jurisdiction of the courts of the Republic in all matters the cause and action of which take place within its territory. It shall never claim, with respect to matters connected with this contract, any rights as an alien, under any form whatsoever, and shall enjoy only the rights and the measures for enforcing them that the laws of the Republic afford to Mexicans, foreign diplomatic agents being unable therefore, to intervene in any manner with relation to the said matters.[3]

The majority of the commission, consisting of Mr. Alfaro and Mr. MacGregor, upheld the motion of the Mexican agent to dismiss the claim as falling outside the jurisdiction of the commission because of the Calvo Clause.[4] The case does not contain any new arguments in regard to the validity of the Calvo Clause. Its importance lies in the fact that it explicitly accepted and approved the principles and rule enunciated previously in the *Dredging* case.

[2] *Ibid.*, p. 207.

[3] *Ibid.*, p. 212. This provision, unlike the Calvo Clause in the *Dredging* case, contained the subjection of the claimant to the jurisdiction of the Mexican courts "in all matters the cause and action of which take place within its territory." However, the key phrase is similar to the *Dredging* clause in that diplomatic intervention was forbidden "with respect to matters connected with this contract." Contrast this with the much broader prohibition in the *Mexican Union* case. See *infra*, p. 242, n. 30.

[4] *Ibid.*, p. 224.

Commissioner MacGregor, speaking for the commission, asserted that events since the *Dredging* opinion was handed down indicated a tendency in the usage of nations to accept the validity of the Calvo Clause as interpreted and applied in the 1926 decision. He made reference to the fact that the *Dredging* decision had been accepted as good law by the Anglo-Mexican Claims Commission [5] and also by a number of nations replying to the League Codification Questionnaire on the point involving the validity of the Calvo Clause.[6] In this connection, the commissioner stated:

With respect to the research work conducted by the League of Nations it may be observed that not all of the replies received from 19 States were unfavorable to the contention of the validity of the Calvo Clause. The replies submitted by Germany, Australia, Bulgaria, Denmark, Great Britain, Hungary, Norway, New Zealand and the Netherlands, are in practical accord with the opinion expressed in the decision of the *North American Dredging Company of Texas*.[7]

To buttress this interpretation of the replies of the various governments, the commissioner quoted the "Basis of Discussion" drawn up by the Committee for the Codification Conference as being representative of the views of the governments that had replied:

An undertaking by a party to a contract that he will not have recourse to the diplomatic remedy does not bind the State whose national he is and does not release the State with which the contract is made from its international responsibility.

If in a contract a foreigner makes a valid agreement that the local courts shall alone have jurisdiction, this provision is binding upon any international tribunal to which a claim under the contract is submitted; the State can then only be responsible for damage suffered by the foreigner in the cases contemplated in Bases of Discussion Nos. 5 and 6.[8]

[5] *Ibid.*, p. 209. See *infra*, pp. 240–245.

[6] *Ibid.*, pp. 209–211. See *supra*, pp. 46–56.

[7] *Ibid.*, p. 210. It was previously noted, *supra*, p. 228, that Great Britain, India, New Zealand, and the United States in their replies specifically cited the *Dredging* case.

[8] *Ibid.*, p. 211. "The last named bases refer only to what is properly called denial of justice in its most restricted acceptance . . ." *Ibid.*

The commissioner went on to assert:

It will be seen by the foregoing that such an authoritative international body as the Committee of the League of Nations, after presenting it to the principal States of the world, established a doctrine which can be reconciled in all of its parts to that laid down by this Commission in the decision of the case of the *North American Dredging Company of Texas*.

With respect to the opinion of the Spanish-American nations in this particular it is necessary to bear in mind that they have all maintained the validity of the Calvo Clause and have continued to insert it into all contracts and concessions granted to foreigners, an unquestionable fact which demonstrates that their silence with regard to the inquiry of the League can not be construed as being adverse to the validity of the so often cited Calvo Clause.[9]

Therefore, in view of this widespread acceptance of the *Dredging* decision by international tribunals and by governments, Commissioner MacGregor asserted, "the instant case must be determined in accordance with the doctrine established in the decision of the *North American Dredging Company of Texas* case."[10]

The commissioner then proceeded to examine the Calvo Clause in the present concession, stating:

The contractual provision under examination does not attempt in any manner to impede or to prevent absolutely all diplomatic intervention, but tends to avoid it solely in *those matters arising from the contract* itself, with its fulfillment and interpretation. It certainly comes, therefore, within the doctrine laid down in the decision rendered in the case of the *North American Dredging Company of Texas* . . .[11]

Having upheld the *Dredging* rule and the Calvo Clause in question, the commissioner applied the rule to the instant case. The American agent had argued that the claim arose not from nonfulfillment of contract but from "a claim based upon a denial of justice as the result of an act of the Government of Mexico in decreeing the cancellation of the contract."[12] The commissioner, however, held:

---

[9] *Ibid.*, p. 211. Only Chile of the Latin American republics had replied to the League Questionnaire.
[10] *Ibid.*, p. 212.   [11] *Ibid.*, p. 213.   [12] *Ibid.*, p. 216.

The question, therefore, which arose between the Company and the Mexican Government, was that of ascertaining whether or not the concessionary had become liable to the cancellation provided for in Article 34, and this question must necessarily be considered as included within what this Commission understood by fulfillment or interpretation of the contract containing a Calvo Clause, when it decided the case of the *North American Dredging Company of Texas*. The cancellation in question, in the case which must now be decided, was not an arbitrary act, a violation of a duty abhorrent to the contract and which in itself might be considered as a violation of some rule or principle of international law, requisites to be established in order that the Commission might take jurisdiction, notwithstanding the existence of a clause partaking of the nature of the Calvo Clause in a contract subscribed by a claimant (Par. 23 of the decision cited).[13]

Commissioner MacGregor concluded:

The instant case is included in the principles fixed by the Commission in the decision of the case of the *North American Dredging Company,* and is not therefore within the jurisdiction of the Commission, it being disallowed, without prejudice to the claimant to seek whatever legal remedies he may have elsewhere.[14]

The presiding commissioner, Dr. Alfaro, supported MacGregor in sustaining the doctrine established in the *Dredging* case, stating:

Notwithstanding the extensive discussion by the American Agency of the important question of the validity of the so-called Calvo Clause, I do not find any ground for modifying or revoking the doctrine established by this Commission in the matter of the *North American Dredging Company of Texas*. That decision has received the approval of the highest authorities on international law and constitutes an appreciable contribution to the progress of this science. The decision in question was of material assistance in clarifying the opinions previously expressed on the validity or invalidity of the said Clause.

The decision mentioned, establishes therefore a just and reasonable middle ground. It protects, in a measure, the defendant State, preserving at the same time the rights of the claimant in the event of a denial of justice or international delinquency.[15]

[13] *Ibid.*, p. 218.   [14] *Ibid.*, p. 222.   [15] *Ibid.*, pp. 222–223.

The American commissioner, F. K. Nielsen, entered a long and vigorous dissenting opinion.[16] Since the majority had based their ruling squarely on the *Dredging* case,[17] Commissioner Nielsen devoted most of his attention to a strong and at times even bitter attack on the previous decision. Mr. Nielsen's attitude toward the *Dredging* ruling is represented by this previously quoted statement: "I am constrained to say that the opinion contains nothing of any consequence with which I agree. . . . [The case was decided with an] utter lack of any basis in law for any conclusions submitted in the former opinion." [18]

Although Nielsen's dissent covers no fewer than sixty pages, the core of his reasoning for opposing the *Dredging* rule and its application to the instant case is contained in the first few pages of his opinion.[19] While the objections raised to the *Dredging* rule are not new and have already been discussed in connection with the analysis of that case, it might be well to quote the relevant passages of the dissenting opinion, since they are representative of the school of thought that has been strongly critical of the *Dredging* rule. Commissioner Nielsen stated:

I consider that the Commission construed the language of the contractual provisions involved in that case in such a way as to give them a meaning entirely different from that which their language clearly reveals — a meaning not even contended for by Mexico. In order to do that the Commission resorted to both elimination, substitution and rearrangement of language of the contractual provisions. These artifices were embellished by quotation marks. And the Commission went so far as to ground its interpretation fundamentally on the insertion in a translation of a comma, which does not appear in the Spanish text of the contract. It seems to me to be almost inconceivable that matters involving questions of such seriousness, not only with respect to important private property rights, but with respect to international questions, should have been dealt with in such a manner.

[16] *Ibid.*, pp. 225–286.

[17] There are no fewer than 22 specific references to the *Dredging* decision in the majority opinions, plus a number of indirect references.

[18] *Opinions of Commissioners*, III, p. 226.

[19] De Beus, *op. cit.*, pp. 63–64, suggests that "if the Commissioner had limited his strictures to these two pages, his opinion would not have lost any fundamental value and would have gained much in simplicity and clearness."

I am impelled to express the view that the Commission's treatment of matters of international law involved in the case did not rise above the level of its processes in arriving at its construction of the contractual provisions — a construction based on a non-existing comma.

The Commission's discussion of the restriction on interposition was characterized by a failure of recognition and application of fundamental principles of law with respect to several subjects.

Principally among them are:

(a) The nature of international law as a law between nations whose operation is not controlled by acts of private individuals.

(b) The nature of an international reclamation as a demand of a Government for redress from another Government and not a private litigation.

(c) A remarkable confusion between substantive rules of international law that a nation may invoke in behalf of itself or its nationals against another nation, and jurisdictional questions before international tribunals which are regulated by covenants between nations and of course not by rules of international law or by acts of private individuals or by a contract between a private individual and a Government.

International law recognizes the right of the nation to intervene to protect its nationals in foreign countries through diplomatic channels and through instrumentalities such as are afforded by international tribunals. The right was recognized long prior to the time when there was any thought of restrictions on its exercise. The question presented for determination in considering the effect of local laws or contractual obligations between a Government and a private individual to restrict that right therefore is whether there is evidence of a general assent to such restrictions.

The Commission decided the case by rejecting the claim on jurisdictional grounds, although it admitted and stated that the claim was within the jurisdictional provisions of the Convention of September 8, 1923, which alone of course determine jurisdiction. Although the case was dismissed on jurisdictional grounds, the Commission made reference to international law but did not cite a word of the evidence of that law. A few vague references to stipulations of bilateral treaties have no bearing on the case, except that possibly the language of those stipulations serves to disprove the Commission's conclusions; the most casual examination into abundantly available evidence of the law disproves those conclusions. The Commission did not concern itself with any such evidence.

The Commission seemed to indicate some view to the effect that the contractual stipulations in question were in harmony with international law because they required the exhaustion of local remedies, and that therefore the claim might be rejected. The Commission ignored the effect of Article V of the Convention concluded September 8, 1923, between the United States and Mexico, stipulating that claims should not be rejected for failure to exhaust local remedies.

. . . .

The Commission stated repeatedly that contractual provisions could not bar the presentation of a claim predicated on allegations of "violations of international law" or of "international illegal acts." It also stated that the claimant did not waive his right to apply to his Government for protection against such acts. The claim of the North American Dredging Company of Texas was of course predicated on allegations of that nature. The Commission was authorized to consider such claims, yet it said that it was without jurisdiction in the case and threw out a case of the precise nature which it stated it was required by the Convention to adjudicate.[20]

It would appear that Nielsen's objections to the *Dredging* opinions boil down to these five: (1) the misinterpretation of the contractual clause; (2) the failure to take cognizance of the fact that international law is a law of nations and is not controlled by acts of private individuals; (3) the fact that the Calvo Clause can be valid only if it is specifically recognized as such by the law of nations, and cannot obtain validity by merely demonstrating that the law of nations does not explicitly forbid it; (4) the misinterpretation of the convention, especially Article V; (5) the misinterpretation of the facts upon which the claim was based.

It is undeniable that the *Dredging* decision is open to many of these criticisms leveled against it in Commissioner Nielsen's dissent.[21] Technical deficiencies do not, however, necessarily destroy

[20] *Opinions of Commissioners*, III, pp. 226–228.

[21] See *supra*, pp. 211–214. Commissioner Nielsen, in addition to strongly criticizing the *Dredging* decision as such, raised the fundamental question of whether Calvo Clause defense against an international reclamation has any bearing at

the authority of a case.[22] It may be observed in passing that the fundamental difference between the viewpoint of Mr. Nielsen and that expressed in the *Dredging* opinion would appear to concern the nature of international law itself. As was noted previously, the commission in the *Dredging* case based its decision on what it understood to be the new developments in international law that permitted it to give more emphasis to the actions of individuals. Nielsen, on the other hand, basing his decision on the more or less traditional principles of international law,[23] found it incomprehensible that an international tribunal would take cognizance of the status of the individual in international law to the extent that it would permit an action of an individual to be determinative in the acceptance or rejection of an international reclamation. Since Nielsen analyzed the case on the basis of different premises, conflicting conclusions were almost inevitable.

It is noteworthy, however, that Nielsen's opinion was in the form of a dissent, and that the majority of the commission followed the *Dredging* rule down the line, as have other commissions that have had an opportunity to deal with the validity of the Calvo Clause since 1926. Herein lies the true significance of the instant case. It contained no new theories or even elabora-

all on the question of jurisdiction, or whether it goes to the merits of the claim. International claims commissions have almost invariably dealt with the Clause as a question of jurisdiction, and it was so treated in the *Dredging* decision and in the instant case. Nielsen, however, argued that jurisdiction is solely determined by the *compromis*, and that the Calvo Clause involved the substantive rule of international law with regard to the necessity for recourse to legal remedies before diplomatic intervention, and thus could only be dealt with in determining the merits of the case. It would hence involve the question of whether an international delinquency could exist so long as the claimant did not carry out his contractual obligation to resort in the first instance to the national courts. See *Opinions of Commissioners*, III, pp. 207, 243–244, and also Nielsen's opinion in the *C. E. Blair* case, *ibid.*, II, p. 107. See also De Beus, *op. cit.*, pp. 75–76. Although Nielsen's argument on this point has merit, since a great majority of the various commissions have dealt with the Calvo Clause as a question of jurisdiction, precedent would appear to support the position taken by the commission in the *Dredging* case and by the majority in the instant decision.

[22] For a critical review of Nielsen's dissent, see De Beus, *op. cit.*, pp. 61–82. See also Lipstein, *op. cit.*, pp. 134–135.

[23] See, for example, *Opinions of Commissioners*, III, pp. 252–254, where Nielsen strongly asserts that only nations have a real status under international law.

tion of theories. It is important only because it endorsed and applied the rule set forth in the *Dredging* case to bar a claim that would have been otherwise receivable, thus giving the *Dredging* rule a prestige and precedential impact hitherto unknown in the jurisprudence involving the Calvo Clause. The commission, in vigorously upholding its former ruling, exhibited a consistency that cannot help but add great weight to its rule of the limited validity of the Calvo Clause.

The prestige and precedential impact of the *Dredging* rule became even more evident in the adjudications of the Anglo-Mexican Claims Commission.

The Calvo Clause before the Great Britain and Mexican Claims Commission

On November 19, 1926, Great Britain and Mexico signed a convention providing for the creation of a claims commission to adjudicate claims of British subjects against Mexico for losses or damages arising from the revolutionary turbulence and violence that had characterized Mexican history during the second decade of this century.[24] The British-Mexican Commission had occasion to deal with the validity and effectiveness of the Calvo Clause in no fewer than five cases. In these adjudications, this commission not only accepted and endorsed the *Dredging* case and its rule of law, but actually broadened the scope of the validity and effectiveness of the Clause in international arbitral jurisprudence.

The first and most important of these cases to come before the commission was that of *Great Britain (Mexican Union Railway, Ltd.) v. the United Mexican States.*[25] The claim, in the amount of 200,000 pounds sterling, was based on damages suffered by the company to its property and operations as a result of a long series of acts connected with revolutionary activity in Mexico, including lack of protection, depredations by govern-

[24] See Stuyt, *Survey*, p. 399. The convention with supplements is reprinted in Feller, *Mex. Claims Com.*, pp. 467–482.

[25] Decision No. 21, February, 1930, *Decisions and Opinions of the Commissioners*, pp. 157–175.

ment and rebel forces, forced acceptance of paper currency, requisitions, and arbitrary threats to cancel the concession granted to the claimant by the Mexican government to construct and operate a railway in that country.[26]

The case came before the commission on the motion of the Mexican agent to dismiss the claim because of the existence of a Calvo Clause provision in the contract. Article 11 of the concession read:

The Company shall always be a Mexican Company even though any or all its members should be aliens, and it shall be subject exclusively to the jurisdiction of the Courts of the Republic of Mexico in all matters whose cause and right of action shall arise within the territory of said Republic. The said Company and all aliens and the successors of such aliens having any interest in its business, whether as shareholders, employees or in any other capacity, shall be considered as Mexican in everything relating to said Company. They shall never be entitled to assert, in regard to any titles and business connected with the Company, any rights of alienage under any pretext whatsoever. They shall only have such rights and means of asserting them as the laws of the Republic grant to Mexicans, and Foreign Diplomatic Agents may consequently not intervene in any manner whatsoever.[27]

A majority of the commission, consisting of Dr. Alfred R. Zimmerman of the Netherlands, the presiding commissioner, and Dr. Benito Flores, the Mexican commissioner, sustained the motion to dismiss the claim on the basis of the Calvo Clause,[28] explicitly accepting and applying the decision and rule of the *Dredging* case. The British commissioner, Sir John Percival, was no less enthusiastic about endorsing the *Dredging* opinion, but held it was not applicable to the fact situation in the instant case, and therefore dissented from the opinion of the majority.[29]

Before we analyze the opinions of the commissioners, it should be noted that the instant case differed in three important respects from the *Dredging* decision. First, the Clause involved in

[26] *Ibid.*, pp. 157–159.
[27] *Ibid.*, p. 159.
[28] *Ibid.*, p. 166.
[29] *Ibid.*, p. 175.

the Mexican Union Railway concession is considerably more inclusive in scope than that contained in the Dredging Company contract. The instant Clause applied to "all matters whose cause and right of action shall arise within the territory of the said Republic" whereas the Clause in the *Dredging* case applied only to "all matters related to the contract." [30] Second, the instant claim arose over revolutionary acts and wrongs done to the claimant, while the claim in the previous case had arisen over "doubts and controversies" related to the alleged breach of contract by the government.[31] Third, the waiver of the local remedies rule in the British-Mexican Convention was somewhat more definite than in the United States–Mexican Convention. The former specifically provided, in Article VI, that the commission "shall not set aside or reject any claim on the grounds that all legal remedies have not been exhausted prior to the presentation of such claim," whereas in the latter it was provided that no claim shall be disallowed or rejected by the commission "by the application of the general principle of international law that the legal remedies must be exhausted as a condition precedent to the validity or allowance of any claim." [32]

In spite of these differences, however, the majority held that the *Dredging* rule applied to the present situation. Because of the importance of this case as one which not only accepted and applied the *Dredging* rule but, in its application to the instant case, actually broadened the scope of that rule, it is desirable to

---

[30] This is the distinction drawn by the commission. See *ibid.*, p. 160. More exactly, the distinction would appear to be that while the *Dredging* provision had forbidden recourse to diplomatic intervention "in any matter related to the *contract*," the *Mexican Union* clause stated, in addition to the subjection of the company "exclusively to the jurisdiction of the Courts of the Republic of Mexico in all matters whose cause and right of action shall arise within the territory of said Republic," that diplomatic intervention was forbidden in "everything relating to" the *company*, and "any titles and business connected with the *company*." Italics mine. The key difference is that one prohibition applied only to the contract, while the other applied to the company itself. Compare with the Calvo Clause in the *Fisheries* case, and my comment *supra*, p. 232, n. 3.

[31] *Decisions and Opinions of Commissioners*, p. 173.

[32] The commission was in unanimous agreement, however, that the Calvo Clause overcame this waiver, basing their opinion squarely on the *Dredging* rule that held that such a provision applied only to claims that were "rightfully" presented. See *ibid.*, pp. 166, 174.

quote rather extensively from the opinion of the arbitration commission.

The commission began by asserting that "all the Commissioners are prepared to agree with and to follow" the *Dredging* decision as well as the considerations that led to that decision, "not thinking it necessary to repeat them, or possible to express them better." [33] The majority went on to assert that the instant renunciatory provision was similar enough to that in the *Dredging* case to be included within its rule, and the Clause must therefore be respected and given effect. [34] The commission emphatically reiterated the view that such a contractual provision does not bind the government, stating:

> In holding that under the rules of international law an alien may lawfully make a promise, as laid down in the concession, the majority of the Commission holds at the same time that no person can, by such a Clause, deprive the Government of his country of its undoubted right to apply international remedies to violations of international law committed to his hurt. A Government may take a view of losses suffered by one of its subjects different to that taken by such subject himself. Where the Government is concerned, a principle higher than the mere safeguarding of the private interests of the subject who suffered the damage may be involved. For the Government the contract is *res inter alios acta*, by which its liberty of action can not be prejudiced. [35]

The majority, following the line of reasoning of the *Dredging* decision, went on to assert that an international tribunal could, with propriety, take cognizance of the action of the individual and hold him to his promise not to *seek* governmental intervention in violation of his contractual commitment without interfering with this right of his state to interpose on its own. In a key passage of the opinion, the commission asserted:

> But the Commission is bound to consider the object for which it was created, the task it has to fulfill and the treaty upon which its existence is based. It has to examine and to judge the claims contemplated by the Convention. These claims bear a

[33] *Ibid.*, p. 160.
[34] *Ibid.*, pp. 160–162.   [35] *Ibid.*, p. 162.

mixed character. They are public claims in so far as they are
presented by one Government to another Government. But they
are private in so far as they aim at the granting of a financial
award to an individual or to a company. The award is claimed
on behalf of a person or a corporation and, in accordance there-
with, the Rules of Procedure prescribe that the Memorial shall
be signed by the claimant or his attorney or otherwise clearly
show that the alien who suffered the damage agrees to his Government's acting in his behalf. For this reason *the action of the
Government can not be regarded as an action taken independently of the wishes or the interest of the claimant. It is an action
the initiative of which rests with the claimant.*

That being the case, the Commission can not overlook the
previous engagements undertaken by the claimant towards the
respondent Government. A contract between them does not constitute *res inter alios acta* for the Commission. They are both,
the Mexican Government and the claimant, standing before the
Commission, and the majority is of the opinion that no decision
would be just or equitable which resulted in the practical annulment of one of the essential elements of their contractual relation.

By this contract the claimant has solemnly promised not to
apply to his Government for diplomatic intervention but to resort to the municipal courts. He has waived the right upon which
the claim is now presented. *He has precluded himself by his contract from taking the initiative*, without which his claim can
have no standing before this Commission and can not be recognizable. Quite apart from the right of the British Government,
his claim is such that it can not be pursued before a body with
the jurisdiction intrusted to this Commission and circumscribed
in Articles I and III of the Convention.[36]

This passage illustrates the interpretation and application of
the rule of the *Dredging* case as holding the Clause binding upon
the individual though not on his state in case of internationally
illegal actions.

Commissioner Percival, in his dissenting opinion, emphatically
accepted the *Dredging* decision and its rule of law. Mr. Percival
stated:

The question of the legality of what is known as the Calvo

[36] *Ibid.*, pp. 162–163. Italics mine.

Clause has been long discussed by international lawyers and a number of rather conflicting decisions have been given upon it by various international commissions, which decisions have been cited and debated before us by the Agents of both sides. It is, however, not necessary for me to refer to these decisions . . . for the whole present legal view on the subject has been admirably set out in the lucid and fair judgment in the case of the *North American Dredging Company of Texas* . . .

Not only would this opinion be worthy of the highest respect in itself, but the Agents of both parties have specifically stated before us that they agree in general with what is laid down therein as being a correct statement of the law in the matter. . . .

The Commission, therefore, has no hesitation in accepting the decision referred to above as a guide to the determination of the present motion to dismiss, and it only remains to apply the principles there laid down to the facts of the present case.[37]

It was in the application of the *Dredging* rule to the instant case that Commissioner Percival disagreed with the majority. He agreed that Article VI of the convention did not cancel out the Calvo Clause stipulation, but argued that the scope of the present contractual provision was too broad to be contained in the *Dredging* rule, and that the origin of the Mexican Union claim in revolutionary damages rather than in contractual "doubts or controversies" removed it from the application of the rule of law enunciated in the previous decision. As a consequence of these distinctions, Mr. Percival concluded that the Calvo Clause did not, in this case, serve to bar interposition and therefore the claim should be heard on its merits.[38]

The importance of the *Mexican Union Railway* case lies in the fact that the rule of limited validity of the *Dredging* decision was emphatically endorsed and applied to the instant reclamation with the result that the claim was barred solely because of the Calvo Clause in the contract. In the absence of the Clause the claim would have been receivable, even though local remedies had not been exhausted, because of Article VI of the convention. Thus in the *Mexican Union Railway* case, as in the *International Fisheries* and *Dredging* cases, the Clause was ac-

[37] *Ibid.*, pp. 167–168.   [38] *Ibid.*, pp. 168–175.

corded a legally meaningful and significant degree of validity under the rules of international law.

It should be noted that the *Mexican Union Railway* case not only followed the *Dredging* decision "all the way," [39] but actually broadened the scope of the rule laid down in that case. As G. Godfrey Phillips has stated, "there can be no doubt that the Commission, whether rightly or wrongly, has advanced beyond the *North American Dredging Company of Texas* decision in the direction of upholding the validity of the Calvo Clause." [40] The Clause was held applicable to claims that did not arise from contract, but actually from "an international delinquency independent of contract." [41] Where the *Dredging* decision admitted jurisdiction, in spite of the Clause, in the event of a "denial of justice or other international wrong," the instant decision would appear to leave open only the cases of denial of justice.[42]

While the *Mexican Union Railway* has been criticized on this ground,[43] it should be noted that the clause in this case, by forbidding diplomatic intervention in regard to everything related to the *company* and not just the *contract*, was phrased broadly enough to include revolutionary damages, and this undoubtedly had an influence on the commission in its application of the broader Calvo Clause to pertain to revolutionary as well as to contract damages. The individual, having voluntarily agreed to this broad renunciatory provision, was held to it by a commission which, following the *Dredging* reasoning, took cognizance of the status and actions of the individual in international law. If we take into account the plain meaning of the Clause, and operate on the premise that an individual's actions can have a determinative influence on the admissibility of an international reclamation, the opinion of the majority would appear to be sound. As Lionel Summers has stated:

. . . [If] a foreigner can validly renounce diplomatic protection

[39] Freeman, *Denial of Justice*, p. 482.
[40] "The Anglo-Mexican Special Claims Commission," *Law Quarterly Review* (April 1933), p. 237.
[41] *Ibid.*
[42] *Ibid.*, pp. 236–237.
[43] E.g., Freeman, *Denial of Justice*, pp. 484–485.

for all questions arising out of a contract, it is hard to see why he can not go a step further, provided he does so with his eyes open, and renounce diplomatic protection for all eventualities that may come to pass. But unless a clause is of this all-embracing variety it should certainly not be applied to questions unrelated to the contract.[44]

The commission, by its decision, added further weight to the role of the individual in international law when it determined the effect to be given to the Calvo Clause on the basis of the scope of the contractual commitment voluntarily accepted by the individual, with the exception that such a commitment would be inoperative in the event of a denial of justice.

The problem of the validity of the Calvo Clause next came before the British-Mexican Claims Commission on April 10, 1931, in the case of *Great Britain (Douglas G. Collie MacNeil) v. the United Mexican States*.[45] The claim, in the amount of 1,637.05 pesos Mexican gold, was for compensation for the requisition from the tramway owned by Mr. MacNeil of animals, fodder, and passenger and freight cars by the Constitutionalist Army during the years 1914 to 1916 inclusive.[46] The case came before the commission on a motion of the Mexican agent to dismiss because proof of ownership had not been demonstrated by the claimant, and because the concession contained the following provision in Article 7:

> The concessionaries, or the Company which they organize, may transfer their rights to another Company or to an individual with the approval of the Corporation, under the precise condition that the business will preserve its Mexican character and without rights of foreigners, even if it may be sustained by foreign capital.[47]

The Mexican agent urged the commission to allow the motion to dismiss for same reasons that were decisive in the *Mexican*

---

[44] *Op. cit.*, p. 478. Podestá Costa, "La responsabilidad internacional del estado," *Cursos Monográficos*, II (1952), p. 216, takes a contrary view, although he strongly supports the validity of the Calvo Clause that applies only to the interpretation and execution of the contract.

[45] Decision No. 27, *Further Decisions and Opinions of the Commissioners*, pp. 21–25.

[46] *Ibid.*, p. 21.   [47] *Ibid.*, p. 23.

Union Railway case, arguing that Article 7 in the instant concession was of the same meaning and force as the Calvo Clause provision in the previous case. The British agent pointed out that in this case the wording of the stipulation was so vague that it did not make clear its real meaning. Moreover, he argued, nothing showed that the claimant, in taking over the concession, knew that he thereby deprived himself of his right to appeal to his government.[48]

The commission, in an opinion signed by all three commissioners, refused the motion to dismiss, holding that the wording of the Clause was too vague to reveal an intention to stipulate a Calvo Clause; furthermore since the contract was with a municipal corporation and not with the Mexican government, that government could not derive rights from a contract to which it was not a party.[49]

In regard to the first ground for rejecting the motion to dismiss the claim, the commission asserted:

The Commission has always realized that its decision in the case of the *Mexican Union Railway (Limited)* was of a very serious, momentous and consequential character in so far as *it deprived British subjects of their right to ask through their Government redress before this Commission for damage and loss, suffered in Mexico.* But the words in which the concessionaire had divested himself of the right, were so clear, circumstantial and detailed, that no other decision was justified. In the test of Article 11 [Mexican Union Railway concession] everything seems to have been foreseen; all the actions from which the concessionaire undertook to abstain himself, are enumerated, circumscribed and detailed with a complete fullness.

A single glance at the text of Article 7 of the concession now under consideration, will show that even assuming that the insertion of a so-called Calvo Clause was intended, this object could certainly not be achieved by the limited, vague and obscure wording of the paragraph, in which the stipulation was laid down.[50]

[48] *Ibid.*, p. 22.
[49] *Ibid.*, pp. 24–25. The opinion was signed by A. R. Zimmerman, the presiding commissioner, Benito Flores, the Mexican commissioner, and William Henry Stoker, now the British commissioner.
[50] *Ibid.*, p. 23. Italics mine. It is noteworthy that the commission, reiterating

As a consequence of this vague and obscure language, a majority of the commission found themselves unable "to understand what were the precise rights waived by the concessionaire," and therefore were unable "to accept a similarity between this clause and the clause inserted in the concession dealt with in decision No. 21 [*Mexican Union Railway* case]." [51] The commission asserted, in the key passage of the opinion:

> The majority holds the view that a so-called Calvo Clause to be respected in international jurisprudence, must be drafted in such a way as not to allow any doubt as to the intentions of both parties. The Commission can not see that this has been done in Article 7 of the concession.[52]

The rule of the case would appear to be that, in order to hold the individual to his Calvo Clause commitment, the provision must be phrased in clear and precise language so that the individual is absolutely aware of the right that he is agreeing to forgo. The decision is otherwise uninstructive, and it certainly would be erroneous to cite this case as one that has denied the validity of the Calvo Clause. Nor does this decision represent, in any way whatsoever, a retreat by the commission from its acceptance of the rule of the limited validity of the Calvo Clause, as an examination of subsequent decisions will demonstrate.

The British-Mexican Commission next had occasion to deal with the Calvo Clause in the case of *Great Britain (Interoceanic Railway of Mexico et al.) v. the United Mexican States*, decided on June 18, 1931.[53] The claim, in excess of 77 million pesos Mexican gold, was for indemnification and compensation for losses to property and earnings resulting from revolutionary damages and requisitions.[54] The case came before the commission on a

the distinction between the right of the individual to seek intervention and the right of the state to intervene, held that a Calvo Clause would divest the right of the individual to ask through his government redress before an international tribunal.

[51] *Ibid.*, p. 24.

[52] *Ibid.* The case was later heard on its merits, and, proof of ownership having been established, an award of 1,637.05 pesos Mexican gold was made to the claimant. See *ibid.*, pp. 245–246.

[53] Decision No. 53, *ibid.*, pp. 118–135.

[54] *Ibid.*, pp. 118–120.

motion of the Mexican agent to dismiss because, among other reasons,[55] the concessions granted to the claimant contained a Calvo Clause identical to that in the *Mexican Union Railway* case.[56]

The commission, in an opinion signed by Commissioner Flores and Presiding Commissioner Zimmerman, explicitly adhered to its decision in the *Mexican Union Railway* case.[57] Since the renunciatory provisions in the instant case and in the *Mexican Union Railway* case had "exactly the same wording," the only question before the commission was whether "the said clause in this case must be disregarded because . . . the claimant has been the victim of internationally illegal acts or breaches of international law, such as a denial of justice or undue delay of justice." [58]

Most of the opinion turned on the point of what constitutes a denial or undue delay of justice. It appeared that the claimant had not ignored his obligation under the Calvo Clause and had actually applied to the minister of finance for relief. After six years of negotiation, no agreement on compensation was reached, with the claimant alleging that it had been confronted with unjust and unacceptable conditions. The claimant then had recourse to the *Comisión Ajustadora de la Deuda Pública*, where their appeal had been pending, at the time of this adjudication, for a year and a half.[59]

The commission held that local remedies had not been completely exhausted, as the claimant had contracted to do, and that there had not been an undue delay in justice in view of the amount of the claims and the large docket of the Mexican agency, and consequently there was no reason to relieve the claimant of his obligations under the Calvo Clause.[60]

[55] The Mexican agent charged that proof of British nationality had not been established, and it had not been proved that British subjects owned a sufficient percentage of the stock to enable them to present a claim. The commission summarily rejected these objections to jurisdiction. See *ibid.*, p. 126.

[56] *Ibid.*, p. 121. See *supra*, p. 241. The Spanish text was identical, although the commission's translation differed slightly in unimportant details such as punctuation.

[57] *Ibid.*, p. 126.

[58] *Ibid.*   [59] *Ibid.*, pp. 126–128.   [60] *Ibid.*, pp. 128–129.

The British commissioner, W. H. Stoker, dissented. While he agreed with the majority that no denial or undue delay of justice had been established in this case, and that the rule of the *Mexican Union Railway*, if accepted, would apply here as well, the commissioner felt constrained to dissent on the ground that the *Mexican Union Railway* case was, in fact, an improper application of the rule enunciated in the *Dredging* decision. It is interesting to note that Stoker did not take issue with either the decision or the rule of the *Dredging* case, but rather held that the *Mexican Union Railway* case and the instant case did not fall within the scope of that rule. His reasoning was very similar to that of Sir John Percival's dissent in the *Mexican Union Railway* case, citing the differences between the origins of the claims, the Calvo Clauses involved, and the conventions under which the two commissions operated.[61]

The decision in the instant case emphasizes once again the consistency with which the *Dredging* precedent was followed. The fact that the British-Mexican Commission applied the rule of limited validity to all the Calvo Clause cases that came before it greatly strengthens the contention that the *Dredging* rule is actually the rule of law on this problem in international arbitral jurisprudence.

That the British-Mexican Commission was only embracing the limited validity of the Calvo Clause and was not endorsing it as a full and complete bar to interposition under all circumstances was made clear in a decision rendered on the same day as that in the *Interoceanic* case. This case was that of *Great Britain (El Oro Mining and Railway Company, Limited) v. the United Mexican States.*[62] The claim was for compensation for the transport of troops and goods on behalf of revolutionary and federal forces, for work done, and for material supplied to revolutionary and federal forces during the period from November 20, 1910, to May 31, 1920.[63]

The case came before the commission on the motion of the

[61] *Ibid.*, pp. 129–135.
[62] Decision No. 55, June 18, 1931, *ibid.*, pp. 141–152.
[63] *Ibid.*, p. 141.

Mexican agent to dismiss because of a Calvo Clause provision in the original concession which "was in tenor and wording exactly similar" to that in the *Mexican Union Railway* case.[64]

The commission, by a majority, adhered to the decision rendered in the *Mexican Union Railway* case, asserting that since

. . . it so happens that in the claim now under consideration the Calvo Clause has exactly the same wording as in the former case, the question before them is whether that Clause must in this case be disregarded, because the claimant Company has been the victim of internationally illegal acts or breaches of international law, such as a denial of justice or undue delay of justice.[65]

The commission found that the claimant, by filing an action with the *Comisión de Reclamaciones* in 1922, had, according to the law of Mexico, exhausted all local means of redress. Since in the intervening nine years no action was taken on its petition for relief, the commission held that this was not only an undue delay of justice, but actually constituted a denial of justice.[66] "For this reason the Commission holds that the terms of the concession do not in this case preclude the claimant from appearing before them."[67] The Mexican commissioner, Benito Flores, dissented, arguing that the nine-year period did not constitute an undue delay or denial of justice in view of the large number and the complexity of the claims pending before the *Comisión de Reclamaciones*.[68]

The *El Oro Mining and Railway Company* case does not indicate any change of the basic rule of law governing the Calvo Clause. Both the United States–Mexican and the British-Mexican Claims Commissions, in enunciating the rule of limited validity, emphasized that, while the Clause was binding on the individual, it would not serve to prevent the state from presenting an international reclamation in the event of a denial of justice.

[64] *Ibid.*, p. 146. See *supra*, p. 241.
[65] *Ibid.*, p. 149.
[66] *Ibid.*, pp. 149–150.
[67] *Ibid.*, p. 150.
[68] *Ibid.*, pp. 151–152. The *El Oro Mining and Railway Company* case was later settled with the award of eighteen thousand pesos Mexican gold to the claimant. See *ibid.*, p. 214.

This case merely illustrates the application of this reservation to the full validity of the Calvo Clause.

The final case involving the Calvo Clause that came before this commission was that of *Great Britain (Veracruz Railway, Limited) v. the United Mexican States,* decided on July 7, 1931.[69] The claim, based on alleged losses and damages resulting from revolutionary activity,[70] presented the commission with a situation nearly identical to that in the *Mexican Union Railway* case.

The case came up on the motion of the Mexican agent to dismiss the claim on the ground that the concession contained a Calvo Clause stipulation with "exactly the same wording" as that in the *Mexican Union Railway* case.[71]

In a very brief opinion, the majority reaffirmed their acceptance of the rule of the limited validity of the Calvo Clause, stating:

> The Commission by a majority adhere to their decision taken in the case of the *Mexican Union Railway,* and as it so happens that in the claim now under consideration, the Calvo Clause has exactly the same wording as in the former case, they can not but take the same attitude.
>
> The Motion to Dismiss is allowed.[72]

The British commissioner, W. H. Stoker, once again dissented, stating:

> Whilst appreciating that the Calvo Clause in this case is identical with that in the *Mexican Union Railway* case (Decision No. 21), and that the alleged circumstances giving rise to the claim are similar to those in that case, it is, in my opinion, necessary that I should record my dissent from the decision in this case, as done already in the case of the *Interoceanic Railway Company* (Decision No. 53).
>
> I do so for the same reasons, recording also my opinion that this is a yet stronger case of the inapplicability of the Calvo Clause to cases resting on revolutionary causes, and not relating to contracts containing a Calvo Clause.[73]

[69] *Ibid.,* pp. 207–211.
[70] *Ibid.,* p. 207.
[71] *Ibid.,* p. 209. See *supra,* p. 241.
[72] *Ibid.,* pp. 209–210.
[73] *Ibid.,* p. 210.

The Calvo Clause

Thus the British-Mexican Commission, in this last case as in the first case, adopted and even extended the rule of the limited validity of the Calvo Clause which was first formulated by the United States–Mexican Commission in the *Dredging* case. The consistency with which both these commissions applied the rule would appear to give great weight to this principle as being the rule of law on the Calvo Clause in modern international arbitral jurisprudence.

The Calvo Clause before the Italian-Mexican Claims Commission

There remains to be considered one additional case that involved a form of the Calvo Clause. The matter came before the Italian-Mexican Claims Commission, set up under the Convention of January 13, 1927, to adjudicate the claims of Italian citizens against Mexico as a result of revolutionary disturbances,[74] in the case of *Italy (Ornato Pitol) v. the United Mexican States*.[75]

It appeared that the claimant had acquired land in Mexico as a colonist under a contract with the government. The claimant agreed to cultivate the land for ten years, at the end of this period becoming the full owner of the land. This contract was concluded by virtue of the General Colonization Law of 1883 which contained the following provision:

The colonists shall be considered as having all the rights and obligations which the Federal Constitution imposes on Mexicans and aliens respectively, and shall enjoy the temporary exemptions provided by the present law; but in all questions which may arise, they shall be of the class which remains subject to the decisions of the courts of the Republic, with absolute exclusion of all foreign intervention.[76]

[74] The convention, reprinted in Feller, *Mex. Claims Com.*, pp. 502–510, contained, in Article VI, a waiver of the requirement to exhaust local remedies as a condition precedent to the presentation of a claim. The commissioners were Miquel Cruchaga Tocornal of Chile (presiding commissioner), Isidro Fabela (Mexico), and Mario Serra di Cassano (Italy).

[75] Decision No. 107 (unpublished). The opinion, along with the other jurisprudence of this commission, is unpublished and is available only in the Archives of the Mexican Secretariat of Foreign Relations. The instant case is, however, abstracted in Feller, *Mex. Claims Com.*, pp. 196–198.

[76] Quoted *ibid.*, p. 197.

Although the phraseology of the Calvo Clause in this contract was exceedingly broad, covering "all questions which may arise," the commission by a majority upheld the effectiveness of the provision as a bar to their jurisdiction. The question of the validity of the Clause was accepted without question, the only matter of concern being whether the renunciatory provision survived the expiration of the ten-year period stipulated in the contract. The commission held that it did, thus upholding the Calvo Clause as a bar to its jurisdiction in spite of the fact that the claimant's injuries, arising out of depredations by revolutionary forces, were clearly ones for which Mexico was liable under the *compromis*.[77]

The *Pitol* case, it appears, conformed to the post-*Dredging* trend in international arbitral jurisprudence to recognize and give effect to the rule of the limited validity of the Calvo Clause.

Conclusions Regarding the Role of the Calvo Clause in International Arbitral Jurisprudence since 1926

A decisive test of whether a principle is actually the rule of law on a given problem is how that principle fares at the hands of courts in subsequent adjudications. Here the record of the principle of the limited validity of the Calvo Clause is indeed impressive. In the seven cases that have dealt with this problem since the *Dredging* decision, five have applied the rule of the limited validity of the Clause to bar claims that would have been receivable in the absence of the renunciatory provision.[78] In the sixth case, the Clause did not serve to bar the claim only because it was so vaguely worded that the intent of the parties was not clear to the commission.[79] In the seventh case, the Clause did not bar the presentation of the claim because of the clear and flag-

[77] *Ibid.* Feller points out one distinguishing characteristic of this case. It was a situation in which the claimant had received a special privilege, that of colonizing on government land. "As a price of the privilege it might well be held that Mexico could require such a promise as was made." *Ibid.*

[78] *International Fisheries, Mexican Union Railway, Interoceanic Railway, Veracruz Railway,* and *Pitol* cases.

[79] *MacNeil* case.

rant denial of justice involved.[80] This record would certainly not support the contention of many authorities that the Clause is illegal, futile, and superfluous. On the contrary, it is legal and significant in determining the admissibility of claims.

It would appear from this summation that the rule of the *Dredging* case has become the rule of law on the Calvo Clause in international arbitral jurisprudence. This is even more evident in view of the explicit approval given to this ruling in the decisional law cited above, both in the majority and minority opinions. This consistency in following precedent is unparalleled in the jurisprudence involving this problem.

Although these cases that have followed the *Dredging* rule have been subjected to much the same criticism that was leveled at that decision,[81] it should not be forgotten that the commissions were analyzing this concept against the wider background of a growing integration of international society,[82] and the correlative developments in the field of international law.[83] Traditional concepts — such as the one holding that international law applies only to nations and that individuals cannot, under any circumstances, have a personal standing under it — were rejected as "antiquated." [84] The commissions felt justified in looking behind the presentation of the claim by the government to see whether the individual had fulfilled his obligation so as to be able "rightfully" to present his claim to his government, to be in turn presented to the international tribunal. There seems little question but that these decisions can be criticized if judged by the criterion of the traditional concept of international law. However, in view of the fact that the attitude represented by the commissions in giving weight and emphasis to the actions of the individual has been in the ascendency in recent years, it would seem unlikely that the rule of law evolved in this decisional law will be reversed. This would appear particularly true in view of

---

[80] *El Oro Mining and Railway Co.* case.

[81] See, for example, Freeman, *Denial of Justice*, pp. 482–489; Feller, *Mex. Claims Com.*, pp. 192–198.

[82] Schwarzenberger, *op. cit.*, p. 65.

[83] *Opinions of Commissioners*, I, p. 24.

[84] *Ibid.*, pp. 23–24.

the apparent willingness by the leading nations of the world to accept this rule of law.

This completes the survey of the arbitral jurisprudence that has involved the Calvo Clause.[85] There remain to be considered the precise content and effectiveness of this rule of law on the Calvo Clause. The contention that it is meaningless and superfluous has been rejected because of its impressive record in determining the receivability of claims in recent arbitral law. This decisional law, taken solely at its face value, would mean, at the very least, that a Calvo Clause commitment may apply to both contractual and revolutionary disputes, depending on the phraseology of the renunciatory provision, and that it is effective at least to the extent that it serves to overcome a general waiver of the necessity to exhaust local remedies contained in the *compromis*. But the language of the commissions in applying the rule of limited validity to achieve this result, and the logical and legal implications of this rule, suggest much more as far as the effectiveness of the Calvo Clause is concerned. This will be discussed in the next chapter, where, after a brief summation of the origin and evolution of the Calvo Clause in inter-American and international law and diplomacy, an analysis will be made of the contemporary status of this concept and its possible future evolution in the diplomacy and jurisprudence of the Americas and the world.

[85] The reasons why, in my opinion, there have been no more recent arbitrations involving this concept will be suggested *infra*, pp. 267–268, in the analysis of the contemporary effectiveness of the Calvo Clause.

‹ IX ›

The Future of the Calvo Clause

THE basic objective of this study has been to determine the rule of law on the Calvo Clause. In order to achieve this objective, attention was directed toward the three chief law-determining agencies — governments, courts, and publicists. This has involved an examination of the diplomacy, jurisprudence, and legal publications that have dealt with this problem. Since the Calvo Clause has been peculiarly an American problem, with the Latin American nations the chief advocates of this principle and the United States the chief protagonist of the opposition, major emphasis has been placed on evidence adduced from the law-determining agencies in this hemisphere.

The primary objective of the Calvo Clause is to restrict or, if possible, to eliminate the right of diplomatic protection by a government on behalf of its nationals resident abroad. The Clause in its extreme form, as a complete bar to interposition under all circumstances, has found little support among the diplomats, jurists, and publicists outside of Latin America, and, on the basis of evidence derived from the three chief law-determining agencies, must be considered void under the rules of international law that are now generally recognized and practiced. Developments either in diplomacy or in jurisprudence might some day result in the validation of the Calvo Clause in its full sense. However, this could be accomplished only through a *change* in the rules governing relationships on the international scene. The possibility and probability of such a change will be discussed shortly.

The Future of the Calvo Clause

Although evidence derived from the three chief law-determining agencies does not support the contention of the complete validity of the Calvo Clause, it would be erroneous to conclude that the Calvo Clause is dead or is irrelevant on the point of international law. Although a majority of the publicists are of the opinion that the Clause is void, illegal, futile, and superfluous, a careful survey of the jurisprudence and diplomacy that has dealt with this concept in recent times does not, it is submitted, bear out this contention.

The rule of law on this concept in international jurisprudence, first formulated in the *North American Dredging Company of Texas* case, and subsequently endorsed and applied in later international adjudications, is that the Clause enjoys a limited validity under the rules of international law. It was held that the Calvo Clause commitment is legally binding on the individual in that it requires him to seek redress for his grievances in the local courts, but is not binding on the government of the individual in the face of an international delinquency such as a denial of justice. As an indication of the vitality and the meaningfulness of this rule of limited validity, it has been applied in six recent international arbitrations with the result that a claim was barred that would have been receivable in the absence of the Calvo Clause.[1] Since this rule of limited validity was first enunciated in 1926, not one international tribunal has questioned it or refused to accept it as being determinative on the question of the validity of the Calvo Clause.[2] This consistency in the recognition of the precedential value of the *Dredging* decision is most remarkable if compared with the confusion and contradiction that characterized arbitral rulings on the Calvo Clause in the period before 1926.

But in order to conclude, with propriety, that a given principle has won recognition as the rule of law it is necessary to

---

[1] *Dredging, International Fisheries, Mexican Union Railway, Interoceanic Railway, Veracruz Railway,* and *Pitol* cases.

[2] Even the dissenting opinions in several of these cases accepted the *Dredging* rule as good law, though not applicable to noncontractual damages. See, for example, the *Mexican Union Railway* and *Interoceanic Railway* cases.

demonstrate that this rule has been accepted by a representative number of governments or is at least reconcilable with their official attitudes. This can be done with the present rule. The attitudes of a majority of states that have had occasion to define their position on this problem are fully reconcilable with this rule of limited validity.[3] The Latin American nations, as evidenced by the position of Mexico,[4] are also apparently willing to accept this rule, although, of course, still hopeful for success in their efforts to win acceptance of the complete validity of the Calvo Clause.

Having thus determined the rule of law on the Calvo Clause, there remains to be considered just what this rule of law means. Unfortunately, there has not been enough decisional law involving this rule of law to give a precise or determinative interpretation. But, in the six cases that have applied the rule of limited validity to bar an international claim, some suggestions as to its precise effectiveness may be found.

The very least that can be accorded to the rule of law that holds the Clause binding on the individual though not on his state is that it serves to overcome a general waiver of the requirement to exhaust local remedies contained in the *compromis.* This much effectiveness cannot be denied, for the six recent arbitral rulings can be cited in support of it. Perhaps this is the full effectiveness of the Clause.[5] Even so, it still cannot correctly be maintained that the Clause is superfluous or ineffective, for it has proven to be effective to this extent, at least, in preventing the submission of claims otherwise receivable. Furthermore, it is very important to note that this waiver of the local remedies rule in the *compromis* has become rather common in recent international arbitrations. Such a provision has been included in at least nine recent conventions between major powers, *including the last four major arbitration agreements to which the United States was a party.*[6] Consequently, if future conventions con-

[3] *Supra*, pp. 36–56.
[4] *Supra*, pp. 36–37.
[5] This is the opinion of Phillips, *op. cit.*, pp. 235–236.
[6] These nine claims conventions would include those between the United

form to what would appear to be the recent trend in international arbitration as evidenced by these nine recent treaties, then the Calvo Clause, even if restricted in effectiveness to overcoming a general waiver of the local remedies rule contained in the *compromis*, will continue to have a determinative effect on the admissibility of international claims.

However, this rule of law on the Calvo Clause is at least suggestive of much more. Since no courts have had occasion to give this rule further application, the full meaning of the rule of limited validity must be sought in the language of the tribunals that have formulated the rule and in the interpretations of the governments which have accepted it. To be sure this analysis will be somewhat speculative, since the actual delimitation of the meaning of the rule of law on the Calvo Clause must await further international adjudication.

Great Britain, in accepting the *Dredging* case and its rule as "good law," stated that this rule means that

. . . no rule of international law prevents the inclusion of a stipulation in a contract between a Government and an alien that in all matters pertaining to the contract the jurisdiction of the local tribunals shall be *complete and exclusive*, nor does it prevent such a stipulation being obligatory . . . upon any international tribunal to which may be submitted a claim arising out of the contract in which the stipulation was inserted.[7]

Germany, in stating its position on the validity of the renunciatory provision, asserted that

. . . it is possible to deduce from agreements of this kind that the *individual foregoes his right* to regard himself as injured by

States and Great Britain (Article III of the "Terms of Submission" of the Pecuniary Claims Arbitration Agreement, signed August 18, 1910); the United States and Mexico (Article V of the General Claims Convention of September 8, 1923); the United States and Mexico (Article VI of the Special Claims Convention of September 10, 1923); the United States and Panama (Article V of the Convention of July 28, 1926); France and Mexico (Article VI of the Convention of September 25, 1924); Germany and Mexico (Article VII of the Convention of March 16, 1925); Great Britain and Mexico (Article VI of the Convention of November 19, 1926); Italy and Mexico (Article VI of the Convention of January 13, 1927); Spain and Mexico (Article VI of the Convention of November 25, 1925). See *supra*, p. 198, n. 14.

[7] *Bases of Discussion*, p. 134. Italics mine.

certain events, so that the State's claim would be devoid of any effective basis.[8]

Czechoslovakia, in this same connection, stated that

. . . in principle, the Czechoslovak Government sees no objection to previous declaration by the person concerned that in certain circumstances he will have recourse only to the legal remedies afforded him by the national law in question and *will not invoke* the diplomatic protection of his own country.[9]

The attitudes expressed in these statements, representative of those governments who have accepted the limited validity of the Calvo Clause, suggest that, in their opinion, the Clause makes the local remedies *complete* and *exclusive* in contractual disputes and precludes the individual from *seeking* the interposition of his government in matters covered by the renunciatory provision. This interpretation is clearly expressed by Mexico, which, in what has been described as a compromise with the United States over the validity of the Calvo Clause,[10] asserted: "The Mexican Government therefore does not deny that the American Government is at liberty to intervene for its nationals; but that does not stand in the way of carrying out an agreement under which the *alien agrees not to be the party asking for the diplomatic protection of his Government.*"[11]

That the Clause, in its limited form, might bind the individual from *seeking* the interposition of his government is likewise suggested in the opinions of the tribunals that have formulated this rule of law. The British-Mexican Commission, in the *Mexican Union Railway* case, asserted that

. . . the action of the Government can not be regarded as an action taken independently of the wishes or the interest of the claimant. It is an action the initiative of which rests with the claimant. . . . By this contract the claimant has solemnly promised *not to apply to his Government for diplomatic intervention*

---

[8] *Ibid.*, p. 133. Italics mine.

[9] *Ibid.*, p. 135. Italics mine.

[10] G. H. Stuart, *op. cit.*, p. 177, states that with this Mexican reply, "a compromise seems to have been reached in the correspondence [over the Mexican oil expropriations]."

[11] U.S. Department of State, *American Property Rights in Mexico* (Washington, D.C., 1926), p. 14. Italics mine.

but to resort to the municipal courts. He has waived the right upon which the claim is now presented. *He has precluded himself by his contract from taking the initiative,* without which his claim can have no standing before this Commission and can not be recognizable.[12]

This same commission in the *MacNeil* case, in referring to the Calvo Clause provision in the *Mexican Union Railway* case, asserted: "But the words in which the concessionaire *had divested himself of the right* [to ask through their government redress before this commission for damage and loss, suffered in Mexico], were so clear, circumstantial and detailed, that no other decision was justified." [13] In the *Nitrate* case, in which the Anglo-Chilean Commission had also embraced this rule that the Clause is binding on the individual, though not on his state, the commission asserted that

. . . the individuals or companies which have obligated themselves by contract freely celebrated not to have recourse *personally* to diplomatic action, *likewise can not invoke, directly or personally, the intervention of the British Legation, nor seek the jurisdiction of this tribunal,* for the resolution of questions which may arise between them and the Government with which they have contracted and with which they have made express agreements . . .[14]

In the *Dredging* decision, the commission, in enunciating this rule, asserted:

Under Article 18 of the contract [the Calvo Clause] declared upon the *present claimant is precluded from presenting to its Government* any claim relative to the interpretation or fulfillment of this contract. . . . As the claimant voluntarily entered into a legal contract *binding itself not to call as to this contract upon its Government to intervene* in its behalf, and as all of its claim relates to this contract, and as therefore *it can not present its claim* to its Government for interposition or espousal before this Commission, the second ground of the motion to dismiss is sustained.[15]

[12] *Decisions and Opinions of Commissioners,* p. 163. Italics mine.
[13] *Further Decisions and Opinions of Commissioners,* p. 23. Italics mine.
[14] *Reclamaciones presentados al Tribunal Anglo-Chileno, 1894–1896,* II, pp. 322–323. Translation and italics mine.
[15] *Opinions of Commissioners,* I, pp. 30–33. Italics mine.

It would appear that the language in which these key opinions were phrased suggests that the limited Calvo Clause serves to preclude the individual from *seeking* the interposition of his government. To be sure, all the governments in their statements and the courts in their opinions asserted that the Clause would not bar diplomatic protection in case of a violation of international law. However, if this rule of the limited validity of the Calvo Clause should be strictly applied by future tribunals to preclude the individual from seeking the intervention of his government, this would actually serve, in practice, to prevent the state from intervening at all. As John Bullington has aptly observed: "It is patent that to recognize the right of the state to require the alien not to invoke the aid of his government is effectively to extinguish the right of that government to intervene in his behalf." [16]

Furthermore, if the Clause were applied in this manner, tribunals would be faced with the exceedingly difficult task of determining whether, in fact, the individual had *sought* intervention contrary to his contractual commitment, or whether the state had interposed *spontaneously.* Only the individual concerned, or his government, would be in a position to disclose the full circumstances behind the sponsorship of the claim, and probably such information would not be forthcoming. This practical difficulty in applying the rule might well make it impossible of implementation in international reclamations.

Although it appears relevant to suggest this possible elaboration of the rule of law on the Calvo Clause in view of the language employed by governments and tribunals in enunciating this principle, it should be noted once again that the rule of limited validity, if employed in the manner suggested above, would result in the realization, in practice, of the complete validity of the Clause as a bar to diplomatic interposition. Consequently, in view of the emphatic pronouncements of statesmen and judges that the Calvo Clause could not inhibit diplomatic protection in

---

[16] "The Land and Petroleum Laws of Mexico," *AJIL*, XXII (January 1928), p. 67. It should be noted that under normal circumstances a government would not even be aware of an injury to its national unless the individual took the initiative in seeking interposition.

the face of a denial of justice, it is not probable that this interpretation and application of the rule of limited validity will come
about in the near future. However, if some future tribunal, such
as, for example, an inter-American court of justice, desired to
find support for an interpretation of the Calvo Clause that would,
in practice, effectively bar all diplomatic interposition, it well
might develop the rule of law on the Calvo Clause along the lines
outlined above.

The rule of the limited validity of the Calvo Clause does make
exception for violations of international law such as a denial of
justice. But this exception is not as meaningful as it might at
first appear, especially in view of the confusion and uncertainty
that exists in contemporary international jurisprudence over the
precise meaning of that term.[17] A further implication of this rule
of law on the Calvo Clause might well be that international tribunals, in the face of a Calvo Clause commitment, will require
such a denial of justice to be more patent and flagrant than is
normally the case. The Harvard Research study lent support to
this possibility when it commented that ". . . [unless] the offense
is particularly flagrant or may be deemed a national affront, the
individual's waiver of a right to indemnity weakens the basis of
his government's demand for reparation . . ."[18] It is not to be
forgotten that the British-Mexican Claims Commission, in a decision[19] which Freeman described as "the most amazing utterance upon the Calvo Clause to date,"[20] held that vain efforts
to secure redress over a period of almost eight years did not constitute a denial or undue delay of justice. The commission was
undoubtedly influenced by the Calvo Clause commitment, and
required evidence of a more patent or flagrant denial of justice.
It would appear, then, that another implication of this limited
validity rule is that greater evidence of a denial or undue delay
of justice will be required than is usual in order to by-pass the
Calvo Clause.[21]

[17] *Supra*, pp. 114–116.
[18] *AJIL*, XXIII, Special Number, p. 207.
[19] *Interoceanic Railway* case.
[20] *Denial of Justice*, p. 486.
[21] The decisions of the commission in the *Dredging* and *International Fisheries*

Still another interpretation of this rule of limited validity would be that the state has the right, if the individual seeks diplomatic intervention in violation of his legally binding contract, to rescind the contract. An eminent legal scholar, and one-time solicitor of the Department of State, Charles Cheney Hyde, has asserted that

. . . a state may prescribe the terms on which it grants a concession. Those terms may in fact purport to restrict the freedom of the grantee to invoke the aid of his own state with respect to matters relating to the contract, or even to restrict the freedom of that state to interpose in his behalf. Even though they are designed to restrain the grantee from the exercise of rights which he ought not to be called upon to give up, or to deter the state of which he is a national from interposing under circumstances when interposition is justifiable, action by the grantee in contempt of these conditions should at least confer upon the grantor the right to rescind the contract.[22]

The fear of rescission would undeniably serve to discourage petitions for intervention unless the situation was very serious and the claimant was prepared to abandon entirely his operations under the contract.

An additional implied effectiveness of the rule of the limited validity of the Calvo Clause is suggested by Lionel Summers, who has asserted that "a strict interpretation of the Calvo Clause will preclude good offices."[23]

This rule of law on the Calvo Clause is, then, far from being meaningless. It has already served to bar a number of international claims, and, as suggested above, its implications might well serve in future adjudications to restrict materially diplomatic interposition and the presentation of claims to international tribunals where a Calvo Clause is involved. It should be

cases further suggest that no question of an "immediate" denial of justice, such as would obviate the necessity to refer to local redress, could arise in the face of a Calvo Clause commitment. See *supra*, p. 212.

[22] "Concerning Attempts by Contract to Restrict Interposition," *AJIL*, XXI (April 1927), pp. 298–299. Eagleton, *Resp. of States*, p. 170, states that the alien "may be forced to accept as a penalty for his failure to abide by it [the Calvo Clause] the loss of his contract."

[23] *Op. cit.*, p. 466.

noted once again that the precise meaning and effectiveness of the Calvo Clause must await further interpretation and application by international tribunals. But the fact that its meaning is uncertain and its implications are perhaps contradictory does not argue against its being the rule of law on the subject. Not all rules of law are, unfortunately, well defined or even consistent in their application.

There have not been any international law cases that have involved this concept since the Mexican claims commissions ceased to function in the 1930s. This is not a result of the decreased utilization of the Calvo Clause in Latin American contractual relationships between the government and aliens. On the contrary, as will be seen presently, the Clause is in as widespread use as previously, if not more so.

The reasons for the lack of recent arbitrations involving the Calvo Clause are undoubtedly many and varied.[24] However, in my opinion, by no means the least of the reasons for this dearth of recent claims is the very fact that the Clause has now realized a limited degree of validity under international law. To be sure a great deal of uncertainty exists as to the precise meaning and effectiveness of the rule of limited validity, but this very uncertainty would tend to make a signer of a Calvo Clause think twice before seeking the intervention of his government. The fact that the Calvo Clause has actually barred international reclamations would, in sharp contrast to previous practice, tend to make the individual exceedingly careful about violating his renunciatory commitment unless the denial of justice was, beyond any question, patent and flagrant — particularly since the individual would face possible rescission of his contract and expulsion from the country in which he is carrying on his business and seeking

[24] For example, World War II and international tension in the postwar period; improvements in the standard of justice and the stability of the Latin American republics; no major recent arbitrations involving Latin America and the investor powers; the political considerations involved in perhaps wishing to press only the more serious claims involving the Calvo Clause during a period when the security and economic interests of the United States dictate hemispheric solidarity and good will.

his fortune.[25] Thus the rule of limited validity could have the effect of forcing aliens to seek redress in the local courts, where, contrary to their initial expectation, they might well find the standards in administration of justice satisfactory.

Although the precise status of the Calvo Clause under the contemporary rules of international law has not yet been determined, on the basis of the evidence contained in this study a few generalizations seem to be in order. It should be apparent that the Calvo Clause in its limited interpretation is now recognized by governments and courts as legal under the rules of international law. Moreover, contrary to the contention of a majority of publicists, the Clause is not superfluous or irrelevant but has played a legally significant and meaningful role in international arbitral jurisprudence. The rule of law on the Calvo Clause, holding that it binds the individual, but not his state in the event of violations of international law such as a denial of justice, is likewise far from meaningless. While there is not much doubt as to the right of the government itself to intervene, the fact that the individual is bound by the Clause might operate, in practice, to narrow greatly the exercise of this right. It might well be that this rule of limited validity will, in practice, lead to the accomplishment of the long-cherished dream of the Latin Americans to restrict severely diplomatic interposition.[26] The interpretation and application of this rule of law by future tribunals should be scrutinized closely to determine more precisely the exact degree of validity of the Calvo Clause and the full meaning and effectiveness of its rule of law.

[25] The constitution of Honduras (March 28, 1936) provides, in Article 19, that should the Calvo Clause stipulation "be contravened, and claims are not terminated amicably, resulting in loss to the country, the claimant shall forfeit his right to live in the country." See Fitzgibbon, *Constitutions of the Americas* (Chicago, 1948), pp. 470–471. The constitution of Nicaragua (March 22, 1939) provides, in Article 25, that those who violate the Calvo Clause provision "will lose the right to reside in the country." See *ibid.*, p. 558.

[26] I was unable to secure from the State Department any information on the number of times in the past two decades that intervention had been requested in spite of the fact that an individual had signed a Calvo Clause. The records of the department are not arranged in a manner that would reveal this information. Evidence obtained from the various United States embassies in Latin

The Future of the Calvo Clause

Current Utilization of the Calvo Clause in Latin America

This investigation of the rule of law on the Calvo Clause would not be complete without the documentation in greater detail of the extent of current utilization of the Calvo Clause in Latin America. How widespread is the incorporation of this renunciatory provision in contracts? Has it played a role in any recent controversies between the Latin American governments and resident aliens or foreign business interests? Although several authorities have ventured the generalization that the Clause is still in rather common use,[27] there has never been any published documentation of this observation.

There are a number of different approaches to a determination of the extent of the current utilization of the Calvo Clause. One way would be to scrutinize the various Latin American constitutions and laws dealing with the status of aliens.[28] But this might result in an erroneous impression, for, as will be seen, in some instances the Clause is not legally required by constitutional or statutory provision, and yet is incorporated in all contracts with aliens as a matter of policy, while in other instances the Clause is legally required and yet is used only under special circumstances. A preferable approach is through the medium of the various United States embassies in Latin America, for they should be in the best position to know not only of the existence of the practice of incorporating the Calvo Clause in contracts, but also of any recent controversies between American business interests and Latin American governments that involved the Calvo Clause.[29]

America indicates, however, that requests for interposition under these circumstances have been infrequent.

[27] Summers, *op. cit.*, pp. 469–470 (as of 1933); Lipstein, *op. cit.*, pp. 130–131 (as of 1945).

[28] For examples, see *supra*, pp. 31–32.

[29] I am deeply indebted to the various United States ambassadors and their staffs who so very generously provided much information that was invaluable to this investigation. Most of the embassies spent a considerable amount of time and effort in complying with my request for specific and documented information, which is particularly appreciated in view of their heavy work load resulting from recent reductions in staff and budget.

The Calvo Clause

It is appropriate to begin this survey with the United States' immediate neighbor to the south, the Republic of Mexico, which has perhaps suffered more from the abuses of intervention and diplomatic protection than any other of the Latin American nations. Mexico, in recent years, has been the most outspoken of the Latin American states in its advocacy of the justice and legality of the Calvo Clause, and consequently it is not surprising to find that the Clause is very widely used in this country. The Clause is required not only in all contract-concessions with the government, but also in all cases in which property is purchased by a foreigner in the city or the country. The renunciatory provision is not usually used when the purchase of machinery or other movable property is transacted. The Calvo Clause is incorporated in the Constitution of 1917 under Article 27, Franction I:

I. Only Mexicans by birth or by naturalization and Mexican societies, have the right to acquire the ownership [dominio] of lands, waters and their accessories, or to obtain concessions for the exploitation of mines, waters or combustible minerals in the Mexican Republic. The State may concede the same right to foreigners provided that they enter into an agreement before the Secretariat of Foreign Relations to be considered as nationals with respect to said properties and not to invoke, therefore, the protection of their Governments in anything relating thereto; under the penalty, in the event of disregard of their agreement, to lose to the benefit of the Nation the properties they have acquired by virtue thereof. In a zone [faja] of one hundred kilometers along the frontiers and of fifty on the seashores, under no circumstances can foreigners acquire direct dominion over lands and waters.

The relevant application form, supplied and translated by an official source in Mexico, reads as follows:

C. Secretary of Foreign Relations.   Mexico, D.F.

I, _____(name), a citizen of the United States of North America, of __ years of age, having paid in full my Income Tax to date, and designating the Office of _____(name and address of lawyer) to hear notifications, and authorizing said lawyer to hear them at his said Office (or domicile), in the City of Mexico, before you, with the greatest respect, say:

That I desire to acquire the following real property _____ (describe), which is located in _____, and the boundaries of which are _____(here give the boundaries).

In compliance with the provisions of Clause I of Article 27 of the Constitution of the Republic, I come before the Secretariat in your worthy charge, to agree to consider myself as a Mexican with respect to said real property and not to invoke, therefore, the protection of my Government in regard to it, under the penalty, in case of failing in my agreement, of losing to the benefit of the Mexican Nation the said property which I may acquire by virtue of the said agreement.

For the pertinent effects, I declare to this Secretariat, that I was born in _____ on the __ day of _____ 19__, and that I am duly registered in the Register of Foreigners in the Secretariat of Gobernación, which issued card form No. __ on the date _____.

By reason whereof, I request you please to grant me the permit requested.

I make the necessary protest.

_____(place) _____(date).

_____(signature)

In Cuba, one of the island republics of Latin America, the Calvo Clause is fairly widely used, I have been reliably informed by an official Embassy source. It is interesting to note, however, that while cognizance of the Calvo principle is taken in the drawing up of numerous local contracts involving transfer of title to commodities and real estate, this contract provision is apparently rarely associated in local legal and commercial circles with the name "Calvo." The use of this provision underwent a development in Cuba apart from the general historical evolution of the concept in the rest of Latin America. The contractual provision in Cuba is said to have had its origin in the practice of including in buying or selling operations where the parties resided in different cities in Cuba a paragraph in which one party would waive jurisdictional privilege. From that start, it became common to incorporate a broader Calvo Clause provision in contracts with resident aliens.

The Calvo Clause

Information from the United States Embassy in the Dominican Republic indicates that as far as is known the Calvo Clause is not written into contracts with resident aliens, nor has it been invoked in an attempt to inhibit diplomatic interposition.[30]

The United States Embassy in Haiti has informed me that the Calvo Clause does not exist in Haitian law at the present time. The Calvo Clause was formerly required, but was removed from the Haitian constitution in 1918, largely at the instigation of United States authorities. During the 1915–1934 occupation, I am informed, United States authorities felt that material progress was desirable in Haiti, that this progress depended largely upon foreign investment, and that foreign investment would not become significant unless it were guaranteed better treatment than it had been getting; therefore one of the broad reforms which United States officials undertook to effect was directed toward improving the climate for foreign investment by improving the treatment which foreigners received within the country. Since, by the Calvo Clause provisions in effect before 1918, foreigners did not have, under Haitian law, rights of diplomatic representation, or, in actual fact, recourse to impartial courts, the removal of the Calvo Clause requirements fitted into the United States' effort to create conditions which would make foreign investment more attractive by giving the investors a greater degree of security.[31] It would thus appear, on the basis of this information, that, if it were not for external pressures, the Calvo Clause would probably still be required under Haitian law.

Turning now to the Central American republics, we find that the Calvo Clause is in rather common use. Panama, the smallest of the Latin American republics in population, has, through statutory and constitutional provisions, required that foreigners waive the right to claim protection through diplomatic channels. This obligation is derived generally from Article 21 of the Panamanian constitution which provides that "all Panamanians

[30] Personal communication, dated July 14, 1954, from the United States Embassy at Ciudad Trujillo, Dominican Republic.

[31] Personal communication, dated October 15, 1954, from the United States Embassy at Port-au-Prince, Haiti.

and foreigners are equal before the law," and specifically from Article 164 of the Administrative Code which provides:

Article 164. Contracts entered into in Panamá between the Government and foreign persons, individuals or companies, shall be subject to the Panamanian law; and the duties and rights arising out of said contract shall be exclusively established by the judges and local courts.

An express condition in all contracts of this nature shall be that the foreigner shall waive claiming through diplomatic channels with respect to the duties and rights arising out of the contract, except in the case of denial of justice.[32]

It should be noted that the exception of cases of denial of justice is not, as has been pointed out previously, as significant as it might at first appear, due to the general confusion over the meaning of this term and the extremely narrow definition usually attached to it by Latin Americans.

Costa Rica likewise adheres to the use of the Calvo Clause, although it is not inserted into all contracts between foreign business interests and the government. I am reliably informed that the three principal concerns operating in Costa Rica under contract with the government are the Compañía Bananera de Costa Rica, the Compañía Petrolera de Costa Rica, and the Northern Railway Company. Of these, only the Compañía Bananera's contract contains the Calvo Clause. The Clause was first introduced into the Compañía Bananera's contract in 1938 and has figured in all their subsequent contracts. But, as far as is known, the Clause has not played a role in the company's dealings with the government. On at least one occasion in the past, a Costa Rican administration has indicated its willingness to have the Department of State intervene in negotiations between the company and the government, if only as an interested observer, despite the existence of the Clause. However, the Department of State has never intervened in any way in such negotiations.[33]

In Nicaragua, the Calvo Clause is by law automatically and

---

[32] Information and translations furnished in personal communications, dated July 26, 1954, and August 20, 1954, from the United States Embassy in Panama.

[33] Personal communication, dated July 16, 1954, from the United States Embassy at San José, Costa Rica.

universally included in all contracts between the Nicaraguan government and foreign interests, individual or group. But, according to official information obtained from the United States Embassy, no dispute in which the Calvo Clause has played any role has arisen in many years.[34]

In El Salvador, while one or another variant of the Calvo Clause has been in the past, and undoubtedly still is, included in contracts between the Salvadoran government and American firms, an official source says that any difficulties which may have arisen have generally been settled by arbitration between the two principally interested parties, assisted at times by the friendly, informal good offices of the United States. No objection apparently has been made to this friendly, informal interposition.

Honduras has a provision in Article 19 of the constitution of March 28, 1936, which prohibits recourse to diplomatic channels, but which, like Panama's constitution, makes exception for cases of a denial of justice. For the purposes of this article, "denial of justice is not understood to mean an executed verdict that is unfavorable to the claimant." [35] The Clause itself apparently is not too widely employed, and, according to informed sources, no recent disputes have come up in which it has been involved.[36]

The Republic of Guatemala has in the past adhered to the use of the Calvo Clause. For example, the Clause has been required in all petroleum concessions granted to foreigners.[37] Because of the recent (1954) internal strife which resulted in the overthrow of the regime of Col. Jacobo Arbenz Guzman by Col. Carlos Castillo Armas, the present utilization and future of the Calvo Clause under Guatemalan law is in some doubt. Apparently,

---

[34] Personal communication, dated July 20, 1954, from the United States Embassy at Managua, Nicaragua.

[35] For the text of the article, see *supra*, p. 25.

[36] Personal communication, dated July 15, 1954, from the United States Embassy at Tegucigalpa, Honduras.

[37] J. Filhol, *Législation mondiale du pétrole* (Paris, 1929), p. 32, reported: "L'exploration des gîtes pétrolifères situés dans le territoire de la république du Guatemala est ouverte à tout le monde. Les étrangers désireux d'obtenir un permis de recherches doivent, cependant, se soumettre aux conditions suivantes . . . engagement de ne jamais avoir recours à l'intervention diplomatique . . ."

however, some variant of the Calvo Clause will continue to be employed.

In the South American republics, also, widespread utilization of the Calvo Clause is found. Information obtained from the United States Embassy in Peru indicates that the Clause "is widely used in Peru, to the extent that its provisions are incorporated in a special article of the Peruvian Constitution of 1933." This article, translated by the Embassy, reads:

Article No. 17. Mercantile companies, whether national or foreign, are subject without any restrictions to the laws of the Republic. In all contracts between the Government and aliens, or in concessions granted to aliens, their express submission to the laws and tribunals of the Republic, and their waiver of diplomatic interposition must be expressly stated.

Even before this constitutional provision, "the inclusion of the Calvo Clause was required in all contracts between aliens and the Peruvian Government." [38]

Colombia, by virtue of Article 15 of Law 145 of November 26, 1888, specifically requires that aliens renounce diplomatic representation in contracts which are signed with the Colombian government. In earlier years especially, the Calvo Clause was frequently inserted in agreements with foreign corporations. However, while the Law of 1888 is still technically in effect, it is not, in practice, enforced, and there apparently have not been any recent instances of the invocation of the Calvo Clause in disputes or disagreements.[39]

Argentina appears to be one of the few republics of Latin America that does not adhere to the use of the Calvo Clause. The United States Embassy there has indicated that it knows of no instance of the use or application of the Calvo Clause in Argentina. A principal legal firm in Buenos Aires which represents numerous foreign business interests has informed the Embassy that it has never encountered such a provision in a contract nor

[38] Personal communication, dated August 1, 1953, from the United States Embassy at Lima, Peru.

[39] Personal communication, dated August 10, 1954, from the United States Embassy at Bogotá, Colombia.

does it know of any specific application of the Calvo Doctrine in business affairs.[40]

The law of Ecuador, passed on February 16, 1938, makes mandatory the inclusion of a Calvo Clause in all contracts concluded with foreigners. Article 31 of this law reads in part: "The renunciation of diplomatic claims will be an implicit and essential condition of all contracts concluded by foreigners with the state, or of all contracts obligating the state or individuals to foreigners, or of all contracts whose effects should be felt in Ecuador." [41] However, the issue of the Calvo Clause has not been invoked in any recent dispute, and there has, in fact, been only one controversy involving an American firm recently, and that was settled by extrajudicial means.[42]

According to official sources, Bolivia is also one of the Latin American states adhering to the use of the Calvo Clause. The Bolivian constitution, in Article 18, prohibits appeals to diplomatic interposition, except in cases of denial of justice. The provision, unofficially translated, reads: "Foreign subjects or foreign enterprises are, with regard to property, in the same state as Bolivians, and in no case can they invoke an exceptional situation or appeal to diplomatic interposition, except in the case of denial of justice." In the controversy involving the expropriation of the Standard Oil properties in Bolivia in 1937, the Bolivian government relied on a Calvo Clause defense in resisting United States' diplomatic intervention in the case.

In Brazil, the largest republic of Latin America, no recent incidents have arisen involving the Calvo Clause. An official source has informed me that, while it is difficult to generalize as to the arrangements made by business firms in so vast a country, no widespread use of the Clause has been noted in recent years.

Venezuela has had a long history of being involved in foreign interventions, both diplomatic and armed, in behalf of resident aliens and foreign business interests; and it is not surprising that

[40] Personal communication, dated August 11, 1954, from the United States Embassy at Buenos Aires, Argentina.

[41] For a more complete text of this law, see *supra*, p. 26.

[42] Personal communication, dated July 14, 1954, from the United States Embassy at Quito, Ecuador.

this republic specifically requires the inclusion of the Calvo Clause in contracts with foreigners. The Venezuelan constitution, signed on April 11, 1953, contains the following provision as translated by the United States Embassy:

Article No. 49: In contracts of public interest entered into with the National Government, or with the States or Municipalities, the following clause shall be deemed to be incorporated: "Doubts and controversies of any kind that may arise out of this contract and that can not be settled in a friendly manner by the contracting parties, shall be decided by the competent courts of Venezuela, in accordance with its laws, and they may not for any reason be the basis for foreign claims."

The Venezuelan Hydrocarbons Law which governs enterprises exploiting the national resources and other businesses so related stipulates, in Article 4, that the foreigner cannot invoke any foreign authority in the event of a dispute.

According to an Embassy source, in actual practice the number of cases in which Americans have had bad experiences with Venezuela are few and belong to the past rather than to the present. In a number of cases that arose immediately following the 1945 revolution when the new government canceled various construction contracts with American interests, the Embassy participated on an informal basis in the negotiations over indemnities, and, as far as Embassy officers who were there then recall, there was no protest by Venezuela against the intervention. The American business interests, although sorry to lose the work, declared themselves satisfied with the indemnity granted. The Embassy has also interceded in behalf of an American-owned business firm, La Internacional, C.A., which is seeking compensation for property destroyed by fire after being expropriated by the government. In the course of the litigation involving this case, the Venezuelan government expressed the opinion that the claimant must exhaust legal remedies available to him in Venezuela before he may enlist diplomatic intercession by his own government in his behalf.[43] It would thus appear that while Venezuela's

[43] Personal communication, dated August 10, 1954, from the United States Embassy at Caracas, Venezuela.

constitutional provision would ban diplomatic protection completely, in practice they are not opposed to interposition after the complete exhaustion of local remedies.

Uruguay does not require the Calvo Clause to be included in all contracts with foreigners. Some contracts negotiated by the government with foreign business interests do, however, contain the commitment that the aliens will not have recourse to diplomatic protection until they have exhausted all local remedies. Following this, if the alien still desires to solicit the interposition of his government, Uruguay would not consider any contractual provision to be effective to prevent a request for interposition.[44] According to informal sources, however, there does not appear to be any problem in this country, one of Latin America's foremost democracies, in regard to foreigners' receiving satisfaction in the local judicial process.

The situation in Paraguay is similar to that in most Latin American states. Official sources have indicated that the Calvo Clause is a part of every solicitation for bids made by the Paraguayan government for which it is expected that foreign companies will wish to tender bids. The Clause becomes a part of any contract signed by reason of a provision in the contract stating that the terms of the solicitation are recognized as a part of the contract. The Calvo Clause is also sometimes made a part of contracts for which there has been no public solicitation for bids; however, it is not customary to do so when the contract is for provision of merchandise or personal services.

The Calvo Clause was applied in the expropriation by Paraguay of the Compañía Americana de Luz y Tracción in 1948. This foreign-owned concern was denied the right of diplomatic intervention, and, according to official sources, none of the three foreign governments concerned protested the action, although there was vigorous informal diplomatic action which resulted in favorable terms for the company. In an earlier instance, Paraguay invoked the Calvo Clause with somewhat less success in

[44] Personal communication, dated August 27, 1954, from the United States Embassy at Montevideo, Uruguay.

a suit to settle accounts with the Asunción Port Concession Company when the American firm's concession lapsed in 1944. The Embassy intervened and the suit was settled out of court, in favor of the company.[45]

Chile likewise conforms to the general pattern. The so-called Calvo Clause "is in rather common use" in contracts between government agencies and foreign organizations.[46]

On the basis of this survey of the current utilization of the Calvo Clause in Latin America, it would appear that several generalizations are justified. It can be concluded that the insertion of the renunciatory provision in contracts with foreigners is definitely not just a practice of the past. On the basis of official information, it is seen that in only three countries, Argentina, Haiti, and the Dominican Republic, is the use of the Clause not found at present. In all of the other Latin American republics the Clause is utilized in varying degrees. Widespread use is found in Mexico, Nicaragua, Venezuela, Ecuador, Paraguay, and Peru. The practice of inserting the Clause in contracts with foreigners may be described as common in Cuba, Panama, Costa Rica, El Salvador, Bolivia, Chile, and probably Guatemala. Less extensive use of the Clause, in practice, at least, is reported in Uruguay, Brazil, Colombia, and Honduras. Thus not only do Latin Americans support the validity of the Calvo Clause in theory, but they also take positive steps to implement the Clause in practice. Insofar as Latin American relations among themselves are concerned, there is much evidence to support the contention that the validity of the Calvo Clause has become accepted as a customary principle of law governing intra-Latin American relationships. The strong support for the Calvo principles in the inter-American conferences would further buttress this conclusion.

It is significant to note, however, that while the utilization of the Calvo Clause is not declining, the number of disputes or con-

[45] Personal communication, dated August 2, 1954, from the United States Embassy at Asunción, Paraguay.

[46] Personal communication, dated August 5, 1953, from the United States Embassy at Santiago, Chile.

troversies in which it has been involved in recent years is apparently decreasing. This, I believe, is in line with the recognition of the limited validity of the Calvo Clause which makes it to the best interests of the resident alien or foreign investor to comply with his contractual commitment and be content with the redress obtainable in the local judicial remedies, unless he has suffered a particularly flagrant denial of justice. A number of the Latin American republics make explicit exception to the Calvo Clause commitment in the case of denial of justice. This qualification, while subject to considerable doubt due to the confusion over the meaning of the term "denial of justice" and the restricted interpretation usually accorded to this term by Latin Americans, would tend to bring the contractual waiver more in line with the rule of law on this concept as evolved in recent diplomacy and jurisprudence.

Perhaps the most significant aspect of the information produced by this survey is that, on the basis of formal and informal comment and observation by official sources, the relations between the Latin American governments and foreign business interests are, on the whole, considerably more harmonious than in the past. Specific reference to this development was made in the reports on Nicaragua, Venezuela, and Uruguay, and a considerable number of the other replies indicated a similar pattern. This would suggest that the contentiousness of this issue, while still evident in diplomatic and judicial circles, is becoming less acute in practice. The Latin American republics still invoke the Calvo Clause under sufficiently pressing circumstances, as is evidenced by the reports from Bolivia and Paraguay. But there seems to be less sensitivity on this subject as is indicated by the fact that a number of republics (Costa Rica, El Salvador, Venezuela, and Paraguay) appear to have no objection to informal diplomatic intercession in spite of a Calvo Clause commitment.

Finally, it should be noted that most of the nations in which the Calvo Clause is either not used or not used very extensively would generally fit into the category of Latin American republics that are considered to be the more stable economically and politically, whereas most of the nations in which the Clause is used very extensively are among those that have suffered the most from intervention, both diplomatic and armed.

The significance of these generalizations as to the extensiveness of the current utilization of the Calvo Clause in Latin America will become more apparent in the subsequent discussion of the future of the Calvo Clause.

The Future of the Calvo Clause

It is extremely difficult to venture predictions about a subject that is actually half legal and half diplomatic. The future of the Calvo Clause depends on developments in both inter-American diplomacy and international jurisprudence, which in turn depend on the degree of integration and harmonization of the world community.

Under the contemporary rules governing the interrelationships of states, the Clause has not realized fully its ultimate objective, to bar completely diplomatic intervention. It might, however, achieve this status through a *change* in these rules, either through inter-American conventions as the first and essential step toward world-wide acceptance or through the evolution of international law to grant recognition to the individual as a true subject of that law.

In regard to the first possibility, it should not be forgotten that the basic principles of Calvo's Doctrine, the parent concept of the Calvo Clause, have not fared too badly before inter-American conventions and conferences. One of these principles, that of nonintervention, has been accepted as perhaps the basic rule governing the interrelations among the republics of the Americas, and has made considerable progress toward winning recognition as a basic rule of international law.[47] The other principle, that of equality with nationals as the maximum to which aliens may aspire, has made impressive though not conclusive progress in recent International Conferences of American States.[48] Acceptance of this principle would in turn validate the Calvo

[47] *Supra*, pp. 64–72.
[48] *Supra*, pp. 72–104.

Clause, which is considered by Latin American jurists to be a formalization of the equality principle. The recent inclusion of the equality principle in the Pact of Bogotá and its partial inclusion in the O.A.S. Charter give evidence of the continuing determination of the Latin American republics to win total victory in their fight against diplomatic interposition.[49] The recent efforts to circumvent the minimum standards rule (which is the chief obstacle to the equality principle) have been aimed at establishing by declaration precisely what is included in a minimum standard and then setting up a Latin American–dominated court to enforce this standard. This might, perhaps, be the method by which the Latin Americans can finally end the practice of the unilateral interposition of a state to secure the protection of the rights of its citizens resident abroad. At the Tenth International Conference of American States held in Caracas in 1954, the efforts of the Latin American republics appeared to be concentrated on the objective of setting up an inter-American court, which would be, quite naturally, considerably more receptive to Latin American legal theories than an international court. Because of this latter consideration, and because of the internal political atmosphere of the United States, such a development is not considered probable until greater and more uniform economic, political, and social stability and progress characterize the nations of the Western Hemisphere. It is, nevertheless, a possibility well worth watching.

In the field of international jurisprudence, the most promising possibility of the complete validation of the Calvo Clause lies in the growing recognition of the status of the private individual in international law. It will be recalled that the fundamental legal objection to the complete validity of the Calvo Clause is based on the traditional precept of international law that only states are subjects of that law. Therefore, as Philip Jessup has stated, "all of the law having to do with the responsibility of states for injuries to aliens is law conferring rights on states," which, according to the old Vattelian formula, "are said to be injured by

[49] *Supra,* pp. 100–103.

injuries to their nationals." [50] Consequently, individuals, not being the subjects of international law and not being possessed of rights and duties under it, cannot validly waive a right that is not theirs, but which can only belong to their state. As M. Schücking, in a representative analysis, has stated: "As the exercise of the right of diplomatic protection is an expression of the discretionary power of a state, it can not be limited by the will of a third personality who is not a subject at law in international law." [51] This has been the traditional ground upon which the United States and other leading powers have denied the validity of the renunciatory provision in a contract.[52]

However, if the individual were a subject of international law, this basic objection would lose its force. Jessup, who has given special study to this problem, has asserted: "under the hypothesis that it is the individual himself who has rights under international law, this basic objection loses all logical force. The rights which appertain to the individual may be waived by the individual.[53]

It would appear that the strength of the arguments for or against the full validity of the Calvo Clause will depend on the degree of recognition accorded to the individual as a subject of international law. This close correlation between the validity of the Calvo Clause and the recognition of the status of the individual in international law was seen in the analysis of the *Dredging* decision, in which the commission apparently predicated its recognition of the limited validity of the Calvo Clause as binding on the individual upon the ground that nations are not the only subjects of international law and that individuals under certain circumstances do have a standing under it.[54] The com-

[50] *Op. cit.*, p. 111. See also Feller, *Mex. Claims Com.*, p. 199.

[51] Observation made in regard to the meeting of the Committee of Experts for the League Codification Project on "The Nationality of Commercial Corporations and Their Diplomatic Protection," *AJIL*, XXII (January 1928), Spec. Suppl., p. 211.

[52] See *supra*, pp. 38–41, 60–61.

[53] *Op. cit.*, p. 111. Gómez Robledo, *op. cit.*, p. 174, asserts that "of course, on the day when the individual is recognized as the subject of international law, the debate will close, victory being ours."

[54] *Supra*, pp. 223–226. Gonzalez, *op. cit.*, pp. 25–31, analyzes this close relationship between these two developments.

mission in this leading case not only gave the Calvo Clause vitality and legally meaningful significance, but also added weight to recognition of the individual's status in international law.[55]

The determination of whether or not the individual is at the present time a subject of the law of nations is not within the scope of this study. But it may be observed that the basic principles underlying the law of nations are undergoing fundamental changes. As Jessup has observed: "The function of international law is to provide a legal basis for the orderly management of international relations. The traditional nature of that law was keyed to the actualities of past centuries in which international relations were inter-state relations. The actualities have changed; the law is changing." [56]

An impressive number of leading publicists have recently adopted the view that the individual does actually enjoy the status of a subject of the law of nations, at least in certain areas of that law.[57]

---

[55] It should be noted there have been fairly frequent instances in which the position of the individual has been taken into account by an international tribunal. A. H. Feller, *Mex. Claims Com.*, p. 199, has pointed out: "The law of international claims is replete with inherent contradictions, rules which do take into account the position of the individual claimant in spite of the fact that the state is theoretically the only claimant." It was held in the *Tattler* case, United States–Great Britain Claims Commission (1926), reported in Briggs, *The Law of Nations* (2nd ed., 1952), pp. 723–724, that a claim must be dismissed where the individual has already reached a settlement with the foreign government. In the case of *Emilia Marta Viuda de Giovanni Mantellero*, before the Italian-Mexican Claims Commission (1927), it was held that a claim was inadmissible because the claimant had refused to sign the memorial and informed the Italian agent that she did not desire to have the claim presented. See Feller, *Mex. Claims Com.*, p. 90. For additional comment on the effect of the individual's action on the presentation of an international claim, see Tan Shao-Hwa, "Spontaneous Renunciation of Governmental Protection by Certain Missionaries in China," *China Weekly Review*, XLVII (January 26, 1929), p. 366. Philip Jessup, "Responsibility of States for Injuries to Individuals," *Columbia Law Review*, XLVI (November 1946), p. 923, asserts that "under the contemplated changes in the law, diplomatic interposition could not be extended without the concurrence of the individual since it is his right which is being protected and not the right of his state." See also Summers, *op. cit.*, p. 475.

[56] "The Subjects of a Modern Law of Nations," *Michigan Law Review*, XLV (February 1947), p. 384.

[57] See, for example, H. Lauterpacht, *op. cit.*, *passim*; Dunn, "The International Rights of Individuals," *Proceedings of the American Society of International Law* (1941), pp. 14–15; William B. Cowles, "The Impact of Interna-

The Future of the Calvo Clause

Charles G. Fenwick, in a review of H. Lauterpacht's latest treatise,[58] commented:

A generation ago it was the almost unanimous opinion of writers that individuals were no more than objects of international law, that their rights and duties were such as states might confer upon them by constitutional law, that whatever treaties might be entered into with respect to individuals were strictly agreements between states, from which the individual might derive rights but which he could not claim in his own name. But today, in the presence of the evidence submitted by Professor Lauterpacht and the conclusions which he draws from the evidence, it would be difficult even for the most rigid positivist to continue to adhere to the traditional position. The developments of the last quarter of a century have changed the position of the individual fundamentally, although the change is limited to certain specific fields, the most important of which is that of fundamental human rights.[59]

There is, however, a great deal of disagreement and controversy over this subject.[60] It should be noted that, at least in the present stage of world development, international law still evolves through the action of states. Thus states may, if they wish, accord to the individual a special status as a subject in certain areas by expressing their collective will through treaty or agreement or through an international agency or tribunal deriving its authority from states.[61] On the basis of the evidence presented in this study, there is scant support for the contention that states have at this time indicated an intention of according sufficient status to the individual to give him complete control over the right of diplomatic interposition and thus of accepting the complete validity of the Calvo Clause.

tional Law on the Individual," *ibid.* (1952), pp. 71–85; Eagleton, "The Individual and International Law," *ibid.* (1946), pp. 22–29, with discussion thereon, pp. 29–50; Jorge Americano, *The New Foundation of International Law* (New York, 1947); Ilmar Penna Marinho, *Caracteristicas essenciais do novo direito internacional* (Rio de Janeiro, 1947).

[58] *Op. cit.*

[59] *APSR*, XLV (March 1951), pp. 229–230.

[60] See Briggs, *The Law of Nations* (2nd ed., 1952), pp. 93–98.

[61] See Jessup, "The Subjects of a Modern Law of Nations," *Michigan Law Review*, XLV (February 1947), p. 385; Schwarzenberger, *op. cit.*, p. 153.

Nevertheless, the trend toward placing greater emphasis on the actions, rights, and duties of the individual will undoubtedly have a strong influence on future tribunals that have occasion to deal with the validity of the Calvo Clause, as it did with the *Dredging* commission several decades ago. The evidence of the status of the individual in international law is considerably more impressive today than it was then, and it well might be that future adjudications will strengthen the rule of the limited validity of the Calvo Clause along the lines suggested in this chapter. As the status of the individual in international law increases, so too will the significance of the rule of law that holds the Calvo Clause commitment binding on the individual, though not on his government in the event of an international delinquency such as a denial of justice.

It may be suggested, in conclusion, that the controversy surrounding the validity of the Calvo Clause will, in the not too distant future, be resolved. The Calvo Clause was born out of the legitimate fear of abuses of diplomatic protection. As the danger of these abuses continues to lessen as a result of the increased political importance and collective bargaining power of the Latin American republics, and also as a result of the faithful observance by the United States of the letter and spirit of the nonintervention policy, the fears and suspicions of our neighbors to the south will correspondingly diminish. Likewise, the basic opposition to concepts such as the Calvo Clause was grounded on the equally legitimate fear of the investor powers that their citizens would suffer if subjected exclusively to local standards of justice, something that the Latin Americans tend to forget. The danger of abuses to resident aliens will lessen as this region attains ever greater stability and progress, and the fears and suspicions of the investor powers will also proportionately decrease.

The present conditions of international relations have drawn the republics of the Western Hemisphere more tightly together in their community of interest. The fact that the United States needs Latin America and Latin America equally needs the United

States is resulting in the growing acceptance of *mutual* interdependence, which in turn produces greater trust and more harmonious relations. It is quite clear that diplomatic protection is no longer abused as it once was, nor are the standards of justice to be found in Latin America as deficient as formerly. It is significant that the survey of the current utilization of the Calvo Clause revealed that while the Calvo Clause is still widely employed, there is increasing evidence of more harmonious relationships between the Latin American governments and resident aliens and foreign business interests. Furthermore, the fact that there was found to be less extensive utilization of the Calvo Clause in most of the more advanced republics would appear to suggest that as Latin America continues to progress economically and politically, problems such as the Calvo Clause will become less important.

This does not mean that the Calvo Clause will be discarded, or the fight for its complete validity discontinued. On the contrary, the Latin American republics, led by those who have suffered the most from foreign intervention, will continue to seek greater security by demanding its acceptance in the form of binding legal principles as a necessary protective device against repetition of past abuses. It is my belief that eventually the complete validity of the Calvo Clause might well win recognition, either through the diplomacy of the inter-American conferences or through the emergence of the individual as a true subject of international law. But it should be emphasized that these developments will not come to pass until greater cooperation and harmony characterize relations among peoples on the international level. Eventually, the safeguarding of individual rights, whether at home or abroad, may be entrusted to an international system, with an international court to which aggrieved or injured individuals could appeal directly for redress and compensation. With the establishment of such a system, the present practice of diplomatic protection would cease to operate, and the purpose of the Calvo Clause would be accomplished. But then, too, the *raison d'être* of the Calvo Clause would also disappear.

The Calvo Clause

With the substitution of a more efficacious system of safeguarding the rights of citizens resident abroad, the Calvo Clause would no longer be necessary. Thus it might well be that success for the long and vigorous efforts of the Latin Americans to win validation of the Calvo Clause will also result in its demise.

It might be observed, finally, that while this study has dealt with but a minute phase of the rules governing relations on the international level, the problem surveyed is important not only in itself but also because it is illustrative of how the rules of international law change, through both political and judicial processes, to meet the changing conditions of the world community. This all-important flexibility is greatly encouraging to those who look to international law to fulfill someday the function in the world community that municipal law fulfills in the domestic community.

SELECT BIBLIOGRAPHY
AND INDEX

Select Bibliography

Digests and Arbitral Compilations

Hackworth, Green H. *Digest of International Law*. 8 vols. Washington, D.C.: Government Printing Office, 1940–1944.

La Fontaine, H. *Pasicrisie internationale. Histoire Documentaire des Arbitrages internationaux*. Berne: Imprimerie Stampfli et Cie., 1902. xvi, 670 pp.

Lapradelle, Albert de, and N. Politis. *Recueil des Arbitrages internationaux*. 2 vols. Paris: A. Pedone, 1905, 1923. Vol. III by Albert de Lapradelle, Jacques Politis, and André Salomon. Paris: Editions Internationales, 1954.

Lauterpacht, H., and others. *Annual Digest and Reports of Public International Law Cases, 1919–*. London: Butterworth and Company, 1932–.

Moore, John Bassett. *A Digest of International Law*. 8 vols. Washington, D.C.: Government Printing Office, 1906.

_____. *History and Digest of the International Arbitrations to Which the United States Has Been a Party*. 6 vols. Washington, D.C.: Government Printing Office, 1898.

Ralston, Jackson H. *International Arbitrations from Athens to Locarno*. Stanford, Calif.: Stanford University Press, 1929. xvi, 417 pp.

_____. *The Law and Procedure of International Tribunals. Being a Résumé of the Views of Arbitrators upon Questions Arising under the Law of Nations and of the Procedure and Practice of International Courts*. Stanford, Calif.: Stanford University Press, 1926. xl, 512 pp.

Reports of International Arbitral Awards. United Nations. 5 vols. to date, 1948–1953. Leyden: A. W. Sijthoff's Publishing Company.

Stuyt, A. M. *Survey of International Arbitrations, 1794–1938*. The Hague: Martinus Nijhoff, 1939. xi, 479 pp.

Treatises

Accioly, Hildebrando. *Tratado de derecho internacional público*. 3 vols. Rio de Janeiro: Imprensa Nacional, 1945–1946.

_____. *Manual de direito internacional público*. São Paulo: Saraiva S/A, Editores, 1948. 491 pp.

Alvarado Garaicoa, Teodoro. *La trascendencia de las reuniones interamericanas*. Guayaquil: Imprenta de la Universidad, 1949. 260 pp.

Alvarez, Alejandro. *Le droit international américain*. Paris: A. Pedone, 1910. 386 pp.

The Calvo Clause

Americano, Jorge. *The New Foundation of International Law*. New York: The Macmillan Company, 1947. xvi, 137 pp.

Antokoletz, Daniel. *Tratado de derecho internacional público en tiempo de paz*. 3 vols. Buenos Aires: Juan Roldan y C., 1928.

Ball, M. Margaret. *The Problem of Inter-American Organization*. Stanford, Calif.: Stanford University Press, 1944. vii, 117 pp.

Bello, Andres. *Principios de derecho internacional*. 2nd ed. Paris: Librería de Garnier Hermanos, Imprenta de Gustavo de Lamarzelle, 1864. iv, 302 pp.

Bemis, Samuel Flagg. *The Latin American Policy of the United States*. New York: Harcourt, Brace, and Company, 1943. xv, 470 pp.

Borchard, Edwin M. *The Diplomatic Protection of Citizens Abroad or the Law of International Claims*. New York: The Banks Law Publishing Company, 1915. xxxvii, 988 pp.

Bustamante y Sirven, Antonio Sanchez de. *Derecho internacional público*. 5 vols. Habana: Carasa y Cia, 1933–1938.

_____. *Manual de derecho internacional público*. 4th ed. Habana: Talleres Tipográficos "La Mercantil," 1947. 765 pp.

Callahan, James M. *American Foreign Policy in Mexican Relations*. New York: The Macmillan Company, 1932. x, 644 pp.

Calvo, Carlos. *Le droit international théorique et pratique*. 5th ed. 6 vols. Paris: Arthur Rousseau, 1896.

Carlston, Kenneth S. *The Process of International Arbitration*. New York: Columbia University Press, 1946. xiv, 318 pp.

Clagett, Helen L. *The Administration of Justice in Latin America*. New York: Oceana Publications, 1952. 160 pp.

Crichfield, George W. *American Supremacy. The Rise and Progress of the Latin American Republics and Their Relations to the United States under the Monroe Doctrine*. 2 vols. New York: Brentano's, 1908.

Cruchaga Tocornal, Miguel. *Derecho internacional*. Vol. I. Santiago: Editorial Nascímento, 1944. lxxix, 722 pp.

De Beus, J. G. *The Jurisprudence of the General Claims Commission United States and Mexico, under the Convention of September 8, 1923*. The Hague: Martinus Nijhoff, 1938. x, 342 pp.

Decencière-Ferrandière, A. *La responsabilité internationale des États à raison des dommages subis par des étrangers*. Paris: Rousseau and Company, 1925. 279 pp.

Diego-Fernandez, Salvador. *Los Pactos de Bucareli*. Mexico. Editorial Polis, 1937. 78 pp.

Dunn, Frederick Sherwood. *The Diplomatic Protection of Americans in Mexico*. New York: Columbia University Press, 1933. ix, 439 pp.

_____. *The Protection of Nationals. A Study in the Application of International Law*. Baltimore: Johns Hopkins Press, 1932. x, 228 pp.

Eagleton, Clyde. *The Responsibility of States in International Law*. New York: New York University Press, 1928. xxiv, 291 pp.

Edgington, T. B. *The Monroe Doctrine*. Boston: Little, Brown, and Company, 1905. viii, 344 pp.

Esquível Obregón, Toribio. *México y los Estados Unidos ante el derecho internacional*. Mexico: Herrero Hermanos Sucesores, 1926. 192 pp.

Feller, Abraham H. *The Mexican Claims Commissions, 1923–1934. A Study in the Law and Procedure of International Tribunals*. New York: The Macmillan Company, 1935. xxi, 572 pp.

Select Bibliography

Fiore, Pasquale. *Nouveau droit international public.* 2nd ed. 3 vols. Translated into French by C. Antoine. Paris: Durand and Pedone, 1886.

Freeman, Alwyn V. *The International Responsibility of States for Denial of Justice.* London: Longmans, Green, and Company, 1938. xix, 758 pp.

García Robles, Alfonso. *La Cláusula Calvo ante el derecho internacional.* Mexico, 1939. 56 pp.

Gómez Robledo, Antonio. *The Bucareli Agreements and International Law.* Translated from the Spanish by S. de la Selva. Mexico: National University of Mexico Press, 1940. xiii, 229 pp.

Gonzalez, Francisco Lopez. *México y la Cláusula Calvo.* Mexico: A. Mijares y Hno., Impresores, 1936. 46 pp.

Gordon, Wendell C. *The Economy of Latin America.* New York: Columbia University Press, 1950. xi, 434 pp.

Guerrant, Edward O. *Roosevelt's Good Neighbor Policy.* Albuquerque: University of New Mexico Press, 1950. x, 236 pp.

Hart, Albert B. *The Monroe Doctrine. An Interpretation.* London: Duckworth and Company, 1916. xiv, 445 pp.

Henríquez, Homero. *Origen y evolucion del derecho internacional americano.* Ciudad Trujillo: Imprenta "Arte y Cine," 1948. 262 pp.

Hudson, Manley O. *International Tribunals, Past and Present.* Washington, D.C.: Carnegie Endowment for International Peace and Brookings Institution, 1944. xii, 287 pp.

Humphrey, John P. *The Inter-American System — A Canadian View.* Toronto: The Macmillan Company of Canada, Limited, 1942. xi, 329 pp.

Hyde, Charles Cheney. *International Law Chiefly as Interpreted and Applied by the United States.* 2nd ed. 3 vols. Boston: Little, Brown, and Company, 1947.

Jacobini, H. B. *A Study of the Philosophy of International Law as Seen in Works of Latin American Writers.* The Hague: Martinus Nijhoff, 1954. viii, 158 pp.

Jessup, Philip C. *A Modern Law of Nations. An Introduction.* New York: The Macmillan Company, 1948. xi, 236 pp.

Lauterpacht, H. *An International Bill of the Rights of Man.* New York: Columbia University Press, 1945. x, 230 pp.

————. *International Law and Human Rights.* New York: Frederick A. Praeger, Incorporated, 1950. xvi, 475 pp.

Lawrence, William. *The Law of Claims against Governments.* Washington, D.C.: Government Printing Office, 1875. vii, 432 pp.

Marinho, Ilmar Penna. *Características essenciais do novo direito internacional.* Rio de Janeiro: Imprensa Nacional, 1947. 475 pp.

Masters, Ruth D. *Handbook of International Organizations in the Americas.* Washington, D.C.: Carnegie Endowment for International Peace, 1945. xvi, 453 pp.

Maúrtua, Victor M. and James Brown Scott. *Responsibility of States for Damages Caused in Their Territory to the Person or Property of Foreigners.* New York: Oxford University Press, 1930. v, 67 pp.

Mendoza, Salvador. *La Doctrina Cárdenas; texto, antecedents, comentarios.* Mexico: Manuel León Sánchez, 1939. 79 pp.

Moreno Quintana, Lucio M., and Carlos M. Bollini Shaw. *Derecho internacional público.* Buenos Aires: Ediciones Librería del Colegio, 1950. 837 pp.

Nielsen, Fred K. *International Law Applied to Reclamations, Mainly in Cases between the United States and Mexico.* Washington, D.C.: John Byrne and Company, 1933. v, 715 pp.

The Calvo Clause

Noel, John V. *The History of the Second Pan-American Congress*. Baltimore: Guggenheimer, Weil, and Company, 1902. 375 pp.

Oppenheim, L. *International Law. A Treatise.* 2 vols. Vol I. *Peace.* 7th ed. by H. Lauterpacht. London: Longmans, Green, and Company, 1948.

Perkins, Dexter. *Hands Off. A History of the Monroe Doctrine.* Boston: Little, Brown, and Company, 1948. xiii, 455 pp.

_____. *The Evolution of American Foreign Policy.* New York: Oxford University Press, 1948. 187 pp.

Planas Suárez, D. Simón. *Tratado de derecho internacional público.* 2 vols. Madrid: Hijos de Reus, Editores, 1916.

Podestá Costa, Luis A. *La responsabilidad del estado por daños irrogados a la persona o a los bienes de extranjeros en luchas civiles.* Habana: Carasa y Cia., S. en C., 1939. 103 pp.

_____. *Manual de derecho internacional público.* 2nd ed. Buenos Aires: Artes Gráficas Bartolomé U. Chiesino, 1947. 536 pp.

Rabasa, Oscar. *El derecho interno y el derecho internacional. Un nuevo punto de vista en México del derecho internacional.* Mexico: Imprenta de la Secretaría de Relaciones Exteriores, 1933. 108 pp.

Rowe, L. S. *The Pan American Union and the Pan American Conferences, 1890–1940.* Washington, D.C.: Pan American Union, 1940. 18 pp.

Sanchez i Sanchez, Carlos. *Curso de derecho internacional público americano.* Ciudad Trujillo, R.D.: Editora Montalvo, 1943. xxxiii, 729 pp.

Savelberg, M. M. L. *Le problème du droit international américain.* The Hague: A. A. M. Stoles, Editeur, 1946. xix, 361 pp.

Schwarzenberger, Georg. *International Law.* Vol. I. *International Law as Applied by International Courts and Tribunals.* London: Stevens and Sons, Limited, 1945. xliv, 645 pp.

Scott, James Brown (ed.). *Inter-American Tribunal of International Justice. Memorandum Project and Documents Accompanied by Observations.* Washington, D.C.: Carnegie Endowment for International Peace, 1937. xx, 105 pp.

Seijas, R. F. *El derecho internacional Hispano-Americana.* 6 vols. Caracas: Imprenta de "El Monitor," 1884.

Sepúlveda Gutiérrez, César. *La responsabilidad internacional del estado y la validez de la Cláusula Calvo.* Mexico: Facultad Nacional de Derecho y Ciencias Sociales, 1944. iv, 88 pp.

Stuart, Graham H. *Latin America and the United States.* 4th ed. New York: Appleton-Century Company, Incorporated, 1943. ix, 509 pp.

Stuyt, A. M. *The General Principles of Law as Applied by International Tribunals to Disputes on Arbitration and Exercise of State Jurisdiction.* The Hague: Martinus Nijhoff, 1946. xi, 272 pp.

Turlington, Edgar. *Mexico and Her Foreign Creditors.* New York: Columbia University Press, 1930. x, 449 pp.

Ulloa y Sotomayor, Alberto. *Derecho internacional público.* Vol. I. 2nd ed. Lima: Imprenta Torres Aguirre, 1938. 394 pp.

Urrutia, Francisco José. *Le continent américain et le droit international.* Paris: Rousseau & C., 1928. xviii, 404 pp.

Vattel, Emmeric de. *Le droit des gens, ou Principes de la loi naturelle; appliqués à la conduite et aux affaires des nations et des souverains.* Classic of International Law ed. 3 vols. Washington, D.C.: Carnegie Institute, 1916.

Whiteman, Marjorie M. *Damages in International Law.* 3 vols. Washington, D.C.: Government Printing Office, 1937–1943.

Select Bibliography

Yepes, J.-M. *El panamericanismo y el derecho internacional.* Bogotá: Imprenta Nacional, 1930. xii, 447 pp.

Periodicals

Accioly, Hildebrando. "Memorandum sobre el tema de reclamaciones pecuniarias," *Diario de Sessiones* (Eighth International Conference of American States, Lima, 1938), pp. 338–339.

Alvarez, Alejandro. "Latin America and International Law," *American Journal of International Law,* Vol. III, No. 2 (April 1909), pp. 269–353.

_____. "New Conception and New Bases of Legal Philosophy," *Illinois Law Review,* Vol. XIII, No. 3–4 (October–November 1918), pp. 167–182.

_____. "The New International Law," *Transactions of the Grotius Society,* Vol. XV (1930), pp. 35–51.

Anzilotti, Dionisio. "La responsabilité internationale des états à raison des dommages soufferts par des étrangers," *Revue générale de droit international public,* Vol. XIII (January–February 1906), pp. 2–28; (May–June 1906), pp. 285–309.

Arias, Harmodio. "The Non-Liability of States for Damages Suffered by Foreigners in the Course of a Riot, Insurrection, or a Civil War," *American Journal of International Law,* Vol. VII, No. 4 (October 1913), pp. 724–766.

Baldwin, Simeon E. "The Limits of Active Intervention by a State to Secure the Fulfilment of Contracts in Favour of Its Own Citizens Entered into by Them with Other States," *Report of the Twenty-Fourth Conference of the International Law Association* (1907), pp. 180–188.

Beckett, W. E. "Diplomatic Claims in Respect of Injuries to Companies," *Transactions of the Grotius Society,* Vol. XVII (1932), pp. 175–194.

Beteta, Ramón, and Ernesto Henríquez. "La protección diplomática de los intereses pecuniarios extranjeros en los estados de América," *Proceedings of the Eighth American Scientific Congress,* Vol. X (Washington, D.C., 1940), pp. 27–48.

Borchard, Edwin M. "Basic Elements of Diplomatic Protection of Citizens Abroad," *American Journal of International Law,* Vol. VII, No. 3 (July 1913), pp. 497–520.

_____. "Committee of Experts, Pan American Codification of International Law," *American Journal of International Law,* Vol. XXXI, No. 3 (July 1937), pp. 471–473.

_____. "Contractual Claims in International Law," *Columbia Law Review,* Vol. XIII, No. 6 (June 1913), pp. 457–499.

_____. "Decisions of the Claims Commissions, United States and Mexico," *American Journal of International Law,* Vol. XX, No. 3 (July 1926), pp. 536–542.

_____. "How Far Must We Protect Our Citizens Abroad?" *New Republic,* Vol. L, No. 645 (April 13, 1927), pp. 214–216.

_____. "Limitations on Coercive Protection," *American Journal of International Law,* Vol. XXI, No. 2 (April 1927), pp. 303–306.

_____. "Memorandum sobre el tema de reclamaciones pecuniarias," *Diario de Sessiones* (Eighth International Conference of American States, Lima, 1938), pp. 311–325, 331–332, 333–334.

_____. " 'Responsibility of States' at the Hague Codification Conference," *American Journal of International Law,* Vol. XXIV, No. 3 (July 1930), pp. 517–540.

The Calvo Clause

_____. "Responsibility of States for Damages Done in Their Territory to the Person or Property of Foreigners," *American Journal of International Law*, Vol. XX, No. 4 (October 1926), pp. 738–747.

_____. "The Access of Individuals to International Courts," *American Journal of International Law*, Vol. XXIV, No. 2 (April 1930), pp. 359–365.

_____. "The Calvo and Drago Doctrines," *Encyclopaedia of the Social Sciences*, Vol. III (1930), pp. 153–156.

_____. "The 'Committee of Experts' at the Lima Conference," *American Journal of International Law*, Vol. XXXIII, No. 2 (April 1939), pp. 269–282.

_____. "The 'Minimum Standard' of the Treatment of Aliens," *Proceedings of the American Society of International Law* (1939), pp. 51–63, and discussion thereon, pp. 64–74.

_____. "The Protection of Citizens Abroad by Armed Force," *Annals of the American Academy of Political and Social Science*, Vol. CXLIV (July 1929), pp. 121–127.

_____. "Remarks by Professor Edwin Borchard on Papers of Dr. Beteta and Dr. Cruchaga Ossa," *Proceedings of the Eighth American Scientific Congress*, Vol. X (Washington, D.C., 1940), pp. 69–75.

Bordwell, Percy. "Calvo and the Calvo Doctrine," *Green Bag*, Vol. XVIII, No. 7 (July 1906), pp. 377–382.

Bowen, Herbert W. "The Monroe, Calvo and Drago Doctrines," *Independent*, Vol. LXII, No. 3046 (April 18, 1907), pp. 902–904.

Brierly, James L. "Arbitration between Great Britain and Costa Rica," *British Yearbook of International Law* (1925), pp. 199–204.

_____. "The Theory of Implied State Complicity in International Claims," *British Yearbook of International Law* (1928), pp. 42–49.

Briggs, Herbert W. "The Settlement of Mexican Claims Act of 1942," *American Journal of International Law*, Vol. XXXVII, No. 2 (April 1943), pp. 222–232.

_____. "New Dimensions in International Law," *American Political Science Review*, Vol. XLVI, No. 3 (September 1952), pp. 677–698.

Brown, Philip Marshall. "The 'Cardenas Doctrine'," *American Journal of International Law*, Vol. XXXIV, No. 2 (April 1940), pp. 300–302.

Bullington, John P. "Informe" presented by President (Bullington) to Comité XVII (Problemas juridico-internacionales de la post-guerra), *Cuarta Conferencia, Federación Interamericana de Abogados* (Santiago, 1945), Vol. III, pp. 1387–1396.

_____. "The Land and Petroleum Laws of Mexico," *American Journal of International Law*, Vol. XXII, No. 1 (January 1928), pp. 50–69.

Bustamante y Sirven, A. S. de. "Carlos Calvo," *Encyclopaedia of the Social Sciences*, Vol. III (1930), p. 153.

Campanella, Alfredo. "Estudio sobre la protección diplomática de los ciudadanos en el extranjero," *Cuarta Conferencia, Federación Interamericana de Abogados* (Santiago, 1945), Vol. III, pp. 1414–1423.

Castro Larraín, Osvaldo de. "Estudio sobre la protección diplomática, la Cláusula Calvo y la garantía de los derechos internacionales de hombre," *Cuarta Conferencia, Federación Interamericana de Abogados* (Santiago, 1945), Vol. III, pp. 1396–1407.

Clarke, R. F. "Intervention for Breach of Contract or Tort Committed by a Sovereignty," *Proceedings of the American Society of International Law* (1910), pp. 149–173.

Coudert, Alexis, and Asher Lans. "Direct Foreign Investment in Undeveloped

Select Bibliography

Countries. Some Practical Problems," *Law and Contemporary Problems*, Vol. XI, No. 4 (Summer–Autumn, 1946), pp. 741–759.

Cowles, Willard. "The Impact of International Law on the Individual," *Proceedings of the American Society of International Law* (1952), pp. 71–85.

Cruchaga Ossa, Alberto. "Memorandum sobre el tema de reclamaciones pecuniarias," *Diario de Sessiones* (Eighth International Conference of American States, Lima, 1938), pp. 301–311, 325–331, 332–333, 334–335.

Cutler, John Ward. "The Treatment of Foreigners in Relation to the Draft Convention and Conference of 1929," *American Journal of International Law*, Vol. XXVII, No. 2 (April 1933), pp. 225–246.

Dávila, Carlos. "The Montevideo Conference: Antecedents and Accomplishments," *International Conciliation*, No. 300 (May 1934), pp. 117–158.

Dennis, William C. "The Orinoco Steamship Company Case before the Hague Tribunal," *American Journal of International Law*, Vol. V, No. 1 (January 1911), pp. 35–64.

Drago, Luis M. "State Loans in Their Relation to International Policy," *American Journal of International Law*, Vol. I, No. 3 (July 1907), pp. 692–726.

Dreier, John C. "Organizing Security in the Americas," *Department of State Bulletin*, Vol. XXX, No. 779 (May 31, 1954), pp. 830–835.

Dunn, Frederick S. "International Law and Private Property Rights," *Columbia Law Review*, Vol. XXVIII, No. 2 (February 1928), pp. 166–180.

Eagleton, Clyde. "Denial of Justice in International Law," *American Journal of International Law*, Vol. XXII, No. 3 (July 1928), pp. 538–559.

————. "L'epuisement des recours internes et le déni de justice, d'après certaines décisions récentes," *Revue de droit international et de législation comparée*, 3rd Series, Vol. XVI (1935), pp. 504–526.

————. "The Individual and International Law," *Proceedings of the American Society of International Law* (1946), pp. 22–29, and discussion thereon, pp. 29–50.

Esquível Obregón, Toribio. "Protección diplomática de los ciudadanos en el extranjero," *Memoria de la Tercera Conferencia de la Federación Interamericana de Abogados* (Mexico, 1944), Vol. III, pp. 218–236.

Fachiri, Alexander P. "Expropriation and International Law," *British Yearbook of International Law* (1925), pp. 159–171.

Félix Maurtua, Manuel. "Observaciones a la declaracion del Comité Jurídico Interamericano sobre reafirmación de los princípios fundamentales del derecho internacional," *Revista Peruana de derecho internacional*, Vol. IV, No. 13 (1944), pp. 187–204.

Feller, Abraham H. "Some Observations on the Calvo Clause," *American Journal of International Law*, Vol. XXVII, No. 3 (July 1933), pp. 461–468.

Fenwick, Charles G. "The Ninth International Conference of American States," *American Journal of International Law*, Vol. XLII, No. 3 (July 1948), pp. 553–567.

————. "The Tenth Inter-American Conference: Some Issues of Inter-American Regional Law," *American Journal of International Law*, Vol. XLVIII, No. 3 (July 1954), pp. 464–469.

Finch, George L. "Eighth International Conference of American States," *International Conciliation*, No. 349 (April 1938), pp. 141–249.

Fitzmaurice, G. G. "The Law and Procedure of the International Court of Justice: General Principles and Substantive Law," *British Yearbook of International Law* (1950), pp. 1–41.

The Calvo Clause

_____. "The Meaning of the Term 'Denial of Justice'," *British Yearbook of International Law* (1932), pp. 93–114.

Freeman, Alwyn V. "Estudio sobre los aspectos recientes de la Doctrina Calvo y el reto al derecho internacional," *Cuarta Conferencia, Federación Interamericana de Abogados* (Santiago, 1945), Vol. III, pp. 1436–1457.

_____. "Recent Aspects of the Calvo Doctrine and the Challenge to International Law," *American Journal of International Law*, Vol. XL, No. 1 (January 1946), pp. 121–147.

García Robles, Alfonso. "Estudio sobre la protección diplomática, la Cláusula Calvo y la salvaguardia de los derechos internacionales del hombre y sobre la organización interamericana en la post-guerra," *Cuarta Conferencia, Federación Interamericana de Abogados* (Santiago, 1945), Vol. III, pp. 1458–1466.

_____. "La protección diplomática, la Cláusula Calvo y la salvaguardia de los derechos internacionales del hombre," *Memoria de la Tercera Conferencia de la Federación Interamericana de Abogados* (Mexico, 1944), Vol. III, Apéndice, pp. 5–25.

Garner, James W. "Decisions of the American Mexican Mixed Claims Commissions," *British Yearbook of International Law* (1927), pp. 179–186; (1928), pp. 156–164; (1930), pp. 220–226; (1931), pp. 166–171.

Goebel, Julius, Jr. "The International Responsibility of States for Injuries Sustained by Aliens on Account of Mob Violence, Insurrections and Civil Wars," *American Journal of International Law*, Vol. VIII, No. 4 (October 1914), pp. 802–852.

Inman, Samuel Guy. "The Lima Conference and the Future of Pan-Americanism," *Annals of the American Academy of Political and Social Science*, Vol. CCIV (July 1939), Supplement, pp. 129–136.

Hackworth, Green H. "Responsibility of States for Damages Caused in Their Territory to the Person or Property of Foreigners," *American Journal of International Law*, Vol. XXIV, No. 3 (July 1930), pp. 500–516.

Hershey, Amos S. "The Calvo and Drago Doctrines," *American Journal of International Law*, Vol. I, No. 1 (January 1907), pp. 26–45.

Hill, Charles E. "Responsibility of States for Damages Done in Their Territory to the Person or Property of Foreigners," *Proceedings of the American Society of International Law* (1928), pp. 67–73, with discussion thereon, pp. 73–92.

Hill, Norman L. "British Arbitration Policies," *International Conciliation*, No. 257 (February 1930), pp. 65–124.

Hudson, Manley O. "Arbitration between Great Britain and Costa Rica," *American Bar Association Journal*, Vol. X, No. 7 (July 1924), pp. 486–487.

_____. "The Central American Court of Justice," *American Journal of International Law*, Vol. XXVI, No. 4 (October 1932), pp. 759–786.

Hull, W. I. "The United States and Latin America at the Hague," *International Conciliation*, No. 44 (1911), pp. 3–13.

Hyde, Charles C. "Concerning Attempts by Contract to Restrict Interposition," *American Journal of International Law*, Vol. XXI, No. 2 (April 1927), pp. 298–303.

_____. "Mexico and the Claims of Foreigners," *Illinois Law Review*, Vol. VIII, No. 6 (January 1914), pp. 355–372.

Jessup, Philip C. "Responsibility of States for Injuries to Individuals," *Columbia Law Review*, Vol. XLVI, No. 6 (November 1946), pp. 903–928.

_____. "The Subjects of a Modern Law of Nations," *Michigan Law Review*, Vol. XLV, No. 4 (February 1947), pp. 383–408.

Select Bibliography

Jully, Laurent. "Arbitration and Judicial Settlement — Recent Trends," *American Journal of International Law*, Vol. XLVIII, No. 3 (July 1954), pp. 380–407.

Kunz, Josef L. "The Bogotá Charter of the Organization of American States," *American Journal of International Law*, Vol. XLII, No. 3 (July 1948), pp. 568–589.

Lauterpacht, Hersch. "The Subjects of the Law of Nations," *Law Quarterly Review*, Vol. LXIII, No. 252 (October 1947), pp. 438–460; Vol. XLIV, No. 253 (January 1948), pp. 97–119.

Lipstein, K. "The Place of the Calvo Clause in International Law," *British Yearbook of International Law* (1945), pp. 130–145.

Lissitzyn, Oliver J. "The Meaning of the Term Denial of Justice in International Law," *American Journal of International Law*, Vol. XXX, No. 4 (October 1936), pp. 632–645.

McDonald, John J., and Carlyle R. Barnett. "The American-Mexican Claims Arbitration," *American Bar Association Journal*, Vol. XVIII, No. 3 (March 1932), pp. 183–187.

MacDonell, John. "South American Republics and the Monroe Doctrine," *Nineteenth Century*, Vol. LIII, No. 314 (April 1903), pp. 587–598.

Malca B., Carlos. "El arbitraje internacional," *Revista Peruana de derecho internacional*, Vol. V (1945), pp. 157–187, 306–340.

Moore, John Bassett. "The Relation of International Law to National Law in the American Republics," *Proceedings of the American Society of International Law* (1915), pp. 11–23.

Moulin, H. A. "L'affaire du territoire d'Acre," *Revue générale de droit international public*, Vol. XI (1904), pp. 150–191.

Naussbaum, Arthur. "The 'Separability Doctrine' in American and Foreign Arbitration," *New York University Law Quarterly Review*, Vol. XVII, No. 4 (May 1940), pp. 609–616.

Nolan, Louis Clinton. "The Relations of the United States and Peru with Respect to Claims, 1822–1870," *Hispanic American Historical Review*, Vol. XVII, No. 1 (February 1937), pp. 30–66.

Peaslee, Amos J. "Estudio sobre la protección diplomática, la Cláusula Calvo y la garantía de los derechos internacionales de hombre," *Cuarta Conferencia, Federación Interamericana de Abogados* (Santiago, 1945), Vol. III, pp. 1408–1414.

Percival, Sir John H. "International Arbitral Tribunals and the Mexican Claims Commission," *Journal of Comparative Legislation and International Law*, 3rd Series, Vol. XIX, Part I (1937), pp. 98–104.

Phillips, G. Godfrey. "The Anglo-Mexican Special Claims Commission," *Law Quarterly Review*, No. 194 (April 1933), pp. 226–239.

Podestá Costa, Luis A. "La responsabilidad internacional del estado," *Cursos Monográficos* (Academia Interamericana de Derecho Comparado e Internacional), Vol. II (1952), pp. 157–223.

Potter, Pitman B. "L'intervention en droit international moderne," *Recueil des Cours de l'Académie de droit international* (The Hague), Vol. XXXII (1930–II), pp. 607–690.

Re, Edward D. "Nationalization and the Investment of Capital Abroad," *Georgetown Law Journal*, Vol. XLII, No. 1 (November 1953), pp. 44–68.

Ríos Igualt, Héctor. "Estudio sobre la protección diplomática," *Cuarta Conferencia, Federación Interamericana de Abogados* (Santiago, 1945), Vol. III, pp. 1424–1436.

The Calvo Clause

Root, Elihu. "The Relations between International Tribunals of Arbitration and the Jurisdiction of National Courts," *American Journal of International Law*, Vol. III, No. 3 (July 1909), pp. 529–536.

Scelle, Georges. "Règles générales du droit de la paix," *Recueil des Cours de l'Académie de droit international* (The Hague), Vol. XLVI (1933), pp. 327–703.

Scott, George Winfield. "Hague Convention Restricting the Use of Force to Recover on Contract Claims," *American Journal of International Law*, Vol. II, No. 1 (January 1908), pp. 78–94.

————. "International Law and the Drago Doctrine," *North American Review*, Vol. CLXXXIII, No. 600 (October 5, 1906), pp. 602–610.

Scott, James Brown. "The Settlement of Outstanding Claims between Mexico and the United States," *American Journal of International Law*, Vol. XVIII, No. 2 (April 1924), pp. 315–320.

————. "The Seventh International Conference of American States," *American Journal of International Law*, Vol. XXVIII, No. 2 (April 1934), pp. 219–230.

————. "The Sixth International Conference of American States," *International Conciliation*, No. 241 (June 1928), pp. 275–349.

Shao-Hwa, Tan. "Spontaneous Renunciation of Governmental Protection by Certain Missionaries in China," *China Weekly Review*, Vol. XLVII, No. 9 (January 26, 1929), pp. 364–366.

Staley, Eugene. "Une critique de la protection diplomatique des placements à l'étranger," *Revue générale de droit international public*, Vol. XLII (1935), pp. 541–558.

————. "Un substitut à la protection diplomatique pour le règlement des conflits de placements internationaux," *Revue générale de droit international public*, Vol. XLII (1935), pp. 659–667.

Stassen, Harold E. "The Case for Private Investment Abroad," *Foreign Affairs*, Vol. XXXII, No. 3 (April 1954), pp. 402–415.

Strisower, M. L. "La responsabilité internationale des états à raison des dommages causés sur leur territoire à la personne et aux biens des étrangers," *Annuaire de l'Institut de droit international* (1927–I), pp. 455–562.

Strupp, Karl. "Les règles générales du droit de la paix," *Recueil des Cours de l'Académie de droit international* (The Hague), Vol. XLVII (1934), pp. 259–595.

Summers, Lionel M. "The Calvo Clause," *Virginia Law Review*, Vol. XIX, No. 5 (March 1933), pp. 459–484.

————. "La Clause Calvo," *Revue de droit international* (Lapradelle), Vol. VII (1931), pp. 567–581.

————. "La Clause Calvo: tendances nouvelles," *Revue de droit international* (Lapradelle), Vol. XII (1933), pp. 229–233.

Ténékidès, C. G. "L'epuisement des voies de recours internes comme condition préalable de l'instance internationale," *Revue de droit international et de législation comparée*, 3rd Series, Vol. XIV (1933), pp. 514–535.

————. "Considérations sur la Clause Calvo. Essai de justification du système de la nullité intégrale," *Revue générale de droit international public*, Vol. XLIII (1936), pp. 270–284.

Turlington, Edgar. "The Pact of Bogotá," *American Journal of International Law*, Vol. XLII, No. 3 (July 1948), pp. 608–611.

Ulloa, Alberto. "Los principios fundamentales del derecho internacional y la

Select Bibliography

politica de nuestro tiempo," *Revista Peruana de derecho internacional*, Vol. II, No. 5 (1942), pp. 391–401.

_____. "Memorandum sobre el tema de reclamaciones pecuniarias," *Diario de Sessiones* (Eighth International Conference of American States, Lima, 1938), pp. 335–338.

Visscher, Charles de. "La responsabilité des états," *Bibliotheca Visseriana*, Vol. II (1924), pp. 89–119.

_____. "Notes sur la responsabilité internationale des états et la protection diplomatique d'après quelques documents récents," *Revue de droit international et de législation comparée*, 3rd Series, Vol. VIII (1927), pp. 245–272.

Vollenhoven, C. van. "La jurisprudence de la Commission générale de réclamations entre les États-Unis d'Amérique et le Mexique, en 1926," *Bulletin de L'Institut intermédiaire international*, Vol. XVI (1927), pp. 237–245.

Weinfeld, Abraham C. "The Mexican Oil Expropriation," *National Lawyers Guild Quarterly*, Vol. I, No. 5 (December 1938), pp. 367–399.

Whitaker, Arthur P. "A Half Century of Inter-American Relations, 1889–1940," *Inter-American Affairs*, No. 1 (1941), pp. 3–40.

_____. "Development of American Regionalism. The Organization of American States," *International Conciliation*, No. 469 (March 1951), pp. 121–164.

_____. "Pan America in Politics and Diplomacy," *Inter-American Affairs*, No. 5 (1945), pp. 1–81.

Williams, Sir John Fisher. "International Law and the Property of Aliens," *British Yearbook of International Law* (1928), pp. 1–30.

Wilson, Robert R. "Some Aspects of the Jurisprudence of National Claims Commissions," *American Journal of International Law*, Vol. XXXVI, No. 1 (January 1942), pp. 56–76.

Yepes, J.-M. "La contribution de l'Amérique Latine au developpement du droit international, public et privé," *Recueil des Cours de l'Académie de droit international* (The Hague), Vol. XXXII (1930–II), pp. 691–799.

_____. "Les Problèmes fondamentaux du droit des gens en Amérique," *Recueil des Cours de l'Académie de droit international* (The Hague), Vol. XLVII (1934), pp. 1–143.

International Arbitral Jurisprudence

Claims Commission between Great Britain and Mexico. Decisions and Opinions of the Commissioners in Accordance with the Convention of November 19, 1926, between Great Britain and the United Mexican States. October 5, 1929 to February 15, 1930. London: His Majesty's Stationery Office, 1931. 175 pp.

_____. *Further Decisions and Opinions of the Commissioners in Accordance with the Conventions of November 19, 1926, and December 5, 1930, between Great Britain and the United Mexican States. Subsequent to February 15, 1930.* London: His Majesty's Stationery Office, 1933. 362 pp.

Claims Commission, United States and Mexico. Opinions of Commissioners under the Convention Concluded September 8, 1923, between the United States and Mexico. February 4, 1926 to July 23, 1927. Washington, D.C.: Government Printing Office, 1927. iv, 489 pp.

_____. *Opinions of Commissioners under the Convention Concluded September 8, 1923, as Extended by the Convention Signed August 16, 1927, between the United States and Mexico. September 26, 1928 to May 17, 1929.* Washington, D.C.: Government Printing Office, 1929. iv, 334 pp.

_____. *Opinions of Commissioners under the Convention Concluded Sep-*

The Calvo Clause

tember 8, 1923, as Extended by Subsequent Conventions, between the United States and Mexico. October, 1930 to July, 1931. Washington, D.C.: Government Printing Office, 1931. iii, 287 pp.

Claims on the Part of Citizens of the United States and Mexico under the Convention of July 4, 1868 between the United States and Mexico. Washington, D.C.: Government Printing Office, 1877. 103 pp. Senate Executive Document No. 31, 44th Congress, 2nd Session.

Final Report of George H. Shields, Agent and Counsel of the United States before the United States and Chilean Claims Commission, Held under Treaty Signed at Santiago, Chile, August 7, 1892. Washington, D.C.: Gibson Brothers, Printers and Bookbinders, 1894. 188, 10 pp.

Great Britain–Costa Rican Arbitration under the Convention of March 7, 1923. Opinion of William Howard Taft, Sole Arbitrator. Printed in *American Journal of International Law*, Vol. XVIII (1924), pp. 147–174.

La réparation des dommages causés aux étrangers par des mouvements révolutionnaires. Jurisprudence de la Commission Franco-Mexicaine des réclamations (1924–1932). Paris: A. Pedone, 1933, xv, 228 pp.

O Tribunal Arbitral Brasileiro-Boliviano. Helio Lobo. Rio de Janeiro: Imprensa Nacional, 1910. vi, 171 pp.

Reclamaciones presentadas al Tribunal Anglo-Chileno 1894–1896. 5 vols. Santiago: Imprenta I Librería Ercilla, 1896.

Report of French-Venezuelan Mixed Claims Commission of 1902. Prepared by Jackson H. Ralston and W. T. Sherman Doyle. Washington, D.C.: Government Printing Office, 1906. xii, 471 pp. Senate Executive Document No. 533, 59th Congress, 1st Session.

Report of Robert C. Morris, Agent of the United States, before the United States and Venezuelan Claims Commission, Organized under the Protocol of February 17, 1903, between the United States of America and the Republic of Venezuela. Washington, D.C.: Government Printing Office, 1904. 563 pp. Senate Executive Document No. 317, 58th Congress, 2nd Session.

Report of the Secretary of the United States and Venezuelan Claims Commission. Washington, D.C.: Gibson Brothers, 1890. 41 pp.

United States and Chilean Claims Commission. Conventions, Rules, Report, Briefs, and Printed Evidence. Under the Convention of August 7, 1892, between the United States and the Republic of Chile, for the Settlement of Certain Claims of the Citizens of Either Country against the Other. Washington, D.C.: Gibson Brothers, Printers and Bookbinders, 1894. Separately paged.

United States and Chilean Claims Commission, Organized under the Convention of August 7, 1892. Minutes of Proceedings and Decisions. Washington, D.C.: Gibson Brothers, Printers and Bookbinders, 1894. 206, 216 pp.

United States and Venezuelan Claims Commission, 1889–1890. Opinions Delivered by the Commissioners in the Principal Cases. To Which Is Prefixed a Copy of the Conventions between the Two Governments and of the Rules of the Commission. Washington, D.C.: Gibson Brothers, Printers and Bookbinders, 1890. ix, 520, 34 pp.

Venezuelan Arbitrations of 1903, Including Protocols, Personnel and Rules of Commissions, Opinions, and Summary of Awards, with Appendix Containing Venezuelan Yellow Book of 1903, Bowen Pamphlet Entitled "Venezuelan Protocols," and "Preferential Question" Hague Decision, with History of Recent Venezuelan Revolutions. Prepared by Jackson H. Ralston, Late Umpire of the Italian-Venezuelan Mixed Claims Commission, and Assisted by W. T. Sher-

Select Bibliography

man Doyle. Washington, D.C.: Government Printing Office, 1904. xxviii, 1105 pp. Senate Executive Document No. 316, 58th Congress, 2nd Session.

Documents and Official Publications

American Scientific Congress. *Proceedings of the Eighth American Scientific Congress.* Vol. X. *International Law, Public Law and Jurisprudence.* Washington, D.C.: Government Printing Office, 1943. 698 pp.

Fitzgibbon, Russell H. *Constitutions of the Americas.* Chicago: University of Chicago Press, 1948. xx, 847 pp.

Harvard Law School. *Research in International Law.* "The Law of Responsibility of States for Damages Done in Their Territory to the Person or Property of Foreigners." *American Journal of International Law,* Vol. XXIII (April 1929), Special Number, pp. 131–239.

Inter-American Bar Association. *Inter-American Bar Association. Organization of the Association and Proceedings of the First Conference* (Havana, 1941). Baltimore: Lord Baltimore Press, 1942.

_____. *Federação Interamericana de Advogados. Anais da Segunda Conferência* (Rio de Janeiro, 1943). 6 vols. Rio de Janeiro: Departamento de Imprensa Nacional, 1950.

_____. *Memoria de la Tercera Conferencia de la Federación Interamericana de Abogados* (Mexico, 1944). 3 vols. Mexico: Talleres Tipográficos Modelo, S.A., 1945.

_____. *Cuarta Conferencia, Federación Interamericana de Abogados* (Santiago, 1945). 3 vols. Santiago: Imprenta el Imparcial, 1946.

_____. *Quinta Conferencia de la Federación Interamericana de Abogados* (Lima, 1947). Lima, 1947.

_____. *Proceedings of the Sixth Conference, Inter-American Bar Association* (Detroit, 1949). Washington, D.C., 1952.

_____. *Anales de la VII Conferencia Interamericana de Abogados* (Montevideo, 1951). 2 vols. Montevideo: Editorial. M.B.A., 1952.

International Conferences of American States. *Bibliografía de las Conferencias Americanas.* Prepared by the Columbus Memorial Library of the Pan American Union. Bibliographic Series No. 41. Washington, D.C., 1954. x, 277 pp.

_____. *The International Conferences of American States, 1889–1928. A Collection of the Conventions, Recommendations, Resolutions, Reports, and Motions Adopted by the First Six International Conferences of the American States, and Documents Relating to the Organization of the Conferences.* Edited by James Brown Scott. New York: Oxford University Press, 1931. xliv, 551 pp.

_____. *The International Conferences of American States. First Supplement, 1933–1940.* Washington, D.C.: Carnegie Endowment for International Peace, 1940. xxix, 558 pp.

_____. *Inter-American Conferences, 1826–1933. Chronological and Classified List.* Prepared by Warren Kelchner. Washington, D.C.: Government Printing Office. 1933. v, 34 pp.

International Conference of American States. First. *Minutes of the International American Conference.* Washington, D.C.: Government Printing Office, 1890.

_____. *Reports and Recommendations Together with the Messages of the President and the Letters of the Secretary of State Transmitting the Same to Congress.* Washington, D.C.: Government Printing Office, 1890.

_____. *Reports of Committees and Discussions Thereon.* 4 vols. Senate Executive Document No. 232, 51st Congress, 1st Session. Washington, D.C.: Government Printing Office, 1890.

International Conference of American States. Second. *Message from the President of the United States, Transmitting a Communication from the Secretary of State, Submitting the Report, with Accompanying Papers, of the Delegates of the United States to the Second International Conference of American States.* Senate Executive Document No. 330, 57th Congress, 1st Session. Washington, D.C.: Government Printing Office, 1902. 243 pp.

————. *Minutes and Documents.* Mexico: Typographical Department of the Government Printing Office, National Palace, 1901.

————. *Recommendaciones, resoluciones, convenciones y tratados.* Mexico: Tipographía de la Oficina Impresora de Estampillas, Palacio Nacional, 1902.

International Conference of American States. Third. *Minutes, Resolutions, Documents.* Rio de Janeiro: Imprensa Nacional, 1907.

————. *Report of the Delegates of the United States to the Third International Conference of the American States.* Senate Executive Document No. 365, 59th Congress, 2nd Session. Washington, D.C.: Government Printing Office, 1906. 180 pp.

International Conference of the American States. Fourth. *Message from the President of the United States Transmitting a Letter from the Secretary of State Inclosing a Report, with Accompanying Papers, Relative to the Fourth International Conference of American States.* Senate Executive Document No. 744, 61st Congress, 3rd Session. Washington, D.C.: Government Printing Office, 1911. 296 pp.

International Conference of American States. Fifth. *Report on the Treaty, Conventions and Resolutions.* Washington, D.C.: Pan American Union, 1925. v, 26 pp.

————. *Report of the Delegates of the United States of America to the Fifth International Conference of American States.* Washington, D.C.: Government Printing Office, 1923, 236 pp.

————. *Verbatim Record of the Plenary Sessions of the Fifth International Conference of American States.* Santiago, 1925.

International Conference of American States. Sixth. *Final Act. Motions, Agreements, Resolutions and Conventions.* Havana, 1928.

————. *Report of the Delegates of the United States of America to the Sixth International Conference of American States.* Washington, D.C.: Government Printing Office, 1928. vi, 343 pp.

International Conference of American States on Conciliation and Arbitration. *Proceedings.* Washington, D.C.: Government Printing Office, 1929. 738 pp.

International Conference of American States. Seventh. *Plenary Sessions. Minutes and Antecedents with General Index.* Montevideo, 1933.

————. *Report of the Delegates of the United States of America to the Seventh International Conference of American States.* Washington, D.C.: Government Printing Office, 1934. xi, 346 pp.

Inter-American Conference for the Maintenance of Peace. *Report of the Delegation of the United States of America to the Inter-American Conference for the Maintenance of Peace.* Washington, D.C.: Government Printing Office, 1937. vi, 280 pp.

————. *Report on the Proceedings of the Conference.* Submitted to the Governing Board of the Pan American Union by the Director General. Washington, D.C.: Pan American Union, 1937. 89 pp.

Select Bibliography

_____. *Texts Adopted by the Inter-American Conference for the Maintenance of Peace*. Geneva: League of Nations *Official Journal*, Special Supplement No. 178, 1937. 71 pp.

International Conference of American States. Eighth. *Addresses and Statements by the Honorable Cordell Hull, Secretary of State of the United States of America, in Connection with the Eighth International Conference of American States*. Washington, D.C.: Government Printing Office, 1940. vi, 90 pp.

_____. *Diario de Sessiones*. Lima: Imprenta Torres Aguirre, 1939. 1066, xliv pp.

_____. *Report of the Delegation of the United States of America to the Eighth International Conference of American States*. Washington, D.C.: Government Printing Office, 1941. vi, 229 pp.

_____. *Special Handbook for the Use of Delegates*. Washington, D.C.: Pan American Union, 1938.

Inter-American Conference on Problems of War and Peace. *Report of the Delegation of the United States of America to the Inter-American Conference on Problems of War and Peace*. Washington, D.C.: Government Printing Office, 1946. iii, 371 pp.

International Conference of American States. Ninth. *American Treaty on Pacific Settlement. The Pact of Bogotá*. Washington, D.C.: Pan American Union, 1948.

_____. *Charter of the Organization of American States*. Washington, D.C.: Pan American Union, 1948. 91 pp.

_____. *Final Act of the Ninth International Conference of American States*. Washington, D.C.: Pan American Union, 1948. iv, 57 pp.

_____. *Handbook for Delegates*. Washington, D.C.: Pan American Union, 1947. iii, 154 pp.

_____. *México en la IX Conferéncia Internacional Americana*. Mexico: Talleres Gráficos de la Nacion, 1948. 557 pp.

_____. *Report of the Delegation of the United States of America with Related Documents*. Washington, D.C.: Government Printing Office, 1948. v, 317 pp.

International Conference of American States. Tenth. *Preliminary List of Topics*. Washington, D.C.: Pan American Union, 1953. Mimeographed. 25, 5 pp.

_____. *Final Act*. Washington, D.C.: Pan American Union, 1954. vii, 135 pp.

League of Nations. Conference for the Codification of International Law. *Bases of Discussion for the Conference Drawn up by the Preparatory Committee*. Vol. III. *Responsibility of States for Damages Caused in Their Territory to the Person or Property of Foreigners*. C.75.M.69.1929.V. 253 pp.

Library of Congress. *List of References on International Arbitration*. Compiled under the direction of Appleton Prentiss Clark Griffin, Chief Bibliographer. Washington, D.C.: Government Printing Office, 1908. 151 pp.

Manning, William R. *Arbitration Treaties among the American Nations to the Close of the Year 1910*. New York: Oxford University Press, 1924. xl, 472 pp.

Pan American Union. *Codification of American International Law*. Washington, D.C.: Pan American Union, 1925.

_____. *Handbook. First Meeting of the Inter-American Council of Jurists*. Washington, D.C.: Pan American Union, 1950. iv, 193 pp.

Schiffer, Walter. *Repertoire of Questions of General International Law before the League of Nations, 1920–1940*. Geneva: A. C. Breycha-Vauthier, 1942. 390 pp.

The Calvo Clause

United Nations International Law Commission. *Preparatory Study Concerning a Draft Declaration of the Rights and Duties of States.* Lake Success: United Nations, 1948. vi, 228 pp.

_____. *Survey of International Law in Relation to the Work of the International Law Commission.* Lake Success: United Nations, 1949. iv, 70 pp.

United States Congress, Senate. Committee on Foreign Relations. *Claims of American Nationals against Mexico.* 77th Congress, 2nd Session. Washington, D.C.: Government Printing Office, 1942. iii, 230 pp.

_____. *Correspondence Relating to Wrongs Done to American Citizens by the Government of Venezuela.* Senate Executive Document No. 413, 60th Congress, 1st Session (1908).

_____. *Rights of American Citizens in Certain Oil Lands in Mexico.* Senate Executive Document No. 96, 69th Congress, 1st Session (1926).

United States State Department. *American Mexican Claims Commission. Report to the Secretary of State.* Publication 2859, Arbitration Series 9. Washington, D.C.: Government Printing Office, 1948.

_____. *Papers Relating to the Foreign Relations of the United States.* Washington, D.C.: Government Printing Office.

_____. *The Calvo Clause in American Policy and Practice.* Research Project No. 50. Division of Historical Policy Research, Office of Public Affairs. Mimeographed. Washington, D.C., 1947. 41 pp.

Index

Acre affair, 185

Adee, Alvey A. (acting United States secretary of state), communication on Calvo Clause, 42–43

Ahokas, V. J., communication on Finland's attitude toward Calvo Clause, 49

Aldunate, L.: dissent in *Stirling* case, 147; opinion in *Nitrate Railways Company* case, 149–150; dissent in *Antofagasta* case, 153

Alessandro, Mgr. (umpire in Brazilian-Bolivian Claims Commission), 186n

Alfaro, H. F., 231–232: on rule of *Dredging* case, 217n; opinion in *International Fisheries* case, 235

Aliens: subject to conflict of jurisdictions, 3–4; rights and duties under international law, 3–4; presence of as cause of controversy in underdeveloped regions, 4; protection of rights, 4–5. *See also* Calvo Clause; Calvo Doctrine; Equality of alien with national formula; International law; Minimum standards rule

Alvarez, Alejandro: on Calvo Clause, 114n; and American international law, 117, 118n

Amaral, Ubaldino do, 186n: dissent in *Rogerio* case, 187

American Electric Company case, 192n: analyzed, 174–175; Calvo Clause involved, 174; effect of Clause, 174–175

American international law, 25, 82: and equality of alien with national formula, 73, 77n; would sanction Calvo Clause and Calvo Doctrine, 86, 117–119; ef-

forts to win recognition of, 117–119; evaluation of, 118–119; in *Colombian-Peruvian Asylum* case, 118n

American Mexican Claims Commission (United States national commission), decision on Dredging claim, 230n

American Scientific Congress, Eighth, 71: issue of Calvo Clause before, 64, 89–90

American Society of International Law, 92

Anderson Morúa, Luis, 84n

Andrade, J.: opinion in *Day and Garrison* case, 133–135; opinion in *Flannagan* case, 136–138

Anglo-Iranian Oil case, 128n

Antofagasta case, 192n: analyzed, 152–154; Calvo Clause involved, 152; effect of Clause, 153–154

Anzilotti, Dionisio, 53

Arbenz Guzman, Jacobo, 274

Arbitration: as alternative to intervention, 20, 65; as alternative to diplomatic intervention for collection of pecuniary claims, 84–86. *See also* Calvo Clause, arbitral jurisprudence involving; Claims Commissions

Argentina, 69n, 79n, 86, 101n: proposed draft convention to prohibit diplomatic protection, 83–84; current utilization of Calvo Clause in, 275–276, 279

Arias, Harmodio, on constitutional provisions incorporating Calvo Doctrine, 25n

Asunción Port Concession Company, 279

Australia, 54: position on Calvo Clause,

307

Index

law, 20; theories enthusiastically received in Latin America, 21. *See also* Calvo Clause; Calvo Doctrine

Calvo Clause: definition of, 5–6, 28; designed to limit strictly or eliminate diplomatic protection, 5, 6, 28, 30, 34, 107, 258; question of validity highly controversial, 6–7, 27–28, 29; relation to status of individual under international law, 6, 7, 223–226, 256, 282–286; considered void or superfluous by majority of publicists, 7, 32, 59–60, 116; origins of, 9–32; in statutory provisions, 26, 31–32, 273, 274n, 275, 276, 277; use in concession contracts antedates Calvo's treatise, 27n; is application of Calvo Doctrine to contractual stipulations, 27–28; origins in Calvo Doctrine, 27–28, 32; relation to equality of alien with national formula, 28, 35, 64, 72–73, 86, 109–110; distinguished from Calvo Doctrine, 28–29; based on consent of individual, 28–29, 32; coverage usually confined to contract, 28, 30; example of, 29; elements of, 29–30; recent tendency to expand coverage of, 30; most successful technique to implement Calvo Doctrine, 31, 34; applies to submission of international claims as well as diplomatic protection, 31n; in constitutional provisions, 31–32, 268n, 270, 272–273, 274, 275, 276, 277; governmental attitudes toward, 33–61; attitude of Latin American republics toward, 34–37; attitude of the United States toward, 37–45; codification attempts involving, 56–60; before United Nations International Law Commission, 58n; Harvard research on, 59–60; controversy before inter-American conferences, 62–105; fight to validate led by Mexico, 89, 97; before Eighth American Scientific Congress, 89–90; before Inter-American Bar Association conferences, 90–95; legal issues involved in, 106–120; current utilization of, 267, 269–281; decline of number of disputes involving, 279–280; future evolution of, in diplomacy, 281–282; future evolution of, in international jurisprudence, 282–286

BROAD SCOPE: distinguished from limited Clause, 30–31, 116; objective to bar completely diplomatic protection, 30, 116; validity rejected by majority of governments, 60–61; rejection of complete validity does not result in complete invalidity, 60–61; draft convention submitted by Mexico to validate, 87–88; arguments for, 87–88, 91–93, 107–111; Latin Americans recognize that international law must be changed to validate, 88; arguments for are more political than legal, 108; validity not recognized by international law, 108, 258–259, 281; arguments against, 111–114; held to be void and illegal by majority of publicists, 112–114, 119; rejected in *Dredging* case, 216; valid if individual were subject of international law, 226, 283; possibilities of future validation, 281–286

ARBITRAL JURISPRUDENCE INVOLVING: at issue in more than thirty international arbitrations, 6; specific Clauses as involved in arbitrations, 29, 126, 130–131, 133, 136, 141–142, 146, 148, 152, 155, 159, 161, 164, 166, 167, 168, 169, 172, 174, 175, 179, 186, 189, 190, 200, 232, 241, 247, 250, 252, 253, 254; effect of Clause on non-contractual damages, 30, 147, 150, 153–154, 240–254, 254–255; importance of specific language of Clause, 30n; distinction between pre-*Dredging* and post-*Dredging* cases, 120; arbitral decisions up to *1926*, 121–193; criterion of legally meaningful validity, 123–124; arbitral decisions up to *1926* characterized by inconsistency, contradiction, and confusion, 123, 154, 193, 197; no legally meaningful validity up to *1926*, 123–124, 191–193; jurisdictional question or one of merits, 126n, 175, 177n, 214n, 237, 238n; accorded legally meaningful validity since *1926*, 194–257; *Dredging* case, 194–230; arbitral decisions since *1926*, 231–257; rule of law on Calvo Clause, 259–268; reasons for no recent cases, 267–268

RULE OF LIMITED VALIDITY: held to be meaningless by publicists, 31, 116,

309

Index

Index

196, 211; distinguished from earlier arbitral rulings on Calvo Clause, 197–198; decision of commission, 198–211; Calvo Clause involved, 200; held that Clause is lawful under international law, 202–205; held that Clause does not cover denial of justice, 208, 211; held that Clause must be agreed to by individual, 208–209; held that Clause bound individual but not state, 210; criticism of decision, 211–214; criticized by publicists, 214, 226–228; accepted by governments, 214, 228–229; Clause decisive on admissibility of claim, 215; full validity of Calvo Clause rejected, 215–216; formulated rule of limited validity, 215–223; precedent for, 221; recognition of status of individual under international law, 223–226, 283–284; impact and influence of, 226–229; rule of, adhered to by subsequent arbitral commissions, 228, 231–257; criticism of, by Nielsen in *International Fisheries* case, 236–239; rule of, is rule of law on Calvo Clause, 255–257, 259. *See also* Calvo Clause, rule of limited validity

Dreier, John C., on nonintervention linked with hemispheric security, 70n

Dunn, Frederick S.: on arguments for and against Calvo Clause, 106–107; on importance of *Dredging* decision, 196n; criticism of *Dredging* decision, 227n

Eagleton, Clyde: on decisions by Barge, 184n; on importance of *Dredging* decision, 196n; on effect of Calvo Clause, 266n

Ecuador: statutory provision requiring inclusion of Calvo Clause in contracts, 26, 31–32; on Article *12* of Charter of Organization of American States, 102; current utilization of Calvo Clause in, 276, 279

Eisenhower administration, 105

El Oro Mining and Railway Company case, 256n: analyzed, 251–253; Calvo Clause involved, 252; effect of Clause, 252–253; issue of denial of justice before, 252; accepts rule of limited validity, 252–253

El Salvador, 15n, 21, 79n, 102n: current utilization of Calvo Clause in, 274, 279, 280

Emilia Marta Viuda de Giovanni Mantellero case, 284n

Equality of alien with national formula: Carlos Calvo on, 18–19; key point of Calvo Doctrine, 18–20; in treaties, 23; principle basic to Calvo Clause, 28; in Guerrero report, 56–57; before codification conferences in Western Hemisphere, 58; acceptance of, would validate Calvo Clause, 64, 72, 77, 86, 105, 281–282; before inter-American conferences, 72–105; has not won acceptance, 73, 82, 96–97; arguments for, 82, 108–110; progress of, before inter-American conferences, 104; legal basis for validity of Calvo Clause, 107, 108–110; criticized by publicists, 112–113; in *Dredging* decision, 206; possible evolution in inter-American diplomacy, 281–282. *See also* Calvo Clause; Calvo Doctrine

Esquível Obregón, Toribio: on defects and abuses of diplomatic protection, 90–91, 93; on Calvo Clause and Doctrine being sanctioned by American international law, 117–118

Evans, Alona E., on American international law before International Court of Justice, 118n

Extraterritorial jurisdiction, 4–5

Fabela, Isidro, 254n

Feller, Abraham H.: on foreign claims in Mexican history, 194–195; on importance of *Dredging* decision, 197n; on fact situation in *Dredging* case, 199n; on rule of *Dredging* case, 217n; on position of individual in law of international claims, 226n; on influence of *Dredging* decision, 228n; on decision in *Pitol* case, 255n; on judicial recognition of position of individual claimant, 284n

Fenwick, Charles: on nonintervention as continuing issue of debate, 70n; on legal effect of inter-American resolutions, 81n; on relations between state and citizens of foreign states, 106; on

Index

Italian-Venezuelan Claims Commission (*1903*), 161–163; Italian-Mexican Claims Convention (*1927*), 195, 198n, 254, 261n; Italian-Mexican Claims Commission (*1927*), 254–255

Janssen, Camille: opinion in *Stirling* case, 146–147; opinion in *Nitrate Railways Company* case, 149–150, opinion in *Antofagasta* case, 152–153
Japan, position on Calvo Clause, 51
Jecker claim, 14
Jessup, Philip C.: on loophole in Porter Convention, 15; on Vattelian formula, 282–283; on validity of Calvo Clause if individual were subject of international law, 283; on changing nature of international law, 284; on diplomatic interposition under new rules of international law, 284n

Kellogg, Frank B. (United States secretary of state), 36: communication on Calvo Clause, 40
Kunhardt case, 183n, 191n, 192n: analyzed, 167–168; Calvo Clause involved, 168; effect of Clause, 168
La Guaira case, 183n, 193n: analyzed, 167; Calvo Clause involved, 167; effect of Clause, 167

La Internacional, C.A., 277
Lapradelle, Albert de, on decision in *Milligan* case, 128n
Latin American republics: chief proponents of Calvo Clause, 7; criticism of diplomatic protection by scholars, 12; subject to armed interventions, 12–14; fears of international claims, 13; experiences with loans and bond issues, 13–16; fears of diplomatic protection, 14; legal theories advanced by, to resist diplomatic protection and armed intervention, 14–21; attempts to implement Calvo Doctrine, 21–32; attitude toward Calvo Clause, 34–37; accept limitations on full validity of Calvo Clause, 36–37; efforts to win acceptance of Calvo principles before inter-American conferences, 62–105; arguments for Calvo Clause, 107–111;

record of, before claims commissions, 122n; parties to international claims commissions, 125–255. *See also* Calvo Clause; Calvo Doctrine
Lauterpacht, Hersch, 285
Law of Nullities (Costa Rica), 188–190
League of Nations, 56, 59, 80, 234
League of Nations Conference for the Codification of International Law: Basis of Discussion No. *26* on validity of Calvo Clause, 36n, 55–56, 57, 233; Preparatory Committee of, 40; replies of governments to preliminary questionnaire on Calvo Clause, 46–56; sessions of conference, 56–57; replies of majority of states to preliminary questionnaire on Calvo Clause held to be compatible with *Dredging* rule in *International Fisheries* case, 196, 233
Lena Goldfields case, 129n
Lima, Peru, 69, 84, 125
Lissitzyn, Oliver J., on meaning of denial of justice, 115n
Little, J., 144, 169, 172: dissent in *Day and Garrison* case, 135; dissent in *Flannagan* case, 138–139
Loans, international, experience of Latin America with, 13–14. *See also* Drago Doctrine
Local remedies rule, 80, 278: United States' support of, 103; held to make limited Calvo Clause superfluous, 116; waived in *compromis*, 120, 197–198, 242, 254n, 260–261; in Calvo Clause decisional law, 132, 135–136, 139–140, 145, 146, 151–152, 171, 172, 173, 174, 178, 181–182, 183, 187, 191–193, 197–198, 215, 217, 250, 252. *See also* Calvo Clause; Calvo Doctrine

MacGregor, Fernandez, 56n: on Latin American attitude toward Calvo Clause, 36n; on attitude of governments toward Calvo Clause, 55; opinion in *Dredging* case, 198–210; opinion in *International Fisheries* case, 232–235
McMurdo case, 192n: analyzed, 154–156; Calvo Clause involved, 155; effect of Clause, 156
MacNeil case, 255n, 263: analyzed, 247–

317